FOUNDATION STUDIES IN EDUCATION:

Justifications and New Directions

A Source Book

by
MARGARET GILLETT
and
JOHN A. LASKA

The Scarecrow Press, Inc.
Metuchen, N. J.   1973

Library of Congress Cataloging in Publication Data

Gillett, Margaret, comp.
  Foundation studies in education.

    1. Education--Study and teaching--Addresses, essays,
lectures.   2. Teachers, Training of--Addresses,
essays, lectures.   I. Laska, John A., joint comp.
II. Title.
LB1732.G54   370'.7   73-7899
ISBN 0-8108-0671-1

PREFACE

Foundation Studies in education--areas such as history of education, educational psychology, philosophy of education, sociology of education--occupy a place in nearly every teacher preparation program in the United States and Canada. Yet, probably more than is the case with any other field of study, the intellectual dimensions and functional role of Foundation Studies remain unclear and poorly analyzed. Although many journal articles and portions of a number of books have been devoted to discussions of various aspects of the Foundations of Education, there is no book which is concerned with a comprehensive exploration of the Foundations field. There are, of course, many books entitled "Foundations of Education," but these present material dealing with the substance of one or more of the Foundations rather than material about Foundations as a field of inquiry and instruction.

In order to remedy the deficiency, the editors of this book have collected and interpreted significant statements on Foundation Studies and presented them within a systematic framework. Foundation Studies in Education consists of three sections, each of which covers a major aspect of the field and includes selected essays plus an introduction written by one of the editors.

Part I deals with the basic question: What are the Foundations of Education? It explores their intellectual status as a field of study and confronts the question of whether or not Foundations of Education are worthy of being considered an independent discipline. The second Part presents papers which examine criticisms levelled at Foundation Studies and advance reasons for including these courses in teacher preparation programs. Finally, Part III provides a discussion of the new directions which various writers believe the Foundations will, or should, take in the future. It is to be hoped that the fresh ideas projected here will help bring new vigor to the field.

This sourcebook, Foundation Studies in Education: Justifications and New Directions, will be of value to anyone concerned with the improvement of teacher preparation. Thus, both Foundations specialists and other teacher educators, as well as people in professional educational organizations, will be interested in this collection.

M. G. and J. A. L.

CONTENTS

Page

PREFACE   iii

PART I: PERSPECTIVES ON FOUNDATION STUDIES

PART II: THE VALUE FOR TEACHER PREPARATION

PART I

PERSPECTIVES ON FOUNDATION STUDIES

JOHN A. LASKA

INTRODUCTION

This section will examine answers to the following
basic question: What is or should be the disciplinary status
of Foundation Studies in education? In order to choose the
appropriate selections for consideration here, it has been
necessary to make two preliminary stipulations.

First, it is assumed that Foundation Studies represents an academic or scholarly field. The term "field"
refers to an organized area of inquiry and/or teaching.
The terms "academic" or "scholarly" designate a field
which is different from a "professional" one, the distinction
being that in a professional area of inquiry and/or teaching,
the principal concern of teachers in the field is to provide
the student with the profession's generally accepted opinion
on how the student should actually perform his prospective
professional role, while teachers in an academic or scholarly
field do not have this as their principal concern. An
academic or scholarly area of inquiry and/or teaching may
often, however, have a professional function--for example,
a course in mathematics may be taken by prospective en-
gineers--but the principal concern of its teachers would not
be to give the student specific guidance in the performance
of his prospective professional role. Therefore, by definition, Foundation Studies in education must be a different
area of inquiry and/or teaching from the purely professional
field or fields involved in the training of the teachers, although it may certainly have a professional function.

Second, the term "Foundation Studies" will be used in
a generic sense to refer to the academic field of education.
Three major terms have, in fact, been used in the United
States to designate this area of inquiry and/or teaching.
The earliest was "Science of Education" or some variant,
the second was "Foundations" or some variant, and the third
was "Educational Studies." But only the term "Foundations"
has gained sufficient recognition to be widely used to designate an institutionalized structure for the academic field of

2

education; therefore, "Foundation Studies" has been selected for use in this book as the generic term for the field.

Two major points of view have been advanced concerning the disciplinary status of Foundation Studies. One of these is the view that the scholarly study/teaching of education must be carried out through the use of the established academic disciplines (such as history and psychology), with the academic field of education thus having a dependent relationship to those other disciplines. The other major conception is the view that Foundation Studies in education constitutes an independent and viable field of academic study/teaching in its own right. There are, of course, many specific variations on these two major conceptions; the selections in this section are intended to be representative of the range of these views.

The Science of Education Movement

The latter half of the nineteenth century saw the formal recognition and establishment within the university of many of the present-day social science disciplines. As Michael B. Katz has noted, "it was roughly between 1870 and 1910 that the differentiation of social sciences into their modern form and their institutionalization within universities occurred."[1]

During the same period, a number of scholars became concerned with the status of education as a field of university study. An expression of this concern is given in our first paper, "Education as a Science," which also bears the title usually given to the movement it represents. This selection is dated June 6, 1881; it is part of one of the annual reports prepared by Frederick A. P. Barnard, president of Columbia College. Barnard argues that "there is a science of education" and that this science is deserving of a place in the university curriculum. He advocates the establishment of "a department embracing the history, theory, and practice of education" and indicates what would be covered under these topics. He believes that education should become "a profession into which no one shall be permitted to enter without having first passed through such a course of preliminary training as is required for admission to the practice of other professions." The department that he wished to establish at Columbia would, he contends, help to remedy the existing deficiencies in the professional preparation of public school teachers.

The science of education idea is further developed in
the selection by William H. Payne, which was published in
1886.   Payne presents the view that education is both a
science and an art.   The art of education he defines as its
practice, while educational science refers to "the doctrines,
principles, or laws that are involved in the art of education."
With Barnard, he considers a science of education necessary
for the professional development of education.   Payne also
describes the kind of knowledge that is to be embodied in
the science of education.   He believes that "by far the larger
and more important part of this science is derivative, consisting of general laws borrowed from physiology, psychology,
ethics, sociology, and logic."   But he also adds that "besides this borrowed material, the science of education must
employ general truths of its own gathering."

Thus, although the term "Foundation Studies" had not
yet been coined, by the end of the nineteenth century views
had been offered on the need for an academic field of education that would be different from, but related to, the professional practice of education.   And on the critical question
of what kind of disciplinary status this field would have, the
selection by Payne combines the two divergent lines of thinking that would later emerge: the idea that the scholarly study
of education is dependent on the established academic disciplines, and the view that certain educational topics were to
be investigated by an independent science of education.

John Dewey wrote a book in 1929 entitled The Sources
of a Science of Education in which he carefully examined the
relationship between the established academic disciplines and
the science of education.   Dewey discusses engineering,
pointing out that in its actual practice it is an art.   "But
it is an art," he explains, "that progressively incorporates
more and more of science into itself, more of mathematics,
physics and chemistry."   He goes on to state that "men
built bridges before there was any science of mathematics
and physics.   But with the latter development, with formulae of mechanics, statics, thrusts, stresses and strains,
there arose the possibility of building bridges more efficiently, and ability to build them under conditions which
previous methods were incompetent to deal with."   Dewey
believes that

there is a science of bridge building in the sense
that there is a certain body of <u>independent</u> scientific material, say mathematics and mechanics,
from which selections may be made and the selection organized to bring about more effective solution in practice of the difficulties and obstructions
that present themselves in actual building of bridges.
It is the way the material is handled and organized
with reference to a purpose that gives us a right
to speak of a science of bridge building, although
the building itself is an art, not a science. The
sciences of mechanics and mathematics are, in
themselves, the sciences which they are, not sciences of bridge building. They <u>become</u> the latter
when selected portions of them <u>are focused</u> upon
the problems presented in the art of bridge building.

From this line of argument Dewey reaches a major
conclusion on the sources of a science of education. He
believes that the problems to be investigated by such a science are found in educational practices. Yet, he insists,
"there is no more a special independent science of education
than there is of bridge making. But material drawn from
<u>other</u> sciences furnishes the content of educational science
when it is focused on the problems that arise in education."
What are these other sciences? Dewey contends that "there
is no subject-matter intrinsically marked off, earmarked so
to say, as the content of educational science. Any methods
and any facts and principles from any subject whatsoever
that enable the problems of administration and instruction
to be dealt with in a bettered way are pertinent." Dewey
believes, therefore, that an independent academic field that
embodies the "principles of education" does not exist.

Considerable attention has been given here to an exposition of Dewey's ideas because of their significance in
the development of thinking about Foundation Studies. He
argues very persuasively that the attempt to produce an independent science of education that would be fully supportive
of the practice of education is simply not feasible. In
making his argument Dewey uses the professional field of
engineering as an analogy. But there is another analogy
that Dewey might have taken which could have led him to a
different point of view. The other analogy would be found
in such academic fields as government (political science),
religious studies, and jurisprudence. These fields are

concerned with the scholarly study of a basic social institution and/or social process. The educational system is also a basic social institution, and the educative process is certainly a basic social process. Therefore, the argument can be made that an academic field that is devoted to the study of the educational institution and process should also exist.

Indeed, an examination of the views expressed by Barnard on the need for a science of education reveals that he was interested, for example, in having the history of education taught to prospective teachers. The history of education is really the history of the institution and the process; it is not the presentation of a set of scientific principles which underlie the practice of education. Thus, even when the science of education movement represented the dominant conception of the academic study/teaching of education, an awareness of the importance of studying the educational institution was also in evidence.

Foundation Studies as a Dependent Field

In the early 1930's some changes were made in the organizational structure of Teachers College, Columbia University. The term "Foundations" was used to designate one of the five divisions into which Teachers College was reorganized. The Foundations division, as Dean William Russell explained in his 1934 report, was created out of what was left when the four divisions devoted respectively to administration, curriculum and instruction, guidance, and tests and measurements were formed: "All that was left, once these four groups were abstracted, was the work in the history of education, philosophy of education, educational sociology, educational economics, comparative education, and part of educational psychology." Russell viewed the Foundations division as being "fundamental to all four, providing the general knowledge of the raw material of education, the product desired, and the recognized means of changing the former into the latter."[2]

The establishment of the Foundations of Education division at Teachers College was duplicated in many other American universities, where a department of Foundations of Education was organized within the predominantly professional school of education of the university (but not within the academic liberal arts component of the university). These actions constituted the first and only widespread institution-

alization of the academic field of education. It is for this
reason, as has already been indicated, that the term "Foundation Studies" has been chosen as the generic term for
the scholarly study/teaching of education.

The types of courses usually provided by Foundations
of Education departments include history of education, educational psychology, philosophy of education, comparative
education, sociology of education, social foundations of education, economics of education, politics of education, anthropology of education, and general courses with such titles
as "introduction to education" and "school and society."
There is a clear suggestion in the names of most of these
courses that the areas of study they represent are derivative from some parent academic discipline (e. g., history,
philosophy, economics).[3] Thus it seems fair to conclude
that the conception of Foundations Studies that is found in
most Foundations of Education departments is a dependent
conception of the field. Hereafter, therefore, this view shall
be referred to as the "dependent Foundations approach."

In the 1960's a reaction against the institutionalization
of the academic study of education within Foundations departments took place, on the principal ground that the academic
rigor of the field had failed to attain a sufficiently high
standard. One of the strongest critics of the courses provided by Foundations departments is James Bryant Conant,
whose influential Education of American Teachers was published in 1963. In this book Conant maintains that teachers
of "foundations courses often attempt to patch together scraps
of history, philosophy, political theory, sociology, and pedagogical ideology. The professors are frequently not well
trained in any one of the parent disciplines; certainly very
few have such mastery of all the disciplines as to be able
to talk about them except at a most superficial level."
Conant's solution is to recommend that prospective teachers
"study philosophy under a real philosopher. An additional
course in the philosophy of education would be desirable but
not essential. The same is true of a course in the history
of education." Conant advocates, therefore, a reduced role
for Foundations divisions or departments, although as the
selection from his book indicates, he is more favorable to
educational psychology than to some of the other Foundations
areas.

Many other writers in addition to Conant have

attempted to delineate the relationship which they believe
should obtain between the parent academic fields and the dependent Foundations areas.   One point of view (which is not
too far from Conant's position) is that the connection between
the two should be a close and intimate one.   Representative
of this orientation is the selection by Richard M. Millard,
Jr. and Peter A. Bertocci on the relationship between
philosophy and philosophy of education.

A contrasting point of view is that the relationship
between a Foundations area and the parent academic field
should be relatively tenuous.   This argument is presented
in Mary Anne Raywid's paper.   Raywid takes the position
that at least one of the prominent Foundation Studies areas--
social foundations of education--has only a loose relationship
to any parent academic discipline, and that this relationship,
so far as it exists, is to a multiplicity of parent disciplines.
She also argues that the social foundations of education area
is not an independent discipline: "It seems to me that Social
Foundations (and possibly the other Foundational areas as
well) represents a teaching field, not an academic discipline.
It is put together for instructional not for research purposes,
and there is no reason why it need try to meet or answer to
the criteria marking and measuring academic disciplines,
which are primarily fields of inquiry."

Foundation Studies as an Independent Field

The view that Foundation Studies constitutes an independent field of academic study/teaching has also had its
advocates.   Edward F. Buchner's paper, for example, provides an early and relatively unambiguous statement (1903)
of the view that educational science should be independent
rather than dependent upon other disciplines.   "If education
is ever to become a science," he argues, "in the sense of
working out a particular and acceptable method of supporting
its inductions, it cannot be brought about by wearing a borrowed mantle, but rather by the elaboration of what is inherent in the activity of the teacher, generically regarded,
and of the pupil as the other member of every teaching
equation."

A more recent and much stronger statement about
the need for an independent academic field of education is
contained in the selection by James L. Kuethe.   In this
article Kuethe argues that "education can and should be

studied in the same sense that the disciplines of history and
physics are studied"; he also believes that "there is a developing discipline of education worthy of study in its own
right." Kuethe rejects the notion that a discipline is characterized by the possession of a unique set of concepts and
data or a unique methodology. Instead, he considers a discipline to represent a unique concern:

> Education is a discipline in the sense that there
> is a body of facts and principles organized in a
> framework of a unique concern. In essence, this
> is about the transmittal of human knowledge and
> culture from generation to generation. Central
> to this concern is the involvement of society in
> making formal provisions for the transmission to
> take place. There are, of course, many crucial
> aspects of the education process which are not
> monitored by a formal system. Teachers could
> not start at the level they do were it not for the
> fact that most students have learned the rudiments
> of the language and the culture in their homes.
> Indeed, if this were not true, the entire complex-
> ion of the teacher's job would be changed. I re-
> gard the discipline of education as involving the
> entire educational process as its subject matter,
> but, of course, formal education is usually recipi-
> ent of special concern perhaps because it is most
> susceptible to study, and also because it is sus-
> ceptible to modification by mandate.

Another view on the disciplinary status of Foundations
Studies is provided by David P. Ausubel in his paper, "Is
There a Discipline of Educational Psychology?" Although
he states that educational psychology is a "special branch of
psychology," he also refers to "the two disciplines." Moreover, in discussing the three types of research orientations
that may be applicable to the study of education, Ausubel
comes out in favor of applied research, both for the general
field of education and for the educational psychology area.
He uses the term "applied" to make a distinction "between
sciences which are oriented toward practical ends, as opposed to 'basic' or 'parent' sciences which do not have this
orientation. 'Applied' does not imply that the content of
the practical disciplines consists of applications from the
basic or parent disciplines. The problems rather than the
knowledge of applied sciences are 'applied.'"

On the question of the disciplinary status of education
and educational psychology, Ausubel offers the following conclusion: "The applied sciences are also disciplines in their
own right, with distinctive and relatively enduring bodies of
theory and methodology that cannot be derived or extrapolated
from the basic sciences to which they are related.   It is
simply not true that only knowledge of the basic sciences
can be related to and organized around general principles."

The Concept of Educational Studies

In recent years advocates of an independent status for
the academic field of education have given attention to the
question of the precise nature of such an independent field.
John Walton, in his paper, "Education as an Academic Discipline," points out that

> most major social enterprises have corresponding
> fields of study in the universities that are recog-
> nized or legitimate scholarly disciplines: govern-
> ment is taught and studied under the name of po-
> litical science; commerce, under economics; and
> community organization, under sociology.   Some
> of these enterprises also have professional train-
> ing programs; for example, commerce not only has
> the discipline of economics, but also a curriculum
> in business administration, which relies heavily
> upon, but is distinguishable from, the academic
> study of economics.   The study of education, how-
> ever, is regarded usually as professional prepara-
> tion for practitioners, or as an aspect of other
> disciplines.

Walton's academic models for the scholarly study/teaching
of education are thus the disciplines that are concerned with
the analysis of basic social institutions and social processes.

The conception of the academic field of education advanced by Walton is also held by John A. Laska.   Since no
claim is made that all of the academic knowledge that professional educators require will be provided by the field,
their view on the nature of the academic field of education
is more limited than it is in the science of education approach of the late nineteenth century.   But neither would
the scholarly study/teaching of education necessarily be
limited to the service of prospective educational professionals,

just as courses in government (political science) and religious studies are taken by other students in addition to
prospective politicians and ministers of religion. Thus the
appropriate university locus for the academic field of education could either be the arts and sciences component of
the university or the professional school of education.

A new term, "Educational Studies," has come to be
employed as a designator for this conception of the academic
field of education. It is found in the name of the American
Educational Studies Association (AESA), the national learned
society in the United States that is devoted to the scholarly
study/teaching of education. Although as used in the name
of this organization Educational Studies applies to both the
independent and dependent conceptions of the field, a basic
purpose of AESA is to encourage the increased integration of
the field. Moreover, Educational Studies was chosen instead
of Foundations because "the long tradition of delimiting the
specialized foundations of education areas on the basis of
the supportive disciplines (i. e., the use of such terminology
as 'social foundations of education' and 'philosophical foundations of education') would no doubt be perpetuated if
'educational foundations' were used to designate the general
field, with the result that the greater integration of the
foundations of education would remain difficult to achieve."
Therefore, in contrast to the term "Foundations," the concept of Educational Studies suggests an independent status
for the academic field of education. Whether it will also
serve as the basis for an institutionalization of the field
now remains to be seen.

Conclusions

For about a hundred years scholars have been concerned with the need to have more knowledge about education than the purely professional knowledge accumulated by
practicing teachers. Initially this concern expressed itself
in the view that a science of education must underlie the
art of education. But as Dewey demonstrates in The Sources
of a Science of Education, many sciences (academic fields)
may be contributory to any given area of professional
practice. Therefore, the development of a single, independent supporting science of education that would accomplish
everything that is done by the other supporting sciences is
probably impossible. It was in their view of the kind of
relationship that should exist between the professional and

the academic fields of education, therefore, that the science
of education advocates seem to have erred.

Notwithstanding the improbability of ever creating a
single, all-encompassing supporting science of education,
the need for a more restricted academic field devoted to the
study of the social institution of education and to education
as a societal process has been manifested in both the dependent Foundations approach and in the more recent Educational Studies approach.   The basic difference between these
two conceptions of the field is that the exponents of the Educational Studies approach have opted for an academic model
patterned after other institutional fields such as government
(political science), religious studies and jurisprudence, while
adherents to the dependent Foundations approach have implicitly rejected this model.   Yet, as several of the selections in this section have indicated, the relationship between
the dependent Foundations areas and their parent disciplines
is a topic that is still being explored.

The major question confronting professors in the
academic field of education today would seem to be whether
the social institution model as a focus for the field is an
acceptable one.   As yet no university has established an
academic department staffed, in Walton's words, "with
scholars who will abjure any prior allegiance to another
discipline.   They will become educationalists. ...   They
will devote their energies to the study of education, to
organizing the information that is available to them, and to
developing new methods of inquiry in the field."   It is at
least a possibility that such a department could succeed,
especially since the institutional model for the academic
field of education has not received the kind of critical rejection that Dewey directed against the science of education
approach.

Notes

1.   Michael B. Katz, "From Theory to Survey in Graduate
     Schools of Education," Journal of Higher Educa-
     tion 37 (June 1966), 329.
2.   Ibid., 333-34.   See also Charles J. Brauner, American
     Educational Theory (Englewood Cliffs, N.J.:
     Prentice-Hall, 1964), pp. 198-223.

3.   Hereafter the term "area" will be applied to the various component areas of study/teaching that make up Foundation Studies.   The term "field" will be reserved for references to the entire field of Foundation Studies.

FREDERICK A. P. BARNARD

1. EDUCATION AS A SCIENCE*

To one who thoughtfully inspects the varied and comprehensive program of subjects which all American colleges
profess to teach, there cannot but occasionally occur a sense
of a singular omission. Among all this great multitude of
educational institutions, not one seems to have made education itself the subject of investigation, or to have regarded
instruction in the theory or practice of education as a part
of its business. This is not because philosophy is incapable
of throwing a salutary light upon the processes by which
the powers of the human intellect may be best unfolded, or
upon the form and method in which given subjects of knowledge may be most successfully presented; nor is it because
the philosophy of education is so simple that its principles
may be assumed to be intuitively known. Yet the latter is
the view which our higher educational institutions of learning
generally seem in their practice to accept; since, in the
appointment of their teachers no question is ever raised as
to whether or not the candidate has himself been educated
to teach. No body of professional men is in position to
exert a more powerful influence upon the destinies of the
race than that of educators; and yet no body of men are
left more completely to accident for the attainment of the
qualifications which may properly fit them for the discharge
of their important functions. It is true that we have normal
schools, of which the professed purpose is to train young
persons in the art of teaching, but the instruction there given
is little more than in routine methods of practice, and the
teachers produced are not of high grade. Education is nowhere treated as a science, and nowhere is there an attempt

*Excerpt from the Annual Report for 1880-81 of the Presi-
dent of Columbia College. Text from William F. Russell,
ed., The Rise of a University, Vol. I: The Later Days of
Old Columbia College (New York: Columbia University
Press, 1937), pp. 289-97.

made to expound its true philosophy. In this respect we
are far behind Continental Europe.   In the leading universities of Germany, systematic courses of lectures have long
been given upon pedagogics, or the science of education, in
its history, its theory, and its practice; and some of our
own ablest educators have had the advantage of listening to
such instruction, and of so preparing themselves for the
better performance of their work at home. Great Britain has
been later in the field.   Up to about four or five years ago,
as little attention was paid to the science of education in
England and Scotland as in our own country.   But, in the
year 1876, there was established in the University of Edinburgh a chair of the history, theory, and practice of education, and another having the same title in the University of
St. Andrews.   More recently there has been created at Cambridge, England, an organization called the Teachers' Training Syndicate, under the auspices of which have been instituted lectures on pedagogy to be continued throughout the
academic year, the first course under this arrangement
having been commenced in October, 1879.   In the introductory lecture of this course, the speaker, Professor R. H.
Quick, refers to the singular neglect under which this important subject has so long lain, even at one of the most
distinguished centers and fountains of high learning in the
modern world--a fact which he illustrated with a certain
humor partaking of the satirical.   He supposes a new royal
commission to have been appointed to investigate the condition of the universities, and that by some means or other
the commissioners selected are intelligent persons from
another planet.   These commissioners have been informed
by Dr. Newman and other high authorities that, in a true
university, every branch of human knowledge should be
taught.   They have before them as a witness a distinguished
professor of Cambridge armed with the university calendar.
They have learned that if Cambridge does not completely
fill out the university idea as they have conceived it, still
that every subject of really substantial importance relating
to God and nature, and to man in his relations to both, is
there entrusted to teachers of eminence, who lay before
the students the results of the latest investigations.   The
chairman is supposed to commence questioning the witness
as follows: "We hear that the subjects not cared for by
the university are unimportant.   What do you mean by unimportant?" The witness hesitates, but answers that he is
not there to give opinions, but to state facts.   The chairman
rejoins that it can hardly be matter of opinion whether any
subject is unimportant which seriously affects the welfare

of the great mass of mankind; and to this the witness assents.
The chairman then says, "We understand, then, that all subjects bearing on the well being of the human race receive
attention in the university," and to this the witness responds
by reading copious extracts from the calendar, showing how
thoroughly a knowledge of the languages and institutions of
past ages is taught in the university, and how even the results of investigations now going on into the state of man in
prehistoric times are faithfully given.   The commission is
deeply impressed, and the chairman continues: "All this is
profoundly interesting.   Without a knowledge of man as he
has been, we cannot properly understand man as he is.
Tell us, now, what you teach of man as he is, as he should
be, and as he may become."   The witness reads further
from the calendar something about political economy, which
shows man as he is, and about morality philosophy, which
shows what he should be; but explains that our leading sciences concern themselves very little about human beings
unless they are ill and we want to cure them, or unless they
fall out and we want to pacify them, or unless they commit
crimes and we want to punish them.   The chairman responds:

> Yes, that we understand, the science is useful
> that tells us how, when men go wrong, to get
> them right again.   But there is another more im-
> portant science which you tell us nothing about, the
> science which shows how to make men grow up
> right--which teaches the order in which their
> faculties develop, and the best means of promoting
> their healthy development, and directing them to
> their proper work.

The witness looks puzzled, and a member of the commission
comes to his aid, remarking, "We mean, of course, the
science of education."   The witness abruptly throws down
his book and says bluntly, "There is not a word about it in
the calendar."   And here the Daily Telegraph reporter in-
serts in brackets the word [sensation].   The discovery of so
singular an omission in the program of a leading institution
of learning, among a people claiming to stand in the foremost
rank of human enlightenment, could not but justify sensation
and afford a proper occasion for surprise.   Nor is this surprise diminished when it is perceived that the neglect of the
science of education in educational institutions is not owing
to an absence of a proper sense of the value of the science
on the part of individual educators.   There exists in the

English language a vast educational literature, built up by
contributions from many of the profoundest thinkers and ablest teachers whom this country or Great Britain has produced, out of which might be elaborated, by careful collation
and digest, an admirable compound of systematic pedagogics.
But in the form in which these actually exist, many of them
covering only special topics, and none of them written with
reference to any common method, or connected with the others by any obvious relation, they furnish not so much a science of education, as evidence that the need of such a science
is universally recognized.

The general recognition of the fact that there is a science of education becomes more strikingly obvious when we
notice the efforts which are made by teachers, through voluntary associations, to aid each other by discussing educational questions, and comparing the results of experience in
periodical conventions. The papers produced on such occasions are sometimes able, but it is more frequently the case
that the educational literature which owes its origin to a stimulus of this kind is desultory and weak. In every numerously
attended body the number of those entitled to speak with authority is always a minority; yet all are equally entitled to
speak, though they may not necessarily speak to edification.
It can hardly be doubted, however, that teachers' conventions
do accomplish something in the way of giving to teachers
clearer views of their profession, and thus improving the
character of their work.

The educational system of the country will, however,
never be what it ought to be until education is made a profession into which no one shall be permitted to enter without having first passed through such a course of preliminary training
as is required for admission to the practice of other professions, and such a state of things cannot be possible until in-
strumentalities exist for regularly training men to this profession. Such facilities can only be secured by the creation, in
some of our existing institutions for the higher education of
the young, of chairs of instruction devoted to this express object. There is no possible way in which the usefulness of any
college could be more immediately or more largely increased
than be establishing a chair of this kind, or by creating a
school which might be called a school of pedagogics, designed
to prepare teachers for their work. No American college has
as yet attempted this, but it was a feature embodied in the
plan, never realized, of a university projected more than twenty years ago, to be established in Tennessee under the name of

the University of the South; and it is not without satisfaction
that the undersigned recalls the fact that it was adopted in
that scheme at his own suggestion. The plan of the institution referred to approached more nearly to the ideal of a
true and complete university than any other that was ever
projected upon this continent. It left no branch of human
science unprovided for, and its prospective resources were
so large as to promise to enable it to maintain all its departments in vigorous operation, without any need of relying
on the uncertain revenues to be derived from fees for tui-
tion.   Its scheme had been matured, its site chosen, the
cornerstone of its principal edifice had been laid, when the
desolating wave of civil war which swept over the land in
1861 extinguished its early promise, and, by destroying the
springs of its vitality, made its revival impossible after the
deluge was at length overpast.

It appears to the undersigned that the time has come
when Columbia College may very properly make an attempt
to supply the serious defect in the educational system of our
country which has here been indicated. A department embracing the history, theory, and practice of education, though
it might not contribute largely to the course of undergraduate instruction, would bring the College more directly, and
to more effective purpose, into contact with the outside
world than almost any other. It could not fail to enlist the
interest, and, with a judicious arrangement of hours, to
command the attendance, of every teacher in this great city
and its vicinity, and it would soon become so attractive as
to draw many more from a distance.

In order to insure to a scheme like this the highest
degree of success, it would be advisable, in the beginning,
not to create a chair to be filled by a single individual,
though that has been the plan adopted in the Scottish universities; but to engage a number of distinguished educators to
give lectures upon particular topics according to a prear-
ranged scheme, holding these lectures at night, and only once
or twice a week during the academic year. The history of
education alone would afford material for a large number of
such lectures which would be full of interest and instruction.
The importance of an acquaintance with this history on the
part of every man who enters this profession with a desire
to be useful in it, is strongly insisted on by the Honorable
Henry Barnard, editor of the American Journal of Education,
and formerly United States Commissioner of Education at
Washington, who maintains that there is no department of

human existence in which preliminary historical knowledge
is so next to indispensable as in this.   He says:

> By just as much as young teachers are ardently
> interested, by just as much as their minds are full
> of their occupation and fruitful in suggestions of
> principles and methods for prosecuting it, by just
> so much are they the more liable to re-invent
> modes and ideas which have been tried and given
> up before, and thus to waste precious months and
> years even, in pursuing and detecting errors which
> they would have entirely escaped, had they learned
> the lessons left them by their predecessors.

The history of education has been adirably set forth
in the comprehensive works of von Raumer and Schmidt in
German, and in that of Gabriel Compayré in French; but with
the exception of the collections of Henry Barnard, embracing
the translations from von Raumer and others, entitled "German Teachers and Educators," originally published in the
Journal of Education, we have nothing of a corresponding
character in the English language.   Professor Meiklejohn, of
the chair of education at St. Andrews, discusses under this
head the notions regarding education and the processes employed in its practice which have prevailed among all nations
called civilized, or which, in other words, have endeavored
to found forms of society favorable to the growth of what is
best in man.   He reviews, therefore, the educational ideas
prevalent early among Eastern nations, among the Persians,
Jews, Greeks, Romans, and among the Christians of the
primitive and medieaeval periods, and, since the fifteenth
century, the systems of the Jesuits and of the Reformers.
He gathers and presents in substance the educational views
of such eminent authorities as Bacon, Selden, Locke, Jean
Paul, Goethe, and Herbert Spencer; and considers and com-
pares the ideas of the originators of practical processes like
Comenius, Pestalozzi, Ratich, Jacotot, Diesterweg, Fröbel;
concluding with a critical examination of existing national systems in Germany, France, England, the United States, and
other countries.

The historical part of the course given by Professor
Laurie at Edinburgh covers much the same ground as the
foregoing, beginning with China and ending with the United
States.   He includes in his survey early education among the
Semitic races of the Mesopotamian basin and among the an-
cient Egyptians, gives an analysis of the educational views

of Plato and Aristotle, an exposition of the Institutions of Quintilian, an account of the labors of Erasmus, Colet, Luther, Melanchthon, and Sturm, an exposition of The Scholemaster of Roger Ascham, and an analysis of the didactics of Comenius and of the educational views of Milton.   Of more recent writers, he dwells upon Dr. Arnold and Herbert Spencer, and of recent originators of systems, upon Jacotot, Bell, Lancaster, and Fröbel.   He concludes with the history and state of education among English-speaking peoples.

The theory of education as given in these university courses embraces an inquiry into the psychology of the growing mind, a summary of the knowledge gathered by observation in regard to this, an attempt to estimate the mode, rate, and kind of growth by experiment; and an inquiry into the relation of various kinds of knowledge to the mind, and the influence of certain thoughts, emotions, and sets of circumstances upon the character.   The growth of the power of the senses, the memory, the understanding, the reason, the will, the imagination, the social feelings are next made subjects of examination.   The relation of the religious, moral, and intellectual sides of human nature to each other are discussed, and the best means of building up a sound understanding and the formation of a just habit of action are inquired into.

The portion of these didactic courses which relates to practice is devoted to an examination of all the processes at present going on in the schools of the country or the world, the relation of these processes to the growth of the mind, and their value considered as means to an end.   These processes are necessarily in great degree dependent upon the subject taught.   Thus in regard to languages, the lecturer considers what are the most effectual means of enabling the learner to master them, what are the mental habits to be created, and what the difficulties to be overcome, whether these be inherent in the language itself, or whether they arise out of the circumstances under which the instruction is given; and how these difficulties may be reduced to a minimum.   As the object aimed at in teaching the modern languages is not the same which is proposed when the ancient are the subject of instruction, due account is taken of this difference, with the modification it may suggest of the methods employed.   In regard to science, and especially the sciences of observation, the methods which experience--in this department of education the best guide--has shown to be most advantageous are explained and illustrated.

The conditions under which a love of elegant letters may be most effectually awakened are also inquired into. The different special subjects usually taught in schools-- such as grammar, geography, history, composition--are finally considered in detail, and the order in which their several parts may be most judiciously presented to the learner is pointed out. The adaptation of particular subjects or parts of subjects to particular ages is discussed; and the important question, how much should be done by the teacher and how much must be done by the pupil in order that he may profit by the exercise, is carefully considered. The relations of the various subjects of study to the process of mental development are investigated, that is to say, it is inquired what faculties each particular subject is best fitted to call into exercise, stimulate, and strengthen. And finally the characteristics of the best books on the several subjects are distinguished, and the value of textbooks as helps to the educational process is discussed and weighed....

WILLIAM H. PAYNE

2. SCIENCE OF EDUCATION: ITS NATURE, ITS METHOD,
   AND SOME OF ITS PROBLEMS *

It was not till within about a hundred years [ago] that
a knowledge of method began to be regarded as an essential
element in a teacher's qualification. This ... opinion respecting fitness for teaching is embodied in the Normal
School, whose original intent was to give a sound academic
training in subjects, and at the same time to communicate
the best-known methods of doing school work.

But the slow evolution of opinion has brought forward
a still higher ideal of fitness for teaching. According to this
conception, the teacher should not only have a broad knowledge of subjects, supplemented by a knowledge of the best
methods, but should know the general principles and laws that
underlie methods, and thus give them their validity. In this
progress of opinion, the sequence has been this: (1) knowledge; (2) knowledge and method; (3) knowledge, method, and
doctrine. Or the successive steps may be stated in another
form, as follows: At first, the teacher was not differentiated from the scholar, there was no preparatory training;
next, the teacher was differentiated from the scholar by method, the preparatory training was empirical; now, this preparatory training is to be rational, --method must be the out-
growth of known physiological, psychological, and ethical
laws; the ideal teacher must be a man of science in the same
sense that the reputable physician is a man of science; teaching is no longer to be a trade, a mere calling, or an empirical art, but a rational art, an art deriving its inspiration
from science, and basing its practice on established laws.
All this amounts to saying that, in the slow but sure evolution of human opinion, a science of education is beginning to
emerge from the art of education: and so the purpose of this

*Excerpt from William H. Payne, Contributions to the Sci-
ence of Education (New York: American Book Co., 1886),
pp. 10-18.

chapter is to define, in outline, the nature of this new science, the method of its cultivation, and some of the problems that it must solve.

Throughout this chapter I use the term science as distinguished from art, science denoting a higher order of knowledge, and art, a correlated, but lower order, of knowledge. To make my use of these contrasted terms as clear as possible, I discriminate two orders of knowledge as follows: We may suppose a farmer to know the mere processes or rules of his art, but to be in absolute ignorance of the physical and chemical laws that are involved in the art; he can do, but cannot explain what he does. On the other hand, we may suppose a scholar to know all the physical and chemical laws that are involved in agriculture, but to be absolutely unable to succeed in a single branch of this art. He can explain all its processes, but can perform none of them. In the first case, there is art without science; and in the second, science without art. This contrast runs through all forms of human labor. There is no art that does not imply a science, for there is no effect without a cause. There may be sciences, however, without correlative arts, because there may be laws that human skill has not employed.

The contrast now pointed out has been expressed as follows: "Science consists in knowing, art in doing;" "the principles which art involves, science evolves." The contrast is broadly expressed by the terms theory and practice, as the theory and practice of teaching. Some of the relations of science to art, or of theory to practice, are the following: 1. The ideal knowledge comprehends both doing and knowing--it is theory embodied in practice, or practice guided and inspired by theory. 2. The largest element in trades is practical knowledge; the largest element in professions is theoretical knowledge. 3. The lower order of knowledge is the easier of attainment; it will, therefore, be the more common, and hence the cheaper; the labor of highest market value will be that which involves the largest use of the intelligence. 4. The direct route to the perfecting of an art is through a clear comprehension of the principles that are involved in the art.

What is meant by educational science must be apparent--the doctrines, principles, or laws that are involved in the art of education. This art has been practiced from time immemorial, but whatever progress has been made in it has, for the most part, been instinctive, slow, and wasteful. It

is now proposed "to take stock of our progress," to discover
the principles that underlie the processes of human perfecti-
bility, and to bring educational methods into conformity with
law, thus making our progress rational, continuous, and eco-
nomical.

This ... movement in educational thought, which we
may call the rational or the scientific, is attested by (1) the
fact, that in Germany, in Scotland, and even in our own
country, education, in its three aspects, as an art, a science,
and a history, has been made a subject of university instruction; (2) by the fact that books on the scientific aspect of education are beginning to be written and read; (3) and also by
the fact that normal schools have begun to superadd to their
instruction in subjects and methods instruction in principles
and doctrines.

This movement towards making education a rational
art has been a genesis or an evolution; it has not been forced
into notice by resolutions and popular demonstrations, but has
been, the rather, instinctive and spontaneous. It has come in
the fulness of time, and it has come as a permanent factor
in educational history.

The new thought will insist on its right of domicile,
and we must gradually adjust ourselves to the changes that
are imminent and inevitable. The newspaper, the reaper, the
sewing-machine, and the telephone are instances of a similar
evolution. They are births rather than inventions. Civilization is a progress, and these elements in our progress may
possibly be superseded by something of a higher type; but it
is not conceivable that the world will go back to the state of
things that preceded these inventions. The particular truth I
wish to emphasize is this: a new day has dawned on the educating art; henceforth teaching is to be allied with philosophy,
and to furnish a field for the exercise of the highest gifts of
mind and heart. Henceforth, the teacher may be inspired to
his highest efforts by the hope of a career; he may see in his
profession an opportunity to rise in public consideration by
the exercise of his ability, his versatility, or his genius.
And, infinitely better than all this, the succeeding generations
of men will attain a higher type of manhood, because from
their training will gradually be eliminated the elements of ignorance, empiricism, and waste.

The general nature of educational science may be gathered from the following statements: Among every people, and

in every age of the world, there has been a conception of
what a human being ought to be; and, in every case, the
purpose of education has been to cause the young to grow
into this ideal. This conception has varied from age to
age, and from place to place; but, in every case, the purpose has been to mould the rising generation into the likeness of some ideal. Animal cunning, physical endurance,
and a contempt for suffering were the elements of the Indian's conception of the perfect man; and so the Indian boy
was trained into habits involving these qualities. The Jewish conception was reverence, piety, and passive obedience
to authority; Jewish instruction, was, therefore, religious
and literary, making the law of Moses and sacred history
the chief studies of the schools. The ideal Athenian was
cultured and aesthetic; the ideal Roman, patriotic, brave,
and practical; and, in each case, education was directed to
the attainment of these ideals. In our own time, education
is moulded after two conceptions or two ideals. First,
there is the conception of the typical man, or of man as the
most perfect specimen of his kind, without regard to any
special use that is to be made of him; and to turn out this
finished product is the purpose of what we call a liberal education. Again, there is the conception of man as a crea-
ture who must "get on in the world," or earn a livelihood
by being serviceable to his fellows; and so, to turn out this
product, we institute what we call technical or practical education. We may now define liberal education as the complex process by which a human being is helped to grow into
the highest ideal of his kind; and technical or practical education as the process by which a human being is to be fitted
to earn a livelihood by some form of industry. The science
of education must start with these two conceptions, and, having made an analysis of them, must formulate methods for
attaining the ends in view.

These two conceptions, the higher and the lower, have
three elements in common: (1) There is the substratum, or
body; (2) the mind, as the seat of intellectual activities; and
(3) the spirit, as the seat of moral activities. In other
words, man, the most perfect specimen of his kind, and
man, as an instrument or toiler, have passed through three
forms of training--physical, intellectual, and moral. If this
complex process of education is to be rational, physical
training must be based on the laws of physiology; mental
training, on the laws of psychology; and moral training, on
the laws of ethics. In other words, the basis of the science
of education must be general laws derived or borrowed from

the sciences of physiology, psychology, and ethics.

Again, education, both liberal and technical, will be modified according to the genius of the people for whom and by whom it is administered. Thus, English education differs from German, German from French, French from American --each from every other. The science of education must provide for these variations, and so it must borrow some of its principles from sociology, general or special.

The medium of communication between teacher and pupil is language; all instruction involves the use of symbols; speech is the instrument of the teacher's art. It follows, then, that the part of education which has to do with the communication of knowledge must be based on principles of logic.

Thus far education is an applied or a derived science. That is, it assumes the principles or laws that have already been established in other departments of thought, and upon these it bases its modes of procedure. But, besides this borrowed material, the science of education must employ general truths of its own gathering. For example, each of the studies upon which the pupil's mind is employed serves a distinct purpose. As Bacon has it: "Histories make men wise; poets, witty; the mathematicks, subtill; naturall philosophy, deepe; morall, grave; logick and rhetorick, able to contend.... So every defect of the minde may have speciall receit." ("Of Studies.") Now, the doctrine of education values is of the first importance in education; but, as there is no independent science for determining these values, this becomes a function of educational science. Other independent investigations falling within the province of this science are the following: the action of examinations; education as affected by sex; modes of organization; the supervision of schools; the training and examination of teachers; school economics; and, in general, the testing and formulating of results. So much as to the general nature of educational science.

If the foregoing outline has been correctly drawn, it is not difficult to state the general method of this science. By far the larger and more important part of this science is derivative, consisting of general laws borrowed from physiology, psychology, ethics, sociology, and logic. In the use of this material, the process must therefore be deductive. Deduction is, then, the general method of investigation in educational science. Assuming the truth of a given psycho-

logical principle, the effort must be to exhibit its application
in the practice of teaching.   In other words, within the com-
pass now under consideration, methods must be the direct
deductions from principles.

Now, leaving out of account the principles borrowed
from other sciences, and directing our attention to the investigations falling within the field of educational science itself, we see that the initial process in several cases must
be inductive.   Take, for example, the influence of sex on education.   Here the most direct method is the analytical examination of results.   If accurate statistics have been kept
in the case of mixed schools, the influence of sex upon scholarship, attendance, etc., if any, will be readily detected.
So far, the process is inductive; but when these inductions
have been merged in a law, this law is deductively applied,
as in the first case.   But, throughout the entire science,
there is the need of this analytical examination of results,
both for the purpose of testing deduced methods, and as the
means of confirming general laws.   For a law may be true,
while deductions drawn from it may be false.   In respect of
method, therefore, the case may be stated in this way: the
greater part of the material composing the science of education is borrowed from other sciences; and these first principles, thus taken on trust, must be applied to use by the
deductive method.   There are other principles, however,
that the science of education must find, and the method of
this finding must be inductive; but when actually found, these
laws, like those that are borrowed, must be applied deductively.   But a concurrent factor throughout the whole science
must be the verification of laws and their applications by the
analytical study of results; and this verification is an inductive process.

JOHN DEWEY

3.   EXCERPT FROM "THE SOURCES OF A SCIENCE
OF EDUCATION" *

Education as a Science

The title may suggest to some minds that it begs a
prior question: Is there a science of education?   And still
more fundamentally, Can there be a science of education?
Are the procedures and aims of education such that it is possible to reduce them to anything properly called a science?
Similar questions exist in other fields.   The issue is not un-
known in history; it is raised in medicine and law.   As far
as education is concerned, I may confess at once that I have
put the question in its apparently question-begging form in
order to avoid discussion of questions that are important but
that are also full of thorns and attended with controversial
divisions.

It is enough for our purposes to note that the word
"science" has a wide range.

There are those who would restrict the term to mathematics or to disciplines in which exact results can be determined by rigorous methods of demonstration.   Such a conception limits even the claims of physics and chemistry to
be sciences, for according to it the only scientific portion of
these subjects is the strictly mathematical.   The position of
what are ordinarily termed the biological sciences is even
more dubious, while social subjects and psychology would
hardly rank as sciences at all, when measured by this definition.   Clearly we must take the idea of science with some
latitude.   We must take it with sufficient looseness to include all the subjects that are usually regarded as sciences.

*John Dewey, The Sources of a Science of Education (New
York: Liveright, 1929), pp. 7-13, 32-42, 48-51. Reprinted
with the permission of Kappa Delta Pi, an Honor Society in
Education, owners of the copyright.

The important thing is to discover those traits in virtue
of which various fields are called scientific. When we raise
the question in this way, we are led to put emphasis upon
methods of dealing with subject-matter rather than to look
for uniform objective traits in subject-matter. From this
point of view, science signifies, I take it, the existence of
systematic methods of inquiry, which, when they are brought
to bear on a range of facts, enable us to understand them
better and to control them more intelligently, less haphazard-
ly and with less routine.

No one would doubt that our practices in hygiene and
medicine are less casual, less results of a mixture of guess
work and tradition, than they used to be, nor that this difference has been made by development of methods of investigating and testing. There is an intellectual technique by which
discovery and organization of material go on cumulatively,
and by means of which one inquirer can repeat the researches
of another, confirm or discredit them, and add still more to
the capital stock of knowledge. Moreover, the methods when
they are used tend to perfect themselves, to suggest new
problems, new investigations, which refine old procedures and
create new and better ones.

The question as to the sources of a science of education is, then, to be taken in this sense. What are the ways
by means of which the function of education in all its branches
and phases--selection of material for the curriculum, methods
of instruction and discipline, organization and administration
of schools--can be conducted with systematic increase of intelligent control and understanding? What are the materials
upon which we may--and should--draw in order that educational activities may become in a less degree products of
routine, tradition, accident and transitory accidental influences? From what sources shall we draw so that there shall
be steady and cumulative growth of intelligent, communicable
insight and power of direction?

Here is the answer to those who decry pedagogical
study on the ground that success in teaching and in moral direction of pupils is often not in any direct ratio to knowledge
of educational principles. Here is "A" who is much more
successful than "B" in teaching, awakening the enthusiasm of
his students for learning, inspiring them morally by personal
example and contact, and yet relatively ignorant of educational history, psychology, approved methods, etc., which "B"
possesses in abundant measure. The facts are admitted.

But what is overlooked by the objector is that the successes
of such individuals tend to be born and to die with them:
beneficial consequences extend only to those pupils who have
personal contact with such gifted teachers.   No one can
measure the waste and loss that have come from the fact
that the contributions of such men and women in the past
have been thus confined, and the only way by which we can
prevent such waste in the future is by methods which enable
us to make an analysis of what the gifted teacher does intuitively, so that something accruing from his work can be
communicated to others.   Even in the things conventionally
recognized as sciences, the insights of unusual persons remain important and there is no levelling down to a uniform
procedure.   But the existence of science gives common efficacy to the experiences of the genius; it makes it possible
for the results of special power to become part of the working equipment of other inquirers, instead of perishing as they
arose.

The individual capacities of the Newtons, Boyles,
Joules, Darwins, Lyells, Helmholtzes, are not destroyed because of the existence of science; their differences from others and the impossibility of predicting on the basis of past
science what discoveries they would make--that is, the impossibility of regulating their activities by antecedent sciences
--persist.   But science makes it possible for others to benefit systematically by what they achieved.

The existence of scientific method protects us also
from a danger that attends the operations of men of unusual
power; dangers of slavish imitation of partisanship, and such
jealous devotion to them and their work as to get in the way
of further progress.   Anybody can notice to-day that the effect of an original and powerful teacher is not all to the good.
Those influenced by him often show a one-sided interest;
they tend to form schools, and to become impervious to other
problems and truths; they incline to swear by the words of
their master and to go on repeating his thoughts after him,
and often without the spirit and insight that originally made
them significant.   Observation also shows that these results
happen oftenest in those subjects in which scientific method
is least developed.   Where these methods are of longer standing students adopt methods rather than merely results, and
employ them with flexibility rather than in literal reproduction.

This digression seems to be justified not merely be-

cause those who object to the idea of a science but personality and its unique gifts in opposition to science, but also
because those who recommend science sometimes urge that
uniformity of procedure will be its consequence.   So it
seems worth while to dwell on the fact that in the subjects
best developed from the scientific point of view, the opposite
is the case.   Command of scientific methods and systematized subject-matter liberates individuals; it enables them to
see new problems, devise new procedures, and, in general,
makes for diversification rather than for set uniformity.
But at the same time these diversifications have a cumulative effect in an advance shared by all workers in the field.
. . . .

Sources vs. Content

        The net conclusion of our discussion is that the final
reality of educational science is not found in books, nor in
experimental laboratories, nor in the class-rooms where it
is taught, but in the minds of those engaged in directing educational activities.   Results may be scientific, short of
their operative presence in the attitudes and habits of observation, judgment and planning of those engaged in the educative act.   But they are not educational science short of this
point.   They are psychology, sociology, statistics, or whatever.

        This is the point upon which my whole discussion
turns.   We must distinguish between the sources of educational science and scientific content.   We are in constant
danger of confusing the two; we tend to suppose that certain
results, because they are scientific, are already educational
science.   Enlightenment, clarity and progress can come about
only as we remember that such results are sources to be
used, through the medium of the minds of educators, to
make educational functions more intelligent.

Educative Processes as a Source

        The first question which comes before us is what is
the place and rôle of educative processes and results in the
school, family, etc., when they are viewed as a source?
The answer is (1) that educational practices provide the data,
the subject-matter, which form the problems of inquiry.
They are the sole source of the ultimate problems to be in-

vestigated. These educational practices are also (2) the
final test of value of the conclusion of all researches. To
suppose that scientific findings decide the value of educational undertakings is to reverse the real case. Actual activities in educating test the worth of the results of scientific
results. They may be scientific in some other field, but not
in education until they serve educational purposes, and whether they really serve or not can be found out only in practice.
The latter comes first and last; it is the beginning and the
close: the beginning, because it sets the problems which
alone give to investigations educational point and quality; the
close, because practice alone can test, verify, modify and
develop the conclusions of these investigations. The position
of scientific conclusions is intermediate and auxiliary.

Illustration from Engineering

        The development of engineering science affords a per-
tinent illustration and confirmation. Men built bridges before there was any science of mathematics and physics. But
with the latter developments, with formulae of mechanics,
statics, thrusts, stresses and strains, there arose the possibility of building bridges more efficiently, and ability to build
them under conditions which previous methods were incompetent to cope with. Bridge building sets problems to be dealt
with theoretically. Mathematics and mechanics are the sciences which handle the question. But their results are tried
out, confirmed or the contrary, in new practical enterprises
of bridge building, and thus new material is acquired which
sets new problems to those who use mathematics and physics
as tools, and so on indefinitely.

        There is a science of bridge building in the sense
that there is a certain body of independent scientific material, say mathematics and mechanics, from which selections
may be made and the selections organized to bring about
more effective solution in practice of the difficulties and obstructions that present themselves in actual building of
bridges. It is the way the material is handled and organized with reference to a purpose that gives us a right to
speak of a science of bridge building, although the building
itself is an art, not a science. The sciences of mechanics
and mathematics are, in themselves, the sciences which they
are, not sciences of bridge building. They become the latter when selected portions of them are focused upon the problems presented in the art of bridge building.

Science of Education Not Independent

Two conclusions as to the sources of educational science are now before us.

First, educational practices furnish the material that sets the problems of such a science, while sciences already developed to a fair state of maturity are the sources from which material is derived to deal intellectually with these problems. There is no more a special independent science of education than there is of bridge making. But material drawn from other sciences furnishes the content of educational science when it is focused on the problems that arise in education.

Illustrations from Measurements

Illustrations may be given of the use of measurements to guide the intelligence of teachers instead of as dictating rules of action. Thus it is reported that teachers in a high school were puzzled by discrepancies between achievements and intelligence quotients. So one of the teachers was relieved of some of her classes to visit parents and homes and interview students. Within two years this had become a full time position, contacts with clinics and other public agencies established, and there was an extension of the concept "problem student" to include other types of maladjustment than the intellectual. Again it is reported that psychological ratings were used as tentative guides to shift children about till the place was found where they could do their best work. In other schools that have taken over more or less of the work of the juvenile court, truant officers, medical inspectors and visiting nurses, the I. Q. reports are correlated with factors ascertained in these other lines before there is direct use of them. (The illustrations are taken from Thomas, W., and D.W. "The Child in America.") A homogeneous grouping without intervening inquiries approximates dangerously to transforming a theoretical finding into a rule of action.

It is empirically noted that one teacher has upon pupils an effect that is qualitatively termed inspiring, awakening, and that the personality of another teacher is relatively deadening, dulling. Now here is a problem set for inquiry, whether the sciences which have to be drawn upon are suf-

ficiently advanced to provide material for its solution or not.
In this case, the science upon which a draft must be made
is presumably that of social psychology, dealing with the in-
teractions of persons. The original facts are raw material,
crude data. They are not part of the science save as they
set the problem and give direction to inquiry: in so doing
they may lead to developments within social psychology itself.
But it is the latter which is the direct source of the content
of educational science in this case.

If it is empirically noticed that the stimulating effect
of some teachers is followed later on by a blasé indifference,
or in emotional over-excitability, on the part of some students, a further problem is set, new discriminations have to
be made, and so on.

It is noted that children in some rooms, or at certain
times of day are languid and dull and work inefficiently.
This condition, even on an empirical basis, raises the question of ventilation, heating, etc. There is a problem set for
scientific inquiry. Not education but physiology and chemistry are the sources drawn upon. Some statement of the detailed correlation between conditions of air, temperature and
moisture and the state of organic efficiency of pupils may be
reached; a solution in terms of a definite mechanism, of how
things are linked together.

Difficulties arising in temperament and deep-seated
habits may be so great that the scientific result in the first
case will not seriously affect the teacher whose influence on
pupils is undesirable. But it may be of aid in correction of
attitudes; and, in any case, it gives useful information to administrators in dealing with such persons. In the other instance, teachers have an intellectual ground for alertness in
observing physical conditions in their classrooms and organic
symptoms in their children that they did not have before.
There is then a case of educational science in operation.
What is done consists of acts, not of science. But science
takes effect in rendering these activities more intelligent. If
teachers are sufficiently alert and intelligent, they go on to
notice conditions of the same general nature, but more subtle,
and set a problem for further more refined inquiry. In any
case, there will be a distinct difference in attitude between
the teacher who merely puts into effect certain rules about
opening windows, reducing temperature, etc., and the one
who performed similar acts because of personal observation
and understanding.

The Scientific Sources of Education

A further conclusion follows regarding the sciences
that are the source of effective means for dealing with them.
We may fairly enough call educational practice a kind of social engineering. Giving it that name at once provokes notice that as an art it is much more backward than branches
of physical engineering, like land surveying, bridge-building
and construction of railways. The reason is obvious. After
all allowance is made for less systematic training for persons who engage in the art of education, the outstanding fact
is that the sciences which must be drawn upon to supply scientific content to the work of the practitioner in education
are themselves less mature than those which furnish the intellectual content of engineering. The human sciences that
are sources of the scientific content of education--biology,
psychology and sociology--for example, are relatively backward compared with mathematics and mechanics.

This statement is not an innocuous truism, for important consequences flow from taking it to heart. In the
first place, just as the problems arising on the practical
side in modern industry, for example, have been an important factor in stimulating researches in heat, electricity and
light, so the problems that show themselves in educational
practice should furnish agencies to direct the humane sciences into intellectually fruitful channels. It is not practice
alone that has suffered from isolation of thinkers in the social and psychological disciplines from the occurrences taking place in schools. Indifference to the latter, a hardly
veiled intellectual contempt for them, has undoubtedly
strengthened the rule of convention, routine and accidental
opinion in the schools. But it has also deprived the sciences
in question of problems that would have stimulated significant
inquiry and reflection. Much of the barrenness and loose
speculation in the humane sciences is directly due to remote-
ness from the material that would stimulate, direct and test
thought. Nothing in our recent situation is more promising
for scientific development than the fact that the intellectual
distance between university and elementary school, for example, is lessening.

In the second place, frank recognition of the relative
backwardness of the sciences that must form the main content of educational science is a protection as well as a stimulus. Recognition that genuine growth in educational science

is dependent upon prior advance in other subjects prevents
us from entertaining premature and exaggerated expectations.
It would, if fully recognized, deter workers in the field from
efforts at premature introduction into school practice of materials whose real value lies only in the contribution they
may make to the further building up of scientific content; it
would militate against exploitation of results that are as yet
only half-baked. And it would impress upon workers in the
field of educational science the need for thorough equipment
in the sciences upon which the science of education must
draw.

At this point, the fact that educational practices are
a source of the problems of educational science rather than
of its definite material is especially significant. Adequate
recognition that the source of the really scientific content is
found in other sciences would compel attempt at mastery of
what they have to offer. With respect to statistical theory
this lesson has been pretty well learned. Whether it has
been with respect to other disciplines, or even with respect
to the separate and exclusive application of statistics to the
solution of educational problems, is open to doubt.

Finally, recognition of this obvious fact would be a
protection against attempting to extract from psychology and
sociology definite solutions which it is beyond their present
power to give. Such attempts, even when made unconscious-
ly and with laudable intent to render education more scientific, defeat their own purpose and create reactions against
the very concept of educational science. Learning to wait
is one of the important things that scientific method teaches,
and the extent in which this lesson has been learned is one
fair measure of the claim to a hearing on the part of workers in the field of education....

No Intrinsic Educational Science Content

If we now turn to the subjects from which are drawn
the materials that are to be brought to bear upon educational problems, we are forced to recognize a fact already incidentally noted. There is no subject-matter intrinsically
marked off, earmarked so to say, as the content of educational science. Any methods and any facts and principles
from any subject whatsoever that enable the problems of administration and instruction to be dealt with in a bettered
way are pertinent. Thus, in all that concerns the bearing

of physical conditions upon the success of school work--as
in the case of ventilation, temperature, etc., already men-
tioned--physiology and related sciences are sources of scientific content. In other problems, such as making budgets,
cost-accountings, etc., economic theory is drawn upon. It
may be doubted whether with reference to some aspect or
other of education there is any organized body of knowledge
that may not need to be drawn upon to become a source of
educational science.

This consideration explains many phenomena in the
present situation. It accounts for the rapid growth of interest in the development of scientific content for educational
practices in so many different lines of activity. We have
become only recently alive to the complexity of the educative
process and aware of the number and variety of disciplines
that must contribute if the process is to go on in an intelligently directed way. In accounting for the manifestation of
enthusiastic activity on the part of some, the situation also
explains the skeptical indifference of many about the whole
matter. Not merely inert conservatives in the general public but many professors in other lines in universities have
not been awakened to the complexity of the educational undertaking. Hence, such persons regard the activities of those
in departments of education as futile and void of serious
meaning.

Failure to perceive that educational science has no
content of its own leads, on the other hand, to a segregation
of research which tends to render it futile. The assumption,
if only tacit, that educational science has its own peculiar
subject-matter results in an isolation which makes the latter
a "mystery" in the sense in which the higher crafts were
once mysteries. A superficial token of this isolation is found
in the development of that peculiar terminology that has been
called "pedageese." Segregation also accounts for the tendency, already mentioned, to go at educational affairs without
a sufficient grounding in the non-educational disciplines that
must be drawn upon, and hence to exaggerate minor points
in an absurdly one-sided way, and to grasp at some special
scientific technique as if its use were a magical guarantee
of a scientific product.

Recognition of the variety of sciences that must be
focused when solving any educational problem tends to
breadth of view and to more serious and prolonged effort at
balance of the variety of factors which enter into even the

simplest problems of teaching and administration.   The uncontrolled succession of waves of one-sided temporarily
dominating interests and slogans that have affected educational practice and theory could thus be reduced.

JAMES BRYANT CONANT

4. THE THEORY AND PRACTICE OF TEACHING[*]

In the majority of the institutions I visited, the future teacher starts his or her sequence of professional courses by taking the same introductory courses irrespective of whether the eventual goal is to teach in an elementary or a secondary school. Sometimes the first course is a course in educational psychology; but often it is of the type I shall describe as "eclectic." Frequently the type I describe as "eclectic" carries the label "foundations of education."

Those in charge of these foundations courses often attempt to patch together scraps of history, philosophy, political theory, sociology, and pedagogical ideology. The professors are frequently not well trained in any one of the parent disciplines; certainly very few have such mastery of all the disciplines as to be able to talk about them except at a most superficial level. They are far from being the kind of intermediary or middleman professor I described a few pages back. Occasionally, to be sure, one encounters a mature scholar who has ranged so broadly and so deeply over the fields of philosophy and social science that he can organize data from many fields to give his students a clear and exciting picture of the relationships between formal schooling and other cultural patterns. If an institution has one of these rare scholars, it might wisely encourage him to offer a social foundations course. In general, however, I would advise the elimination of such eclectic courses, for not only are they usually worthless, but they give education departments a bad name. I have rarely talked with students or school teachers who had good words to say for an eclectic foundations course. Perhaps the kindest word used to describe most of these courses was "pathetic."

---

*Excerpt from James Bryant Conant, The Education of American Teachers (New York: McGraw-Hill, 1963), pp. 126-137. Reprinted with the permission of Conant Studies of American Education, Educational Testing Service.

As an example of such an eclectic course I might
cite a course entitled "American Foundations" in a large private metropolitan university. The course is described in
the prospectus as follows:

> An introduction to the professional sequence. A
> field of study in which the student becomes ac-
> quainted with the development of the contemporary
> school; with the teaching profession, its opportuni-
> ties, requirements, and expectations; with the be-
> liefs and aspirations of our people as they apply to
> the school and other agencies; and with the funda-
> mental problems in American education. The his-
> torical development of ideas, events, and laws are
> reviewed in relation to the organization, purpose,
> and program of today's school. Satisfies require-
> ments for (1) American Public Education, and (2)
> Philosophy of Education. 4 semester hours.

One characteristic of this course and of similar courses
with which I have become familiar is the very impressive
list of reference books. In this particular course no fewer
than 23 titles are listed under the heading "Personalities,
Ideas, and Events"; the titles range from Ulich's History of
Educational Thought to Rugg's Foundations for American
Culture. In the third section of the course, which is entitled "Purposes of the School in Our Society," the suggested
reading runs to 34 titles ranging from Counts' Education and
American Civilization to Caswell & Foshay's Education in
the Elementary School. Such lists are impressive indeed,
but in the institutions I visited I found on inquiry that only
one copy of each suggested book was available, and not by
any conceivable stretch of the imagination would a student
find time to read even two or three of the books listed for
each section. It must be remembered that such a course is,
as a rule, a one-semester course carrying three semester
hours of credit.

Another sample of an eclectic course is one entitled
"Introduction to Teaching" at a well-known state university.
This course is even more of a potpourri, since bits of educational psychology and references to the literature on instructional methods have been stewed in. The 18 main headings of the outline of the course, each of which has two or
three subheadings, will indicate the range of material covered:

1. The Challenge of Being a Teacher
2. Planning a Career in Education
3. Competencies and Certification Standards for Educators
4. Preparation for Teaching
5. Opportunities in Teaching
6. School and Community Responsibilities of Teachers
7. Learning to Guide the Growth of Pupils
8. Professional Organizations and Publications
9. Salaries of Teachers
10. Other Economic Benefits
11. Historical Development of Our Schools
12. The Development of Modern Concepts of Education
13. Community Aspects of Education
14. Purposes of Education in American Democracy
15. Problems, Issues, and Inservice Professional Growth
16. Organization and Administration of Schools
17. Financing our Schools
18. Moving Ahead.

I have found little evidence that these courses stimulate a
student to read either deeply or widely. Quite the contrary.
The classes I have visited are far too reminiscent of the less
satisfactory high school classes I have seen. The course is
dominated by a textbook or a syllabus, and the instruction
seems to be wedded to the dogma that a discussion must take
place whether the talk is lively or the class is bored. The
pace and the intellectual level seemed geared to students far
less able than those in the top 30 per cent group from which
we should recruit our teachers.

The eclectic courses may be said to be a conglomera-
tion of bits of the history of American education, the philosophy of education, educational sociology, the economics and
politics of the school, together with an introduction to education as a profession as well as a glimpse at the application
of psychological phraseology in the observation and teaching
of children. From the point of view of education, I see no
reason for the existence of these courses. One suspects
that they exist to meet (on paper) state requirements! Since
virtually every state has differing course titles and descriptions in their requirements, one must respect the versatility
of the professors of education in designing courses that they
can reasonably argue meet these diversely defined requirements. I have found the type of foundations course I have
described being given in institutions approved by NCATE.
I consider the existence of such courses, which is encour-

aged by the present certification requirements and accredita-
practices, one of the arguments for the reforms I have recommended.

Courses in the philosophy, history, or sociology of
education are, unlike "eclectic" courses, intended to apply
the disciplines of specific academic areas to education.   But
these, too, may be of limited value; the crucial question is
how they are taught and by whom.

The word philosophy, as used by many professors of
education, is like a thin sheet of rubber--it can be distorted
and stretched to cover almost any aspect of a teacher's interest.   Under the best conditions, it seems to me a course
in the philosophy of education would legitimately presuppose
that the students had been exposed to the basic issues of
epistemology, ontology, and ethics in an introductory philosophy course required of all teachers as part of their general
requirements.   Such a course would not, however, have addressed itself to the problems of education.   In the philosophy of education course a well-trained philosopher should
turn his, and his students', attention to the problems, the
language, the assumptions, and the value premises that enter
into educational theory and practice.   Using the new tools of
the logical analysts, and demonstrating by his own behavior
the philosophic impulses for comprehensiveness and clarity,
the professor of the philosophy of education should train his
students to think clearly and critically about educational issues, including those raised by the psychologists, other professional educators, and informed laymen.   Occasionally one
finds a course in philosophy of education so taught.   Far
more often one finds that it represents little more than the
professor's attempt to indoctrinate the student with his own
educational values, or to make the student vaguely familiar
with the views of eminent men who have written about education, a few of whom may have sought to put their views into
practice.   Even if one assumes that it is important to know
what these people have written about education, I doubt that
the students have time to gain an understanding and appreciation of the material presented.   What is most likely to be
the consequence is a superficial knowledge.   The same criticism may be made of some of the courses in the history of
education: those that in fact, are more in the nature of histories of educational theories or philosophies.

The worst type of philosophy of education course I
have encountered is one that attempts to combine a survey

of a few well-known philosophies with an anlysis of problems
in a school.   One textbook--the worst I have seen--attempts
to give the student an understanding of such words as realism, scholasticism, and pragmatism by a paragraph each in
the appendix.   As my suggestion of a program in general education makes evident, I believe it is important for a teacher
to have some appreciation of the way philosophers have
tackled the problems that come under the headings of epistemology and ontology.   But I am very certain that a glib attempt to summarize certain philosophers' views can only
leave the future teacher with the most dangerous of misunder-
standings: that he knows what he is talking about when, in
fact, he does not.   There are exceptions to my general con-
demnation of courses in the philosophy of education.   Some
are given by the type of person I have called an intermediary.
If I were participating in faculty appointments in an institution that certifies future teachers, I should do all in my
power to see to it that all who gave courses in the philosophy of education were approved by the philosophy department
as well as the department or faculty of education.   Graduate
schools of education should cease trying to train professors
of the philosophy of education without the active and responsible participation of the departments of philosophy.   The
latter should move into this field as fast as possible, though
they have been unwilling to do so in the past.   Well-trained
philosophers who turn their attention to problems of American education have an opportunity to make a real contribution to overhauling the philosophic foundations of education,
which today consist of crumbling pillars of the past placed
on a sand of ignorance and pretension.

        The future teacher, as I have said, would do well to
study philosophy under a real philosopher.   An additional
course in the philosophy of education would be desirable but
not essential.   The same is true of a course in the history
of education.   Again, the professor should be an intermediary or middleman; he should be approved by a department
of education and a department of history or an outside committee containing eminent historians.   The explanation of the
history of the schools of the United States under the guidance
of a first-rate American historian would be a valuable experience for any teacher.   It would strengthen his understanding of the political basis of our educational system and
relate what he should have learned in his American history
courses to his own professional work.   Some of the material presented might be considered sociological rather than
historical.   If a competent sociologist is investigating social

problems closely related to the schools and is ready to give
a course in educational sociology, the desirability of such a
course is evident. As to whether the present group of professors who consider themselves educational sociologists
should perpetuate themselves, I have the gravest doubts. I
would wish that all who claim to be working in sociology
would get together in the graduate training and appointment
of professors who claim to use sociological methods in discussing school and youth problems.

The discipline of pyschology is, as I have indicated,
more closely related to the work of the teacher than are philosophy, history, and sociology. As one would therefore expect, every teacher-training institution with which I am familiar includes in the program a course in educational psychology (under one name or another). In addition, a few institutions require a course in general psychology. Advanced
courses in various branches of educational psychology given
in summer schools are popular among teachers and are often
included in graduate programs.

Many laymen and professors of academic subjects are
skeptical about psychology. Those who disparage the subject
can easily produce examples of trivial and even inane statements in textbooks of psychology and in particular of educational psychology. But the harsh critic must remember that
in this century the word "psychology" has come to cover a
vast field of knowledge. Furthermore, unlike the fields of
chemistry, physics, or biology, there is relatively little separation between "pure science" and "applied science." The
reason is clear. "Pure chemistry" could be defined, at
least in the nineteenth century, as systematized knowledge
(including wide generalizations) applicable to procedures in a
laboratory. Without specifically so restricting the definition,
this meant procedures dealing with relatively small amounts
of homogeneous material. Applied chemistry, on the other
hand, was concerned with practical operations like sugar
purification, beermaking, or even the manufacture of large
quantities of chemicals like sulphuric acid, soda, and quick-
lime. Because the materials were never homogeneous, there
were many limitations to the applications of "pure chemistry"
to applied chemistry.

The contrast with psychology is striking. From the
beginnings right down to the present day, the applications
were in the forefront. Teachers, for example, have been
eager each generation to avail themselves of what psycholo-

gists were claiming as new knowledge of the human brain
and its workings.   Professor Boring, in his history of psychology, has written, "The most important and greatest puzzle which every man faces is himself, and, secondly, other
persons." What over the years different schools of psychology have presented to the public has been "the key to the
mystery, a key fashioned in the scientific laboratory and
easy to use."

        In a sense one might define psychology as the search
for the key to the mystery every man faces--"a key easy to
use." Philosophical speculation and religious dogma still
provide for many persons a satisfactory key to the puzzle
every man faces.   Thus, even in the mid-twentieth century,
psychology is bounded on one side by metaphysics.   It is
bounded on a second side by anatomy and physiology, and on
a third side by the vast domain of commonsense generalizations about human nature.   These are for the most part highly limited and unsystematized generalizations, which are the
stock in trade of everyday life for all sane people.   But
from these generalizations a science is slowly emerging that
enables us to predict to some degree the future behavior of
an individual from a knowledge of the past.   If one defines
psychology as the area within the triangle I have just outlined, it is clear that much depends on whether one approaches the subject as a philosopher, a neurophysiologist, or a
practical man concerned with human nature--an advertiser,
for example, or above all an educator.   If one examines the
texts in general psychology used in introductory college
courses, one will find material that can be classified in
terms of the triangle I have drawn, though the triangle is
far from equilateral; the metaphysical side is apt to be quite
short!   The amount of space devoted to physiological psychol-
ogy--sense perception, brain construction, and nerve action--
will vary with the author.   But this aspect of the subject is
certain to be emphasized far more in texts on general psychology than in those on educational psychology.   The material in the latter falls under four major headings: growth and
development, learning, personality adjustment, and evaluation. [1] In terms of my triangle, the line representing common sense marks the boundary between educational psychology and the art of teaching.

        My own classification of the psychological material I
have seen treated in different courses would be as follows:
individual differences, child growth and development, tests
and measurements (evaluation), adolescent psychology, men-

tal health and abnormal psychology, learning theory, results
of animal experimentation (Pavlov's dogs, Thorndike's cats,
Kohler's apes, Skinner's pigeons), and neurophysiology.   In
any introductory course, an account of psychology as a science based on experiment should include, of course, considerable space devoted to the description of animal experimentation and an evaluation of the evidence thus obtained.

If those who write and read books in psychology were
not always concerned with finding the "key to the mystery
every man faces" and keen to use it, a good introduction to
the establishment of a new science might be presented with
little or no reference to human beings.   As it is, most authors make the extropolation from animal experimentation to
human behavior seem so self-evident as to blur some important philosophic and methodological issues.   Having had some
experience with attempting to explain to students what is involved in the advances of science, I can be sympathetic with
the writers of the general texts in psychology.   The focus of
attention, they feel, must be not only on science but also on
its applications--on what the reader is going to apply tomorrow in his day-to-day dealings with people.   Yet it must be
demonstrated that the statements made are "scientific,"
which implies careful evaluation and analysis of the evidence.
Furthermore, a vast range of phenomena must be considered.

The role of psychology in the education of teachers
is a subject of much controversy.   This is the case not only
in the United States but also in other countries.   In a recent
report of a joint working party appointed by the British Psychological Society and the Association of Teachers in Colleges of Education (in Great Britain), the following statement
occurs:

> Child centered teaching, in the sense of teaching
> based on a study of learning and development in
> the child, forms a distinctive feature of present-
> day education....
>
> ... All this involves an understanding of the pu-
> pil's processes of maturation and learning and what
> he is ready for in the class situation.   These top-
> ics form an important part of the subject matter
> of educational psychology.   Although classroom
> techniques, observations and experiments have been
> and are carried out in their own right, the theo-

retical models and languages used to account for
the results of these activities are essentially psychological. It may be that educational science will
evolve its own language but it is difficult to see
such a language being independent of psychological
terms. Certainly at the present time nearly all
its terms are psychological.... We should make
use of psychology wherever, as a theory or
through its experimental results, it appears relevant to Education.... More specifically it should
provide students with knowledge of the major aspects of child development and the nature and conditions of classroom learning; and with certain
skills in the use of tests and other devices for as-
sessing children, diagnostic procedures, case history techniques, etc. At the same time, it should
provide skill in recognizing when to call in specialist help.

In another section the authors of this report point out
certain difficulties and precautions. They state:

There must always be a cautious use of psychological theory, particularly when arguing by analogy.
This refers particularly to some of the more speculative suggestions emanating from learning theory
based on animal studies or on human learning in
situations much simpler than those of the classroom.... The language of psychology should be
taken over with the full context of its psychological
use. Often this language is taken over in a slip-
shod way and subsequent casual usage can see it
applied in situations far removed from the origi-
nator's mind.... A further difficulty is in securing the effective transfer of psychological knowledge to classroom circumstances; that is, in teaching the subject in such a way as to cultivate a student's psychological insight and judgment in concrete situations.

For my part, on the basis of my observations and
reading of textbooks on educational psychology, I would sub-
scribe to what the British group has written. But by no
means all American professors of education (as apart from
professors of educational psychology) would agree with my
emphasis on the importance of a course in educational psychology as such. Those who believe in a science of educa-

tion, whose attitude I described earlier, would be particularly reluctant to accept my argument. To them the interpretation of the results of research, or perhaps even the carrying out of such research, can be left to those who are trained as "educators," not as educational psychologists.

It would be my contention that the validity of principles of psychology applicable to teaching depends on whether, from these principles, one can deduce such specific predictions as "If I (as a teacher) do so and so, such and such will probably happen" or "If he (the pupil) behaves in this or that way in situation X, he will behave in a certain way in situation Y."

What is at issue here is the applicability of the research work of psychologists in this century to what goes on in the classroom. Do the writings of psychologists help the teacher in understanding children? Are there principles of child growth and development that can be demonstrated by laboratory experience--that is, in a classroom? After listening to many arguments, eliciting the opinions of many teachers, and reading some of the textbooks used in courses in education, I have come to the conclusion that there are perhaps a few principles of psychology--as well as a considerable amount of purely descriptive material--which are relevant. They are particularly relevant to the total task of teachers for the kindergarten and the first six grades. My quotation from the British report indicates what those principles are likely to comprehend.

Despite the present limitations on the scientific aspect of psychology as applied to teachers, I have been convinced, largely by the testimony of students and teachers, that for those who teach children, psychology has much to say that is so valuable as to warrant the label "necessary," at least for elementary teachers. I believe that research will continue that will yield generalizations sufficiently wide as to be called scientific. As an introduction to the point of view of those concerned with the behavior of animals (including man), a general course in psychology would seem essential. One would hope for close coordination between those responsible for such a general course and those who were teaching and advancing the applied science of educational psychology.

The principal complaint I have heard from undergraduate students about psychology is that there is a great deal of duplication between what is presented in the general course

and what is presented in the courses in educational psychology and sometimes in the "methods courses" (which I shall
discuss later).   In one institution, at least, a valiant attempt is being made to coordinate the teaching of general
psychology and educational psychology.   In some colleges or
universities, on the other hand, those who give the two types
of course are barely acquainted with one another.

Except for aspects of educational psychology that deal
with the field of tests and measurements, I am doubtful
about the significance of educational psychology for the teachers in a senior high school.   I venture to question the width
and solidity of the so-called scientific generalizations that
some professors of education claim are the product of research.[2]   If my conclusion is at all sound, the role of psychology in the education of future elementary teachers should
be greater than in the education of teachers for secondary
schools.

I am aware that there exists a vast body of literature
concerning the unique problems and behavioral traits of adolescents, and stressing the fact that American culture impos-
es severe strains on many young people of this age group.
Any literate adult can scarcely avoid extensive contact with
this literature.   But the overwhelming proportion of students
found in secondary school classrooms are stable enough in
their personality structure, and are capable of learning and
thinking in a sufficiently adult manner, that the classroom
teacher can rely on his general education and experience in
understanding them.   Remember that I have recommended a
course in general psychology for all teachers.   Beyond this
a school district in whose classes a disproportionate number
of disturbed youngsters are found might well provide special
instruction in adolescent psychology as part of its efforts to
introduce the new teachers to the problems of the schools
within the district.   This is particularly true of the large
cities.   The time for a consideration of many psychological
and sociological factors is clearly during the first few years
of a new teacher's experience.

Notes

1.   Hendrickson and Blair reported on 13 books which were
far from uniform in Encyclopedia of Educational
Research, W. S. Monroe, ed., a product of the
American Educational Research Association (page

349).   The Macmillan Company, New York, 1950.
2.   I am here discussing the preservice education of second-
         ary school teachers.   An experienced teacher may
         have sufficient insight to gain much from psycholog-
         ical instruction that would mislead the novice.

RICHARD M. MILLARD, Jr.
and PETER A. BERTOCCI

5.   PHILOSOPHY AND PHILOSOPHY OF EDUCATION [*]

To talk about the relation between philosophy and philosophy of education or educational theory as though one were
talking about two totally different disciplines or areas of investigation is to confuse issues at the outset and to perpetuate a relatively recent divorce which the authors feel should
never have occurred.   When in 1954 a joint committee of the
Boston University graduate department of philosophy and the
department of Social Foundations in the School of Education
began discussion of the possibility of a program for a doctorate of philosophy in philosophy of education we found that
only eleven institutions in the country offered such a degree
and that of these only two required any specific course work
in the field of philosophy as such.   To many members of the
American Philosophical Association philosophy of education
has tended to be an unrecognized stepchild.   The inclusion of
a symposium on philosophy of education at the fifty-second
meeting of the Eastern Division held at Boston University in
1955 caused more than a few raised eyebrows.

This indifference of men in the general field of philosophy to philosophy of education has had its counterpart in
an almost equal indifference to philosophy of education by
professional educators.   Far too frequently philosophy of education disappeared from education curricula altogether or, if
it did appear, as former Dean Kandel has so strongly pointed
out,[1] it too often was offered by persons with little or no
philosophic training who had little to present in terms of philosophic content.   This is not to say that through the second
quarter of our century there were not exceedingly able men
working in the area of philosophy of education, but it is to
suggest that far too frequently these men were voices in the
wilderness spurned both by "technical" educators and those

---

*Journal of Education (Boston University), Vol. 141 (1958-
59),   pp. 7-13.   Reprinted with permission.

who would call themselves "technical" philosophers.

And yet we would insist that not only philosophy and philosophy of education but also education in general are inseparably linked.   The failure to recognize the inseparability of the link constitutes a peculiar sort of professional myopia on the part of all concerned.   At the point at which communication among any of the three breaks down all three tend to be the losers.   This is not to claim that all three are identical, nor is it to agree with Max Black that "in practice, philosophy of education becomes nothing less than philosophy, without qualification or restriction."[2]   It is, however, to insist that each necessarily involves the other to a greater or lesser degree.

Our task at this point cannot be an exhaustive analysis of the relations among the three.   Such an analysis would involve not only developing a complete philosophy of education but a detailed philosophy about philosophy of education. But we can at least suggest some of the major areas of mutual involvement and some of the dangers of misunderstanding the character of these involvements, as they appear from at least one philosophical perspective.

If philosophy is conceived of not as an oracular deliverance of Olympian insights but as the persistent, critical, and systematic attempt to discover and consistently formulate in relation to each other the basic characteristics, meanings, and values of our experience in its widest perspectives, then a person engaged in philosophic investigation, of all persons, can least afford to overlook or fail to think critically about educational experience.   From Plato to Dewey and Whitehead recognition of the central relation of educational philosophy to other specialized areas of philosophic investigation has characterized western thought.

It is exactly in the educational process that the problems of knowledge, of value, of what constitutes the good life or lives, of the kind of world we live in and what we can do about it become most crucial.   Philosophically one is concerned with drawing out and making explicit presuppositions and meanings, with developing tools for critically evaluating these presuppositions and meanings in relation to each other and all available additional areas of experience.   To a large extent it was the practical business of education and the need for clarification of what education is about that gave rise to the typical areas of philosophical investigation and not vice

versa. It is no accident culturally or logically that the
sophists (Greek educational practitioners) preceded and set
the stage for Socrates, Plato, and Aristotle. Nor was it an
accident that Plato's central work, The Republic, is basically a philosophy of education for the good society and the
good life.

    To put the matter in a slightly different way, philo-
sophic investigation is not something that does or can occur
in a cultural or personal vacuum. Of all disciplines it can
least afford to remain indifferent to any pervasive area of
human experience, for to do so is to deprive it of its content. The major philosophic positions, as Professor Brameld has suggested,[3] may well be described as critical "interpretations of cultural experience and hence, of the pervasive human problems always indigenous with that experience" or "as the articulated effort of any culture to give
maximum meaning to itself." To this it must be added that
few of the major philosophic positions are intentionally culturally exclusive, for, ideally at least, each of them must
deal with cross-cultural reference and criteria of cross-cultural or intercultural as well as intracultural judgments.
Nevertheless, insofar as education (not conceived of as restricted to the schools alone) is "the supreme human activity
whereby any organized group seeks to perpetuate and modify
its own way of life,"[4] education provides some of the most
important data areas for philosophic investigation on the one
hand, and philosophic investigation becomes a prerequisite to
critical and directed as opposed to non-reflective and accidental education and educational planning on the other. A
philosopher who is not willing to listen to and learn from the
educator may be a linguistic technician in some restricted
area but hardly a philosopher. An educator who is not philosophically literate in relation to his aims and presuppositions
educationally may be an educational technician but he is operating blindly. The philosopher of education whose function it
is to keep the vital discussion alive by bringing the resources
of philosophy to bear on educational problems and the results
of educational practice and discovery to bear on philosophic
investigation needs to be particularly well grounded both theoretically and practically in both areas.

    Every educational system or body of educational prac-
tices does involve some set of ends or aims felt to be of
sufficient importance or value to be perpetuated, or strengthened, or created in individuals and the community by the particular processes of education as such. Without these no edu-

cation would, in fact, occur. Quite apart from "schooling,"
the primitive father who teaches his child to fish and hunt
does so for some end which he feels is of vital importance
for the child, for himself, and for the community. This
would seem to be obvious, and yet, what may not seem
quite so obvious is that education is thus in its root conception purposive in character. As such, it inevitably involves
a theory of value, including both a general theory of value
or criteriology of values and an ethics and social philosophy
(conceptions of the life and the community worth attaining).
Today, for example, someone needs to face such questions
as the following: Are we to educate for self-realization in
community or efficiency in industrial production? Is com-
munal adjustment more important than individual initiative?
Is education for conformity or for creativity of prime importance?

       The particular theory of value involved in a particu-
lar educational system or set of educational practices may
be implicit or explicit, may be critically adopted in the light
of thought through value criteria and awareness of the problems of value criteria or uncritically adopted via tradition,
authority, inertia, or hasty judgment induced by crisis.   In
the light of present post-sputnik proposals, someone needs
to ask: Is a crash program in the physical sciences with
de-emphasis on the social sciences and humanities the most
adequate way to meet the challenge of the "space age"?
What kind of scientists and society would such a program
produce?   Are we willing to educate for security at any
price?

       In addition to a theory of value, every educational
system or body of educational practices involves an epistemology, that is, a series of hypotheses or assumptions of
presuppositions which constitute, when made explicit, a theory of knowledge.   Such a theory of knowledge includes assumptions about the possibility and limits of knowledge, a
conception of truth, and a criterion or criteria determining
when truth is obtained or approached and how one goes about
obtaining it.   The form and techniques an educational system
utilizes will be and have been rather strikingly different in
a society in which it is assumed that the final court of appeal for truth and falsity lies in some one institution or doc-
ument as contrasted with a society in which truth or the approach to it is considered to be determined by rational
weighing of evidence.

Further, every educational system or body of educational practices involves at least some metaphysical presuppositions, that is, some conception of the nature of man and
his place in the universe in the light of one's conception of
the kind of universe this is. The segregationist and the de-
segregationist in actual practice hold quite different conceptions of what men really are. Somewhere this issue of what
men in fact are needs to be faced. Such assumptions as
the following lead to quite different educational practices and
conceptions of the nature of education itself: All men are
selfish; all men are altruistic; all men are economically determined; all men are only physiological organisms determined by stimulus-response patterns and conditioning; all
men are children of God. The social sciences may help
throw light on the accuracy of such assumptions but even
this help may be limited. In some cases at least, particular schools within the social sciences make such assumptions at the outset themselves and to appeal to these for
proof is to beg the question. Again, in the educational process, these and other assumptions may be more or less explicit, more or less complete, and more or less critically
assumed. Those who guide the educational processes may
or may not have some explicit criteria or criterion of what
constitutes reality. And yet the unavoidability of metaphysical assumptions is strikingly demonstrated by the fact that
even those contemporary thinkers who would deny that a
metaphysics is possible are asserting something about the
amenability of the universe to human intelligence and thus
are making metaphysical statements.

The function of a philosophy of education may be conceived in two ways--ways which are not mutually exclusive.
On the one hand an educational philosopher may be concerned
primarily with a critique of the philosophic assumptions of
existing educational systems and practices. On this level
his task is primarily analytic, that is, he is concerned with
making explicit the implicit assumptions in any particular
educational system and looking at them from the standpoint
of their compatibility, consistency, and adequacy in the light
of the growing body of knowledge in the social and physical
sciences as well as the humanities and philosophic disciplines. He is concerned with developing critical acumen and
purging discussion of fogginess, meaninglessness, and incon-
sistency. He is the educator become self-aware and self-
critical. We have heard a great deal, for example, about
education for democracy, but what kind of democracy are
we educating for? Mussolini, Stalin, and Dewey agreed (sur-

prisingly enough) that we should educate for "true" democracy, but each one's conception of "true" democracy was
three worlds apart and so was each one's conception of education.   To talk about education for democracy without clarification of terms is to compound confusion under cover of a
warm feeling.

On the other hand, an educational philosopher may be
primarily concerned not with a critique of existing educational systems so much as with developing a philosophy of education, that is, a positive conception of what education ought to
be in the light of as much information about man, society,
and the universe as he can muster from all available areas
of experience and knowledge.   This has been essentially the
concern of educational thinkers such as Plato and Dewey.
Contemporaneously, one question of such an order raised on
the level of a United Nations Commission as well as in more
restricted philosophic and educational circles, is that of
whether or not there are any basic human rights that apply
to all men as men and, if there are any such, what do these
mean in terms of education?   Is the right to education one
such right?   If so, what kind of education?   It is not difficult to see that the first, what we called the analytic function, and the second, what we shall call the theoretical function, of educational philosophy are intimately related.   One
can hardly carry the critical function very far without developing critical norms nor can one carry out the theoretical
function with any hope of relevance unless he relates it critically to existing educational systems and practices.

Each function, however, critical or theoretical, is
apt to be truncated if the investigator is philosophically naive
or if he lacks adequate background in the practices and sciences of education.   If for no other reason than to avoid past
blind alleys and to keep one's critical tools sharp the continuing conversation between educators and those in the general
field of philosophy via the educational philosopher or philosophical educator is of vital importance.

But if such cooperative endeavor is vital then why the
seeming divorce between the two areas of philosophy and education we noted above?   Is it apt to be permanent or is a
reconciliation likely?   A number of factors might be suggested in answer to the first question.   High on the list
would have to be placed the indifference of many persons in
the field of philosophy to educational problems.   Part of this
indifference has been due to the intense concern in philo-

sophical circles in the second quarter of this century with
the problems of philosophy of science and linguistic analysis
and had not been due to any basic antagonism to educational
questions.

A second factor has been the dominance in educational circles of one major philosophic position which, not in
terms of its founder or leading proponents in the field of education but in some educational quarters, has seemed on theoretical grounds to disparage the importance of theory in fav-
or of an almost exclusive emphasis on practice. [5]   This in
practice has tended to give rise to what might be described
as a naive empiricism which has forgotten its theoretical
foundations and the fact that it is not self-evident or self-
justifying.   Still another factor in educational circles has
been the rapid development of the sciences of education with
a resulting preoccupation with these to the exclusion of seeing these sciences in the perspective of the total educational
process, its aims and goals.   This growth of the sciences of
education, while temporarily shifting attention from theoretical questions, has and will continue to have a salutary effect on rethinking the foundations of education.   If for no
other reason, it will do so because of the tremendous increase in data which these sciences plus the social sciences
in general have made available for the task, data which call
for assimilation in educational theory.

One other deterrent to effective communication in the
past and not wholly absent today has been the assumption on
the part of some educators (not without some justification)
and some philosophers (though few philosophers like to admit it) that once the philosopher has his foot in the door he
will proceed to legislate what education must be from some
privileged pinnacle.   It must be admitted that some men in
the field of philosophy have attempted to deduce philosophies
of education with little regard for the demands of educational practice.   But nothing less befits a person in the field of
philosophy than intellectual pride.   Two things must be said
to the contrary: It is not the business of the philosopher
to tell the educator or anyone else what he must do.   There
is a legitimate place for developing the educational implications of major philosophic positions.   This is particularly
desirable insofar as the philosophic positions themselves form
part of the cultural context in which and for which education
occurs.   But even when the philosopher, educational or otherwise, is so engaged, his function is not dictation.   Rather the
function he may be able to perform is that of opening up new

vistas and suggesting aspects of experience that may previously have been overlooked or underestimated. This is exactly the kind of a task in relation to education that John
Dewey, for example, helped to perform. But a philosopher
who under such circumstances failed to work closely with
the professional educator or who did not grasp the practical
problems of education would undermine the relevancy and the
effectiveness of his work.

But far more basically the philosopher may serve as
a resources person; one who can in cooperation with the educator bring the methodology and alternatives of philosophic
investigation to bear upon common educational philosophic
problems. One might put the matter another way: The educator, whether he realizes it or not is, as we have suggested
earlier, inevitably involved on a day to day basis with philosophic problems and issues. To perform his educational task
as effectively as possible, he needs enough philosophic sophistication to recognize the problems for what they are in
their historical context and the alternatives available. Here
the philosopher may be of direct aid in the common task of
helping human beings become as fully aware as possible of
what is involved in evaluating the direction of their experiences with a view to the fullest and most worthwhile life possible.

Fundamentally, the contention of the authors is not
that those who are called professional philosophers ought to
be called in on every educational problem. This would be
nonsense. Rather our contention is threefold: (1) that the
lines of communication be kept open for the mutual enrichment of both areas, (2) that those persons who specialize in
the field of philosophy of education have the opportunity to
develop competence in philosophy commensurate with their
competence in education or vice versa, and (3) that all persons who intend to teach should have some acquaintaince with
the aims, presuppositions, and alternatives in educational
theory through work in philosophy of education offered by
persons competent in both fields.

Turning to the second question: "Is the divorce between philosophy and education apt to be permanent?" the
answer would seem to be an encouraging "No." A number
of things point to increasing reconciliation and recognition of
the mutual involvement in common problems in both educational and philosophic circles. As early as 1942 the National Society for the Study of Education devoted the first part of

its Forty-first Yearbook to philosophies of education.[6]   A
more expanded and inclusive treatment appeared in the Society's Fifty-fourth Yearbook in 1955.[7]   In 1950, Educational Theory as the organ of the growing Philosophy of Education Society, along with the John Dewey Society and the College of Education of the University of Illinois began publication.   The Symposium on Philosophy of Education at the
Eastern Division of the American Philosophical Association
in 1955 (noted above) participated in by Professor Harry
Broudy and Professor Kingsley Price was followed up by the
spring issue, 1956, of the Harvard Educational Review, devoted wholly to comments on the symposium papers by an
extensive list of philosophers, educational philosophers, and
educators.[8]   Another symposium on value theory in education
is scheduled for the 1958 Meeting of the Eastern Division of
the American Philosophical Association.   The number of articles dealing with philosophy of education both in education
and philosophic journals has noticeably increased in the last
eight years as has the number of important new books.   As
cases in point on the preparatory level, advanced degree programs in social foundations and philosophy of education with
greater emphasis on philosophic adequacy have been developed and continued at the University of Illinois, New York
University, and Columbia.   The development at Boston University of the first joint program for a Ph.D. in philosophy
of education by a school of education and a graduate department of philosophy has stimulated much inquiry from other
institutions.   These are only sample cases of the renewed
interest and growing communication between fields.

In a period of shifting values, of national and international cultural crises such as our own, the educational philosopher stands in a peculiarly responsible and sensitive spot,
for his task is the articulation and development of the aims
and presuppositions of the educational processes.   To a remarkable degree failure to keep educational philosophy vital
and to translate it into educational process can mean the demise of a culture itself.   Accordingly the educational philosopher not only needs every encouragement but the active
cooperation of all the disciplines, philosophic and scientific,
that bear upon his task.

Notes

1.   I. J. Kandel, "Philosophy of Education," Harvard Educational Review, 26 (1956), pp. 134-136.

2. Max Black, "A Note on 'Philosophy of Education'," Harvard Educational Review, 26 (1956), p. 155.
3. Theodore Brameld, "Philosophy, Education, and the Human Sciences," Harvard Educational Review, 26 (1956), p. 137.
4. Ibid.
5. An instance to the contrary that advances the role of unifying theory in the education of the teacher is: Theodore Brameld, Cultural Foundations of Education. New York: Harper & Brothers Publishers, 1957, Chapter XIII, "The Study of Culture in Teacher Education," with particular reference to pp. 269-273.
6. Nelson B. Henry (ed.), The Forty-First Yearbook of the National Society for the Study of Education. Part I, Philosophies of Education, Chicago: University of Chicago Press, 1942.
7. Nelson B. Henry (ed.), The Fifty-Fourth Yearbook of the National Society for the Study of Education, Part I, Modern Philosophies of Education. Chicago: University of Chicago Press, 1955.
8. The original symposium papers were published in The Journal of Philosophy, 52 (1955), pp. 612-633. Harry S. Broudy's paper was entitled "How Philosophical Can Philosophy of Education Be?" (612-621) and Kingsley Price's paper was entitled "Is a Philosophy of Education Necessary?" (622-633).

MARY ANNE RAYWID

6. SOCIAL FOUNDATIONS REVISITED[*]

In Search of a Genre

One of the interesting sidelights of the discussion on the nature of Social Foundations of Education is its apologetic tone. Even some of the more extensive contributors have tended, like Professor Miller in the spring 1972 issue of Educational Studies, to offer a demurrer conceding the sterility and uselessness of the task. What follows will differ from some of the literature, for I do not think the investigation useless; indeed, insofar as deliberate scrutiny of one's own activities seems to be one of the surest routes we know to enhancing them, I take it that such discussion is highly desirable. Furthermore, even had the definitional discussions to date proved logically adequate, I suspect that the very nature of Social Foundations necessitates frequent re-examination of what it is up to. For its contemporaneous focus is one of its clearest features; and as the scene and context change, it seems reasonable that an enterprise identifying itself so largely on its responsiveness to the contemporary might change accordingly.

But we are getting ahead of ourselves. Before coming to focus on this or any other single attribute of Social Foundations, it might be helpful to try to locate the field within Foundations generally--hoping, with the help of the larger framework to establish a logical starting point and thus lend greater meaning and validity to our efforts. Such attempts have frequently foundered in the past, however, on such questions as "What are Foundations foundational to?" "Unless education is a discipline--which is questionable-- how can it have 'foundations'?" "Why is it that only education or educationists claim 'foundations,' while other disciplines, arts, and endeavors do not seem to think in such

---

*Educational Studies, Vol. 3 (1972), pp. 71-83. Reprinted with permission.

terms at all?" and "What sort of relationships are implicit
in the notion that certain claims and concerns are 'founda -
tional' to certain other claims and practices?"

It is, I think, because we have never made logically
adequate reply to these and similar questions that there remains an important job to do in identifying Foundations of
Education generally--others as well as Social Foundations.
But far from representing the distasteful and counterproduc-
tive chore some might suggest, this offers a challenge that
ought to claim some of our best efforts. To date, it seems
largely just the critics who have given the matter much at-
tention--so that most inquiries into education's Foundations
have not only yielded negative assessments, but have also
displayed a sufficiently unsympathetic tone as to rule out
constructive suggestions. Perhaps, then, those who want to
claim viability for the general notion of foundations for education ought to begin trying to wrestle with the challenges
and hard questions that have been raised--not just in the off-
hand fashion of an outsider like James Conant, but also in
the far more responsible manner of philosophers of education like Charles Brauner and George Newsome.[1] Such an
attempt might help to clarify one's own efforts and to facilitate decision on whether "Social Foundations of Education"
is an enterprise worth trying to pursue, or whether it ought
instead be laid to rest as the academic abomination or historical accident some claim. It is hoped that this article
will contribute to further friendly scrutiny. And as additional stimulus, I am appending a bibliography of all the relevant discussions I have seen.

I am not prepared to offer a logical topology of the
field and its parts. But perhaps I might contribute a little
to advancing the attempt, in the following way: When we ask
about Foundations of Education as a genre, and the possible
nature of this broad category that in some way seeks to subsume and render as parallels "History of Education," "Anthropology and Education," "Educational Psychology," and
"Comparative Education," it seems immediately evident that
no simple thread of likeness or relation is likely to suffice
by way of reply. If this seems obvious or trivial, it is by
no means accepted by all, however--as witness the view of
one analyst, for instance, that either the relation of logical
reducibility obtains between the claims of education's Foundations on the one hand, and educational assertions and practices on the other, or else education cannot claim to 'stand
on foundations' at all.[2] It seems far more likely that what-

ever similarities and connections may hold among such disparate subjects, and link them in turn to education, the ties
are considerably more complicated than that.

   The four-so-called Educational Foundations enumerated above (out of a far lengthier possible list, of course)
seem quite different sorts of cat; and if all are appropriately viewed to offer some kind of potential contribution to the
preparation of teachers and other educational specialists,
perhaps the four contributions differ quite markedly from
one another. That this be so might, perhaps, be suspected
even from the titles of the enterprises: in "History of Education," the term of as the connective or binding link suggests quite a different set of relations than the and which
has to articulate "Anthropology and Education." The very
form of the name "Educational Psychology," on the other
hand, seems to imply a much more integral connection between these two areas. Now given this spread of difference
in the way each of these three 'foundational' areas is internally constituted, it seems unlikely that any single pattern
will describe the way it is joined to and serves or illumi-
nates education. Any similarities among the connections
yielding these three areas of study are far more likely to
be of the looser "family resemblance" type than the rigorous,
tightly ordered relations logicians often seek.

   One of the important ways that at least some foundational fields differ from others is in the sort of contribution
they are expected to make to the professional preparation of
a teacher or other educational specialist: One would very
probably expose a prospective teacher to Educational Psychology to very different sorts of purposes than those which
might recommend a Philosophy of Education course. One
way to express the contrast in these purposes is by resort
to the distinction between applicative and interpretive uses
of knowledge. [3] From a logical standpoint, we can locate
Educational Psychology, and Philosophy of Education, better
than some other Foundations just because we have a fair
idea of the sort of contribution we want them to make to the
practitioner. On this basis, we might conclude that one of
the problems in identifying "Comparative Education" as a
Foundations area is that we are less clear about just what
prospective use to make of the knowledge it offers. It seems
to deal heavily with applicative-type material--as generally
adduced, however, to interpretive-type purposes. One of
the things which prominently divides Social Foundations specialists among themselves involves this very issue: Does

Social Foundations aim at providing knowledge primarily for
interpretive or for applicative use? Or, to put the matter
in terms more familiar: Are Social Foundations courses
intended to produce and equip social and educational activists
and reformers? Or is their purpose rather to provide understanding and interpretation of educational arrangements
and processes?

One of the things which make it difficult to consider
the broad question of the nature of Foundations of Education
--even to grab onto an adequate beginning--is the inevitably
circular or question-begging nature of almost any attempt to
do so. For example, the foregoing paragraph suggests that
there may be something different about Educational Psychology, marking it off from all other Foundations fields (with
the possible exception of Comparative Education) in that it
proffers knowledge for direct application rather than primarily for interpretive purposes (e.g., an Educational Psychology course would offer information about a method of teaching reading, to the purpose of having students put that information to immediate use in classrooms; material presented
in other Foundations areas, however, is not ordinarily projected as directly applicative to managing classrooms or conducting instruction). But this feature represents a difference
only if we designate the enumerated fields as "Foundations
of Education." If we call them, "Educational Studies" instead, this particular difference disappears--along with the
identification of any particular audience or sort of use for
the subject matter. The "Educational Studies" label does
not seem to promise, that is, that its offerings will stand in
any particular relation to any group or enterprise (educators
or educating) or, consequently, that it has any sort of special professional contribution to make. Readers will recognize this as the designation chosen, and the conception of the
field recently advanced by John Laska and others.[4] It is, of
course, one of the conceptions undergirding this journal and
the organization which publishes it. As is readily apparent,
the name is associated with the view that the several pursuits others call "Educational Foundations" ought to identify
and align themselves with liberal arts purposes, functions,
and administrative units. There are good sociological and
political reasons to recommend this,[5] and additionally, advocates claim that the liberal arts association would serve
to upgrade the calibre of the field. I am not sure I find
that sort of potential magic in such a switch. But it would
certainly have the merit of freeing us from the logical confines of the 'construction' metaphor which "Foundations" in-

evitably brings to mind, and perhaps also from such related
corruptions as "Fundamentals of Education." But the divorce
entailed--from the preparation of educators--proposes a separation of many of us would want quite strongly to reject.

Even such preliminary notes for a topology of Educa-
tions would be incomplete without adding that there have been
other proposals too, for reconstituting the category. The
University of Illinois identified its program some years ago
as the "Theoretical Foundations of Education," consisting of
"Historical, Comparative, Philosophical, and Social."[6] More
recently, Syracuse University subsumed these, plus a few
more, under the designation "Cultural Foundations of Education." The areas denoted may shift with changes in labels,
however, so that it is not always clear whether the increasingly popular term "Policy Studies" is intended in lieu of
"Foundations of Education" or more often in substitution just
for "Social Foundations." Thus, as this excursion has been
intended to show, there is more than a little conceptual spade-
work to be done in straightening out the terminological difficulties associated with the field. It is not primarily or just
names and labels at stake, of course, but far more importantly such matters as who is to profess and study the content in question, under what sorts of auspices, and for what
purposes. And, of course, changes introduced to exclusively nominal or other extraneous purposes can have far-reaching effects with regard to these critical questions.

Social Foundations or Policy Studies

In turning from trying to characterize the broad area
of Foundations to the presumably narrower and more specific
Social Foundations, we bear the burden of the difficulties already described, plus a few more. Occasional usage seems
to make Social Foundations exhaustive of the foundational
field, either by rendering it co-extensive with Foundations
generally, or by leaving it to the sole survivor after discon-
necting all those foundational concerns that can cleanly be assigned to one discipline or another (as in the case of Sociology of Education, History of Education, Philosophy of Education). Furthermore, even in such a disparate and uneven list,
Social Foundations seems a uniquely non-parallel entry in the
Foundations of Education roster. In contrast to Sociology of
Education, History of Education, and Philosophy of Educa-
tion--each of which suggests its own content, perspectives,
and inquiry procedures--Social Foundations represents an en-

terprise that is in some way fashioned from these, and
hence both related to and yet unlike them.   It is thus an
even more difficult enterprise to characterize than other
Foundations areas; and there may well be, as critics have
charged, an even wider range of conceptions of the field
among those who profess it.   I concluded an initial analysis by identifying four major approaches that rendered Social Foundations courses largely as social philosophy; social science (or sciences); a combination of these; or an introduction to teaching, serially displaying matters of official concern to teachers (e.g., curriculum, methods, child
development).   D. Bob Gowin, who inquired into the nature
of Social Foundations offerings at about the same time,
found five different types: "a philosophical approach, a social scientist or sociological approach, an historical approach, a social action, and social policy approach."[7]   The
considerable range undoubtedly reflects institutional accident
or administrative error in teaching assignment, as well as
real differences about the field among people with specialized preparation for teaching it.   But even so, there remains a considerable spread of opinion among those who
identify themselves primarily as Foundations specialists.
Thus, a survey of current practice may be more likely to
obstruct than to advance our inquiry into Social Foundations.[8]

Let us look, then, to some selected formulations of
the nature of Social Foundations of Education (or differently
named entities apparently proffered as equivalents):

(1)   The University of Illinois statement cited earlier
has this to say: "Social Foundations, as a field, is concerned with those aspects and problems of society which
need to be taken into account in determining educational policy, especially as this policy concerns the social role of the
school, and in determining broader social policies which affect educational policy."   And elsewhere: "The problems of
social foundations are the problems of policy-formulation and
policy-evaluation set by contemporary social conditions."[9]

(2) The late Stanley Ballinger, in a paper issued by
the University of Indiana "Center for the Study of Educational Policy," concluded that "educational policy can and ought
to be made a distinctive (but not isolated) field of study....
The study of educational policy ought to be one of the foundational disciplines of professional preparation of educational
workers, in close association with other foundational fields
of study, particularly philosophy of education, educational

sociology, history of education, and comparative education. It ... is to be centrally normative in its conception."[10]

(3) R. Freeman Butts called several years ago for a component in all doctoral programs at Columbia aimed at yielding "a disciplined sense of policy-oriented educational responsibility"--through (a) an understanding of "the deepest social and cultural crises of our civilization as they bear upon the educational enterprise" and (b) "competence in the use of disciplined methods of analysis and judgment." On the question of labels, Butts claimed that he has no objection to the traditional "Foundations of Education" designation but that his description, "Policy Orientation With Educational Responsibility," does yield a tempting substitute in the form of a timely acronym, "POWER."[11]

(4) James Shields accepted but enlarged the POWER conception, associating policy-oriented knowledge and its responsible use with enabling students (a) "to analyze American educational patterns and practices within the context of the ideals rooted in the democratic tradition" and helping them (b) "define for themselves the role they can and should play as professional educators in shaping educational policy." The first of these aims primarily involves focus on "the disparity between educational ideals and prevailing practices" or "the analysis of the general conceptions of human beings and human behavior implied in existing educational practices." And "responsible use could be most appropriately defined for now at least as raising the sensibilities of a wide range of the population to the realities of our American educational system in terms of a more humanized vision of man's place in the universe."[12]

There seem to be sufficient liknesses in these several renderings to permit identification of major common elements and shared presuppositions. Perhaps the clearest, most prominent of these is the policy preoccupation and focus. This is of considerable consequence in identifying and delineating the field within several universes of discourse. In the first place, logically speaking, the policy focus suggests a one-step or one-level removal from particular instances, but a less abstract level than those at which philosophy or social science might operate. Within professional preparation, then, the policy focus would serve to separate the concern of Social Foundations of Education from the detail of daily classroom practice, on the one hand and on the other, from such logically prior considerations as the

nature of man and knowledge, and the patterns of human
growth and development. Or, in the terminology of standard
course labels, it is this policy focus which distinguishes Social Foundations from Methods courses, and from Philosophy
and Educational Psychology courses.

A second similarity in these several conceptions is
that all assume Social Foundations to be <u>unifying</u> in nature,
drawing on the yield of disparate fields and considerations.
The policy-decision focus requires combining content from
several disciplines-recurringly from philosophy, plus one or
more social sciences--and of treating normative as well as
descriptive elements. The criterion on the basis of which
these concerns are selected is the demands of decisions
about educational arrangements and practices. Thus, policy
questions, problems, and issues become the organizing principle in Social Foundations, and content is chosen, ordered,
and articulated in terms of such questions, problems, and
issues. It is perhaps just this insistence which most clearly
and permanently denies Social Foundations disciplinary status,
for that would call for eventual development of its own logical structure, content, and procedure. Instead, Social
Foundations in effect makes the claim that the demands
of policy formulation span several disciplines, and are not
to be contained with the boundaries of academic disciplines.

A third attribute shared among the several conceptions of Social Foundations cited is the extensive implication of interpretive material. This deserves attention, because people have so accustomed themselves to contrasting facts with value judgments that they tend to minimize
or overlook what is, in some respects, the even greater
contrast between descriptive claims. Many descriptions
are immediately and extensively judgmental in nature. A
number of the sorts of descriptive claims involved in policy determination are perhaps more appropriately and accurately understood as characterizing or descriptive <u>judg-
ments</u> than as "facts" in any simple or immediately
sense-accessible sort of way.

This leads to a fourth element of presupposition associated with Social Foundations: It is that the particular
combining or integrational nature of the field calls for considerable self-consciousness about method. The Butts formulation makes this trait most explicit--in rendering "compe-

tence in the use of ... methods of analysis and judgment"
one of two major features of his program. Even where less
explicit, the focus remains important to the adequate performance of the Social Fundations functions, because the attempt to combine the yield of several disciplines must occur
without the usual methodological guidelines directing work
within any single discipline. In effect, Social Foundations
seeks to reassemble in an experiential context, the abstractions the several disciplines create as they separate for analysis what is connected empirically. In making such an attempt, the field is engaged in the logical challenge of span-
ning the gap dividing theory from practice. To seek to do
this in any scholarly and deliberate way calls for considerable methodological sophistication. In academic terms, it
is the sort of understanding and analytic skills one might
seek from work in Epistemology and Philosophy of Science.
These areas of philosophy, then, seem as centrally implicated in the doing of Social Foundations as the more frequently recognized areas of Social Philosophy and Value Theory.
(If the further demands of the methodological seem difficult
of realization for beginners, see Fischer and Thomas, Social Foundation of Educational Decisions,[13] as one attempt
at initiating the relevant instruction.)

A fifth similarity is the contextual preoccupation called
for by policy-formulation. Policy can hardly be advised, or
ill-advised, apart from the circumstances and conditions
within which it arises and is to apply. Ergo the very impetus for "social" foundations, or the weighing of social considerations, in arriving at educational policy. Furthermore,
the evaluation of educational policy cannot consist simply of
the one-way process this might suggest. The "context" to
be considered is not just a simple, linear situation in which
all extra-educational or 'other' institutions shape education:
the actual situation is a far more intricate one of reciprocal
impacts and influences. Hence, Social Foundations is typically concerned with viewing education's effects on society
as well as society's formative impact on the schools. Furthermore, the effect of such close and reciprocal relations is,
as the University of Illinois statement put it, that the concern of Social Foundations must extend to include "broader
social policies which affect educational policy." Thus, the
issue Counts made explicit in asking "Dare the Schools Build
a New Social Order?" must remain an ever-present accom-
paniment to the doing of Social Foundations. For although
most analysts might deny such innovative force to schools,
there is considerably less doubt as to their power as exerted

in the opposite direction, and their ability to opt to retard
and impede change. For this reason, as both the Butts and
Shields statements strongly suggest, the object of the policy
formulation and evaluation shifts back and forth, from school
to society. If this seems vague or imprecise, that is virtually unavoidable, given the school's raison d'être as the institution in which society makes its most deliberate commitment as to what it wishes to be.

A sixth feature typical of Social Foundations conceptions is the assumption that ideas form a critical part of the
social context to be examined. If this seems too obvious
and unexceptionable an assumption to warrant much attention,
it might be noted that it is one of the major points of contrast between Social Foundations of Education and a great
deal of Sociology of Education--the latter often taking institutional practice and structure as the significant context of the
school's operation, rather than the ideas which articulate and
justify those. This particular assumption as to the power
and significance of belief in human affairs would account, then,
for a prominent part of the difference between one of Shields'
courses as described above, and a Sociology of Education
course. It would also account for the Social Foundations
concern with general ideology (as distinct from the products
of formal science and technical philosophy).

Finally, as the contextual focus would imply, these
and other conceptions of education's Social Foundations are
marked by an insistently contemporaneous orientation--a preoccupation with present circumstances, events, and conditions. The pursuit must obviously be firmly rooted in examining the here and now, given the articulating purpose of exploring which educational arrangements and practices seem
currently best advised. Questions about the past may become one facet of the examination, but the contemporary focus of Social Foundations assigns any historical content its
role and function--in the same way that the policy-framing
context may call for, but restricts and assigns the use of,
philosophic and social scientific material.

As I noted at the outset, it is this 'contemporaneous-
ness' and the demand that education respond to the present,
that calls for such periodic surveys of the state of the field
as the foregoing, and by implication at least, for reconstituting Social Foundations when time and circumstances seem to
recommend that. Is today such a juncture? Is the conception of Social Fundations--with the roots identified above--a

sound and viable one? I think that it is, and furthermore
timely and responsive to the current than to the previous
Foundations idea even more timely and responsive to the current than to the previous Foundations idea even more timely
and responsive to the current than to the previous decade.
But if such timeliness is necessary to viability for the field,
it is not sufficient. Not all that is timely is proper grist
for the academic mill. Thus, a case for Social Foundations
must be able to claim academic validity for the pursuit, as
well as responsiveness. And this requires a look at the arguments in principle that have been raised in challenging it.

The Question of Academic Validity

Those questioning the academic respectability of Social Foundations of Education have in effect maintained that
the enterprise violates certain logical and disciplinary boundaries that academia has come to observe.[14] Thus, Social
Foundations has been questioned not only for its insistence
on borrowing widely from the several social sciences, but
also for its failure to observe such distinctions as is and
ought or normative and descriptive, philosophic and scientific, academic and professional. Since the analytic or 'divide
and conquer' approach has been the dominant essential strategy for academic research--with new disciplines emerging
largely from the discovery and observance of ever finer distinctions and categories--the obliterating or ignoring of such
lines has been in opposition to academic fashion. Even more
fundamentally, Social Foundations has stood against the Posi-
tivist-inspired academic withdrawal from the advocacy function generally. As the result of a series of philosophic
moves, the view which eventually came to dominate academia
at large was that advocacy (in the guise of evaluational conclusions and recommendations as well as outright urgings) is
just so much 'sermonizing': Since no amount of description
can, in logical terms, ever ground any prescription, then
the advocacy function simply has no place in academia. Furthermore, not only should the barrier separating description
from prescription be observed, but also the integrity of each
of the several disciplines at stake. The social sciences differ, it has been argued, as to concept and theory, presuppositions, and methodology. To attempt, then, to combine their
yield apart from any principle of systematic combination (i.e.,
short of formulating an explicit methodology for a new discipline) is to invite academic hash--an eclectic mess.

Social Foundations advocates have attempted a variety
of rejoinders, but in my own view these objections would
weigh heavily against any attempt to claim Social Foundations of Education as a discipline in its own right with unique
content, perspective, and method. But why need any such
claim be asserted? It seems to me that Social Foundations
(and possibly the other Foundational areas as well) represents a teaching field, not an academic discipline. It is put
together for instructional not for research purposes, and
there is no reason why it need try to meet or answer to the
criteria marking and measuring academic disciplines, which
are primarily fields of inquiry. The particular 'package'
constituting Social Foundations is assembled on the grounds
that it unites disparate material bearing on educational issues, using the issues themselves as the selecting and organizing principle. In a professional school context, what
further logical justification is needed for assigning such a
central, articulating function to issues surrounding the professional practice and setting?[15]

It has recently been held (and continues to be, among
many 'academic studies' advocates) the prospective professionals, like others, would do far better to examine the institution instead through the lenses (concepts, methods, etc.)
provided by a single discipline. I have never been convinced that this is so, since it seems so patently reasonable
to assume that education's problems might better be illum-
ined with the aid of a number of research fields: political
science, anthropology, history, philosophy, sociology, economics may all offer valuable input to the display of a particular educational policy issue, so why not seek and exploit
such aid? To rely exclusively on anthropology or economics
as the means or lens for exploring education--even for the
duration of a single course--is to accept, among other things,
the categories or logical organization of the discipline chos-
en, along with its tools for working within them. These
categories and structures are obviously not coincidental with
those of education as an art or field of professional study
(which is, indeed, why education is not simply applied anthropology or economics). Thus, to insist that content be
chosen and courses organized to the intent of displaying anthropology's contribution to understanding education may be
better calculated to obscure than to illuminate education.
Cutting the academic pie in this way seems plausible enough
for the purpose of preparing an anthropologist or economist,
but far less so for preparing an educator.

It seems to me, then, that the case for Social Foundations of Education as an instructional enterprise seeking to render some aspect of the universe most intelligibly would be quite similar to the case made for social studies in the schools, in preference to social sciences. The over-riding considerations might properly be more psychological than logical--more closely tied to the empirical question of 'Which approach seems to lead to the greatest amount of most meaningful learning for more students?' than to questions of epistemological credentials. And on this sort of criterion, it seems to me that Social Foundations is at no disadvantage whatsoever. Indeed, its superiority to the alternatives we have been considering seems a highly plausible hypothesis,[16] partly on the grounds that it is far easier to catch and sustain student engagement with Illich's de-schooling proposal or Jerry Farber's impetus to total de-institutionalization than with the far more logically adequate and academically respectable treatments of quite similar substance by Joseph Grannis and Robert Dreeben.[17] All four stress the instructional effects of education's institutional structure. But the difference in appeal and impact displays the critical pedagogical role of context, and offers a key to the special timeliness of the Social Foundations approach for today. Grannis and Dreeben provide careful examination and insightful sociological description of the ways in which classroom and school structure teach, and of the particular messages they impart. Illich and Farber, on the other hand, forage widely to round out their indictments of the school, charging a "hidden curriculum" deliberately exploited to the purpose of making "niggers" of students. The appeal of the Illich and Farber versions (even despite Illich's formidable prose) seems to reside in considerable part in their advocacy posture. Since it is the argument that determines the material to be included, both also call on content from several disciplines, in disregard of academic bounds. These two attributes reflect themes of increasing contemporary prominence--and themes to which Social Foundations is remarkably responsive.

Timeliness and Relevance

One of the most insistent demands of today's young is for "getting it together" and, as they also put it, for "getting it together in a new way." The press is in part for a new unification or articulation of life that would put an end to the weird contradictions and awful dysfunctions. Such ills occur, it is charged, because of contemporary life's frag-

mentary and disjointed character (which is, in turn, the consequence of our failure to insist on rendering conditions and
events more immediately and adequately responsive to human
concerns).   The demand is a call, then, for the re-shuffling
and re-constituting of traditional categories: the obliteration
of present boundaries and the recombining of present elements so as to create different ones.   Applied to institutions,
"getting it together differently" would mean an end to some
and the emergence of new ones.   As it applies within the
school as a particular institution, the message is a call for
dividing education into different sorts of parts or elements.
As Postman and Weingartner expressed it, "it's the damned
sequences, lines, compartments, and categories that need to
be split, rearranged, and integrated."[18]   The formal ordering of content, according to disciplines established to research purposes, yields academia's most prominent and pervasive compartments and categories.   On the academic
scene, it is these that are being challenged in the complaint
against fragmentation and the demands to "get it together in
a new way."

       Again, these are complaints and demands to which
Social Foundations is highly responsive, as an enterprise constituted precisely from its insistence on "getting it together."
Moreover, the resulting integration proceeds on a principle
of combination (the policy-formulation function) that is both
somewhat exceptional within academic practice and responsive to the heightened human concern with decision-making.

       This brings us to a second and very important sense
in which Social Foundations of Education seems particularly
attuned to the spirit of the times.   It is directly responsive
to our growing preoccupation with commitment and our increasing rejection of the Positivist withdrawal from advocacy.
Academics seem to be emerging from a long period of reti-
cence about advancing conclusions and solutions in the realm
of practical affairs.   Ours is a day and age increasingly impatient with such technicalities as is-to-ought fallacies, and
an academic's resulting hesitancy to range beyond the descriptive of his own bailiwick.   Within Foundations departments, the press is understandably great, given the widespread social criticism of the day; and the ensuing demands
cause real consternation.   For on the one hand, our road to
academic respectability has seemed to lie in ever closer emulation of traditional liberal arts procedure and practice; and
on the other hand, we are being pressured from various
quarters to depart radically from that practice.   Meanwhile,

the breech is being filled by a number of figures who seem
in an important sense to be doing Foundations of Education,
and doing it better and with more success than those who
formally profess it.   Such seems to be the case with Paul
Goodman, Edgar Friedenberg, Jonathan Kozol, and John Holt,
to name just a few.   The hearing they have obtained is not
only a function of the particular views they urge, but also of
their very willingness to prescribe for us all.   As of a decade ago, the cautious academic's response to all this might
well have been to charge insufferable hubris in such attempts
to assume the Renaissance Man role and then burden it even
further with the "witness" function tacked on as well.   Today, however, such objections might very well meet with
reasonable if naive questions as to knowledge's worth if it
be unrelated to wisdom and advocacy.   (The question gathers
added force, of course, when put within a professional
school context--of education, or anything else.   For if knowledge does not serve as a warrant for prescribing practice,
then why do we have or need professional schools at all?)

     In some respects, Social Foundations of Education
may almost have come full circle since its official beginnings
in the Thirties. [19]   The open advocacy marking its early
stages came to be muted later, in two associated developments already noted: the Positivist critique, and the search
for academic respectability.   Under such circumstances, the
warrant for the enterprise soon collapsed--for reasons which
seem evident in Harold Rugg's memorable rendering of the
procedure involved, "LET THE FACTS CONCLUDE!"[20]
Subsequent generations of graduate students tended to considerably less intensity and ardor, coming into contact with the
restraining influence--the dash of cold water--of then-current
philosophical fashion.   Some sought to retain general affiliation with the tradition, while disassociating themselves from
"subjective pontificating";[21] others, however, found it unsal-
vageable, simply "a moralizing doctrine."[22]   Perhaps the
full circle can be traced in the career of James McClellan,
who pursued his graduate work at the University of Illinois,
surrounded by the Social Foundations tradition. [23]   As a Philosopher of Education of growing eminence, McClellan joined
in the epistemological objections and rejection alluded to
earlier.   In 1962, however, he co-authored a textbook displaying virtually all of the elements by means of which we
have identified the Social Foundations enterprise: Education
and the New America[24] presses a persuasive case for building a particular sort of ideology, or commitment, in the
young; the recommendation is grounded largely in an exten-

sive socio-cultural diagnosis and appraisal of our time.   It
does not seem inappropriate to take the appearance of such
a book as at least tacid author acknowledgment of the need
for, and legitimacy of, the Social Foundations function.

It would appear that conditions may keep that need
alive for some time to come.   There are significant parallels to be drawn between our time and the Thirties which
gave rise to Social Foundations--a shared sense of urgency
and crisis, and a comparable dearth of plan and program of
sufficient promise to unify and rally large numbers.   Given
such a context, and the contextual commitment of Social
Foundations, it seems possible that the field may once again
be addressing itself largely to the social advocacy function.
That seems highly appropriate to the needs of the time, assuming we can exercise and inculcate that sort of "responsible use of policy oriented knowledge" which would distinguish
academic advocacy from the "Right on!" variety.   I think that
sort of distinction possible.   And I conclude, furthermore,
that it frees us from any academic obligation to abjure advocacy altogether in favor of that exclusively descriptive pose
which, if transferred to the world of daily affairs, could only
counsel a kind of detached suspension within it.

This is the construction of Social Foundations of Education which the contemporary scene seems to call for.   Perhaps it is both boon and bane, boast and embarrassment of
the enterprise that a different context will undoubtedly require
a new construction.   Which is why, as we suggested at the
outset, those who profess Social Foundations need commit
themselves to permanent professional self-consciousness and
continuing re-examination of their field.

Notes

1.   See Brauner's Chapter 11, "A Moralistic Doctrine:
       Foundations of Education," in his American Educa-
       tional Theory (Englewood Cliffs, N.J.:   Prentice-
       Hall, 1964), pp. 198-223, and Newsome's "Social
       Foundations of Education: Where Do They Stand?"
       Educational Philosophy and Theory 3 (May 1971):
       19-27.
2.   C. D. Hardie, "Does Education Stand on Its Founda-
       tions?" Educational Philosophy and Theory 1 (May
       1969):   3-7.
3.   As drawn in Democracy and Excellence in American

Secondary Education (Chicago: Rand McNally, 1964), by Harry S. Broudy, B. Othanel Smith, and Joe R. Burnett. See pp. 50-60.

4. See John A. Laska, "Current Progress in the Foundations of Education," Teachers College Record 71 (December 1969): 179-86.

5. For the discussion of some of these reasons see especially the Laska article (ibid.) and Janice F. Weaver, "Some Additional Questions for Foundations of Education," Proceedings of the Third Annual Meeting of the American Educational Studies Association, 1971, pp. 163-170.

6. In a University of Illinois bulletin written by Archibald W. Anderson, Kenneth D. Benne, Foster McMurray, B. Othanel Smith, and William O. Stanley, and titled The Theoretical Foundations of Education (Urbana, 1951).

7. D. Bob Gowin and M. E. DeYoung, "An Analysis of Conceptions of Social Foundations of Education," Undated ms. (c. 1967), p. 1.

8. It should be noted that differences of construction of a field do not, of course, per se cast doubt upon its respectability or viability. There are a number of quite different notions of the field of Philosophy of Education, held by recognized leaders therein; but it remains comparatively free of a number of the challenges to which Social Foundations is subject. Nor is Philosophy of Education challenged qua field by the misassigned teacher who does not know its content. His uninformed practice has little effect on modifying the field and its literature. Not so, evidently, in Social Foundations.

9. Anderson et al., op. cit., p. iv.

10. "The Nature and Function of Educational Policy: An Introductory Essay," Occasional Paper No. 65-101, Center for the Study of Educational Policy, Indiana University, May, 1965, p. 32.

11. In a widely circulated letter of December 10, 1968, addressed to Dean Robert J. Schaefer of Teachers College, pp. 3, 4, 6.

12. "Foundations of Education: Relevance Redefined," Teachers College Record 71 (December 1969): 187, 194, 198.

13. Louis Fischer and Donald R. Thomas, Social Foundations of Educational Decisions (Belmont, Calif.: Wadsworth, 1965).

14. This section deals with some of the direct challenges

put to Social Foundations, i.e., with objections
addressed to the conduct of Foundations activities.
For reasons which hopefully will be apparent, it
does not attempt to confront the broader, or indirect case involving the sorts of issues cited on
the first page of this essay.

15. Note that here, as elsewhere, the issue hinges on one's
construction of the genre. The argument above has
force if we want to talk about "Foundations," designed for educators; it seems considerably less
persuasive if we want to construe the genre instead
as "academic studies of education," available as
general education.

16. This article has perhaps already attempted too much to
take on the additional matter of the evidence tend-
ing to support such a preliminary hypothesis. But
it might be of interest to note in this regard that
in their treatment of all sorts of material, peda-
gogues have long attributed motivational value to
the very invitation to consider policy sorts of questions! The strategy of a great deal of discussion
teaching rests precisely on the assumption that the
very process of selecting a stance, or deciding
what ought to be--i.e., framing or evaluating policy decision--is of intrinsic interest, or motivational value per se.

17. The allusion is to numerous publications by Ivan Illich,
most extensively his Deschooling Society (New York:
Harper and Row, 1970); to Jerry Farber's "The
Student as Nigger" appearing in his book of the
same name (North Hollywood, Calif.: Contact
Books, 1969); to Joseph Grannis's "The School as
a Model of Society," in the Harvard Graduate
School of Education Bulletin 12 (Fall 1967); and to
Robert Dreeben's On What Is Learned in School
(Reading, Mass.: Addison-Wesley, 1968).

18. Neil Postman and Charles Weingartner, Teaching as a
Subversive Activity (New York: Delacorte, 1969),
p. 86.

19. For this history, see Brauner, op. cit., and I. James
Quillen, "Education of Teachers: Social Founda-
tions," Society and the Schools: Communication
Challenge to Education and Social Work, ed. Robert
H. Beck (New York: National Association of Social
Workers, 1965), pp. 67-85.

20. Harold Rugg, Foundations for American Education
(Yonkers-on-Hudson, N.Y.: World Book Company,

1947).   See the Foreword and passim.
21.   The phrase is that of Louis Fischer and Donald G.
        Lahr, who used it in designation of the sort of ma-
        terial excluded from their survey of recent inquiry
        related to "Social Policy and Education," in Review
        of Educational Research 37 (February 1967), p. 34.
22.   This is Charles Brauner's title phrase, op. cit.
23.   Brauner, ibid., assigns a central role to the University
        of Illinois program as furthering and elaborating up-
        on the Social Foundations tradition begun at Colum-
        bia.
24.   By Solon T. Kimball and James E. McClellan (New
        York: Random House, 1962).   The book's jacket
        identifies it as "a basic reappraisal of America's
        emergent form of civilization."

Bibliography

Anderson, Archibald W.; Benne, Kenneth D.; McMurray,
        Foster; Smith; B. Othanel; and Stanley, William
        O.   The Theoretical Foundations of Education.
        Urbana: University of Illinois, 1951.
Ballinger, Stanley E.   "The Nature and Function of Educa-
        tional Policy."   Occasional Paper No. 65-101,
        Center for the Study of Educational Policy, Indiana
        University, 1965.
Beck, Robert H.; Borrowman, Merle L.; Callahan, Raymond
        E.; and Stanley, William O.   Social Foundations of
        Education: An Essential in the Professional Educa-
        tion of Teachers.   Cedar Falls: Extension Service,
        State College of Iowa, 1966.
Brauner, Charles J.   "A Moralistic Doctrine: Foundations
        of Education."   In American Educational Theory,
        pp. 198-223, Englewood Cliffs, N.J.:   Prentice-
        Hall, 1964.
Broudy, Harry S.   "Teaching: Craft or Profession?"   Edu-
        cational Forum 20 (January 1956):   175-84.
Butts, R. Freeman.   Letter to Dean Robert Schaefer, De-
        cember 10, 1968.
Campbell, Jack K.   "The 'Black Status' of Teacher Educa-
        tion in Academia."   Proceedings of the American
        Educational Studies Association, 1971, pp. 152-
        162.
Derr, Richard L.   "Social Foundations As a Field of Study
        in--Education."   Educational Theory, April, 1965,
        pp. 154-160.

Eason, Elmer. "Sociology of Education Is Not Enough."
    Journal of Educational Sociology 35 (November
    1961): 141-43.
Gowin, D. B., and DeYoung, M. E. "An Analysis of Concep-
    tions of Social Foundations of Education," Unpub-
    lished ms., c. 1967.
Hansen, Donald. "The Uncomfortable Relations of Sociology
    and Education." In On Education: Sociological
    Perspectives, edited by Donald A. Hansen and Joel
    E. Gerstl. New York: Wiley, 1967.
Hardie, C.D. "Does Education Stand on Its Foundations?"
    Educational Philosophy and Theory 1 (1969): 3-7.
Laska, John A. "Current Progress in the Foundations of
    Education." Teachers College Record 71 (Decem-
    ber 1969): 179-86.
Levit, Martin. "The Study of Education." Address to the
    National Standing Conference on Humanistic and
    Behavioral Studies in Education, April 14, 1971.
Lipkin, John P. "Thoughts Toward Defining the Social Foun-
    dations of Education." Education Review 5 (1967)
    [University of Virginia].
Miller, Steven I. "The Social Foundations of Education:
    Issues and Concerns." Educational Studies 3
    (Spring 1972): 1-4.
Newsome, George L. "Social Foundations of Education:
    Where Do They Stand?" Educational Philosophy
    and Theory 3 (1971): 19-27.
Quillen, I. James. "Education of Teachers: Social Founda-
    tions." Society and the Schools: Communication
    Challenge to Education and Social Work, edited by
    Robert H. Beck. New York: National Associa-
    tion of Social Workers, 1965.
Raywid, Mary Anne. "Response to Jan Weaver." Middle
    Atlantic States Philosophy of Education Society,
    April 16, 1967.
_____. "Social Foundations: Notes for a Concept Analy-
    sis." Unpublished ms., February, 1968.
_____. Review of Social Foundations of Education: A
    Cross-Cultural Approach, by Cole Brembeck. Ed-
    ucational Forum, March, 1968, p. 380.
_____. Review of Social Foundations of Educational De-
    cisions, by Louis Fischer and Donald R. Thomas.
    Educational Forum, March, 1967, p. 371.
Rugg, Harold. Foundations for American Education.
    Yonkers-on-Hudson: World Book Company, 1947,
    pp. 578-582.
Rust, Val. "Experiencing Foundations of Education." Pro-

ceedings of the American Educational Studies Association, 1971, pp. 102-112.

Shields, James J., Jr. "Foundations of Education: Relevance Redefined." Teachers College Record 71 (December 1969): 187-98.

_____. "Social Foundations of Education: The Problem of Relevance," Teachers College Record 70 (October 1968): 77-87.

Urban, Wayne J. "Social Foundations and the Disciplines," Teachers College Record, 71 (December 1969): 199-205.

Weaver, Jan. "Some Additional Questions for Foundations of Education," Proceedings of the American Educational Studies Association, 1971, pp. 163-170.

_____. "An Analysis of Conceptions of Social Change as an Illustration of Social Foundations of Education." Lecture at Ohio State University, April 25, 1972.

EDWARD FRANKLIN BUCHNER

7. EDUCATION AS A SCIENTIFIC PURSUIT[*]

The last half century or more has revealed great
outbursts of interests in every form of education. Not only
have these outbursts appeared and effected reforms, but the
interests have been cumulative in their power. In the present decade our pedagogical passions have become intensely
consuming. There is grim determination written across the
face of every school community. Citizens are demanding a
more vital and practical training for the children of the
state. Educational leaders are multiplying schemes for re-
sponding to these public demands, while teachers are flitting
to and fro, and expending their well-worn energies in making efforts to fit themselves anew to the demands of the
hour. Schools and school studies are multiplied in number.
The total enrollment in the secondary schools, for example,
during the decade has increased eighty-six per cent. The
percentage of increase of students in these schools taking the
so-called secondary studies during the ten years has been
more than one hundred per cent, on the whole, reaching as
high as one hundred and seventy-four per cent in the case
of Latin, and one hundred and forty-seven per cent in the
case of geometry. The proportionate number of students
taking Greek in these schools is eight per cent greater than
the proportionate increase in the total enrollment during the
decade.

Established institutions of learning, on the other hand,
have created a veritable field of competition in trying to provide substantially for an academic recognition of education.
Trustees and professors are surmising that education, even,
may be made a "liberalizing" study. On the professional
side of these higher interests these institutions have been
providing "courses for teachers," establishing chairs for
"the science and art of teaching," and forming organic departments in which a full-orbed study of education can be

---

[*]Education, Vol. 24 (1903), pp. 129-32, 137-38, 142-44.

carried on.   About one tenth of the total number of so-
called normal students in the United States four years ago
were pursuing their studies in universities and colleges.
Ten years earlier the statistical records made no mention
of students of "pedagogy" in our higher institutions!

Again, the history of educational thought and practices is being studied as never before, and great numbers
are listening to fresh expoundings of the philosophy of education.   Teachers have been led to believe, by the goadings of
those who have urged them on, that the repository of educational traditions is a many-doored chamber.   Every form of
educational effort finds some representation of its material
therein.   Teachers, however, have not gone to this repository through the impulse of their pedagogical instincts, or
the history of education would have been known long before
Schwartz, ninety years ago.

If we turn from this more scholastic interest in education, and regard the practical phases of the upheavals and
reforms, we find on every hand intenser interests and a
more varied expression thereof.   There are the educational
"committees," to whom is committed authority on certain
specialties.   There are the conventions, submerging the local and the national teacher alike.   There are the round-
tables, all maintaining that the teacher should be trained into something more than merely an appreciative state of mind.
It would add nothing to our purpose to be reminded of the
material interests which have gained in such enormous expressions during these years.

These really violent changes which have appeared, and
will continue to appear, in educational thought and endeavor,
essentially regarded, are due to an apparent attempt to rec-
oncile the claims of science with the deeds of education.
Some time since, in a conversation with a mature woman,
trained and learned in the physical sciences, I was informed
of the absolute impossibility of calling education a science,
or of its ever possessing a scentific character.   The brief,
and for her mind, the clinching argument, ran thus: "I have
been so long accustomed to the exact sciences that I do not
see that you prove anything in psychology." (I was not in-
sensible to the double thrust at both pedagogy and psychology
made in this criticism.)   As over against this echo from the
mathematical view of scientific knowledge, the student of the
hour must recognize two things: first, the willingness of
educators to look for fundamental principles which shall give

birth to rules suggesting an education according to the natural conditions of the human individual; second, the student
must at the same time observe a contemporaneous openness
on the part of science to appropriate every natural sequence
to itself, whether that sequence appears among masses of
matter, living cells, or in human history. Hence there has
been a gradual admission by many among us that education
is open to a treatment similar to that which science tries to
give to the material which it has recognized hitherto.

One evidence of this reconciliation, it is well to note
in passing, can be found in the usual form of expression
prevalent during the last twenty-five years. It has been a
well-established custom to speak of "education as a science,"
rather than to say that it is a science. Men have not been
willing to apply so pretentious, consoling and convenient a
name as science to any and every attempt to expound the uncertain art of the teacher. This mode of expression might
even be taken as implying that every systematic statement
of law and maxim which has relation to the task of educating
is really specious. One could follow along this line and
easily work out very serious insinuations against every effort to make the problems of education really intelligible.
We may yet have enough occasion to see just how much spe-
ciousness there is in the current aspect of education, which
shelters itself behind the all-protecting shield of the adjec-
tive which appears in our theme. We should not fail to notice, however, a delicate modesty which has pervaded this
pedagogical attitude. It has a better side, in which the
claim of the educational aspirant merely reads thus: In all
treatment of educational problems one should insist upon
"the utmost precision and rigor in the statement, deduction
and proof" of the various conclusions which represent the intellectual side of educational activity....

The outcome of the discussion so far leads one to see
that the teacher is a dominant factor in the work of education. This work is not automatic in its execution. This
should be instructive to the ready definers of educational activity, and lead them to observe that in every valid definition there should be implicit, if not explicit, reference to
the nature of education as limited by the possible achievements
of the teacher. In other words, if education is to be regarded as a scientific pursuit, the first necessity to be heeded
and the first condition to be fulfilled is that we sould deal
with real facts, real events, and real possibilities. Ideali-
zation is alluring in no form of human interest more than in

that of education. It is not implied that there are not ideal
interests and obligations to be thought of in connection with
the great art of human training and human formation. But
for the present, it cannot be insisted upon too urgently that
the teacher and he who thinks about the teacher's efforts
must address their attention to specific forms of empirical
reality.

This leads to the next step in our consideration, where
we are obliged to notice some descriptive facts of teaching.
Here is where, if anywhere at all, must be found those facts
of possible experience which comprise the data of a pedagogical science. Our first observation is to the negative effect that one phrase is not sufficient to describe teaching as
a real thing. To teach is not to enact a simple occurrence;
to teach is not to convey one idea; to teach is not the production of a simple movement; to teach is not an elementary
adjustment. On the contrary, the present epoch of scientific
analysis is enabling us to see the complications which are
carried into the schoolroom and developed there to a high degree. We must recognize that the character of a science
and that the attitudes of those who pursue it are determinable
in terms of the material constituting the experience of which
it seeks description and offers explanation. Now, to be
frank, what is the so-called material in educational experience? For the time being, there should be no hesitancy in
maintaining that the primary facts of educational science are,
and must be, found in acts of teaching, and these are the
most empirical of all pedagogical data. A boy draws a blackboard picture of a hen, or a girl memorizes and recites a
selection of poetry, or a third child succeeds or fails in getting certain geometrical concepts. In these apparently isolated cases lurk the generalities which are sought in ascer-
taining the scientific basis of the maxims to be offered for
the next thing to be done in any given case....

There are those among us who would have education
become truly scientific merely as a result necessarily following from the fact of having teachers study particular sciences.
To all intents and purposes, the study of hydrostatics or of
chorology would be regenerative on the part of the teacher.
It is supposed that science is a universal spirit that breathes
over all. But dry bones can never be made to grow dead
flesh! If education is every to become a science, in the
sense of working out a particular and acceptable method of
supporting its inductions, it cannot be brought about by wearing a borrowed mantle, but rather by the elaboration of what

is inherent in the activity of the teacher, generically regarded, and of the pupil as the other member of every
teaching equation.   Let us therefore abandon the hope of
making ourselves scientific merely by forcing ourselves to
study the sciences as sciences.

It is high time that we look upon education somewhat
more favorably.   In the first place, it must be recognized
by ourselves, and we must lead others to see, that a quantitative analysis is not the fundamental trait of the scientific
attitude.   This, of course, has been the historic claim of
the scientists.   The details of the known objects or events,
it is said, must be counted and measured.   Amounts of
things are supposed to give us accurate knowledge, and
changes are supposed to succeed one another volumetrically.

Now, it is just as true that a qualitative analysis is
necessary in every form of knowledge, and, in fact, must
precede every attempt to measure.   The distinction of "what
kind" must be made before an arbitrary or a natural standard of quantitative estimation can be established.   There is
a disposition in many of the sciences at present to sneer at
a merely qualitative treatment of their facts.   Let us insist,
however, that there is "exact" knowledge essentially given in
the detection of the marks or attributes of any object in
which the scientist has an interest.   The work of education
is to be understood, then, not in terms of months and grades,
nor in numbers of studies and examination percentages.   The
mathematical refinement, which has usurped almost entirely
the modern schoolroom, is a most vicious trait of the current pedagogical attitude.   No doubt it is quite proper that
the educational machinery should be reported, and it can be
reported only in terms of number.   This necessity has over-
flown its channels, and has transformed itself into the spirit
of our pedagogical thought, ramifying the whole structure
from the United States Bureau to the smallest school.

When it is said that a qualitative analysis of the work
of education must be undertaken, one must not jump immediately into the realm of ideals or the determination of ultimate values.   This is done too often, and results in giving
us an education based on abstractions.   Long before the
teacher can present ideals, and long before the pupil mind
can entertain notions of value, the progress of teaching is
dependent upon kinds of material, kinds of methods, and
kinds of attitudes, to which the teacher must resort in order
to accomplish the ends of teaching.   We are all apt to rec-

ognize this now and then in a sporadic way.   But the num-
bering and percentage spirit has so engrossed our interests
that the recognition of qualitative values has but little force
in our reflections.

JAMES L. KUETHE

8. EDUCATION: THE DISCIPLINE THAT CONCERN BUILT*

This conference on the discipline of education comes
at a time when the entire process of formal education is under a spotlight more brilliant and more searching than ever
before in history. Never before have so many individuals
been involved, so much money been spent; and never before
has there been so much doubt about the nature and methods
of education and its practitioners. There is far less agreement today about the goals and methods of education than
there was twenty years ago. Of what is this a symptom?
Does this mean we know more? Does it mean we are attempting to include more? Or does it simply mean that our
concern has increased and as a result our doubts are greater?

It is my contention that we know quite a bit more
about the process of education, and this, together with increased concern, is one source of the prevalent confusion.
It is not my intention, if, indeed, it is in my capacity, to
go into the reasons for the increased concern which serves
to produce this confusion, or at least to give it publicity.
The challenge of conflicting ideologies in the modern world
and the staggering increase in population would no doubt be
high in the list of factors that have awakened concern. It is,
rather, my intention to argue that some degree of order can
be brought out of the chaos by the study of education as an
entity in it own right. I believe that education can be and
should be studied in the same sense that the disciplines of
history and physics are studied and are in turn developed
through study. When I say that it is important to study education, I run the risk of being regarded as having made a
statement of the quality and significance of "Love your moth-

---

*From John Walton and James L. Kuethe, eds., The Disci-
pline of Education (Madison: The University of Wisconsin
Press; c 1963 by The Regents of the University of Wisconsin), pp. 73-84.

er" or "Let us all be loyal citizens." This is the climate of thinking at the moment in this country as a result of the publicity, favorable and unfavorable, that the educational enterprise has been receiving. It almost seems at times that the topic of education has become like classical music-- many people show great interest in it because they feel they should, even if they are bored by what they hear.

I want now to come back to my statement that education should be studied. The climate is such that I could expect with almost any audience to receive vigorous nods of approval, much as if I had said we should eliminate slums. Allow me, though, to point out a quite basic assumption that I have made, an assumption easily obscured by the prevalent level of concern. My central assumption, indeed my contention, is that there is something here that can be studied. This is what I meant when I said education can and should be studied in the same sense that history or physics are studied.

It is, then, my belief that there is a developing discipline of education worthy of study in its own right. What does this mean? A discipline implies a set of teachings: at least this is the meaning of disciplina from where the term discipline derives. However, there is a tendency to require more of a discipline than simply that there be a set of teachings or principles. In defining a discipline many look for what might be called unique or internally developed facts and principles. This would mean unique in the sense that gravity belongs to physics and the story of 1066 is part of history.

Many will say that education is not a discipline because it does not possess a corpus of facts and principles of its own. They will perhaps say that education is an unrelated mass of borrowings, a patchwork quilt of psychology, sociology, philosophy, history, economics, and so on. If the situation were really this simple, educators would be in a position to demand of their critics, "Are you saying that what we have borrowed is wrong or are you saying that we have borrowed the wrong things?" It is hard to believe that what education has borrowed is wrong. The disciplines to which education is in debt seem quite solid and respectable. It also seems unlikely that the wrong facts and principles have been incorporated from the traditional disciplines. For many years there has been ample opportunity for empirical evaluation of principles derived elsewhere and now incorporated into the matrix of the formal education process. Many of the

individuals involved in the total educational effort and its
evaluation have been very capable people. Considering the
magnitude of the enterprise, a very successful job has been
done in this country. The United States stands out in the
world as the nation that has carried the maximum benefits
of education to the maximum number of its people.

It is not the possession of a unique corpus of facts
that characterizes a discipline. If this were true, the disciplines of political science and economics might be hard
put to demonstrate how they are more than a particular combination of psychology, sociology, statistics, and law. Disciplines can not be identified by the possession of a unique
method. The methods of physics and chemistry are similar,
as are the methods of psychology and sociology. If I wanted
to argue that there is a discipline of education on the basis
of unique concepts and practices, such things as curriculum
could be stressed. If arguments were to be made on the
basis of method, the idiosyncratic nature of the instructional
process would receive emphasis.

Instead, I want to approach the problem from the
viewpoint of concern. [Education is a discipline in the sense
that there is a body of facts and principles organized in a
framework of a unique concern. In essence, this concern is
about the transmittal of human knowledge and culture from
generation to generation. Central to this concern is the involvement of society in making formal provisions for the
transmission to take place. There are, of course, many
crucial aspects of the education process which are not moni-
tored by a formal system. Teachers could not start at the
level they do were it not for the fact that most students have
learned the rudiments of the language and the culture in
their homes. Indeed, if this were not true, the entire com-
plexion of the teacher's job would be changed. I regard the
discipline of education as involving the entire educational
process as its subject matter, but, of course, formal education is usually the recipient of special concern perhaps because it is most susceptible to study, and also because it is
susceptible to modification by mandate.]

In what way does a unique concern make itself felt in
the structure of a discipline? What is unique about a discipline, I believe, is a concern with certain relations between
facts. Certain relations and principles may be unique to a
discipline even though they are derived from principles
shared by one or more other disciplines. I would argue that

concern with the economic behavior of man permits the continued existence of an independent discipline even though there
is another discipline called psychology that according to its
textbooks is the discipline that studies human behavior. As
psychology defines its discipline it embraces economics, sociology, political science, and the languages, to name a few of
the traditional subjects. Even history could, perhaps, be
viewed as a chronology of behavior, or there could be a psychological approach to the understanding of history. Certainly to the extent that education is concerned with the learning
process, it is concerned with something that lies within the
domain staked out by psychology. These last remarks are of
course the sort of things one might have expected a psychologist to say.

The increasing difficulty of drawing lines between disciplines is certainly part of the problem. I would say that
biochemistry and biophysics are disciplines in their own right
because of their specific concern. The fact that they appear
to be manufactured out of other disciplines is not important.
As a matter of fact, although I do not intend to press the
point, it is possible to take the view that all of knowledge is
continuously related. According to this concept all facts, all
truths, are interlocking parts of some total pattern. If this
is so--and it certainly is attractive to believe that it is--
then any classification of knowledge into discrete disciplines
is obviously arbitrary. To identify any body of knowledge
and methods as a discipline would be forcing a discontinuous
classification upon a continuous system.

It seems that a classification based upon unique or at
least central concerns about relations is the most reasonable.
Most economists are concerned with the economic behavior of
people while most psychologists have specific concerns such
as how people see or how they hear or how they adjust to the
demands of the environment.

When many individuals have a specific concern, this
concern directs their efforts, their experimentation, and their
thinking. Specific concern with the process of education leads
to experimentation and thinking directed at this problem.
When facts, ideas, or techniques are incorporated from other
areas of interest, these are taken for only one reason and
this is relevance or adaptability to the problem of concern to
those involved in education. I have heard Paul Tillich say
that every man has a god, it is that with which he has ultimate concern. Perhaps there is the problem that concern

leads to irrational involvement in a problem.   This would
certainly explain the utter breakdown of communication between individuals with different goals, different concerns.

At this point there is a rather obvious question that
can be asked: If classification into disciplines is arbitrary,
if knowledge is continuous in nature, why bother at all with
the question of whether or not there is a discipline of education?   Once again let us come back to the question of concern: the process of education is something that has received concern.   Because we are concerned about it we shall
go on studying it.   Because we are concerned we shall take
facts and methods from other interests to the degree to which
they are of help to us in our concern.

A specific concern is a basis for the organization of
principles and ideas in a unique way.   In a class in educational psychology students are told how the teacher should react when a student volunteers an answer and is wrong.   They
are told that the teacher should inform the student that he is
wrong in such a way that, while the student knows his answer
was not correct, he also knows that the teacher is not angry
at him and does not like him less in any way.   Discussion of
this point would include consideration of the manner in which
this can be done.   Obviously there is not going to be a scientifically exact prescription that can be given.   For example,
while observing at a high school, I observed a teacher handle
this situation by saying, "Where is my baseball bat? I am
going to bop that guy real good." The student and the class
were amused but the job was done.   The student knew he had
been wrong but at the same time he did not feel personally
rejected; he knew that the teacher would never have joked
that way if he did not like him very much.

I have given this example because it serves to illustrate an important point.   It embodies a principle that is, as
a totality, unique to education.   As a principle of formal education it might be stated: "Tell a student whether or not
he is correct and, at the same time, associate this information with the student's response.   Reduce as much as possible
the tendency of the student to perceive such information as
personal criticism." This principle is unique to education
because it has to do with a process that is of concern to education.   One might argue that this concept does not include
anything that cannot be found in traditional psychology.   It
could be argued that we know from psychology that immediate knowledge of results provides the greatest efficiency of

learning and this is why the teacher should bother to tell the
student whether he is right or wrong in the first place.   It
would also be possible to find within clinical lore or in concepts of adolescent personality dynamics, information to the
effect that the adolescent is especially likely to take criticism very personally and perhaps be quite disturbed.

However, nowhere in traditional psychology are these
items of fact or theory combined into a unified principle in
the way they are combined as a principle of education.   It
is quite obvious why this principle, this unique combination
of fact and theory, does not occur in traditional psychology.
It does not occur because it does not deal with something
that is of concern to traditional psychology.   The unique responsibility of education for providing for the transmittal of
the culture has led to the development of this principle both
from what theory has offered and results in the classroom
have justified.   It is the existence of a central concern that
produces the body of knowledge which constitutes a discipline.
In the case of education, the corpus of the discipline has
several aspects: there are the direct contributions of the
traditional academic disciplines, there are new formulations
originating in other disciplines but modified by the specific
concern of education, and there is the knowledge that has
resulted directly from the practical experience of those concerned with the education enterprise.   My own background in
psychology causes me to emphasize that discipline when illustrating the relation between education and other areas of
interest.   Foundations of education in philosophy, sociology,
and history will, I trust, receive more emphasis from my
colleagues.

The concern of education produces selection and modification of the contributions of other disciplines on the basis
of many values; dominant among them are humanitarian values.   An illustration of this may be seen through the analysis of a classroom situation involving a child in conflict.
Let us suppose that an animal, perhaps a raccoon, has been
brought in for the children to maintain and observe.   If a
child is afraid to approach the animal he is placed in an ap-
proach-avoidance conflict.   Out of curiosity he probably does
want to approach, and it is also quite likely that the other
children will exert considerable social pressure.   Now if the
teacher were to handle the situation on the basis of the analysis afforded by traditional psychology there would be two
main alternatives: the teacher could increase the child's
tendency to approach or decrease the child's tendency to

avoid.   Either tactic would result in the child's coming into
closer contact with the animal.   However, the concern of
education includes consideration of developing certain valued
attitudes which would be lost were the child, already motivated to approach, made more anxious.   The teacher would,
therefore, employ techniques for reducing the tendency to
avoid--perhaps by allowing the child to become more familiar with the source of fear gradually and by indirect methods.
The body of knowledge that is evolving in education is selected and unified by the total concern of education.   Concern,
unlike many systematic approaches to the analysis of a discipline, implies that specific values are a critical part of the
framework.

These examples of the way in which knowledge from
another discipline has been assimilated into the discipline of
education illustrate an important point.   The substances of
educational theory and practice is not a crazy quilt of odds
and ends from the rest of the campus.   What has been taken
from elsewhere has been taken only because it is relevant to
the concern of education, and in almost every case this concern has produced modification of what has been incorporated.

Some have said education is philosophy, while a smaller number have claimed that it is a social science.   As a
discipline organized by a concern, education would be regarded as both philosophy and method.   Research in education
and in the traditional social sciences provides new data, new
information; but it is the philosophy of education that attempts
to clarify the meaning and the values these facts have.

At this point it might be mentioned that there are concepts that are completely the concern of education.   One example would be theory of curriculum.   However, it is not
the intention of this paper to argue that education should be
studied because it is capable of generating unique content.
What is unique to education is its primary concern with the
transmittal of the culture.   Topics as diverse as the teaching of attitudes and the most effective way to illuminate the
classroom are generated by this concern.

It is a serious mistake and an unfortunate loss when
capable individuals come to the conclusion that there is nothing in education that can be studied.   The magnitude and
complexity of the education enterprise tends to obscure the
existence of a central theme, namely the concern which has
produced this admittedly unwieldy mass.   Of course there

will always be people of ability who are made anxious by
confusion and the absence of precision. Some react to this
by attempting to introduce order; others react by seeking
areas of interest that already have considerable structure.
The study of education is not going to appeal to those who
are unable to tolerate considerable ambiguity.

Aspects of education have been studied by psychologists, philosophers, historians, and many other people with
special orientations. It may well be that the body of knowledge that has evolved in education can produce a new generation of scholars. These would be scholars of education,
men who would regard education as their discipline, not
merely as the name of their department or as a collection of
method courses. These second-generation scholars will be
concerned with all aspects of the transmittal of the culture,
an endeavor as valid and at least as worthy as the study of
the traditional social sciences. These will not be people
whose primary goal is to improve their own skill as instructors; there will be relatively more emphasis on studying education because it itself is a challenging area of knowledge.
These scholars might even be similar in sentiment to the
pure mathematician who considers the possibility of practical application an inadequate justification of his interest. It
is quite possible that these scholars will not think of themselves as educators; that label already has too many connotations and the connotations are not all favorable. These
men will be a different breed from most people now referred
to as educators, and the term would perhaps be an unfortunate handicap to inflict upon them. A different label does
not come readily to mind, at least not one that is neither
cumbersome nor pretentious.

On the other hand, it might be well if such people remained identified clearly with education; the public image of
education might be upgraded as a result. Education at the
moment does have renewed status, not because we have suddenly done better but as a result of both international development and the changing basis of evaluating personal status
in this culture. Education has become related to personal
status somewhat by default. Family background has become
an unreliable criterion now that families have become scattered, and money gives less status than it once did because
of the decreased variability of the population's buying power.

When the hucksters of Madison Avenue use educators
as a status symbol to sell cigarettes, it is evident that the

climate has changed.   True scholars of education are in a
better position to receive moral and financial support than
they have been for some time.   There is the possibility of
a bright future for the discipline if the new breed can avoid
insulting the intelligent with nonsense and can restrain itself
from generating the jargon which has encouraged ridicule in
the past.

Some may feel that concern with transmittal of the
culture involves many facets of our society that go beyond
the proper boundaries of any discipline of education.   There
are those who would limit their concern to the formal or institutionalized provisions that society has set up for the instruction of its citizens.   It might be argued by the advocates of this position that, even with this restriction, the diversity of topics included, ranging from constitutional law to
audio-visual aids, prohibits the unification of concepts required for a discipline.   Once again I would emphasize the
view that the central concern of education is the source of
unity and the basis for the study of the discipline.

The learning that occurs in the home, on the streets,
and in the motion-picture houses is an essential part of the
transmittal of the culture.   It would not be a difficult task
to argue that the real substance of the culture, the most important attitudes and response predispositions, are acquired
outside of the classroom.   Perhaps it is because people are
little and inadequate when they start school and large and
articulate when they emerge that the schools get some credit, as well as blame, that is not completely deserved.   It
certainly is true that the nature of formal education should
be determined by what it can assume is learned elsewhere
as well as by the instruction that it feels to be its particular responsibility.   For example, if the school could not assume that most of the students already had the basic rudiments of the language, the type of activities carried on the
first years would be quite different.   The fact that the teacher can communicate to a moderate extent with beginning elementary students makes possible the method of instruction
usually employed.   If the schools had to start at a different
level, they would; in fact this is what occurs in some cases.
What this means is that the schools should not be committed
to teaching what they do in the way they do; the important
thing is that there is a goal.   The schools cannot rigidly
identify themselves with a particular part of the job that
must be done; the schools must respond to the total concern.
Those entrusted with providing formal education can only re-

spond to the total concern of education through a comprehension of the total process of education. It is the formal system that is in a position to perceive what is lacking, what part of the culture is inadequately transmitted elsewhere, and to dedicate the large part of its effort toward completing the aim of education.

Where do we go from here? If we accept the existence of a discipline of education based on a central concern and guided in its development by the ramifications of this concern, would not scholars of education be mere monitors of the process? The answer is of course, No. The foreman knows that he must supervise the production of an automobile, but the process of education does not produce such an objective result. In the factory the specifications of the end product are agreed upon before work begins; in education there has been very little consideration of the ultimate goal. To the extent goals are verbalized, one hears "Children need algebra" or "The colleges require us to give two years of a language."

Lack of a unified approach to carefully considered goals results in waste that can no longer be afforded. A student in high school in the eleventh grade will take a chemistry course in which he is required to memorize the valences of the common elements. One year later most of this information is forgotten. The following year the student memorizes the valences again as part of his college freshman chemistry course. Three years later when he is receiving his degree from the department of Romance Languages he will have forgotten the chemical valences a second time. Perhaps it is not really disastrous that he has twice learned and forgotten this information, for no one will ever notice!

The study of education can lead to clarification of the concern of education. The question of what things are worth teaching lacks systematic consideration. Perhaps the now popular attempts to program instruction will force a partial answer to this problem. When material is programmed, the requirements of continuity and relatedness force the programmer to concentrate on where he is headed as well as what he is presenting at a given moment. This is a consideration lacking in many textbooks and most lectures with the result that often the student does not actually know what it is that he should learn. The importance of letting the student know what he should learn is, of course, another basic principle of education.

The teaching of attitudes remains on a hit-or-miss
basis even though attitudes toward the education process acquired by students in elementary school are crucial in shaping future progress. Study of the culture and the process
by which it is transmitted is fundamental to full consideration of this problem. What attitudes should be taught and the
optimum way in which to teach them is another topic that
needs systematic study.

These questions and many others are basic to the aims
of education. Principles of transmitting the culture are principles of education. Only scholars who share the concern of
education will be able to develop these principles and inte-
grate them into the discipline of education. But the rigorous
study of education will proceed, for the concern about education and its relations will demand proof and explanation.

DAVID P. AUSUBEL

9.   IS THERE A DISCIPLINE
OF EDUCATIONAL PSYCHOLOGY? [*]

Is there such a discipline as educational psychology?
I have a very strong personal stake in hoping to be able to
convince you that there is, because if I fail in this attempt
I shall be concomitantly demonstrating that as a scholar, a
researcher, and a theorist, I myself do not exist.   For however else I may perceive my academic and professional role,
I regard myself primarily as an educational psychologist.   It
is certainly not the case that I perceive this question as irrelevant or irreverent.   Quite the contrary, it follows very
pertinently if one examines many textbooks of educational
psychology that were written during the past thirty years. In
fact, from the conception of educational psychology inferable
from analysis of the contents of these textbooks--that is, as
a superficial, ill-digested, and typically disjointed and water-
ed-down miscellany of general psychology, learning theory,
developmental psychology, social psychology, psychological
measurement, psychology of adjustment, mental hygiene,
client-centered counseling and child-centered education--one
would be hard put not to give a negative answer to the question raised by the title of my paper.

Definition of the Field

My thesis, in brief, is that educational psychology is
that special branch of psychology concerned with the nature,
conditions, outcomes, and evaluation of school learning and
retention.   As such, the subject matter of educational psychology consists primarily of the theory of meaningful learning and retention and the influence of all significant variables
--cognitive, developmental, affective, motivational, personal-

[*]Psychology in the Schools, Vol. 6 (1969), pp. 232-44.
Reprinted with the permission of the publisher and the author.

ity, and social--on school learning outcomes, particularly
the influence of those variables that are manipulable by the
teacher, by the curriculum developer, by the programmed
instruction specialist, by the educational technologist, by the
school psychologist or guidance counselor, by the educational administrator, or by society at large.

Psychology versus Educational Psychology

Since both psychology and educational psychology deal
with the problem of learning, how can we distinguish between
the special theoretical and research interests of each discipline in this area? As an applied science, educational psychology is not concerned with general laws of learning per
se, but only with those properties of learning that can be related to efficacious ways of deliberately effecting stable cognitive changes which have social value (Ausubel, 1953). Education, therefore, refers to guided or manipulated learning
directed toward specific practical ends.   These ends may be
defined as the long-term acquisition of stable bodies of
knowledge and of the capacities needed for acquiring such
knowledge.

The psychologist's interest in learning, on the other
hand, is much more general. Many aspects of learning,
other than the efficient achievement of the above-designated
competencies and capacities for growth in a directed context,
concern him.   More typically, he investigates the nature of
simple, fragmentary, or short-term learning experiences,
which are presumably more representative of learning in
general, rather than the kinds of long-term learning involved
in assimilating extensive and organized bodies of knowledge.

The following kinds of learning problems, therefore,
are particularly indigenous to psychoeducational research:
(a) discovery of the nature of those aspects of the learning
process affecting the acquisition and long-term retention of
organized bodies of knowledge in the learner; (b) long-range
improvement of learning and problem-solving capacities; (c)
discovery of which cognitive and personality characteristics
of the learner, and of which interpersonal and social aspects of the learning environment, affect subject-matter
learning outcomes, motivation for learning, and typical ways
of assimilating school material; and (d) discovery of appropriate and maximally efficient ways of organizing and presenting learning materials and of deliberately motivating and

directing learning toward specific goals.

Another way of epitomizing the difference between the
two disciplines is to say that general aspects of learning interest the psychologist, whereas classroom learning, that is
deliberately guided learning of subject matter in a social
context, is the special province of the educational psychologist. The subject matter of educational psychology, therefore, can be inferred directly from the problems facing the
classroom teacher. The latter must generate interest in
subject matter, inspire commitment to learning, motivate
pupils, and help induce realistic aspirations for educational
achievement. He must decide what is important for pupils
to learn, ascertain what learnings they are ready for, pace
instruction properly, and decide on the appropriate size and
difficulty level of learning tasks. He is expected to organize subject matter expeditiously, present materials clearly,
simplify learning tasks at initial stages of mastery, and in-
tegrate current and past learnings. It is his responsibility
to arrange practice schedules and reviews, to offer confirmation, clarification, and correction, to ask critical questions, to provide suitable rewards, to evaluate learning and
development, and where feasible, to promote discovery
learning and problem-solving ability. Finally, since he is
concerned with teaching groups of students in a social environment, he must grapple with problems of group instruction, individualization, communication, and discipline.

Thus the scope of educational psychology as an applied science is exceedingly broad, and the potential rewards
it offers in terms of the social value of facilitating the subject-matter learning of pupils are proportionately great.

In What Sense is Educational Psychology an "Applied" Discipline?

Few persons would take issue with the proposition
that education is an applied or engineering science. It is an
applied science[1] because it is concerned with the realization
of certain practical ends which have social value. The precise nature of these ends is highly controversial, in terms
of both substance and relative emphasis. To some individuals the function of education is to transmit the ideology of
the culture and a core body of knowledge and intellectual
skills. To others, education is primarily concerned with
the optimal development of potentiality for growth and achieve-

ment--not only with respect to cognitive abilities, but also with respect to personality goals and adjustment.   Disagreement with respect to ends, however, neither removes education from the category of science nor makes it any less of an applied branch of knowledge.   It might be mentioned in passing that automobile engineers are also not entirely agreed as to the characteristics of the "ideal" car; and physicians disagree violently in formulating a definition of health.

Regardless of the ends it chooses to adopt, an applied discipline becomes a science only when it seeks to ground proposed means to ends on empirically validatable propositions.   The operations involved in such an undertaking are commonly subsumed under the term "research." The question under discussion here relates to the nature of research in applied science, or, more specifically, in education.   Is educational research a field in its own right with theoretical problems and a methodology of its own, or does it merely involve the operation of applying knowledge from "pure" scientific disciplines to practical problems of pedagogy?

Despite the fact that education is an applied science, educational psychologists have manifested a marked tendency uncritically to extrapolate research findings from laboratory studies of simplified learning situations to the classroom learning environment.   This tendency reflects the fascination which many research workers feel for the "basic-science" approach to research in the applied sciences, as well as their concomitant failure to appreciate its inherent limitations.   They argue that progress in educational psychology is made more rapidly by focusing indirectly on basic-science problems in general psychology than by trying to come to grips directly with the applied problems that are more indigenous to the field.   Spence (1959), for example, perceived classroom learning as much too complex to permit the discovery of general laws of learning, and advocated a straightforward application to the classroom situation of the laws of learning discovered in the laboratory; he saw very little scope, however, for applying the latter laws to problems of educational practice.   Melton (1959) and E. R. Hilgard (1964) take a more eclectic position.   They would search for basic-science laws of learning in both laboratory and classroom contexts, and would leave to the educational technologist the task of conducting the research necessary for implementing these laws in actual classroom practice.

My position in other words, is that the principles governing the nature and conditions of school learning can be discovered only through an applied or engineering type of research that actually takes into account both the kinds of learning that occur in the classroom as well as salient characteristics of the learner. We cannot merely extrapolate to classroom learning general basic-science laws that are derived from the laboratory study of qualitatively different and vastly simpler instances of learning. Most attempts to do so, as, for example, Mandler's (1962) attempt to explain complex cognitive functioning in terms of the laws of association, or Sheffield's (1961) recent explanation of the hierarchical learning of sequentially organized materials in terms of the principle of contiguous conditioning, are extremely tortuous.

Laws of classroom learning at an applied[2] level are needed by the educational technologist before he can hope to conduct the research preparatory to effecting scientific changes in teaching practices. He can be aided further by general principles of teaching which are intermediate, in level of generality and prescriptiveness, between laws of classroom learning and the technological problems that confront him. Contrary to Spence's (1959) contention, the greater complexity and number of determining variables involved in classroom learning does not preclude the possibility of discovering precise laws with wide generality from one educational situation to another. It simply means that such research demands experimental ingenuity and sophisticated use of modern techniques of research design.

Basic Science versus Applied Approach

Three different kinds of research orientations have been adopted by those who are concerned with scientific progress in applied disciplines such as medicine and education: (a) basic-science research, (b) extrapolated research in the basic sciences, and (c) research at an applied level (Ausubel, 1953).

The basic-science research approach is predicated on the very defensible proposition that applied sciences are ultimately related to knowledge in the underlying sciences on which they are based. It can be demonstrated convincingly, for example, that progress in medicine is intimately related to progress in general biochemistry and bacteriology; that

progress in engineering is intimately related to progress in
physics and chemistry; and that progress in education is
similarly dependent upon advances in general psychology,
statistics, and sociology. However, two important qualifications have to be placed on the value of basic-science research for the applied sciences: qualifications of purpose or
relevance and qualifications of level of applicability.

By definition, basic-science research is concerned
with the discovery of general laws of physical, biological,
psychological, and sociological phenomenology as an end in
itself. Researchers in these fields have no objection, of
course, if their findings are applied to practical problems
which have social value; in fact, there is reason to believe
that they are motivated to some extent by this consideration.
But the design of basic science research bears no intended
relation whatsoever to problems in the applied disciplines,
the aim being solely to advance knowledge.   Ultimately, of
course, such knowledge is applicable in a very broad sense
to practical problems; but since the research design is not
oriented to the solution of these problems, this applicability
is apt to be quite indirect and unsystematic, and relevant
only over a time span which is too long to be meaningful in
terms of the short-range needs of the applied disciplines.

The second qualification has to do with the level at
which findings in the basic sciences can be applied once their
relevance has been established. It should be self-evident
that such findings exhibit a much higher level of generality
than the problems to which they can be applied. At the applied level, specific ends and conditions are added which demand additional research to indicate the precise way in which
the general law operates in the specific case. That is, the
applicability of general principles to specific problems is
not given in the statement of the general principle, but must
be explicitly worked out for each individual problem. Knowledge about nuclear fission, for example, does not tell us how
to make an atomic bomb or an atomic-powered airplane.

In fields such as education, the problem of generality
is further complicated by the fact that practical problems often exist at higher levels of complexity with respect to the
order of phenomenology involved than do the basic-science
findings requiring application. That is, new variables are
added which may qualitatively alter the general principles
from the basic science to such an extent that at the applied
level they have substrate validity but lack explanatory or

predictive value. For example, antibiotic reactions that take place in test tubes do not necessarily take place in living systems, and methods of learning that children employ in rotely mastering lists of nonsense syllables in the laboratory do not necessarily correspond to methods of learning children use in classrooms to acquire a meaningful grasp of subject matter.

The basic-science approach in educational research, therefore, is subject to many serious disadvantages. Its relevance is too remote and indirect because it is not oriented toward solving educational problems; and its findings, if relevant, are applicable only if much additional research is performed to translate general principles into the more specific form they have to assume in the task-specialized and more complex contexts of pedagogy.

These limitations would not be so serious if they were perceived. In the latter event, it would be defensible for educational institutions to set aside a small portion of their research funds for basic-science research as a long-term investment. But since the limitations of this approach are not generally appreciated, some bureaus of educational research confidently invest their major resources in such programs, and then complacently expect that the research findings which emerge will be both relevant and applicable in their original form to the problems of education.

Naiveté with respect to the second premise, that is, of immediate applicability, is especially rampant and has led to very serious distortions in our knowledge of those aspects of the psychology of learning that are relevant for pedagogy. The psychology of learning that teachers study is based on findings in general psychology which have been borrowed wholesale without much attempt to test their applicability to the kinds of learning situations that exist in classrooms. It would be a shocking situation indeed if a comparable procedure were practiced in medicine, that is, if physicians employed therapeutic techniques validated only in vitro or by animal experimentation.

The second general research approach in the applied disciplines is "extrapolated basic-science research." Unlike pure basic-science research, it is oriented toward the solution of practical or applied problems. It starts out by identifying significant problems in the applied field, and designs experiments pointed toward their solution on an analogous but highly simplified basic-science level. In this way it satisfies

the important criterion of relevance, but must still contend
with the problem of level of applicability. The rationale of
this approach is that many practical problems are so complex that they must be reduced to simpler terms and patterned after simpler models before one can develop fruitful
hypotheses leading to their solution.   Once the problems are
simplified, control and measurement become more manage-
able.

Depending on the nature of the problem under investigation, this approach may have genuine merit provided that
the resulting research findings are regarded only as "leads"
or hypotheses to be tested in the applied situation rather than
as definitive answers per se to problems in pedagogy.   As
already noted, however, educational researchers have a tendency to extrapolate basic-science findings to pedagogical
problems without conducting the additional research necessary
to bridge the gap between the two levels of generality involved.

The third approach to educational research, research
at the applied level, is the most relevant and direct of the
three, yet paradoxically is utilized least of all by professional research workers in the field.   When research is performed in relation to the actual problems of education, at the
level of complexity at which they exist, that is, in situ (under the conditions in which they are to be found in practice),
the problems of relevance and extrapolation do not arise. [3]
Most rigorous research in applied disciplines other than education is conducted at this level.   The research program of
a hospital or medical school would be regarded as seriously
unbalanced if most of its funds and efforts went into pure
biochemical or bacteriological research instead of into applied and clinical research.   The major responsibility for
furthering research in the former areas belongs to graduate
departments of chemistry and bacteriology.   On the other
hand, unless medical schools undertake to solve their own
applied and clinical problems who else will?   And the same
analogy obviously holds for education as well.

Although applied research presents greater difficulties
with respect to research design, control, and measurement,
the rewards are correspondingly greater when these problems
are solved.   Certainly such problems cannot be solved when
they are deliberately avoided.   If other applied disciplines
have been able to evolve satisfactory research methodologies,
there is no reason why education cannot also do so.   In fact,

if any applied discipline with unique and distinctive problems
of its own is to survive as a science it has no choice in the
matter--it is obliged to do so.

Many of the better-known geralizations in educational
psychology--the principle of readiness, the effects of over-
learning, the concrete to abstract trend in conceptualizing the
environment--illustrate the pitfalls of the basic-science approach to educational research. They are interesting and
potentially useful ideas to curriculum specialists and educational technologists, but have little utility in educational practice until they are particularized at an applied level of operations. The prevailing lack of practical particularization
damages the "image" of educational psychology insofar as it
induces many beginning teachers to nurture unrealistic expectations about the current usefulness of these principles.
Subsequently after undergoing acute disillusionment, they may
lose whatever original confidence they may have felt in the
value of a psychological approach to educational problems.

The need for applied research in these areas is well
illustrated by the principles of readiness. At the present
time we can only speculate what curriculum sequences might
conceivably look like if they took into account precise and
detailed (but currently unavailable) research findings on the
emergence of readiness for different subject-matter areas,
for different subareas and levels of difficulty within an area,
and for different methods of teaching the same material.
Because of the unpredictable specificity of readiness as shown,
for example, by the fact that four- and five-year-olds can
profit from training in pitch but not in rhythm (Jersild &
Bienstock, 1931, 1935), valid answers to questions, such as
those of readiness, cannot be derived from logical extrapolation; they require meticulous empirical research in a school
setting. The next step involves the development of teaching
methods and materials appropriate for taking optimal advantages of existing degrees of readiness, and for increasing
readiness wherever necessary and desirable. But since we
generally do not have this research data available, except
perhaps in the field of reading, we can pay only lip service
to principles of readiness in curriculum planning.

The basic-science-extrapolation approach, of course,
offers several very attractive methodological advantages in
verbal learning experiments. First, by using nonsense syllables of equal meaningfulness, it is possible to work with
additive units of equal difficulty. Second, by using relative-

ly meaningless learning tasks, such as equated nonsense syllables, it is possible to eliminate, for the most part, the
indeterminable influence of meaningful antecedent experience,
which naturally varies from one individual to another. But
it is precisely this interaction of new learning tasks with
existing knowledge in the learner that is the distinctive feature of meaningful learning.

Thus, although the use of nonsense syllables adds undoubted methodological rigor to the study of learning, the
very nature of the material limits the applicability of experimental findings to a type of short-term, discrete learning that is rare both in everyday situations and in the classroom. Nevertheless, even though there are no a priori
grounds for supposing that meaningful and nonmeaningful
learning and retention occur in the same way, the findings
from rote-learning experiments have been commonly extrapolated to meaningful learning situations. One cannot have
one's cake and eat it too. If one chooses the particular
kind of methodological rigor associated with the use of rote
materials, one must also be satisfied with applying the findings from such experiments to only rote learning tasks.

In conclusion, therefore, educational psychology is
unequivocally an applied discipline, but it is not general psychology applied to educational problems--no more so than
mechanical engineering is general physics applied to problems of designing machinery or medicine is general biology
applied to problems of diagnosing, curing and preventing human diseases. In these latter applied disciplines, general
laws from the parent discipline are not applied to a domain
of practical problems; rather, separate bodies of applied
theory exist that are just as basic as the theory undergirding
the parent disciplines, but are stated at a lower level of
generality and have more direct relevance for and applicability to the applied problems in their respective fields.

The time-bound and particular properties of knowledge
in the applied sciences have also been exaggerated. Such
knowledge involves more than technological applications of
basic science generalizations to current practical problems.
Although less generalizable than the basic sciences, they are
also disciplines in their own right, with distinctive and relatively enduring bodies of theory and methodology that cannot
simply be derived or extrapolated from the basic sciences to
which they are related. It is simply not true that only basic-
science knowledge can be related to and organized around gen-

eral principles. Each of the applied biological sciences (e.g., medicine, agronomy) possesses an <u>independent</u> body of general principles underlying the detailed <u>knowledge</u> in its field, in addition to being related in a still more general way to basic principles in biology.

The Decline of Classroom Learning Theory

The serious decline in knowledge and theorizing about school learning that has taken place over the past half century, accompanied by the steady retreat of educational psychologists from the classroom, has not been without adequate cause. Much of this deliberate avoidance can be attributed to the scientific disrepute into which studies of school learning fell as a result of both (a) glaring deficiencies in conceptualization and research design, and (b) excessive concern with the improvement of particular narrowly conceived academic skills and techniques of instruction rather than with the discovery of more general principles affecting the improvement of classroom learning and instruction in any subject-matter field. The vast majority of studies in the field of school learning, after all, have been conducted by teachers and other nonprofessional research workers in education. In contrast, laboratory studies of simple learning tasks were invested with the growing glamour and prestige of the experimental sciences, and also made possible the investigation of general learning variables under rigorously controlled conditions.

Thus the more <u>scientifically</u> conducted research in learning theory has been <u>undertaken</u> largely by psychologists unconnected with the educational enterprise, who have investigated problems quite remote from the type of learning that goes on in the classroom. The focus has been on animal learning or on short-term and fragmentary rote or nonverbal forms of human learning, rather than on the learning and retention of organized bodies of meaningful material. Experimental psychologists, of course, can hardly be criticized if laboratory studies of nonverbal and rote verbal learning have had little applicability to the classroom. Like all pure research efforts in the basic sciences, these studies were designed to yield only general scientific laws as ends in themselves, quite apart from any practical utility. The blame, if any is to be assigned, must certainly fall upon educational psychologists who, in general, have failed to conduct the necessary applied research and have succumbed to the temp-

tation to extrapolate the theories and findings of their experimental colleagues to problems of classroom learning.

Finally, for the past three decades, educational psychologists have been preoccupied with measurement and evaluation, personality development, mental hygiene, group dynamics, and counseling. Despite the self-evident centrality
of classroom learning and cognitive development for the psychological aspects of education, these areas were ignored,
both theoretically and empirically (Ausubel, 1963).

Although the withdrawal of educational psychologists
from problems of meaningful classroom learning was temporarily expedient, it was, in the long run, highly unfortunate
on both theoretical and research grounds. In the first place,
rotely and meaningfully learned materials are represented
and organized quite differently in the student's psychological
structure of knowledge (cognitive structure), and hence con-
form to quite different principles of learning and retention.
Not only are the respective learning processes very dissimilar, but the significant variables involved in the two processes are also markedly different, and, where similar, have
very different effects. Second, it is evident that a distinction must be made between learning tasks involving the short-
term acquisition of single, somewhat contrived concepts, the
solution of artificial problems, or the learning of arbitrary
associations--in a laboratory--and long-term acquisition and
retention of the complex network of interrelated ideas characterizing an organized body of knowledge that is presented
to the learner for active incorporation into his cognitive
structure.

Hence the extrapolation of rote learning theory and
evidence to school learning problems has had many disastrous
consequences. It perpetuated erroneous conceptions about the
nature and conditions of classroom learning, led educational
psychologists to neglect research on factors influencing meaningful learning, and hence delayed the discovery of more effective techniques of verbal exposition. And, finally, it convinced some educators to question the relevance of learning
theory for the educational enterprise, and to formulate theories of teaching that attempt to conceptualize the nature, purposes, and effects of instruction independently of its relationship to learning.

Still another reason for the decline in classroom learning theory can be found by examining its historical develop-

ment during the twentieth century. First, E. L. Thorndike
initiated a movement that separated school learning theory
from its relevant concern with the acquisition of large bodies
of organized knowledge (as represented by the scholastic and
humanistic philosophers and by such educational theorists as
Herbart), and focused theoretical attention on a mechanistic
and reductionistic concern with explaining the rote acquisition of discrete units of such knowledge. This concern was
reinforced later by behaviorism, neobehaviorism, Pavlovian
psychology, a revival of associationism, the functionalism of
the Twenties and Thirties, and Skinnerian psychology and the
teaching machine movement it spawned. Second, the immediate theoretical reaction to connectionism, associationism, and
behaviorism, namely, Gestalt and field theory approaches,
failed to provide a viable theoretical alternative for educational psychology. Their doctrinaire overemphasis on a perceptual model of learning and retention led to a vastly over-
simplified interpretation of the actual learning task involved
in the acquisition of subject matter, an overvaluation of the
role of stimulus properties and stimulus organization and a
corresponding undervaluation of the role of existing cognitive
structure in school learning, an emphasis on nativistic explanatory principles that was quite alien to the very spirit of
education, and an unrealistic preoccupation with discovery
learning and problem solving that diverted attention from the
more basic reception aspects of classroom learning. Lastly,
John Dewey and the Progressive Education movement dero-
gated expository teaching, verbal learning, structured learning experience and the importance of practice and testing,
and also placed undue emphasis on direct, nonverbal, con-
crete-empirical experience and on learning by discovery.

Prerequisites for a Discipline of Educational Psychology

The foregoing historical considerations and substantive propositions regarding the definition of the field of educational psychology, its relationships to general psychology,
and its status as an applied discipline lead to the conclusion
that a minimum number of crucial prerequisites must first
be met before educational psychology can emerge as a viable
and flourishing discipline. First the acquisition of certain
basic intellectual skills, the learning and retention of subject-
matter knowledge, and the development of problem-solving
capabilities must be regarded as the principal practical concerns toward which theory and research in this area of inquiry are directed. Second, the attainment of these objec-

tives must be conceptualized as products of meaningful verbal or symbolical learning and retention, and a cogent theory
of such learning and retention must be formulated in terms
of manipulable independent variables. Third, the elaboration of this theory implies the delineation of unambiguous distinctions between meaningful learning, on the one hand, and
such other forms of learning as classical and operant conditioning, rote verbal and instrumental learning, perceptual-
motor and simple discrimination learning, on the other, as
well as clear distinctions between such varieties of meaningful verbal learning as representational or vocabulary learning, concept learning, and propositional learning, and between
reception and discovery learning. Finally, meaningful verbal
learning must be studied in the form in which it actually occurs in classrooms, that is, as the guided, long-term, structured learning in a social context of large bodies of logically
organized and interrelated concepts, facts, and principles
rather than as the short-term and fragmented learning of discrete and granulated items of information such as is represented by short-frame and small-step-size teaching machine
programs.

The Predicted New Look in Educational Psychology

It is obviously difficult to separate the objective delineation of future research trends in educational psychology
from a statement of personal values and preferences in this
area. Nevertheless, although frankly conceding this serious
limitation at the very outset, I still venture to predict the
emergence of four major trends in the coming decade. First,
I am confident that educational psychologists will return to
the classroom to study the kinds of learning processes that
are involved in the meaningful acquisition of subject-matter
knowledge, instead of continuing to extrapolate to such processes theories and evidence derived from highly simplified
instances of nonverbal or rote verbal learning in laboratory
situations. Second, I think we will shortly cease pretend-
ing that meaningful classroom learning consists merely of a
designated series of problem-solving tasks, and will also
make a serious attempt to study the learning of ideas and information presented by teachers and textual materials. Third,
I feel reasonably certain that we will devise appropriate
methods of investigating the effects of general variables influencing meaningful learning, both singly and in combination,
instead of vainly seeking to speculate about these effects from
the results of particular curriculum improvement projects

(e. g. , the PSSC, the UICSM) in which an indeterminate number of variables are manipulated in uncontrolled and indeterminate fashion. Lastly, I am hopeful that we will focus our attention increasingly on the long-term learning and retention of large bodies of sequentially organized subject matter rather than on short-term mastery of fragmentary learning tasks.

What about the product of this research activity, that is, the future shape of the discipline? I am hopeful that the educational psychology of tomorrow will be primarily concerned with the nature, conditions, outcomes, and evaluation of classroom learning, and will cease being an unstable and eclectic amalgam of rote learning theory, developmental and social psychology, the psychology of adjustment, mental hygiene, measurement, and client-centered counseling. Thus, hopefully, the new discipline will not consider such topics as child development, adolescent psychology, the psychology of adjustment, mental hygiene, personality, and group dynamics as ends in themselves but only insofar as they bear on and are directly relevant to classroom learning. It will confine itself only to such psychological theory, evidence, problems, and issues that are of direct concern either to the serious student of education or to the future teacher in his role as facilitator of school learning. It will also eliminate entirely many normally covered topics in educational psychology courses which are typically drawn from general and developmental psychology and which bear little or no relation to classroom learning. Examples of such topics include the nature and development of needs, general determinants of behavior, general reactions to frustration, developmental tasks, mechanisms of adjustment, parent-child relationships, noncognitive development during infancy and the pre-school years, and physical development. It is true, for example, that physical development during childhood affects motor coordination, writing, and popularity in the peer group, and that physical changes in adolescence affect the self-concept, emotional stability, peer relations, and athletic skills. But an educational psychology course cannot cover everything. Prospective elementary school teachers will presumably have a course in adolescent psychology. Similarly, certain aspects of motivation are obviously relevant for classroom learning, but a general discussion of needs, their nature, function, development, and classification, such as would be appropriate in a course in general psychology, hardly seems necessary.

One might reasonably anticipate that the new discipline of educational psychology will be principally concerned

with the kinds of learning that take place in the classroom,
that is, with meaningful symbolic learning--both reception
and discovery. Some kinds of learning, such as rote learning and motor learning, are so inconsequential a part of
school learning as to warrant no systematic treatment in a
course on educational psychology. Other kinds of learning,
for example, the learning of values and attitudes, are not
indigenous to the primary or distinctive function of the school,
and should be considered only insofar as they affect or are
part of the learning of subject matter; their more general
aspects may be left to such courses as general and social
psychology. And still other kinds of learning, for example,
animal learning, conditioning, instrumental learning, and
simple discrimination learning, are wholly irrelevant for
most learning tasks in school, despite the fact that wildly
extrapolated findings in these areas quite commonly pad the
learning chapters of many educational psychology textbooks.
The new discipline also, will hopefully not be eclectic in
theoretical orientation, but will proceed from a consistent
theoretical framework or point of view based on a cognitive
theory of meaninful verbal learning. Greater stress would
be placed on cognitive development than was true in the past,
and this material would be integrated more closely with related aspects of cognitive functioning.

     Finally, an effort should be made to employ a level
of discourse in teaching educational psychology that is appropriate for prospective teachers and mature students of
education, that is, to avoid over-simplified explanations, language, and presentation of ideas. Educational psychology is
a complex rather than a simple subject. Hence to over-
simplify it is to render the beginning student a serious dis-
service. Clarity and incisiveness of presentation, also, do
not require reversion to a kindergarten level of writing and
illustration. In fact, it is the writer's firm conviction that
much of the thinly disguised contempt of many prospective
teachers for courses in pedagogy and educational psychology
stems from the indefensible attempt to expose them to water-
ed-down, repetitive content and to an unnecessarily elementary level of vocabulary, sentence structure, illustration, example, and pedagogic device.

     It is true, of course, that if educational psychologists
limit their coverage of learning to meaningful verbal learning,
the unfortunate paucity of experimental evidence in this area
becomes painfully evident. This situation is a reflection of
the prevailing tendency, over the past three or more decades,

for educational psychologists to extrapolate findings from animal, rote, and perceptual-motor learning experiments rather
than to conduct research on meaningful verbal learning.   In
my opinion, presenting certain significant theoretical propositions to students without definitive empirical support for the
time being would be preferable to leaving large gaps in theory
or filling them by means of unwarranted extrapolation.

Organization of New Discipline

        How will the subject matter of the new discipline of
educational psychology be organized?   Inasmuch as classroom
instruction involves the manipulation of those variables influencing learning, a rational classification of learning variables
can be of considerable value in clarifying both the nature of
the learning process and the conditions that affect it.   Such
a classification also provides, in a sense, an organizational
framework for the field, since any course in educational psychology must, of necessity, be organized largely around the
different kinds of factors influencing classroom learning.

        One obvious way of classifying learning variables is to
divide them into intrapersonal (factors within the learner) and
situational (factors in the learning situation categories.   The
intrapersonal category includes: (a) cognitive structure vari-
ables--substantive and organizational properties of previously
acquired knowledge in a particular subject-matter field that
are relevant for the assimilation of another learning task in
the same field.   Since subject-matter knowledge tends to be
organized in sequential and hierarchical fashion, what one already knows in a given field, and how well one knows it, obviously influence one's readiness for related new learnings;
(b) developmental readiness--the particular kind of readiness
that reflects the learner's stage of intellectual development
and the intellectual capacities and modes of intellectual functioning characteristic of that stage.   The cognitive equipment
of the fifteen-year-old learner self-evidently makes him ready
for different kinds of learning tasks than does that of the six-
or ten-year-old learner; (c) intellectual ability--the individual's relative degree of general scholastic aptitude (general intelligence or brightness level), and his relative standing with
respect to particular more differentiated or specialized cognitive abilities.   How well a pupil learns subject matter in
science, mathematics, or literature obviously depends on his
general intelligence, verbal and quantitative abilities, on his
problem-solving ability, and on his cognitive style; (d) moti-

vational and attitudinal factors--desire for knowledge, need
for achievement and self-enhancement, and ego-involvement
(interest) in a particular kind of subject matter. These general variables affect such relevant conditions of learning as
alertness, attentiveness, level of effort, persistence, and
concentration; (e) personality factors--individual differences
in level and kind of motivation, in personal adjustment, in
other personality characteristics, and in level of anxiety.
Subjective factors such as these have profound effects on
quantitative aspects of the learning process.

The situational category of learning variables includes:
(a) practice--its frequency, distribution, method, and general
conditions (including feedback or knowledge of results); (b)
the arrangement of instructional materials--in terms of
amount, difficulty, step size, underlying logic, sequence,
pacing, and the use of instructional aids; (c) such group and
social factors as classroom climate, cooperation and competition, social-class stratification, cultural deprivation, and
racial segregation; and (d) characteristics of the teacher--
his cognitive abilities, knowledge of subject matter, pedagogic competence, personality, and behavior. Intrapersonal and
situational variables

> ... undoubtedly have interative effects upon learn-
> ing. ... The external variables cannot exert their
> effects without the presence in the learner of cer-
> tain states derived from motivation and prior learn-
> ing and development. Nor can the internal capabil-
> ities of themselves generate learning without the
> stimulation provided by external events. ... As a
> problem for research, the learning problem is one
> of finding the necessary relationships which must
> obtain among internal and external variables in or-
> der for a change in capability to take place. In-
> struction may be thought of as the institution and
> arrangement of the external conditions of learning
> in ways which will optimally interact with internal
> capabilities of the learner, so as to bring about a
> change in these capabilities [Gagné, 1967, p. 295].

Another equally meaningful and useful way of classify-
ing the same set of learning variables is to group them into
cognitive and affective-social categories. The former group
includes the relatively objective intellectual factors, whereas
the latter group includes the subjective and interpersonal determinants of learning. This scheme of categorization is

perhaps somewhat more convenient for the researcher, and
is also more familiar to the classroom teacher than is the
interpersonal-situational scheme.

Notes

1. The term "applied" is used here to distinguish between
   sciences which are oriented toward practical ends,
   as opposed to "basic" or "parent" sciences which
   do not have this orientation. Applied does not imply that the content of the practical disciplines consists of applications from the basic or parent disciplines. The problems rather than the knowledge
   of applied sciences are "applied."
2. These laws are just as "basic" as basic-science laws.
   The terms "basic" and "applied" refer to the distinction between basic ("pure," "parent") and applied ("practical") sciences made earlier. "Basic"
   does not mean "fundamental." In the latter sense,
   applied research is just as basic for its distinctive
   domain as research in the pure sciences is for its
   domain.
3. Applied research is also directed toward the discovery
   of general laws within the framework of its applied
   ends. The generalizations it discovers, therefore,
   exist at a different plane of generality than those of
   "basic" science research.

References

Ausubel, D. P. "The nature of educational research." Edu-
   cational Theory, 1953, 3, 314-320.
   _____. The psychology of meaningful verbal learning.
   New York: Grune & Stratton, 1963.
Gagné, R. M. "Instructions and the conditions of learning."
   In L. Siegel (Ed.), Instruction: Some contempo-
   rary viewpoints. San Francisco: Chandler, 1967.
   Pp. 291-313.
Hilgard, E. R. "A perspective on the relationship between
   learning theory and educational practices." In
   Theories of learning and instruction, 63rd Yearbook
   National Society for the Study of Education, Part I.
   Chicago: University of Chicago Press, 1964. Pp.
   402-415.
Jersild, A. T. , & Bienstock, S. F. "The influence of train-

ing on the vocal ability of three-year-old children."
Child Development, 1931, 2, 277-291.
_____ & _____ . "Development of rhythm in young children." Child Development Monographs, 1935, No. 22.
Mandler, G. "From association to structure." Psychological Review, 1962, 69, 415-426.
Melton, A.W. "The science of learning and the technology
of educational methods." Harvard Educational Review, 1959, 29, 96-106.
Sheffield, F.D. "Theoretical considerations in the learning
of complex sequential tasks from demonstration and
practice." In A. A. Lumsdaine (Ed.), Student response in programmed instruction. Washington,
D.C.: National Academy of Sciences, National Research Council, 1961. Pp. 13-32.
Spence, K.W. "The Relation of learning theory to the technology of education." Harvard Educational Review,
1959, 29, 84-95.

JOHN WALTON

10.   EDUCATION AS AN ACADEMIC DISCIPLINE *

The most serious gap in our intellectual system is the lack of a reputable academic discipline of education. Most major social enterprises have corresponding fields of study in the universities that are recognized as legitimate scholarly disciplines: government is taught and studied under the name of political science; commerce, under economics; and community organizations, under sociology.   Some of these enterprises also have professional training programs; for example, commerce not only has the discipline of economics, but also a curriculum in business administration, which relies heavily upon, but is distinguishable from, the academic study of economics.   The study of education, however, is regarded usually as professional preparation for practitioners, or as an aspect of other disciplines.   This lag in scholarship should be attended to by those individuals and institutions whose business it is to advance knowledge.

Why concern ourselves about an autonomous academic discipline corresponding to the great practical art of education?   The same question can be asked about economics or political science, and the answer is the same in all cases. It is generally agreed that systematic study of social phenomena is desirable.   Such organized knowledge increases our understanding, leads to further knowledge, and, often indirectly, enhances our control over our social environment.

Many who accept this justification for the study of education will ask, Why is an autonomous discipline of education necessary or even desirable?   Why not study the various aspects of education in other appropriate disciplines? School learning can be studied in psychology, the government of education in political science, and the normative and logical aspects of education in philosophy.

---

*School and Society, Vol. 92 (1964), pp. 264, 265, 268.
Reprinted with permission.

There are three reasons why a separate discipline of
education is necessary. First, there are some extremely
important aspects of education that have no place in other
disciplines; for example, teaching and the curriculum. Second, the other disciplines do not have education as their central and primary interest. Sociologists may be intensely interested in education as a mechanism of social change, and
they may use education as a source of information for the
enhancement of their own subject; but the results of their research will be absorbed into and obscured by the original
discipline rather than related to other information about education. And, third, students of the various aspects of education should belong to a community of discourse that has
education as its major focus. These reasons for an autonomous discipline of education indicate the fallacies in the current argument that the other disciplines should assume the
responsibility for the study of education. And if we sub-
scribe to the inter-disciplinary approach to the study of social phenomena, there is need for a discipline of education.

Why do we not now have such a discipline? First,
those who have set out to study education in its own right
have exhausted their energies in the professional training of
teachers and administrators, either because of temperament
or the conditions imposed upon them, in arriving at solutions
for urgent practical problems and in attempting to build a
profession of education out of odds and ends of knowledge
found in ad hoc investigations and in other disciplines. The
humanitarianism of professional educators, laudable though it
is, probably has prevented the concept of the "disinterested"
scholar in the field from taking hold. Second, there has
been a maidenly reluctance--to understate the case-- on the
part of other disciplines to encourage a new discipline that
might have something to say about the school, the college,
and the university that would carry more weight than cher-
ished opinions. However, the demand for systematic knowledge about education is so great that universities soon will
be forced to provide for scholars in education whose concern
about the subject will be considerably less cavalier than that
now assumed by other disciplines.

The first step will be the staffing of a department of
education with scholars who will abjure any prior allegiance
to another discipline. They will become educationists, as
will their graduate students. The educational theorist will
be analogous to the social theorist in sociology and to the political theorist in political science, and the scholar in the

empirical aspects of education may become a professor of experimental education. In like manner, the professors of comparative education, curriculum, and methodology will be identified with education. They will communicate with one another rather than be drawn by the centrifugal force of other allegiances into diverse communities. This does not mean that they will not have considerable training in some of the other disciplines. Certainly, the educational theorist will be eminently qualified in those aspects of philosophy that are pertinent to the study of education, and the professor of school learning should be a brilliant scholar in the psychology of learning. However, they will devote their energies to the study of education, to organizing the information that is available to them, and to developing new methods of inquiry in the field.

A reputable discipline of education can be developed. Interesting, complex, and identifiable phenomena are present, and various methods of investigation are within the academic domain. If government, economics, and community organization can become the subjects of disciplines, education surely can. Its subject matter can well be limited to the phenomena of formal schooling from nursery school through the university. At first, its structure would be archipelagic, but more comprehensive organizations can be expected from prolonged study and reflection. Since the study of education must deal with both normative and factual matters, C. P. Snow's two cultures will stand side by side. A synthesis should not be forced, but, perhaps, this close proximity may result in new and promising relations between them.

Education can well become one of the most intellectual exciting disciplines in the curriculum of higher education. Most people have a keen interest in the subject, and we are moving into a time when education will become truly one of our major occupations. It is weird, indeed, to think that it will not be studied as one of the major social sciences. The study which the scholars rejected may well become the cornerstone of their temple.

JOHN A. LASKA

11. CURRENT PROGRESS IN THE
FOUNDATIONS OF EDUCATION *

The appearance of a recent article by James J.
Shields, Jr., entitled "Social Foundations of Education: The
Problem of Relevance," calls attention to the fact that scholars in the foundations of education are still re-examining the
state of their field.[1] They have obviously been unwilling to
follow Conant's dictum of a few years ago that they should
relinquish their role in teacher preparation to representatives
of the traditional disciplines, such as psychology and history.
Instead, they have attempted candidly to assess the weaknesses of their field and take appropriate steps to overcome
these deficiencies.

Within the past two years, probably the most important single development affecting the foundations of education
field was the establishment of the American Educational Studies Association in February, 1968. This new learned society
has over 500 members, most of whom are professors in the
foundations of education. As stated in its constitution, the
purpose of this organization is

> to promote the academic study of the educative
> process and the school as a fundamental societal
> institution. All analytical and interpretive ap-
> proaches that are appropriate for the academic
> study of education shall be represented in the mem-
> bership of the Association. The increased integra-
> tion of the field of educational studies shall be en-
> couraged by providing closer contacts between gen-
> eralists and specialists in the academic study of
> education, and between educational scholars and
> those from the traditional disciplines who also have
> an interest in education.

*Teachers College Record, Vol. 72 (1969-70), pp. 179-86.
Reprinted with permission.

At least four important points of view on the foundations of
education are embodied in this brief statement of purpose.
First, the statement suggests that education can be studied
as an academic field. Second, it contains the notion that
this field derives its independent validity from the study of
a fundamental societal institution. Third, the statement expresses a concern for the attainment of greater integration
of this field. And fourth, it uses the term educational studies as a designation for the academic study of education.
An elaboration of each of these concepts follows.

Academic and Professional Fields. The distinction
between the study of education as an academic field and the
study of education as a professional field is seldom made,
yet it is a distinction that is of critical importance if the
role of the foundations of education in the professional training of teachers and other school personnel is to be properly
understood. Briefly, we can say that an academic field is
one in which knowledge is sought without explicit regard for
its utilization, while a professional field is one in which
knowledge is sought to meet the requirements of an identifiable occupation (or occupations). For example, in the typical American university physics, economics and sociology are
taught as academic fields, while engineering, business administration and social work are taught as professional fields.
But this way of differentiating between academic and professional fields of study should not be interpreted to mean that
an academic field is impractical or totally divorced from the
occupational objectives of the students in the field. Indeed,
for many students in the American university, the work they
do at the advanced levels of an academic field of study is
very much related to their occupational objectives--to become
a university teacher or research specialist, for example.
The exposure of students to the elementary levels of an academic field is also usually justified by its practical benefits
in the preparation of "informed citizens," "well-rounded individuals," and so forth.

The basic distinction between an academic and a professional field, therefore, is in the amount of explicit attention that is given to the practical applications and occupational aspects of the field. In the teaching of an academic field,
the impartation of a body of scholarly knowledge is the principal concern; it is assumed that anyone possessing this body
of knowledge will be able to make whatever practical applica-
tors are later required. By contrast, the teaching of a pro-

fessional field is primarily oriented toward the preparation
of an individual for a specific occupational role and stresses
the applications of knowledge in the performance of that role;
in fact, the occupational focus in a professional training program may be so explicit as to include actual practice in the
occupational role.

The organization of the American university generally exhibits a structure which is differentiated according to
academic and professional fields: instruction in the academic fields is usually given by departments in the arts and sciences division of the university; instruction in each of the
professional fields is often provided by a separate college
or school that is outside the arts and sciences division. But
the structural differentiation of the university into academic
and professional segments is by no means complete. In the
smaller universities and those institutions of higher education which are primarily liberal arts colleges, some of the
professional fields may be constituted as professional departments within the arts and sciences division of the university
or college.

Moreover, the professional departments, schools and
colleges may also offer academic instruction. Since a student enrolled in a professional training program generally
requires academic instruction as well as purely professional
training, some of the academic instruction that is an essential component of the professional training program may (for
reasons of convenience) be provided within the professional
department, school or college. Thus, for example, a law
student ordinarily receives his instruction in jurisprudence--
which is an academic subject--from the faculty of the law
school, rather than from the arts and sciences faculty of the
university.

The study of education in the typical American university is quite comparable to the study of law. Although the
departments, schools and colleges of education are primarily
involved in purely professional training, they also provide
courses which deal with the academic study of education.
These academic courses--for example, "educational psychology" and "social foundations of education"--are known collectively as courses in the foundations of education. The
courses in the foundations of education are a component of
the total professional training program in education and thus
have a professional function, but their subject matter is academic in the same sense that the subject matter of jurispru-

dence courses is academic.

Educational Foundations as an Independent Institutional Field. If it is granted that courses in the foundations of
education are fundamentally academic courses, can we regard the foundations of education as comprising an area of
study which possesses independent validity? Much futile discussion has taken place over whether education does or does
not constitute a discipline. [2] Rather than enter into this essentially sterile controversy, the founding members of the
American Educational Studies Association have chosen to use
the general term "field" to designate their area of study.
Thus, if it can be agreed that, for example, demography,
genetics and ecology constitute fields of study (though perhaps not disciplines), there should be no difficulty in regarding the academic study of education as a field of study, re-
serving for later years the question of whether it has at-
tained disciplinary status or not.

The argument for the legitimacy of educational foundations as an independent academic field of study rests on an
analogy with the field of government (or political science) and
the emerging field of religion (or religious studies). The
fields of government and religion are both devoted to the
study of particular social institutions. [3] They constitute academic fields because they are concerned mainly with a search
for knowledge about government and religion rather than with
the training of personnel for particular governmental or religious occupations. Although sociology is the field that is
concerned with the general study of societal institutions, the
existence of government and religion as independent fields of
study can be justified on the basis of the convenience that
such institutional fields afford to their students, who presumably are more interested in obtaining a specialized understanding of the institutions of government or religion than in
acquiring information on the operation of social institutions
in general. If, therefore, the study of the institutions of government and religion can be the basis for legitimate academic fields, the study of the basic educational institution of so-
ciety--the national school system--also can be the basis for
an independent field.

It should not be inferred, however, from the preceding discussion that education as an institutional field of study
would involve only the sociological aspects of the educational
system, any more than the fields of government and religion

are limited to the sociological aspects of their respective institutions. For example, the psychological, historical and
philosophical aspects of the educational system would also
need to be included. Nor could education as an institutional
field of study fail to give considerable emphasis to the study
of the educative process, just as the field of government
must encompass the political process.

          Achieving Independent Status. But the foundations of
education as an independent field of academic study has not
yet achieved a status that is comparable to the field of government, or even the field of religion. One of the problems
which the academic study of education faces is that of attaining an organizational identity within the university that is distinct from the professional field of education and from other
academic fields. The academic study of government and religion is ordinarily provided by separate departments in the
arts and sciences division of the university; there is no professional training program for the training of politicians with
which the academic study of government can be confused,
while the professional training programs of the seminaries
and schools of theology are ordinarily clearly distinguished
from the academic departments of religious studies. However, the courses in the foundations of education (as we have
already indicated) are usually offered within a predominantly
professional department, school or college of education.
Furthermore, these courses usually are not the responsibility of a single, clearly-labeled administrative subdivision of
this department, school or college of education, often a separation is made which administratively divides the social
foundations from the psychological foundations of education.

          Related to this lack of organizational distinctiveness
is the absence of a generally accepted name to apply to the
academic study of education other than the term "foundation
of education," which does not unequivocally suggest an academic field (we have had to resort in this article to the cumbersome terms "academic study of education" and "professional study of education" to make the desired distinctions).
Quite often, in fact, the single term "education" is used to
refer to either the professional or the academic field of education. The same difficulty does not arise in the case of
most other academic fields and the professional fields that
are closely related to them. For example, even though the
academic study of sociology or economics may sometimes
be provided by the same department of the university in

which the training of prospective social workers or business
administrators takes place, the professional fields are usually identified as "social work" and "business administration,"
respectively, thus keeping them terminologically separate
from the fields of sociology and economics.

   Need for Greater Integration.   Even more serious
than these problems of obtaining a satisfactory organizational and terminological identity for the academic study of education is the problem of developing a coherent and systematic
body of scholarly knowledge within the field itself.   This difficulty arises from the fact that an independent institutional
field is still dependent to a considerable extent upon the more
general behavioral sciences and the humanities for its methodologies and general concepts.   The important question for the
institutional field, therefore, is whether the need to draw upon the supportive disciplines will result in a compartmentalization of knowledge around the supportive disciplines or
whether the institutional field will be able to organize its
body of scholarly knowledge in such a way that the integrity
of the institutional field is maintained.   The field of government has largely managed to avoid a compartmentalization
of knowledge around its supportive disciplines.   For example,
some of the major subdivisions within the field of government are "political parties," "public opinion" and "political
theory"; the designations for these subdivisions are distinctively governmental and do not imply the relegation of the
study of government to other academic fields, as might be
the case if the labels "sociology of government," "psychology of government" and "philosophy of government" were
used instead.   But in the fields of religion and educational
foundations, the major subdivisions of these fields do reflect
an orientation toward the supportive disciplines.   The major
subdivisions in the field of religion, for example, bear such
labels as "sociology of religion" and "history of religion";
similarly, in the foundations of education the designations for
the major subdivisions of the field include "sociology of education," "history of education" and "philosophy of education."

   In recent years the foundations of education field has
tended to split apart even further along the lines of the supportive disciplines.   It was this tendency, in fact, that provided the specific impetus for the creation of the American
Educational Studies Association as one means of bringing together the several specialized foundations of education areas.[4]

Primarily responsible for the enhanced tendency toward frac-
tionation has been the widespread conviction that the foundations of education represents a somewhat unscholarly field
and that the only way to obtain increased rigor is to draw
more heavily upon the related disciplines. As a result of
this emphasis on other fields of study, many of the teachers
and researchers concerned with the academic study of education have come to regard themselves as being primarily psychologists or historians, for instance, rather than scholars
in the foundations of education. Also, the preparation afforded to prospective teachers of educational foundations
through many of the existing programs of graduate training
has been limited in a similar way, with the prospective
teacher gaining proficiency in a single specialized area such
as "philosophy of education" or "psychology of education"
but never being systematically exposed to the total body of
knowledge in the foundations of education field.

The Introductory Course. The absence of an integrated body of scholarly knowledge within the foundations of
education field is perhaps best illustrated by reference to the
problem of the introductory course in the foundations of education. Obviously, one would expect in any field of academic study that an introductory course would be offered to beginning students and that this course would constitute an acceptable overview of the body of scholarly knowledge represented by the field. And because of the fundamental coherence that is expected in the field, the topics covered in the
introductory course schould tend to be similar regardless of
where and by whom the course is taught. In the foundations
of education, however, the actual condition of the introductory course is far from the ideal. Two separate introductory
foundations of education courses are usually provided within
the undergraduate professional training program for prospective teachers: one of these is a course in the "psychology
of education" and the second is a course covering in some
fashion the social, historical and/or philosophical aspects of
education.

Although we might nevertheless expect that together
these two courses would comprise a comprehensive introduction to the academic study of education, this rarely happens.
This difficulty is due in part to a failure to regard these
courses as completely academic courses--all too often they
offer a mixture of the academic and the professional, reflecting an uncertainty as to their basic purpose.[5] But the basic
difficulty lies in the choice of topics in the two courses.

Apart from the inevitable overlapping and confusion that results when two (often uncoordinated) foundations of education
courses are given, there is simply no general agreement as
yet on what should constitute the basic subject matter of an
introductory foundations of education course.   Unlike the situation in other academic fields, the content of the existing
introductory courses in the foundations of education does
vary markedly from university to university and from instructor to instructor.

Only through a concerted attempt to achieve greater
integration within the foundations of education field can the
problem confronting the introductory course be resolved.
(It hardly seems necessary to point out that the introductory
course is by far the most important one that is offered in
the foundations of education, since relatively few prospective
teachers are required to pursue the advanced courses in the
field.) Although there may be some utility for the purposes
of advanced courses and research to retain such labels as
"social foundations of education," "history of education,"
"educational philosophy" and "psychological foundations of
education," there is little merit in such terminology when it
serves to prevent the development of inherently educational
subdivisions for the introductory foundations of education
course.   One of the immediate goals of the American Educational Studies Association, therefore, is to provide a forum through which discussions on the nature of the introductory educational foundations course can take place and through
which a consensus may eventually be reached.[6]

Educational Studies Instead of Educational Foundations.
At least two objections can be made to the use of "foundations of education" as the designation for the academic study
of education.   First, the term "foundations" does not readily
suggest a field of academic study.   And second, the long
tradition of delimiting the specialized foundations of education areas on the basis of the supportive disciplines (i.e.,
the use of such terminology as "social foundations of education" and "philosophical foundations of education") would no
doubt be perpetuated if "educational foundations" were used
to designate the general field, with the result that the greater integration of the foundations of education would remain
difficult to achieve.

For the purpose of promoting greater integration,
therefore, a different name seemed desirable to the founders
of the American Educational Studies Association.   Rather than

adopt a new coinage for the academic study of education,
such as "educology" or "educationology" (or even "educational science" as a term parallel to "political science"), the
term "educational studies" has at least for the present
seemed more appropriate.   The latter term is also parallel
to "religious studies," which is widely used to designate the
academic study of religion--a field in approximately the same
state of development as the academic study of education.

But the several new points of view on the foundations
of education field that are exemplified in the establishment of
the American Educational Studies Association notwithstanding,
there is a close connection between the present approach and
the earlier tradition.   It would certainly not be possible to
consider integrating the body of scholarly knowledge in the
academic study of education if much of this knowledge had
not already been generated within the general foundations of
education field and the various specialized foundations of education areas.   More than symbolic of this basic continuity,
therefore, is the fact that the first (and current) president
of the American Educational Studies Association is Dr. R.
Freeman Butts of Teachers College, Columbia University,
an educational scholar who remains firmly dedicated to its
advancement.

Notes

1.   James J. Shields, Jr., "Social Foundations of Educa-
         tion: The Problem of Relevance," Teachers Col-
         lege Record, Vol. 70, No. 1, October 1968, pp.
         77-87.
2.   See, for example, John Walton and James L. Kuethe,
         Eds.   The Discipline of Education.   Madison,
         Wisconsin: The University of Wisconsin Press,
         1963.
3.   It is sometimes maintained that the field of government
         is fundamentally concerned with the study of politi-
         cal behavior or the political process, rather than
         with a societal institution.   This contention can be
         easily refuted, however, by examining a represent-
         ative sample of the textbooks used in the introduc-
         tory course in government (such as textbooks are
         assumed to offer an overview of the field), and
         noting their predominant emphasis on the institution
         of government and the behavior which takes place
         within that institution.

4. The term "specialized foundations of education areas"
    will be used hereafter interchangeably with the ex-
    pression "subdivision of the foundations of educa-
    tion field." It refers, of course, to the special-
    ized areas which presently exist, such as "educa-
    tional psychology" and "social foundations of educa-
    tion."

5. This problem is especially noticeable in the "psychology
    of education" courses. Sometimes these are con-
    ceived of as introductory courses in the academic
    field of psychology, diluted somewhat to meet the
    presumably less stringent requirements of prospec-
    tive teachers, at other times these courses are
    the means through which suggestions for profession-
    al practice are offered, using a psychological per-
    spective; only rarely do these courses concentrate
    entirely on the academic study of education.

6. The argument that a satisfactory introductory course in
    the academic study of education represents a vir-
    tually impossible undertaking owing to the diverse
    psychological, social, historical and philosophical
    elements comprising the field seems untenable.
    Satisfactory introductory courses are provided in
    such fields as anthropology and geography, which
    have more diverse elements than the academic
    study of education.

PART II

THE VALUE FOR TEACHER EDUCATION

MARGARET GILLETT

INTRODUCTION

It is only fair to start with a warning: this section is an attempt to justify a place for Foundation Studies* in teacher preparation programs. It is not merely a description, nor is it an objective analysis. The point of view is partial. It favors Foundation Studies. Nevertheless, this is not a whitewash and there are no extravagant, unsupported claims. On the contrary, there will be considerable scrutiny of assertions and assumptions relating to the value of the various Foundational Studies, as well as warnings about the hostility that is generated among students when unrealistic claims for Foundations are not honored. In short, this section offers a marshalling of learned opinion to support the case for Foundation Studies.

It should be clear, then, that this is a defense. While there may be merit in the notion that the best method of defense is to attack, that is not the approach used here. Supporters of Foundation Studies do not seem to try to "save their own skins" by attacking the other components of teacher education. This is a defense without apology and without disguise. It is a defense, simply because Foundation Studies are under constant attack and need defending. While it may be more dignified to ignore one's detractors, it is now too late for that. We have to face the issue squarely--Foundation Studies occupy an embattled position. Some of the sub-disciplines may suffer more than others in particular institutions and at different times, but all are being battered by curriculum committees, administrators, students, alumni, professors in other fields, and the professional muckrakers of education. In response to all this, a defense is inevitable and is supported by people who believe that Foundation Studies are indeed worth defending.

_____

*No attempt at definition is made here. This was done in Sect. I.

One of the salutory outcomes of this situation is that
people are required to consider consciously why they believe
Foundation Studies are worth defending.   Many people are
already doing this.   One of the most readily identifiable efforts of this kind can be found in the Standing Conference
of Foundational Societies which was formed from representatives of six concerned learned societies (American Educational Studies Association, History of Education Society, Philosophy of Education Society, John Dewey Society, Comparative and International Education Society, and Society of Professors of Education).   The Standing Conference first met in April
1971 with a mandate "to assess the role of the humanistic and
behavioral studies in teacher education." It did so against a
background of pressures, uncertainties, and doubts.   In the
words of Ursula K. Springer, there were questions of whether
"the foundation disciplines failed in substance and image-build-
ing."[1]   The answers that will emerge from the Standing
Conference, as well as from other sources, are not all in,
of course, but there is plenty of strong opinion with which
to begin the defense of Foundation Studies.

But first, we must examine the nature of the attack.

A Synopsis of the Charges

Part of the criticism of Educational Foundations derives from the general disaffection with institutionalized education in all its forms.   Thus, simply because courses in
the History of Education, Philosophy of Education and the
rest exist, they are being attacked.   Part of the criticism
is derived from a broad dissatisfaction with all aspects of
teacher education.   Numerous commentators have identified
teacher education as the single greatest weakness in the
American education enterprise.   Despite increased expendi-
tures, despite the transformation of teachers colleges into
universities, despite the expansion of the graduate study of
Education, teacher preparation still falls far short of per-
fection, and Foundation Studies are attacked along with other elements of the curriculum.   It has been claimed that
teacher education appears to make little difference to the
effectiveness of the practicing teacher--indeed, decades of
educational research have failed to yield unequivocally even
what is meant by "effective teaching."   Foundation Studies
are also criticized quite specifically.   Part of this attack
seems to stem from a new demand for that which is immediately practical, instantly applicable.

The major criticisms are devastating in their simplic-
ity and their completeness: Foundation Studies are held to
be irrelevant in content and to be badly taught. They are
seen as vapid, useless timewasters providing neither intellectual substance nor methodological models. They are retained
because of the inertia, conservatism, even downright stupidity
of teacher educators. There can be no real justification for
them in a modern curriculum other than the obvious ones:
"Because they are there," or because they are supported by
the vested interests of Foundations professors, or because
they have become locked into State certification requirements.
Their value has never been established, say the critics, it is
only taken on faith. This faith is now reinforced by custom
as well as the pressures of the fearful and defensive professors involved, yet it is a faith rejected by thousands of
people who have actually taken, because they were required
to take, Foundation courses.

Such criticisms cannot be dismissed lightly for they
are based on more-or-less objective surveys, observations
and interviews, as well as derived from second-hand sources
which tend to repeat old, uninvestigated complaints. Attacks
were led by people like Bestor and Barzun in the fifties,
Koerner and Conant in the sixties. Who in the seventies?
Illich and Nader?

In any event, for the last decade, the views of James
D. Koerner and James Bryant Conant have both dominated and
epitomized the criticisms. Koerner wrote with vigor, almost
with gusto, that Education as and academic field had failed to
develop a significant body of knowledge and techniques; that
the professional courses required of teachers are not con-
structed around programs of proven worth but are the result
of "a half-century's haphazard accretions" for which no specific rationale exists; that there is no evidence to support the
assumptions that courses now part of pedagogical preparation
have anything to do with teacher competence; that graduate
Education courses proliferate anti-intellectualism.[2] He included Foundation courses in all these complains and was at
some pains to put philosophy of education in sneering quotation marks.[3] It was perhaps unfortunate for true educational
reform that Koerner's attacks were so global that they could
actually produce complacency on the part of some Foundations
people, since anyone could think of an exception to his broad-
sides and could thus label him "unfair." Supporters of Foundations could even look at the evidence Koerner supplied and
draw comfort. True, he cited students who said they detested

various Foundations courses and found them ridiculous, repetitious, superficial and a greal deal of "busy work." But in the Appendix there were also admissions such as: "Education courses, except in the philosophy and student teaching areas, seem on the whole useless";[4] "... all, with the exception of a grad. course in philosophy of education were a waste of time";[5] "The course in history of ed was one of the few ed courses worth taking. It had content and was well presented";[6] "Philosophy of education was stressed in my program, and I feel that this was one of the most valuable parts of my preparation for teaching and should be emphasized in any teacher's program of education."[7]

Conant's equally well-known study expressed little sympathy for Education courses in general. Dr. Conant did grant that courses in the History of Education and so forth could have value, especially if taught in the academic department concerned, but he found no merit in eclectic foundation courses.[8] His proposals for change emphasize more practice teaching and, in the last few years, practicums, workshops, field work, internships have noticeably increased. This is not without irony. At a time when much of the intellectual activity in other disciplines is being devoted to the search for broad understandings and general principles, there is a real danger that the reformers who criticize Education for the anti-intellectual fragmentation of its courses, may be helping direct teacher education toward a return to a non-intellectual apprenticeship program. Even more curious is the fact that teachers-to-be are to get their preparation in the schools--schools which everyone, including the same reformers, criticize as authoritarian, uncreative, non-relevant. Inevitably, the apprenticeship movement involves an emphasis on the present and the practical. And such an emphasis means that basic theories and broad integrating ideas are in danger of being overlooked or undervalued.

In the selections which follow, the need for these broad, integrating ideas is encountered consistently. This is perhaps the key which has been missing in teacher preparation programs. The defenders of Foundation Studies presented here not only make claims for the value of broad, integrating ideas, but also put forward some advice about making these ideas usable, about tranferring them from the realm of theory to the reality of practice. The common rationale, whose absence has so long been bemoaned by the critics, may at last be emerging in Foundations. Perhaps an answer is now being given to question raised forty years ago in Abraham Flexner's scrutiny

of higher education. As he reviewed the catalog of Teachers
College, Columbia, he noted:

> A few instructors offer courses in education phi-
> losophy, in foreign or comparative education; prob-
> lems of elementary and secondary education are
> not slighted. But why do not these substantial and
> interesting fields suffice? Why should not an edu-
> cated person, broadly and deeply versed in educa-
> tional philosophy and experience, help himself
> from that point on? Why should his attention be
> diverted during these pregnant years to the trivial-
> ities and applications with which common sense can
> deal adequately when the time comes?[9]

Professors in Foundation Studies today may be as
puzzled as Flexner, for they see their "substantial and interesting fields" as basic, not peripheral, to the development of the contemporary teacher. They consider the insights they offer extremely valuable for an understanding of
the rapidly changing world of learning and they wonder why
their courses are attacked while so many of the "triviali-
ties" Flexner saw still remain. They may, as the critics
have noted, try to bolster their position by quoting themselves to themselves on the importance of their courses.
Yet they can take a firm stand on general statements such
as this one from Jerome S. Bruner:

> What then of subject matter in the conventional
> sense? The answer to the question, 'What shall
> be taught?' turns out to be first the answer to the
> question, 'What is non-trivial?' then it is not dif-
> ficult to distinguish between the aspects of it that
> are worth teaching and learning and those that are
> not. Surely, knowledge of the natural world, knowl-
> edge of the human condition, knowledge of the na-
> ture and dynamics of society, knowledge of the
> past so that it may be used in experiencing the
> present and aspiring to the future--all of these, it
> would be reasonable to suppose, are essential to
> an educated man. To these must be added another:
> knowledge of the products of our artistic heritage
> that mark the history of our aesthetic wonder and
> delight.[10]

In precisely these terms, Foundation Studies professors
claim that they are contributing to the education of teachers,

that Foundation Studies are, indeed, worth knowing about.

"These Substantial and Interesting Fields"

One of the consistent claims for Foundation Studies is that they are humanizing. The argument is a simple one: "Teachers are human beings who spend their professional lives working with other, generally younger, human beings. If teachers are not to become less than human beings, that is mere technicians, they must have in their preparation some humanizing courses. Foundation Studies are the humanizing courses. Therefore teachers must have Foundation Studies." If the assumed connection between Foundation Studies and the humanizing effect is rarely tested, it is tacitly legitimatized by the whole weight of the Western intellectual tradition. If, for example, history and philosophy are part of the humanities, then philosophy of education and history of education as specialized branches of those disciplines are also part of the humanities. The question then becomes the global one, "Do the humanities humanize?" Despite Thorndike's dictum that if a thing exists, it exists in some amount and can thus be measured, measuring techniques for the effect of the humanities remain unconvincing and crude, regardless of their sometimes elaborate design and the use of computers. The effects of most courses in the College of Arts, as well as those in the Foundations of Education Departments, elude scientific pinpointing. Who can say that such courses do make a significant difference? Who can say they do not make a significant difference?

The question of the humanizing effect of Foundations Studies is further complicated because it involves not only amounts of information, but there is also the obvious and difficult problem of quality as well as the question of time. Few people would claim that the effect of Foundation Studies is immediate and direct. Thus, if the effect is not linear, how does it work? The architectonics of learning in Foundation Studies must be considered here. What is the structure of Foundations learning? It is clearly not built on the model of the skyscraper with one storey piled neatly, sequentially upon the last, leading ever upwards until, suddenly, it stops. Nor is it of the ranch-house plan, with connecting but branching lateral developments. A more appropriate model for Foundations learning is the agglutinative one of the beehive. Here, knowledge is built up layer upon layer for storage in a construction that is fragile but sturdy and from which ideas may be extracted long after they were formed. It is impossible to predict when concepts from Foundation Studies may be drawn upon, or in what order. They will probably not be called forth in linear sequence and they will, at least partially, have been integrated into the persona of the learner so that they may re-emerge modified and colored by other ideas.

It is this that has often given the impression that Foundation Studies are irrelevant to the practical business of school teaching. This may be discouraging, but it is not fatal, especially since it has lately been recognized that the teacher's job is not just that of instructor. It is now commonly agreed that the teacher's responsibility goes well beyond the classroom, and he has (or should have) a voice in decision-making through school committees, P.T.A. meetings and the like, so there is an obvious need for him to have a grasp of the principles that are at work in the evolution of new educational policy, to have an understanding of what happened in the past, and to have insights into the sociological, economic, and political factors impinging upon the educational process. Some few graduates of teacher education programs will become officials in teachers' unions and will actually spend their professional lives grappling with the ideas and issues that are really the main substance of Foundations courses. Likewise, others, who become administrators, are elected members of school boards, or join government departments of education, or are appointed members of commissions of inquiry into education. Such people may be a small minority, but they are certainly an important group and they cannot be effective, cannot communicate to their confreres in the schools, unless those teachers also have some exposure to the basic ideas of education as well as to the techniques of teaching.

The average graduate of any teacher education program will, of course, become a classroom teacher. He will doubtless sympathize with the views expressed in 1971 by a student in an open-ended evaluation of a Foundations course based on "Contemporary Issues in Education." With a colorful mixing of metaphors which did not obscure his concern, this student appeared to dismiss Foundations-type courses.

> While at the University, one is in the spirit and
> atmosphere of advanced thinking, philosophy, hu-
> manitarianism, good will to all, and advanced con-

cepts. Realities such a discipline, truculent and
lazy students, and the pecking order of the staff
are as remote as Pluto.

But, once in the schools, one is in noise, chaos
and turmoil. The essential element is SURVIVAL.
A very mild analogy would be that of a general in
the Pentagon finding himself instantly transposed
to Khe Sahn, where he is only a private. The good
will, order and progressive ideas somehow are
lost in the boiler-room of schools.

Who cares what Aristotle said, when one is in a
small pool with twenty-seven hungry sharks? Who
thinks of Dewey, when in the staff room the main
concern is whose turn is it to run the coffee machine, or what the pro-strike faction thinks? One
looks at faces and sees, not philosophic humanitarianism but hard, unsmiling mill workers; the older
the face the harder it's set. Somehow the people
we had come to rescue have become the enemy, and
our allies are a cynical and corrupt ruling class
who resent our intrusions and the attempts to free
the people. And the more one realizes this, the
greater the cynicism and what's worse, the despair.
Yet the antidote is sheer persistence: 'Into the
breach once more ... '

Back to the Pentagon, one has time to reflect, and
compare battle-scars with others. And the process
of studying what Aristotle said continues ...

The sentiments are probably familiar enough to any
Foundations Studies professor. But how valid are they?
Does it make any difference that, in the course in question,
there was never any formal presentation of or emphasis on
Aristotle, or any of the other classical philosophers, either?
Does the apparent rejection of theory and the cry for the
practical ring entirely true? What are we to make of the
phrase, "the people we came to rescue"? Is this practical
young man, after all, an idealist?

Yes, he is. And Foundation Studies are the courses
which have helped nourish his ideals. Yet they take the
brunt of his attack. And that's the paradox, for the Foundations professor and the student teacher are really on the
same side. What the student-teacher really wants is to do

some good, to "rescue" someone; he is oriented, not toward
an immediate aim like order in the classroom, but to an ultimate goal of some kind like the individual self-fulfilment of
his students.   He becomes angry and frustrated because he
has to be diverted from this to attend to a proximate aim
and cannot get on with the business of the real or ultimate
Aim (spelled with a capital "A").   At this point one remem-
bers R. S. Peters' arguments that "These very general aims
are neither goals nor are they end products.   Like 'happi-
ness' they are high-sounding ways of talking about doing
some things rather than others and doing them in a certain
manner."[11]   Peters goes on to claim, "The crucial question
to ask, when men wax enthusiastic on the subject of their
aims, is what procedures are to be adopted in order to im-
plemente them.   We then get down to moral brass tacks."[12]
Peters suggests that "principles of procedures"--which he
does not clearly specify--are what one needs to help cope
with practical problems and to devise ways of teaching.   The
ultimate, high-sounding Aims are not only remote, but unnecessary.   Other philosophers of education endorse this
view which, on the face of it, would seem to deny the necessity for philosophy of education (and would therefore put
Peters out of business).   Michael Oakeshott, for one, defends
such a position and rebutts those who would ask, "Why travel
if there is no prefigured and final destination?" by pointing
out that poetry, science, art are among the human pursuits
which have no ultimate goal but are, nevertheless, considered worthwhile "journeys."[13]

    The hitchhiking student of today who has abandoned
the systematic, secure ways of the Establishment, can probably appreciate this kind of argument.   The thing is to trav-
el--the going itself, the experiences, the sidetracks, the adventures, even the bummers, these are what matter.   Still
the West Coast beckons!   There remains the achievement,
the glow of being able to say, "I made it from coast to
coast."   But even a relaxed, unprogrammed hitch has more
common sense to it, more zest, if there is a general notion
of a desired direction.   Even to begin, you have to decide
which side of the road you are going to stand on!   In the
long run, then, one may choose to agree with Jonas Soltis
when he says simply, "Practically speaking, it would be impossible to intentionally educate without some value commitment or some desired program being operative."[14]

    Even if one rejects Peters' rejection of Aims, one is
grateful for the attention he focuses on procedure and for the

irreverence with which he treats lofy goals.   Foundation
Studies professors have so often tended to overlook procedures and methods, and may have helped wreck their courses
with high moral tone.   That was the way to respectability.
However, things are changing.   The straight, linear path--
seen most clearly in the chronological survey in the History
of Education--is no longer the sole, or even the principal,
approach to Foundation Studies courses.   There is an increasing number of options and more flexibility of procedures.
Thus, a modified "hitchhiking" approach to Foundation Studies
is possible; so that the student can be met on his own terms,
in a milieu that he appreciates.   This would not be random
wandering; rather, it might tend to stay on the highways
(contained within the parameters of the basic disciplines), although there would be many intersections and possibilities of
exploring other routes (interdisciplinary studies); nor would
it be aimless (irrelevant to the function of the professional
teacher); rather, it would recognize the enriching value, the
potential for personal development in a variety of (intellectual) experiences.

It still remains for the Foundation Studies professor
to convince the harried student-teacher that their goals coincide.   The student who stopped his hitchhiking in the fall and
now sees himself on a direct professional course toward a
degree, a job, and a career, may remain skeptical.   The
papers in this section provide many arguments to show that
the idealistic young and the ivory tower professor should
stick together if they want to make it to the Coast.

A Summary of the Support

The following statements in support of the various
Foundation Studies are extracted from the papers in this section.   By no means do they represent all the arguments set
forth, but they do provide a small compendium of significant
ideas about the place of Foundation Studies in teacher preparation programs.

--"Either teachers are to have a craft training only, in which
case their right to a share in policy making is no better than
that of any other citizen; or the preparation of teachers has
to become genuinely professional, which means more foundational study, not less, than is now prescribed."--Harry S.
Broudy

--Foundation Studies "are the base of operations, the hub so to speak, to which other studies or activities in teacher education and training relate and in which they find their unity of movement and purpose. They provide the orientation to his functions that the teacher needs and give meaning and direction to what otherwise would be merely fortutious and certainly ill-understood by the teacher. This assumes, of course, that they are treated with reference to the student teacher's actual teaching experiences."--Andrew F. Skinner

--"Much of the dissatisfaction which students express about training courses could probably be traced to unrealistic expectations concerning much of what they are taught. From the student's interest in educational matters it might be possible to lead him on to explore some history, philosophy, sociology and anthropology, and we may well believe that it would be worthwhile to encourage such interests, but it would be fraudulent to suggest that they will help him to cope with 4B more successfully."--J. P. Powell

--"... the teacher, like every other human being, achieves dignity as he makes effectual choices in the world, as he creates and recreates himself as a teacher day by day, month by month, by dint of making the kinds of decisions and employing the kinds of strategies which will enable young people to learn. The relevance of history for such a person depends, I believe, on the degree to which a study of the educational past enables him to organize his own experience in the situation of the present, to refine his strategies, to enlarge his conceptual scope. Its relevance depends on the degree to which (as in the case of the statesman who studies political history) it enables him to discern a range of possibilities for action, to perceive both limitations and what Arthur Schlesinger, Jr., calls 'ambiguities'."--Maxine Greene

--"The significance of educational history has not been so evident, in spite of the proliferating foundations courses in colleges throughout the country. It seems to me that the discipline may be justified, however, as other subject matters are justified today, as long as its distinctivness is identified--perhaps as one of the humanities."--Maxine Greene

--"History of Education does not have to be revered as a foundation nor written off as a frill. Its place in teacher education can be justified, even if the reasons advanced are more intrinsic than instrumental ... Taught well, it can both humanize and help legitimatize teacher education as an academic endeavor."--Margaret Gillett

--"If philosophy of education is to remain an integral element in teacher preparation programs, it must have a purpose. In other words, the work of the philosopher of education or the business of philosophical clarification generally, must have some relevance to professional practice in education. This relevance, as has been explained by many, cannot be direct; the philosopher of education cannot legislate for the practitioner. But his work of clarification and examination must exhibit the range of reasonable and desirable choices confronting educators in their professional work ... This is, in fact, another way of saying that teachers must learn to think for themselves."--N.C. Bhattacharya

--"One would hope the philosopher of education is uniquely qualified to present a partisan position. He may wish to wxhibit the range of alternatives in a given situation. But, finally, his discussion ought to terminate with a recommendation--about curriculum, school organization, instruction, or whatever. It is significant to note that those few philosophical theorists whose voices have been heard in the market place of ideas inevitably do espouse a position. In an age that eschews commitments in favor of moral neutrality, the greatest service the philosopher can render is to provide intellectual leadership. Although his views may not find acceptance, educational controversy will be informed by a measure of the philosophical insight it so sorely requires."
--Christopher J. Lucas

--"The successful ordering of society ... depends on the growth of integrative understanding, along with the advance of specialized inquiries ... Social and intellectual advances do require the development of the capacity for powerful generalization. This task is essentially philosophical. The goal for comprehensive understanding will not be achieved simply by juxtaposing separate specialized disciplines. It requires a different quality of thinking that is integrative in nature. The deliberate cultivation of this integral perspective is the most distinctive task for the philosopher ..."--Philip Phenix

--"Opportunities, through anthropology, to enrich educational experience in its manifold dimensions are vastly wider and deeper than have thus far been explored. Nevertheless, such opportunities, especially those emerging within scarcely two decades, have already begun to prove their own extraordinary usefulness ... My discovery of anthropology in any intensive

way occurred some years after primary concentration in
philosophy, and my first prolonged effort was to draw these
two disciplines closer together by means of a third: education. Subsequent research inter-relating all three fields has
continued to build upon the theoretical foundations earlier
laid ... The intent of our field experiences is a ... humble
one: to introduce professional educators to some of the
techniques by which anthropology approaches, examines, and
interprets cultural experiences, with particular regard for
that important feature of such experience known as education."--Theodore Brameld

--"The issue here is the teacher's view of his world, as
distinct from the practice of his craft.
        Sociology badly taught will be as useless as any other
discipline ... [But] the social context of education is now
predominant. The world has moved--from elitism to democracy; from colonialism to nation-states; from isolated peasant cultures to mass communications. All these changes
arise from, and generate, social forces which must be understood."--Leonard Marsh

--"The teacher is much involved in the activities of the modern world. Its challenge increasingly requires a comparative attitude of mind and the continuous appraisal by international comparison of whatever is done domestically."--Ed-
mund King

--"If we are inquiring about a possible place for comparative education in teacher training we should be able to show
1.   that it employes an intellectually rigorous method af-
fording useful explanations of educational phenomena;
2.   that, moreover, the claims usually made for comparative education--that it accords "perspective," that it engenders sensitivity for the relative range of national experience, etc.--really amount to a theoretical understanding,
through cross-cultural comparison, of education as a system;
3.   that we really have here that integrating approach which,
as is often said, leads to an understanding of the politics of
education and, consequently, to political alertness and a reforming attitude;
4.   that, finally, the cross-cultural study of education is of
practical value, both in an applicative sense--the critical use
of a repertory of devices and solutions--and in an interpretive sense--an improved orientation in the wide field of educational institutions and practice. We may call these four
aspects the relevance of method and of theory, the political

and the practical relevance. --Saul B. Robinsohn

These, then, are some of the arguments put forward
to justify the continuation and development of Foundation
Studies in the teacher preparation curriculum.   These extracts, and more especially the papers from which they
come, show that contemporary supporters of Foundation
Studies in Europe and Canada, as well as in the United
States, do indeed have faith in their subjects--in their integrative, intellectual and practical effects.   But it is a faith
tempered by reason and analysis.   While none of the papers
is naively optimistic, only Christopher Lucas' really strikes
a gloomy note--but it is the more interesting for that.   In a
published response to Lucas, James E. McClellan says:

> My advice to Lucas and to all who are concerned
> about the demise of educational philosophy is to
> forget it.   The crises of our times will keep phi-
> losophy alive despite what we professionals do or
> don't do.   Our only obligation is to maintain a
> deep and conscious commitment to the tradition
> of rational thought which we have undertaken to
> sustain.   If our commitment focuses on philosophy
> of education, then, Deo volente, we will find that
> the language and action of educators reveals us
> questions, puzzles, tensions, ambiguities, dilem-
> mas--which we will want to treat in continuity with
> our own tradition of thought.   If we are lucky and
> resourceful, practical men (including the students
> in our classes) will find insight and enlightenment
> in what we are doing. [15]

No one claims that the benefits of Foundation Studies
are automatic and universal.   Explicitly or implicitly, the
papers presented here raise the old, fundamental problem of
transfer of learning.   They therefore invite the professors
of Foundation Studies to point out consciously how the work
of their areas can and, indeed, must, be applied to the real
concerns of education.

Notes

1. Ursula K. Springer, CIES Newsletter, June 1971, p.3.
2. James D. Koerner, The Miseducation of American
      Teachers, Boston: Houghton Mifflin, 1963, passim.

Notice, however, that surveys in other countries
have not produced quite the same harsh results.
See, for example, Helen Menzies-Smith, "Desirable Training of Teachers," Teachers in Australia,
Melbourne: F.W. Cheshire, 1966, pp. 60-93. In
the study cited, students at undergraduate and
graduate levels rated as of major importance
courses dealing with "Aims and Purposes of Education in Changing Society," though they were not
quite so kind to Comparative Education or to
courses dealing with "Ideals and Ethics of Traditional Education."

3. Koerner, op. cit., p. 50.
4. Ibid., p. 332.
5. Ibid., p. 336.
6. Ibid., p. 344.
7. Ibid., p. 349.
8. James Bryant Conant, The Education of American
   Teachers. New York: McGraw-Hill, 1965.
9. Abraham Flexner, Universities: American, English,
   German. New York: Oxford University Press,
   1930, p. 99.
10. Jerome S. Bruner, On Knowing. Cambridge, Mass.:
    The Belknap Press of Harvard University Press,
    1962.
11. R. S. Peters, Authority, Responsibility and Education.
    London: George Allen and Unwin, Ltd., 1959,
    p. 86.
12. Ibid., p. 94.
13. Michael Oakeshott, "Political Education," in Israel
    Scheffler, ed., Philosophy and Education. Boston:
    Allyn & Bacon, (2nd ed.), 1966, p. 342.
14. Jonas F. Soltis, An Introduction to the Analysis of Ed-
    ucational Concepts. Reading, Mass.: Addison-
    Wesley, 1968, p. 15.
15. James E. McClellan, "Educational Philosophy Resur-
    rected," School Review, February 1971, pp. 280-
    81.

HARRY S. BROUDY

1. THE ROLE OF THE FOUNDATIONAL STUDIES
IN THE PREPARATION OF ELEMENTARY TEACHERS*

I shall begin the discussion of the role of the foundation studies in the preparation of elementary teachers by
registering some dissatisfaction with the terms "foundation"
and "foundational. " A brave band of professors at Columbia
Teachers College deserve our gratitude for the idea of foundational studies, but not for the term.

Inevitably the word makes one think of the building
trades, or those great philanthropic geese that lay the golden
eggs for educational reform, or the art of corsetry. All
these connotations have their roots in the notion of a beginning. The foundation of the edifice is the first layer of the
building, and when one founds an establishment he institutes
or originates it; presumably an establishment is called a
foundation when its goal is to assist in the founding of other
enterprises. As for the foundation garments worn by women,
they too are supposed to be the first layer of clothing, as
well as the means of establishing a basic contour for the
figure's subsequent adornment.

Along with the connotation of initiation or beginning
goes the idea of importance. What is foundational is supposed to be fundamental, basic, supportive. Without foundations, one is led to believe, there can be no buildings, no
fashionable figures, no research, no first-class trips on jet
airplaines to esoteric conferences, and no innovations in education, especially in teacher education.

These images and their penumbral meanings are quite
unsatisfactory. To begin with, the foundational studies are
rarely first in order of instruction. For the most part,

---

*The Journal of Educational Thought (University of Calgary),
Vol. II, No. 1 (April 1968), pp. 30-9. Reprinted with the
permission of the Journal and the author.

they are reserved for the later phases of teacher preparation. Some schools--as a matter of fact, theory, or con-
venience--reserve these studies for in-service training or
postpone them until after student teaching. The delay is
urged on the ground that the student will be more mature
and consequently more ready for the history, philosophy,
and the sociology of education. The psychology of education
(or the psychological foundations of education) is an exception, because one expects (over-optimistically) it to be applied immediately to problems of the classroom, and therefore should precede practice teaching.

In the second place, the metaphor of a foundation as
holding something up, as something on which one builds,
fails badly when used in connection with educational history
and philosophy, and limps even with regard to the psychology and sociology of education. Their placement at various
stages of the training indicates that they are not uniformly
thought of as prerequisites for later studies that incorporate
them as elements. On the contrary, they themselves require (or should require) the study of the parent disciplines
of history, psychology, sociology, and philosophy as prerequisites. However, the sciences of education, if we ever
develop them, might well qualify as prerequisites for large
segments of the teacher-preparation curriculum.

Distracting as foundational imagery may be, it is
less damaging than the unrealistic expectations it spawns in
the teacher, and the hostility to the foundational studies that
results when the expectations are not fulfilled. Two sorts
of expectations come to mind. One is that study of the philosophy, history, psychology, and sociology of education
will equip the teacher with technical solutions to classroom
problems. The other is that these courses or studies will
build into the teacher a set of values that will keep her
headed in the right direction regardless of the pressures
and turmoil of time and circumstance. I regret to report
that foundational studies will do neither. They will not provide tricks for evading classroom predicaments, because
they do not deal with particular cases, whereas teaching always does. And they will not provide firm guides for morality because, for the most part, the philosophy of education, which is expected to do this, examines the validity of
values and usually ends up by questioning all of them. So
the prospective teacher is more likely to be less sure of
her values after the course than before. To be sure, she
will be able to discuss her unsureness with greater preci-

sion, but that is not, I take it, what has been expected or even promised.

Now there may come a time when the psychology of education, the sociology of education, and perhaps the anthropology and economics of education will be so well developed as sciences that we can milk them for important empirical generalizations. These may, in turn, help us create a technology that will be applicable to the everyday problems of the teacher. When that happy day arrives, these subjects will not be called "foundational"; they will be taught to prospective teachers as methods, i.e., as rules for applying the generalizations of educational science. Some aspects of educational psychology are already in this phase, e.g., when we use tests of various sorts, or when we change the curriculum to accommodate the mentally retarded.   The philosophy and history of education, however, will never give this sort of help, and even the other behavioral sciences are still a long way from doing so in any substantial way.

On what grounds then can we reasonably ask prospective elementary school teachers to devote time to what seems so remote from their immediate needs?   How can we avoid their reporting the foundational courses as the ones that have helped them least in their teaching career?

First of all, it is quite possible that foundational studies can be dispensed with altogether.   This is especially plausible if one conceives of elementary teaching as a craft in which the teacher is a person who loves children and treats them humanely while teaching them how to read, spell, write, and do arithmetic while introducing them to the subject matter fields.   As a craftsman all the teacher really needs is a set of rules and the techniques for applying them in more or less standard situations.   The untypical situation can be referred to the supervisor or the principal.   If this is so, one can understand why so many "good" teachers do so "well" with so little theory; why the prospective teacher is so impatient with theory, and why student teaching is the heart of teacher preparation, both elementary and secondary.   (It is to be noted that all prospective professions--not merely teachers but also doctors, lawyers and engineers--are impatient with theory precisely because it is the craft aspect of their work that excites them, that will confront them first and trouble them most. The difference is that in the established professions the impatience of the students is not taken seriously by those in charge of their training.)

The recent wave of teacher strikes in the United States demonstrates the ambiguous status of classroom teachers. On the one hand, they behaved as craftspeople unsatisfied with their pay and working conditions. Their leaders "jeered" at remonstrances that this direct defiance of the "authorities" was unprofessional and smacked of proletarianism. On the other hand, at least in New York City, the striking union insisted that teachers have a voice in the making of educational policy. But by virtue of what do teachers claim this right? By virtue of their skill as craftspeople? But are matters of policy simply matters of technical skill? Are the issues of schooling for the disadvantaged simply matters of technique? Or do the teachers claim the right to share in the determination of educational policy by virtue of their being citizens of the community in which they teach? Certainly nobody would deny their rights as citizens, but the mechanism for registering citizen opinion on matters of community policy is not, as a rule, a strike. I would think that the teachers should claim this right by virtue of their thorough understanding of the problems of the school in all their social and philosophical ramifications, as well as on their experience in the classroom. In other words, they presumably have studied what schooling ought to be, what the relation between teacher and pupil, teacher and administrator, school and community ought to be. And one would like to believe that they not only have beliefs on these issues, but that they would also be willing and able to defend these views, rationally.

What in their formal preparation for teaching provided them with the conceptual tools for such an understanding, an understanding superior presumably to that of the craftsman and the ordinary well-intentioned citizen? I submit that the foundational studies, or their equivalent, can take some of the credit (or blame), for this is precisely the proper content of these studies. Philosophy of education studies the problems of education--the problems of aims, curriculum, organization, teaching-learning--in the light of the concepts of philosophy; the history of education is the history of these educational problems; the psychology of education concentrates on this same set of problems in their psychological aspects, while other behavioral sciences study these problems in their anthropological, economic, and sociological dimensions.

Perhaps teacher strikes will force teachers, the public, the self-appointed critics, and saviors of education to choose. Either the teachers are to have a craft training only, in which case their right to a share in policy making is no better than that of any other citizen; or the preparation of the teacher has to become genuinely professional, which means more foundational study, not less than is now prescribed.

One of the major obstacles to understanding these alternatives is that classroom teachers, at least in the United States, believe that they have had a professional training. Partly they believe it because college catalogues told them so; their training, insofar as it is not general education or the study of the subject they are to teach, is often called "professional preparation." They also believe it because they are not blue collar workers, and because they have had more general education, as a rule, than the electrician or the plumber. Moreover, they are working with human beings in a very important human enterprise. The last point certainly makes it reasonable to argue that they ought to be professionally trained, but wearing white collars and having some general education do not prove that they are so trained. Scanning the requirements for the teaching certificate in most states, one is led to the conclusion that the majority of classroom teachers have less theoretical training than the graduate of a good school of nursing and far less technical training than that of a master electrician or carpenter. Most of the schools preparing teachers are, so to speak, schools of nursing masquerading as medical schools.

To become genuinely professional, the curriculum for teacher education will have to become more theoretical, so that teachers can rationalize techniques and rules of procedures, just as the engineer and physician use theory to understand why a rule of practice applies. Knowing the theory behind the rule gives the professional the right to depart from the rule, and perhaps even to formulate new rules. This right and freedom are not accorded to the craftsman who merely knows the rules and uses the techniques.

Two uses of theory are involved in the preparation of teachers at the professional level: applicative use and interpretive use. The first, if well developed, furnishes the basis for a rational technology to solve our problems of practice; the second enables us to conceptualize and thereby to understand these problems, and to evaluate the tech-

nology itself. Sociology, economics, and other behavioral
sciences of education may have both an applicative and an
interpretive use; history and philosophy of education are restricted to the interpretive use.

What then is this interpretive use of knowledge and
how does it function in the work of an elementary teacher?[1]

Let us take, first, a problem that is not educational
at all and note the difference between the applicative use of
knowledge and the interpretive. Suppose on a frosty morn-
ing your automobile does not start. What use can you make
of knowledge to help you get it started? Did you take a
course in physics in high school or college? Do you know
the principles of the internal combustion engine? Can you
apply this knowledge to vitalizing your cold automobile? Do
you know how a carburetor is put together or how the igni-
tion system of an automobile works? If you know all this
you have all the theoretical knowledge needed to start your
car. But like many motorists who have all this knowledge
you probably will not apply it. For one thing, you may not
know what your car's carburetor looks like nor where it is
in the metal jungle under the hood. If you could identify it,
could you tell what parts operate in what ways to make it
work? And even if you can pass this test, do you have the
tools and skill to do what knowledge indicates might be necessary?

Your automobile mechanic may know little or much
about physics and the theory of internal combustion engines,
but one can rightfully expect him to know the anatomy of
your automobile and the rules of procedure well enough so
that with the appropriate tools he can do the proper things
to get the car started. As a matter of plain fact, the
knowledge that most motorists, with or without the benefit
of courses in physics, do apply is that which enables them
to look up the telephone number of the nearest automobile
mechanic.

Much of our knowledge of automobiles--especially
that which we remember from the general science course--
is strictly for interpretive use. It enables us to understand
how and why an internal combustion engine works and to discuss it with others who have the same sort of knowledge;
but in and of itself it does not enable us to cure ailing automobiles. For this one needs to translate the theory of the
internal combustion engine into the principles of automobile

design and construction. One needs intimate familiarity with many instances of automobiles and their troubles, and above all, one needs to know the techniques used to manipulate automobile engines. It is this type of professional knowledge that entitles its possessor to be called an expert within a given domain of practice.

Yet the more developed the profession and the more its domain of practice is linked with other domains, the more does the professional need to know the total field of which his speciality is a part. But because he cannot possibly have applicative knowledge of the total field, he must make do with interpretive knowledge in all fields outside of his speciality. He cannot <u>solve</u> problems in these adjacent fields, but he can understand them and know what knowledge is relevant to them. It is precisely this type of <u>interpretive professional</u> knowledge that the foundational studies, especially the humanistic ones, supply to the professional worker in education.

Professional interpretive knowledge is especially necessary in education, because education finds it virtually impossible to dismiss any field of knowledge as wholly irrelevant to its own problems. Can we become expert even in one related field, such as psychology, not to speak of all the behavioral sciences that seem to have something important to say about teaching? And ought we to become experts in electronics in order to understand the technology of teaching instruments, of which we are promised more and more esoteric models each year? If by becoming expert we mean knowing how to apply this knowledge, the answer is obvious. However, if we mean interpretive knowledge, the answer is not so obvious, for there is a possibility that we can get this sort of knowledge, or at least some of it, as part of teacher preparation.

To make more concrete what I have in mind, let us take the problem of teaching the disadvantaged. It is a problem that affects all levels of schooling and all phases of schooling, and it certainly concerns the elementary teacher. What sort of applicative knowledge do we have in solving this problem? What sort of interpretive knowledge might we have for understanding and structuring this problem?

I think you will agree that the social psychologists, together with the sociologists, have made it clear that a great many factors that have little to do with formal school-

ing, make the problem of teaching the disadvantaged almost
hopelessly complex. Consider, for example, how the family
structure, economic conditions, low level of aspiration, and
restricted verbal environment all combine to make the stra-
tegically crucial teaching of reading a special problem.

Can we <u>apply</u> this knowledge to handling a mixed
classroom of nine-year-olds? Can the teacher change these
conditions? Can she use it to change the level of aspiration, the dirty and deprived home? No, we do not as yet
have either the scientific theory or the technology to effect
such changes. We are accumulating experience and conducting a few experiments. Not long ago <u>The Educational For-
um</u> published an article by a man experienced in teaching
the disadvantaged.[2] The article was a mixture of sociological and psychological principles plus sets of very detailed
rules for teaching in a disadvantaged classroom. The author claimed that these rules work, but these rules follow
no more necessarily from current psychological and sociological theories than do a half dozen other sets of rules that
perhaps work equally well. In other words, in this area
the elementary teacher may profit from experience, but one
can hardly say that there is scientific knowledge that can be
applied with the confidence of the expert.

Yet even in the absence of applicative knowledge, is
the knowledge we do have useless? Is understanding the
class structure of our society, its economic system, the
role of schooling in economic life useless? Would the teaching of the disadvantaged be possible or even tolerable without such understanding? How would one guide the search
for applicable knowledge, if one did not first conceptualize
these problems? So the interpretive knowledge is not useless. Without it the teacher is reduced to desperate trial
and error. Often this results in intolerable frustration and
a general reluctance to teach in schools for the disadvantaged. To fill the vacuum, messianic, high-minded ama-
teurs rush in with every conceivable variety of project to
redeem the disadvantaged. In time, one might hope, the
interpretive knowledge we do have will be supplemented by
applicative knowledge. When that comes to pass, we shall
be on the way to making the teaching of the disadvantaged a
professional speciality. Professional knowledge and skill will
then replace some of the missionary zeal and the evangel-
ism that now are needed to sustain it. This will make the
work less exciting, perhaps, but far more effective.

Is then the interpretive knowledge furnished by foundational studies merely a stop-gap until the behavioral sciences provide us with knowledge that one can apply to solve the problems of schooling? Will educational science one day solve all educational problems, pretty much as medical science will solve all problems of health and disease?

Unfortunately, or fortunately, to define education is to define human life itself, and not all solutions are equally human. Suppose, for example, it could be shown that taking all disadvantaged children from their homes at the age of two and having them brought up in government nurseries according to the rules laid down by the psychologists and social workers would do the trick. There is some reason to believe that this would be a very efficient way not only of solving the problem but perhaps even of getting rid of it altogether. However, even a rudimentary understanding of the value system to which citizens of the United States seem to be committed will indicate why the scientists had better seek other ways of solving the problem.

The value system of a multi-culture society cannot be understood by reading the weekly opinion polls. Defining standards of value and justifying them are the most puzzling problems in philosophy, and yet they are rehearsed every time the movies, television, long hair, and miniskirts come up for discussion. Some understanding of the value problem teachers do acquire in their general studies, and there are those who argue that the study of value questions in the general courses in literature, philosophy, and history is all the classroom teacher will need. But if so, why do the daring remarks of the young college professor of literature sound so strange in the mouth of a high school teacher? Why do the clever comments that sound so deliciously bold at the ladies' literary club become frightening if uttered by a teacher to one's own offspring? The answer, of course, is that values of prime importance to parents are the welfare of their child, not the learning of the professor or his academic freedom. What, then, is the appropriate perspective for the classroom teacher, who mediates between the world of learned opinion and that of the parent? Perhaps this difference of context accounts for the disappointingly meager contributions to the solution of educational problems emanating from the mouths of liberal arts professors. Unless they become educationalists in the non-prestigious sense of that word, they are more valuable as agents provocateurs than as front line troops.

There are, of course, many other problems facing
the elementary teacher that could have been used as examples of the usefulness of interpretive knowledge. One is
that of innovation, especially the kind of innovation that is
connected with programmed instruction and teaching machines. The relation between the elementary school teacher
and the pupil has not yet been reduced to that between a
sender and a receiver of information. Every elementary
teacher knows that it takes all sorts of maneuvering to get
a live human pupil to play the role of a receiver. He persists in being something else. Inevitably, the young child
will try to establish a personal relationship to the teacher;
he can be distracted from this only momentarily and perhaps never completely. Will automated instruction be an
aid or a hindrance to this relation? If the teacher's instructional role can be decreased, will the personal relationship gain or suffer? Is individualized instruction the same
as personalized instruction? Is this difference important or
not?

I shall in all charity refrain from saying anything
about the antics of schoolmen who are innocent of history in
general and of the history of education in particular. The
word "innovative" at the moment is the magic word. The
U.S. government through its Office of Education has decreed
that the schools shall be innovative. It has put researchers
in battalion strength to work not only to find innovations,
but also to find out how to get these disseminated. The
search for innovation has become a large-scale industry.

Now the charisma of innovation, if one may so speak,
lies in the supposition that the new is bound to be better
than the old. In a couantry where obsolescence is planned
for, the one absolute value is to be up to date. In a culture where all values are challenged as being relative, subjective, or classbound, the word innovation divides the world
into two clearly differentiated camps; the good guys who are
willing to try anything, and the bad guys who drag their
feet.

Such idolatry of the innovative is possible only with
people who have kept away from the study of history, of society, and of the school itself. As a result, the Dalton
Plan and fairly ancient variations of the activity-programs
are being rediscovered and promulgated as imaginative innovations. In a field where the applicative knowledge is
ample, as in engineering and medicine, the new is likely

to be really an advance and not merely different. In a
field where applicative knowledge is still meager, only
teachers with rich interpretive knowledge can distinguish
the merely innovative from genuine advances.

For a long time to come, therefore, teachers can
profit from extensive study of the history, philosophy, psychology, and sociology of education--what have been called
the foundational studies. I would also like to suggest, in
passing, a possible answer to those who say, "But teachers
report that these courses were of the least use and often of
the least interest in their teaching-preparation curriculum."

I would suggest, first of all, that interpretive knowledge gets used quite often without the person being aware
of either its use or its source. For it is the virtue of interpretive knowledge that it becomes so integral a part of
our perceiving, thinking, and feeling that we do not consciously think of when and how we learned it. In the case
of the foundational studies, as in that of general education,
it is easier to discern the man who lacks it than to justify
the trouble of getting it.

In the second place, we tend to value most that which
relieves our most immediate difficulties--and these are, of
course, those of daily practice.

Thirdly, not all courses labeled "Philosophy of Education" or "History of Education" are equally good as to
content and presentation. This prompts one to urge schools
of education that unless they can afford to hire well-trained
specialists to teach these courses, they would be well advised not to offer them at all.

There is one other way of evading the conclusion
that foundational study is essential to the elementary school
teacher. This is to say that economic conditions and the
shortage of teachers make it unlikely, and perhaps impossible, that all elementary teachers will be trained to a genuinely professional level; that, therefore, the training time
had better be spent on student teaching, methods, techniques,
and as much general education as one can manage.

This is a cogent argument because it so closely describes the reality. It may be that the United States can afford to have only one out of fifteen of its elementary teachers
trained to the professional level, just as it can manage to

have only so many physicians on a hospital staff.   If this is
the case, it would be wise to face this possibility and to
differentiate between two classes of school personnel.   There
is nothing mean or lowly about being a nurse.   On the contrary, much of the effectiveness of modern medicine depends
on the existence of a large corps of competent nurses.   But
it does no one any good to make believe that all the nurses
are physicians, and calling them by the same name only
compounds the confusion.

The theoretical studies--both the scientific ones that
can yield rules for practice and the humanistic ones that
can only help us interpret educational problems--are indispensable only for those elementary teachers who hope to
operate at the professional level; for the large cadre of
craftspeople who have to be turned out in a minimum of
time and with a minimum of cognitive strain, neither type
of theory is indispensable; rules, techniques, and apprenticeship are sufficient.   Like good nurses they are invaluable, but only as adjuncts of a strong albeit fairly small
core of professionals.

This may have to be the solution, but if it is, the
public will not be happy with it, especially in the elementary grades.   Rightly or not the public has more faith in
the elementary school than in the secondary one.   Why this
is so, is not clear, but if I were to speculate I would attribute it to the fact that the public respects the elementary
school teacher as more of a specialist than the high school
teacher of history of mathematics.   Mistakenly or not the
public believes that anyone who has studied history or mathematics can teach it.   A college graduate who might not be
averse to taking a fling at teaching in a high school would
be scared witless at the prospect of substituting for even a
day in the second grade.   How many educated parents would
be willing to teach their own children to read, write, or
spell?

The respect for the elementary school teacher goes
well beyond the acknowledgment of esoteric craftsmanship--
of knowing how to do something one cannot do himself.
Parents also appreciate the importance of childhood, and
when they entrust a young child to the school they do so with
the confidence that the teacher is not merely a mother substitute, but an ideal mother substitute--a substitute who loves
children not only well but wisely.   In this sense, the public
attributes to the elementary teacher a degree of profession-

alism that she may not always deserve, but in expecting it the public is well ahead of many schools of education which are willing to settle for something less.

Notes

1. For a more thorough and technical discussion of the applicative, replicative, associative and interpretive uses of knowledge and schooling the reader may wish to consult H. S. Broudy, B. O. Smith, and Joe R. Burnett, Democracy and Excellence in American Secondary Education (Chicago: Rand McNally, 1964), Chaps. 3 and 4; "Philosophy and the Curriculum," in Philosophy and Education--Proceedings, International Seminar, March 23-25, 1966 (Toronto: The Ontario Institute for Studies in Education, Monograph Series, No. 3, 1967), pp. 59-71; also "The Role of the Foundational Studies in the Preparation of Teachers," in Improving Teacher Education in the United States, Stanley Elam, editor (Bloomington, Ind.: Phi Delta Kappa, 1967), pp. 1-35.
2. A. O. Ornstein, "Teaching the Disadvantaged," The Educational Forum 31 (January, 1967), pp. 215-223.

ANDREW F. SKINNER

2. TEACHER-TRAINING AND THE FOUNDATIONAL STUDIES [*]

A Personal Statement

Innovation and Resurgence

"There is a flaw in the Kingdom of Fife. ... There are too many alternative roads to everywhere in Fife." Because of my native and indestructible affiliations this statement was drawn to my attention recently. It was not news to me, but there followed the question as to which roads, in these days of rush and planning, should be signposted as main routes. This, it seems to me, is the kind of dilemma, of bafflement, that confronts anyone who is rash enough to undertake to write on the theme of this article. And the sense of dilemma is magnified as one thinks about education in this permissive, relativistic age. Go-go in education today is impressive. Yet one wonders if we are going anywhere or if indeed there is anywhere to go. The means are plentiful--but to what end is seldom clear.

Teacher-training is a realm that is marked by uncertainties and has been, perhaps in consequence, open to criticism from many sources. In many ways we are still, and doubtless under ever-changing circumstances we always will be, groping towards an understanding of what is essentially involved. Moreover, there are so many different routes followed in our Western world, and indeed in Canada itself, that it is hardly possible to write in general terms about any aspect of teacher-training and perhaps least of all about the so-called Foundational Studies. They have been given the hardest knocks of all by the critics, and certainly the effectiveness of their treatment is bound to depend on the matur-

*Reprinted from Teacher Education (University of Toronto), Spring 1968, pp. 26-38, with the permission of the journal and the author.

ity and experience of students and the time allocated for
their study. The question of their place in a short post-
secondary-school course, or even in a post-university top-
dressing year, is a very different matter from that of the
more flexible possibilities of integrated four- or five-year
courses.

In spite of all that, one can at least attempt to write
in general terms, though perhaps it should be said that the
circumstances and arrangements in the College I now know
best may intrude and be uppermost in my mind.

Besides variety of routes, one has to recollect too,
in attempting to see this theme in appropriate perspective
today, that, as in schooling and education generally, there
is in teacher-training an atmosphere of innovation, of ongoing change and indeed, in the view of some, of revolution.
Amongst the plethora of books and articles about education
in recent years, have appeared those with the title "Revolution in Teacher-Training" and the like. The "new" in
teacher-training, in other words, must keep pace with, and
ought perhaps more urgently to anticipate and lead the "new"
in teaching. Teachers must be appropriately prepared for
the increasing responsibilities that accompany the "new" developments in modern education. And so the influence of
colleges of education is likely to become all the greater, or
at least the conditions and opportunity are there to make
this possible.

It ought to be said, however, in view of the rhythm
of arrogance and recession of claims made in education today, that to those who know their history of education the
use of the word "new" is not new. What is different today
is not change but the rather overwhelming rapidity of change,
and the urgency of overhaul and of attention to new demands
and modern features. There is consequently a scrutiny and
recasting of curricula, an extension of the resources of
teaching, and a redefining of the processes of learning and
of the nature of learning appropriate to a "new" age. To
the colleges of education as to the schools, the winds of
change have brought and continue to bring a new atmosphere:
there is an infusion of new purpose, a seemingly continuous
reassessment of approach and organization, and an improving sense of the significance and responsibility that belong
with the preparation of teachers.

Whatever is new, however, whether in schools or

teacher-training institutions must always relate to something
substantial retained, if confusion and discontinuity are to be
avoided.   As Professor Frankel said in the course of an address on Kilpatrick's philosophy of education, "Change when
nothing is fixed, is not merely dizzying, it isn't change, but
mere motion or succession."   There is no virtue at all in
falling behind and being out-of-date, but neither is there any
particular virtue in unquestioning acceptance of whatever
claims to be "new" or in over-estimating the claims of new
techniques.   A kind of permanent weakness exists in education towards claiming too much too soon for "innovations."
In any case what is relevant here is that evidence increases,
rather than diminishes, that the real and central qualities of
"good" teaching dwell in the qualities of the "good" teacher.
It is still essential too, indeed with increasing reason, to
consider "the deeper concerns of education," the needs of
education, and not simply the "skilfulness of the processes."
In short the key to good schooling is still the all-round
preparation, enlightenment, and competence of individual
teachers.   There are ingredients that continue to be essential in teacher-training though their admixture, and indeed
the texture of the product, may differ with differing circumstances and different ordering of arrangements.

        Considerable reassurance is to be found in the con-
templation of the general accelerating trends of change in
teacher-education in the many countries of the Western
world.   As someone has said, "there is a common market
in educational ideas but they are not readily exportable."
The comment applies to teacher-training as to other parts
of educational systems, yet the advances in a number of
countries in recent years show much in common and are for
that reason all the more striking.   This is not an occasion,
of course, for reviewing these trends.   Two of them must
be mentioned here, however, and their general effects may
be noted as we proceed.   The lengthening of the period of
preparation of teachers, beyond the high-school years, is
highly significant in itself, but perhaps the most striking
movement of all has been that towards ever stronger association with universities.   Indeed it is not uncommon to find
that universities have taken over full responsibility for the
education and training of teachers, and it becomes more and
more usual for intending teachers to qualify both for teaching and for university degrees.   This has long been an aspiration of teacher organizations, in the expectation that the
standards and prestige of universities and the degrees they
award would ensure both respected preparation of teachers

and advancement of their professional status.

Strangely enough the recognition of the importance of this trend is not "new." For instance, in the course of one of his lectures, given as long ago as 1880 in Cambridge University, J. G. Fitch maintained: "It is to the universities that the public look for those influences which will prevent the nobler professions from degenerating into crafts and trades. And if the schoolmaster [teacher] is to become something more than a mere pedant ... it is to his University that he ought to look for guidance, and it is from his University that he should seek in due time the attestation of his qualifications as a teacher; because that is the authority which can testify that he is not merely a teacher, but a teacher and something else."[1] Intriguing surely, and to be examined, is that "something else"!

In all of this there is clear recognition, or confirmation, if one may summarize, that greater maturity than previously is required in the beginning teacher today; that the trained teacher might better be better educated and the educated teacher better trained; that in relating academic studies to teaching, the educated mind should have a chance to become the educating mind required in teaching; that a clearer appreciation of the complexity of the teacher's task might be sought; and, above all, that more time be spent in seeking greater understanding of the meaning and purposes of education and in fostering the sense of direction and personally dependable professional knowledge and resources that the young teacher requires more than ever today. It is not at all surprising then, in view of all that is involved, that in the teaching profession as a whole there are rising aspirations, that in colleges and faculties of education there is increased interest, inquiry and action, and, in this special context I venture to add, professional studies are thought to have a larger role to play in the all-round preparation of the teacher.

The Teacher's Task Viewed in Totality

One may conclude from what has been said, first that increasing emphasis is being placed on those qualities and qualifications in the teacher that are distinctively professional, and secondly, that there is correspondingly increasing acknowledgment that teachers are professionally qualified to share more than ever before in all matters of

educational policy and practice.   It is not difficult at all to
associate with these conclusions the increasing value of the
professional or foundational studies, and the need, which
these studies go a long way to meet, for seeing and understanding the teacher's task in its totality.   This need presents the chief and underlying purpose of professional studies.   The prospective teacher is thereby brought into touch
not simply with the more immediate practical affairs of
teaching, but with great thinkers and great teachers who
have generally presented education as something whole, and
teaching as concerned with something whole.   He learns to
confront and think about educational problems and issues
that include, but are larger than, those of classroom and
school.   He begins to see that the more complex issues and
movements are likely to be better understood and more intelligently considered if studied in historical, philosophical,
and psychological context.   Without this kind of study and
scrutiny there may be little of the power of the critical assessment, and little evidence of the coherent thought, that
would be expected to characterize the teacher as professional.

        Throughout the history of education it is clear that
while the necessarily practical, technical, or "doing" side
of education has always been in evidence, and at times even
regarded as exemplary in its practical purposes and accom-
plishments, there has also been something over and above
and altogether more inclusive.   I. L. Kandel, for example,
was ever keen to stress that every teacher must in a sense
be a specialist but must also be aware of a common frame
of reference to which his special work must stand related.
That frame of reference can best be acquired and understood, he maintained, "through the study of the history and
philosophy of education, of comparative education, and of
educational sociology."

        It is unlikely that teachers can ever have as good a
chance as in the period of their professional training to see
education clearly and to see it whole.   And this kind of opportunity becomes more important when, in a time of rapid
change, increasing demands are made upon the intelligence,
adaptability, and resourcefulness of teachers.   The difficulty
is that the opportunity, coming as it still normally does before the responsibilities of full-time teaching are assumed,
may seldom be recognized for what it is by students.   This
would seem to suggest that any attempt to stress wholeness
in teacher-training and to give the student-teacher a "princi-

pled understanding of the task in hand," is a matter for concerted attention by the staff of colleges of education and depends on their corporate sense of direction. As it is--and
it is not to be wondered at, with all the urgent demands
made of the several departments in a college of education,
and the tendency towards proliferation of courses--speciali-
zation seems to become more emphatic and divergence the
more likely.

Time was, not so long ago, when the "generalist"
would overlook and oversee studies and lines of inquiry and
give cohesion and meaning to the whole enterprise. When
the Bell chairs of "Paedeutics" were founded in 1876 in
Edinburgh and St. Andrews, Scotland, which some claim
were the first full-time professorial chairs of education in
the English-speaking world, the incumbent's duties in each
case were to give courses in the history of education, the
principles of education, and methods of school instruction,
school discipline, and school organization, so that "persons
intending to become schoolmasters may, while pursuing general studies in the university, learn within the university
walls all that has hitherto been arrived at as to the philosophy and technique of their profession."[2] Such were the inclusive and integrative functions and purposes of men who
yet had time to become widely influential and even internationally well known. Even up to the time of the Second
World War a professor of education became such after considerable breadth and depth of study of both an academic and
a professional kind, and subsequent varied and fairly extensive school-teaching experience; he had a chance to see education whole and its practical problems in clear relation to
its theoretical foundations.

The position today is very different, no doubt inevitably so, but not necessarily for the better. The explosion
of knowledge has set off its consequent and corresponding
explosion in education. There has been an increasing splint-
ering of the broad field of study of education into fragmented
studies. And the fragments themselves are splintered in
turn, with the bits and pieces apparently demanding their
own specialists and specialized attention. If one could be
sure that specializations arise from a broad base of study,
knowledge, experience, and understanding, one's confidence
might remain secure, and there might be a chance of restoration, by some, of the bits and pieces to something relevant, helpful, and meaningful--something whole. In institutions that are more concerned with advanced studies in edu-

cation, the designation of Co-ordinators acknowledges the
need of some comprehensive conception of what goes on.
Perhaps with even greater reason some such conception of
co-ordination is necessary in teacher-training if the desired
wholeness in the preparation and outlook of the teacher is
to be preserved. This conception has little chance if on the
one hand members of staff become exclusively concerned
with their specialisms, and on the other the student-teachers
become too preoccupied with the more immediate demands
of methods and practice of teaching. One does of course
understand and can sympathize with both of these tendencies
and interests. Nevertheless, as L. A. Reid points out,
"When things go wrong in teacher education, it is usually
because some of the parts of it get unduly emphasized, or
become separated from the others."[3]

Professional studies find their place in a well-bal-
anced curriculum of teacher-preparation, and in finding their
place contribute focally to the understanding of education as
a whole and of the total meaning of the teacher's task in
particular. "If there is any justification," says Broudy, "for
the general professional studies, it is a professional justification, viz. , that they are essential to being a first-rate
professional, not to a scholar as scholar nor to a craftsman. They are essential for the understanding and interpretation of the educational enterprise as a whole as well as of
one's specialty."[4]

Requisites for Today's Teaching

Perhaps I should now outline, without claim to any
substantial "innovation," and without discussing them in full,
what might be regarded as the teacher's main broad requisites, if anything like the totality of meaning and task, which
we have regarded as important, is to be borne in mind.
These broad requisites, which are not necessarily independent of each other, may be described somewhat as follows:

1.   Knowledge of subjects to be taught.
2.   Knowledge of aims and methods that are relevant to the teaching of these subjects.
3.   A right attitude towards teaching, and one that
ensures some effort to keep up to date.
4.   Interest in, and knowledge about, students in
schools and the various relationships involved.
5.   Some over-all sense of direction and inclusive

purpose.

The first two of these need not be discussed here at all, although under examination they very quickly begin to intertwine with the other three.

The third should not be dispensed with so summarily. S. J. Curtis, in writing of teacher-training, expresses the view that "The main aim of training is to give the learner the right attitude towards his future work."[5] One might hesitate to regard this as the aim, but one readily agrees that right attitude is of fundamental importance. In particular, in view of the need to understand and keep pace with relevant advances and changes in subjects taught and in the teaching of them, and to be intelligent in deriving assistance from the various teaching media and resources that invade the schools of today, the desire to keep abreast as far as possible is to be fostered.

The fourth requisite obviously requires a study of the psychology of human development, of individual differences, of learning theories and processes, of human relationships, and some knowledge of the social and cultural limitations (or advantages) of their homes and community. If one wishes to name professional subjects here, three are clearly involved: psychology of education, sociology of education, and (especially if one associates with it what has evidently come to be called "professional practice") administration and organization.

These studies with a fairly direct, obvious practical relevance to teaching belong with the behavioural or social sciences. The studies appropriate to the fifth and last requisite are of a different character, concerned as they are with the theoretical rather than the practical, and yet practical in the fullest, most comprehensive sense, and more aptly to be thought of as humanities. These are the studies that most directly convey the sense of continuity in educational development and an over-all sense of meaning, direction, and purpose. Through these studies the prospective teacher may acquire a meaningful framework of educational thought, a well-sustained coherent point of view about education. The teacher's "freedom" to teach or in teaching, to which all these requisites contribute, through his mastery of his subjects for instance, is advanced much more inclusively if he is well grounded in history and philosophy of education. The effectiveness, the expertness, of his teach-

ing require and indeed arise from the enlightenment and
sense of purpose that these foundational studies can give.
It is through them that the teacher becomes at once the "intelligent" teacher and the "independent" teacher, descriptions which one would wish to associate with the profession
of teaching.

The Role of Foundational Studies

        Some find the description Foundational Studies unap-
pealing and somewhat misleading perhaps, since it seems
to conjure up comparisons with foundations in all kinds of
other concerns. They are, to my mind, foundational in the
sense that they are central or focal. They are the base of
operations, the hub so to speak, to which other studies or
activities in teacher education and training relate and in
which they find their unity of movement and purpose. They
provide the orientation to his functions that the teacher needs,
and give meaning and direction to what otherwise would be
merely fortuitous and certainly ill understood by the teacher.
This assumes, of course, that they are treated with reference to teaching and to the student-teacher's actual teaching
experiences. Moreover, these studies themselves might
well be so organized as to exemplify and illustrate the sense
of the integration that we have thought should characterize
teacher-training and the whole educational process.

        There is a good deal to be said for what might be
called the British way of designating the compulsory professional studies as simply Education (or perhaps Educational
Theory) and Educational Psychology, and, wherever numbers
allow, of preserving and sustaining this unifying point of
view under tutorial systems of training. The student has a
chance to see something integral and meaningful, and practical indeed in the sense that the benefit of such studies sus-
tains observation and practice-teaching in schools. These
general headings of course subsume mainly history of education, philosophy of education, psychology of education, social studies, and comparative education. But even when
these studies are pursued separately, as indeed they must
be if any depth of interest or knowledge is to be established,
they can be thought of as presenting a unity because of common purpose, common relevance to teaching, and the many
cross-references that reflect common themes and overlapping
content.

The general intent of the professional studies is therefore to provide such professional groundwork as would enable students to examine and appreciate the aims, ideas, values, influences, and assumptions that underlie the approved practices of an educational system. When they are thought of and treated as entities in themselves, and when there may be involved the dual purpose of preparation for teaching and preparation for university degree examinations, additional questions and difficulties are bound to arise, especially in courses that are as short as a one-year course taken after university graduation.

Moreover, if degrees are involved, the balance of studies may be affected according to the type of degree, or inversely the type of degree may differ according to the emphases made in the course of training as a whole. A degree in Education would imply considerable emphasis upon the professional subject; if the emphases are upon academic subjects, chiefly those the students will be preparing to teach, upon practical subjects involved in schooling, and upon methods and teaching practice, the degree might better be one in Teaching after a more recent North American fashion.

In any case, whatever the arrangements, important questions and serious differences of opinion concerning approach and selection of material to be discussed arise within each of the professional subjects themselves. One may be wrong, but one tends to think of psychology of education as having least difficulty in these respects, since it can be so firmly related to the practices and problems of the schools, and for this reason its relevance can quickly be seen and appreciated by students in training. With other foundational studies, in which there is such a variety of possible approaches and whose practical and generally professional value cannot quickly be exposed, it can become a greater problem to dispel from the minds of students a distrust of what may appear to them, especially if they are sensitive about and preoccupied with practice in teaching, to be theory in isolation. Discussion procedures of course have their appeal and can help in this regard, if staff-student ratios allow, but discussion without some basis of knowledge, and prior experience and thought, may well destroy the whole intent of serious introduction to such studies.

It is quite a problem, for instance, to determine in

history of education what is or ought to be involved. Nevertheless, even if the question about the content and purpose
of history of education can lead to a variety of answers there
is no gainsaying, to my mind, that the benefit its "cumulative wisdom" can bring and the measure of assurance it can
offer, when the young teacher can so readily feel overwhelmed by the demands of new developments in schooling,
are not lightly to be set aside.

So also with philosophy of education. And the problem becomes more complex when the two are conjoined, in
courses that can be all too short, under the cumbersome
overloaded title, history and philosophy of education. Even
then, however, one would wish, if time allowed, at least to
introduce students to the outstanding thinkers and teachers of
the centuries, to expose those principles of education and
teaching that seem to be characteristic and that survive, to
present the origins and development of major educational institutions, and to trace the roots and growth of the problems
of the system in which the students will qualify to teach.
Others of course would think of entirely different outlines.

There has been in recent years a great thriving of
interest in philosophy of education, though it seems to be
less directly, less inclusively helpful than previously. The
newer schools of philosophers and philosophers of education,
applying their restrictive "verification principle" under which
they reject reliance upon the speculative and precriptive aspects of philosophical thought, maintain it is not their function to give direction or guidance in any over-all sense in
the practical affairs of education. They are willing to expose and assist in clarifying underlying concepts and issues
in education and to elucidate the meanings of terms that admittedly are used too freely and loosely in the technical jargon of education. Such critical analysis can be of considerable practical assistance, of course, provided the assistance
does in fact reach and influence those actively engaged in
schools and their administration. The more traditionally inclined philosophers and educationists, although they may not
question the value of the assistance given by the analysts,
tend to find that such restriction leaves philosophy of education too narrowly limited, if not gutted. Philosophy of education, it is maintained here, should be concerned with looking at education as a whole and with seeking to benefit, not
simply advanced students, but students who are on the way
to becoming teachers, the purpose being that through better
understanding teachers may become "better" teachers. Its

more traditional function, therefore, of helping the student-
teacher "tie together all his knowledge into a pattern that
has real meaning" is still the more valuable, and it may be
after all that "the maximizing of education and minimizing
of philosophy" in the title philosophy of education is the better choice to make rather than the reverse.

Comparative education has simply been named so far
as one of the professional studies. Its increasing importance merits some greater attention here. It is not a new
field of study by any means, but has generally been featured
in more advanced courses than those for teacher-training.
I. L. Kandel, perhaps the greatest exponent of comparative
education over some 40 or 50 years of this century, regarded it in some ways as an extension of history of education into the present and therefore relevant as a branch of
the professional studies of prospective teachers. More and
more educationists in these years are supporting the view
that all teachers should have the benefit of some of the insight that comes from the study of comparative education.
Indeed in some colleges or departments of education it is
already a compulsory subject. It contributes to the understanding of education and its processes and what its powers
and purposes are or can be. It results too in more objective evaluation of the system of education one knows best,
and possibly in a greater understanding and appreciation of
what others are trying to do, and in their different circumstances have to do.

In recent times there has been an increasing exchange of knowledge, ideas, techniques, and personnel in
the realm of education, and a growing realization that education is a powerful instrument of national policy. Success
of one kind or another in one country leads to comparative
evaluation in other countries and fresh scrutiny of purposes
as well as of practices and achievement. Distant peoples
are now near neighbours and mutual influences become
stronger and require to be recognized and understood.

In short, one would expect student-teachers to be introduced to the study of comparative education and teachers
to keep themselves informed of international movements and
developments in education, including those investigations of
international dimensions that are now being conducted and
that will no doubt increase in number and influence. As
Robert Ulich has emphasized, 'We cannot afford the luxury
of ignorance about the education and ideals which other na-

tions try to commit to the next generation."[6]

It is certainly not surprising to find, for instance, that comparative education is included as part of the compulsory study of the history of education, in courses for intending teachers, in the pedagogical institutes of the U.S. S.R., or that the study there of foreign systems of education, their features and practices, intensifies as the years pass. Without question comparative education is an increasingly important field of study. It belongs with professional studies in the preparation of teachers.

Extension of Effort

I suppose it is trite to say that what one means by professional or foundational subjects depends on the purposes for which they are offered. But it simply has to be said. The intention cannot be to have student-teachers become psychologists or administrators or historians or philosophers or sociologists--certainly not in non-university or one-year post-university courses of training. Students may nevertheless be introduced, effectively, impressively, infectiously, to such studies, and can be shown their relevance to the business of teaching. That is the paramount purpose: to see that such studies contribute in a fundamental way to the initial preparation of teachers, and to encourage interest and further study in them.

Student-teachers are being initiated to what is today a complex, continuously demanding task, and are being given a foretaste so to speak of the responsibilities they will have to assume. More is required, much more, than knowledge of subjects and all the technicalities associated with teaching them. Recognizing what at best is a unity of effort in their preparation, student-teachers should emerge with a sense of direction, some wholeness of outlook towards teaching and education, as well as with a feeling of confidence and competence in teaching in taking up their first appointments.

I have said before elsewhere and it can perhaps stand repetition, that there has been, and there still is, the danger that too little value is attached by teachers in general to those parts of a teacher's preparation and equipment which distinguish the teacher from other professional people. We have here supported the view that teachers should be well educated, but education even to the level of honours degrees,

important as that is, does not distinguish the teacher as
such. Professional studies can assist greatly in providing
this distinction: they are essential in this respect as well
as fundamental to the teacher's training.

There is bound to be some kind of connection between the young teacher's initial training and his later development as a teacher. For this reason one could wish
that student-teachers when they become teachers could continue to be sustained in the attitudes and convictions, and
even in an often ridiculed idealism, which they acquired during their years of training. If students--some of them at
least and when possible--could return from time to time to
their colleges, as to a kind of headquarters, as teachers
of full stature and of experience varied in kind and length,
the advantages of a reappraisal of their professional studies
would be mutually helpful. In any case this could be one
aspect of what could become a developing programme of inquiry and research that in a college of education might surely appropriately concentrate on teaching and on teacher education. As M. V. C. Jeffreys has said, "The training of
teachers is more likely to be alive and effective if it is carried on in an atmosphere of fresh inquiry."[7]

Notes

1. J. G. Fitch, Lectures on Teaching (New York: Mac-
        millan, 1891), pp. 18, 19.
2. From a book of 1884 on Edinburgh University by Sir
        Alexander Grant, II, 150. This reference to the
        writer's alma mater must be excused. During his
        formal induction to this Bell Chair of Education in
        St. Andrews he had to promise to mention at least
        once a year the name of Andrew Bell. His con-
        science remains clear.
3. L. A. Reid, Philosophy and Education (London: Heine-
        mann, 1962), p. 184.
4. Stanley Elam, ed., Improving Teacher Education in the
        United States (Bloomington, Indiana: Phi Delta
        Kappa Inc., 1967), p. 22.
5. S. J. Curtis, Introduction to the Philosophy of Educa-
        tion (London: University Tutorial Press, 1958),
        p. 34.
6. Robert Ulich, in Comparative Education Review, vol.
        1, no. 2, October 1957, p. 4.

7. M. V. C. Jeffreys, Revolution in Teacher Training
    (London: Pitman & Sons Ltd. , 1961), p. 15.

J. P. POWELL

3. ANOTHER LOOK AT THEORY AND PRACTICE
IN EDUCATION

The peculiar character of the theory of educational ideas has passed largely un-noticed and this has led to a great deal of muddled thinking and confusion. Many people have supposed that anything said about education must have something to do with teaching and when theorists have conspicuously failed to produce the required goods their work has sometimes been condemned as being of no value to practising teachers. While this view prevailed, and it is still by no means uncommon, there was little hope of the theoretical study of education getting off the ground since theorists were simply not interested in the daily practical problems which confront teachers.

Evidence of a new appreciation of the nature of theorising about education, and especially of the distinctive character of the theory of educational ideas, can be found in a recent collection of essays on the study of education.[1] Peters claims that the study of philosophy, history or sociology will be of no direct use to intending teachers but that as a result they "will gradually have their view of children, schools, and subjects transformed."[2] Simon argues that "No claim should be made that the study of the history of education directly affects the practice of the teacher in the classroom."[3] Taylor explicitly denies that there is any link between the study of sociology and the improvement of classroom technique. The study of sociology, he says, is justified because it helps the teacher in "thinking logically and rationally about the whole range of social phenomena that he encounters in his personal and professional life."[4]

How will a clearer understanding of the nature of

*Reprinted with permission from The Journal of Educational Thought (University of Calgary), Vol. II, No. 1, (April 1968), pp. 28-9.

educational theorising help those with responsibilities for the
training of teachers?   The theory of instruction is clearly
highly relevant to the needs of intending teachers since it
constitutes a body of knowledge directly connected with the
skills which they will be required to exercise.   If we view
teachers as educators rather than instructors then the theory of education becomes probably even more important in
a course of professional studies since it helps students to
justify and describe what they are doing and to appreciate
its wider social significance.   The theory of educational
ideas, however, is in a different position and its inclusion
in a programme of professional studies requires special
justification.   It might well be argued that teachers should
know something about the history of education, for example,
but it would be difficult to support this on the grounds that
such knowledge would make them more effective in the classroom.   Much of the dissatisfaction which students express
about training courses could probably be traced to unrealistic expectations concerning much of what they are taught.
From the student's interest in educational matters it might
be possible to lead him on to explore some history, philosophy, sociology and anthropology, and we may well believe that it would be worthwhile to encourage such interests,
but it would be fraudulent to suggest that they will help him
to cope with 4B more successfully.

                                Notes

1.   J. W. Tibble, ed., The Study of Education (London:
          Routledge and Kegan Paul, 1966).
2.   Ibid., pp. 79-80.
3.   Ibid., p. 126.
4.   Ibid., p. 210.

MAXINE GREENE

4. THE PROFESSIONAL SIGNIFICANCE
OF HISTORY OF EDUCATION*

History of any sort connotes, for me, searching, exploration, and increasingly complex designs. I think of what Henry James spoke of as a "fineness" of insight and perception, of what he described in Portrait of a Lady as expanded consciousness, the pursuit of a larger, "more plentiful" life. Isabel Archer in that novel is a kind of exemplary figure--one who "carried within herself a great fund of life"--whose "deepest enjoyment was to feel the continuity between her own soul and the agitations of the world. For this reason she was fond of seeing great crowds and large stretches of country, of reading about revolutions and wars, of looking at historical pictures--a class of efforts to which she had often committed the conscious solecism of forgiving them much bad painting for the same of the subject...."

We, too, dealing with the history of education at a moment like this, have much to forgive; and "for the sake of the subject," we obviously need to confront the difficult question of the discipline's significance in teacher education. Not very long ago, such questions were either set aside or resolved by administrative fiat. Educational history tended to be validated by the contributions it made to the public image of the profession. The men who wrote it (as Bernard Bailyn and others have been reminding us) conceived the schools of the past to be but preparations for the common school; and the emergence of that common school was seen to represent one of history's culminations--the fulfillment of a "promise" made (perhaps) at the beginning of time.

The nature of history qua history was a matter of

---

*Reprinted with permission from History of Education Quarterly, Summer 1967, pp. 182-90.

179

indifference to writers like these. The uncertainties which
plagued historians through the ages did not occur to them.
It is doubtful whether they troubled themselves about the issue of historical "reality" or historical "truth." No Colling-
wood appeared among them to speculate about the difficulty
of understanding particular actions, nor to hypothesize that
the historian ought to try to rethink the thoughts of a Horace
Mann or a Francis Parker in an effort to comprehend what
happened and why. No one, in fact, brought up the question
of whether or not the educational historian's concern was
primarily with "rational human action"--whether educational
developments could be adequately explained by a consideration
of the decisions and behaviors of a given number of educational pioneers. Nor did anyone offer as an alternative the
possibility of discovering (in Michael Oakeshott's words)
"greater and more complete detail" with respect to events in
the world of schools. Nor is there evidence that any of the
early educational historians seriously contemplated the sort
of problem which has concerned Carl Hempel: the kinds of
explanations made possible by "an assumption of general
laws." General laws were, it would seem, frequently assumed; but the matter of explanation did not appear to trouble
the writers of educational history any more than did "what
actually happened" in the past.

What happened, it was assumed, could be known
through consultation of the texts of laws, reports, and public
addresses. It could be determined through a reading of the
descriptive accounts left by journalists, social reformers,
statesmen, and--most of all--the schoolmen themselves. Or
it could be worked out by drawing inferences from these,
sometimes for a conception of individual motivation or popular opinion; sometimes for a conception of "tendency," "tradition," or "law." The problem of organization was solved
by a kind of foreshortening: chronologies were developed in
terms of the more visible aspects of institutional development,
or by discovering correlations between the stages of such development and events which were apparently related.

The business of determining the discipline's significance, as well as the discipline's structure, is far more
complicated today, now that we know some historiography and
can no longer write history for strategic reasons or political
ones. We can no longer arbitrarily skim educational history
off the top of cultural history, no matter how we decide to
specialize. We cannot evade the problems fundamental to the
larger discipline of history: the pervasive problems of the

past's "reality," of objectivity, meaning, and truth.   Nor
can we evade the issues of historical explanation and generalization.   We have, each of us, to decide the degree to
which we can be "scientific" about history; we have, each of
us, to define criteria of relevance, particular scales of priorities.

      As I see it, relevance is still the crux of the matter
where the determination of professional significance is concerned; but relevance, to me, signifies relevance for the individual teacher or the teacher-to-be--not simply utility, and
certainly not utility in enhancing the status of the profession.
I am existentialist enough to believe that a teacher, like
every other human being, achieves dignity as he makes effectual choices in the world, as he creates and recreates
himself as a teacher day by day, month by month, by dint
of making the kinds of decisions and employing the kinds of
strategies which enable young people to learn.   The relevance of history for such a person depends, I believe, on the
degree to which a study of the educational past enables him
to organize his own experience in the situations of the present, to refine his strategies, to enlarge his conceptual scope.
Its relevance depends on the degree to which (as in the case
of the statesman who studies political history) it enables
him to discern a range of possibilities for action, to perceive
both limitations and what Arthur Schlesinger, Jr., calls
"ambiguities."

      It is trivial to say simply that history--any kind of
history--illuminates the present.   To say that is to assume
that there is an objective, identifiable state of affairs called
"the present," existing apart from the interpretations of existing individuals who are skilled in various distinctive ways,
responsible, involved.   It seems meaningless now to assert
that knowledge of what happened in the past can prescribe or
offer reliable clues to what ought to be done in the present.
I think we know enough to agree that our inquiries into the
educational past do not equip us to make the kinds of predictions scientists make with respect to the physical universe,
any more than they put us in the position to perform experiments.   They do not give us a warranty for finding analogous situations, nor do they provide the kinds of reliable
generalizations which assure long-range controls.   We can,
I think, devise generalizations by adopting certain principles
from the social sciences; but these ought to serve as organizing principles, permitting us to identify certain recurrences
and similarities while we study singular facts.   At best, they

will help us order an inchoate field and permit us to make
some hypothetical explanations which may be used as resources when we are required to make choices with regard
to teaching, learning, and the schools.

When I ponder the significance of the discipline with
the individual teacher in mind, I believe we have to begin
with a conscious orientation to teaching, learning, and schools
in the contemporary world in which that teacher lives and
works--and with questions variously and skillfully defined by
responsible people functioning in the midst of that world.
They must be questions defined because of the needs of action, because of the exigencies of choice.

Consider the world of the teacher today, with its impinging immediacies, its pressure, the sense of constant innovation, insufficiency, flux. Consider the pervasive uncertainties with respect to the aims of schooling, the absence of
what was once called a "public philosophy," the sometimes
appalling realization that education extends far beyond the professional teacher and far beyond the institutional life of the
schools.

The curricula in teacher-training institutions are built
upon the recognition that the teacher can only deal with such
challenges if he masters certain concepts in selected disciplines, aside from his field of specialization, the subject
matter that he is teaching or planning to teach. He must
learn to conceptualize learning behavior and non-learning behavior, to identify the learning tasks that can reasonably be
performed. He must understand the fundamentals of institutional life, the function of groups in society, something of
the way in which communities and neighborhoods are structured, something of the role of subcultures and the "culture
of poverty" and of the various traditions that pervade American society. He is expected, too, to understand something
about the organization of the schools, about the ways in which
they are controlled, about the making of policies respecting
what is taught, and about the "politics" now involved. The
professional significance of all this knowledge is generally
assumed to be found in its relevance to a teacher's actual
work in the public schools, to the necessity for him to relate
intelligently to the manifold situations that arise in professional life.

The significance of educational history has not been
so evident, in spite of the proliferating foundations courses

in colleges throughout the country. It seems to me that the discipline may be justified, however, as other subject matters are justified today, as long as its distinctiveness is identified--perhaps as one of the humanities. I think it belongs to the area of the humanities because it deals fundamentally, not with the impersonal lives of institutions, but with the continuing, sometimes desperate efforts of groups of men to choose, shape, and maintain what they consider to be a proper human way of life. It deals, I think, with the way men conserve in the midst of change that which they select as worthy of perpetuation--those elements of knowledge, tradition, skill, and belief deemed worthy of keeping alive. It was Jakob Buckhardt who said that history is what one age finds worthy of note in another. History of education, then, may be what the historians of education find significant enough to note in the choices made in ages past. One of the distinctive things about this kind of history, of course, is that the educative "reality" being studied always involves value choices. The historian looks at decisions with respect to what has been considered valuable and to the action on such decisions, whether deliberate or unthinking. He may find that what seems to him worthy of note is precisely the opposite of that found worthy of conversation. He may find what he conceives to have been trivial and inappropriate somehow frozen into the heritage. Educational historians and educators, therefore, face somewhat the same problems: what one generation considers valuable and important may not be what a previous generation prized. A historian of education, in consequence, cannot avoid confronting himself as interpreter. His task is not the simple reconstruction of the past, nor merely the explication of singular things.

All depends on how the singular things are ordered, how experience of past and present is interpreted by a disciplined mind. Both history and education, it seems to me, turn upon such interpretation; and, again, I am reminded of Henry James and what he called "the reflector" or the "central consciousness" which works upon raw materials and orders them. For James, it was art which ordered life; without art, he said, life would be "a splendid waste." I think we can say that about the history of education where a teacher is concerned. Without a conscious process of selection and organization, without a deliberate search for long-range meanings, the educational world, too, would resemble a "waste," although not a very splendid one. It would be a confusion of momentary puzzlements, unfinished inquiries, unexpected cataclysms. Dazzled by presentness, the teacher would be all too likely to find perspective impossible--and interpretation hindered hopelessly.

I am suggesting, of course, that the significance of historical study for the teacher lies in the possibility it offers for the shaping of large perspectives, enabling that teacher to make some sense of the inchoate present through which he moves. To engage in historical inquiry is to seek out organizing principles and ideas to pattern the particularities that compose experience as it widens to include the past. Asking questions about continuities, lines of development, relationships among ideas and events, facts and values, and economic and social changes, the teacher is in a position to pursue meanings, if not answers. He is in a position to orient himself in the continuous universe extending far beyond his personal plight. He is in a position to appropriate the past by making it part of his own life situation, the situations in which his choices are to be made.

I have in mind such large perplexities as those accompanying the struggle over integration in the public schools today. I have in mind the open question respecting the role to be played by the family in the life of the city child, the equally open questions respecting economic opportunity and the viability of "equality" as norm. Also I have in mind the problem of the direction of contemporary education: the aims that are and ought to be defined. I have in mind the connection between those aims and the professed goals of the culture, as well as the commitments of individuals who mediate and interpret for the mass of people: the artists and writers of America; the men who administer the mass media; the so-called "influentials," ranging from block-association leaders in the city slums to corporation executives responsible for the new technologies.

Surely it is important for the individual teacher to make sense of some of this, to relate himself to it, to take a stand.

Beginning with particular questions, preferably those arising out of his affirmed responsibility, he may, if he knows enough, borrow concepts from the social sciences or the behavioral sciences for the sake of ordering his own field. Or, if he finds them workable, he may borrow concepts from the discipline of academic history, with the awareness--whatever the concepts he chooses--that the organization they make possible is but one of several alterna-

tive modes of organization, each of which might permit him
to define a few meanings in a limited sphere.

If, because of his particular involvement, the teacher
is preoccupied with the problem of school integration, he
may productively apply principles taken from sociology.
They may be principles related to the problem of assimilation, a problem confronted repeatedly by teachers for more
than a hundred years. Also, he may draw from what is now
called "urban studies," or from economics, or from one of
the historical specialties. Looking back at the cities of the
past and at their efforts to absorb waves of immigrants who
had to be assimilated, he may be more free than he would
otherwise be to conceptualize the whole matter of the "common school" experience and the tension between demands for
such experience and concurrent demands for group autonomy.

He may be enabled to compare the relationship between such deliberately fostered assimilation and equality of
opportunity with relationships between them at moments in
the past. At once, he may be enabled to define his own
doubts and prejudices with respect to both assimilation and
equality. It seems to me to make a difference when one is
trained to consider this problem in the light of the problem-
atic past and to relate the demonstrable facts of the past to
the actuality of the present, to the end of ordering both by
means of some viable organizing idea.

As interesting to me is the even larger question of
the place of public education, with all the promises made for
it, in the context of the American tradition--pervaded as that
tradition has been with the sense of special mission, of a
promise given at the moment of settlement. The teacher
functions today in the midst of crumbling idols, even as public education becomes increasingly important on the national
scene. The investments in knowledge and schooling grow
apace; yet there appears to be a declining faith in what education can accomplish where the social order is concerned,
a declining faith in what it can do to promote security, to assure individuals opportunities for what was traditionally called
"success."

The dominant emphasis is relatively new in our purportedly anti-intellectualist history: the emphasis upon cognitive mastery, on the ability to conceptualize, on the kind
of intellectual competence which enables people, not necessarily to succeed in any particular sphere, not necessarily

to become businessmen or inventors or hunters of white
whales, but to make intelligent choices in a precarious world.

Given the traditional assurances, the traditional rationale for the public school, this is hard for many Ameri-
cans to accept. Teachers, I find, are ambivalent; but they
also find it difficult (if occasionally comforting) to accept the
notion that it is the business of the schools primarily to
teach young people how to think and to initiate them into the
subject matter disciplines. It is no longer the prime objective of the schools to rebuild the social order, to eliminate
poverty, to guarantee equality--to redeem.

And here, too, there is a place for history of education, perhaps a place where it can play its most significant
role. As historians interpret our educational experience, I
believe, they inevitably dramatize the tragic element in our
national life: the clash between the dream and the actuality;
the persistence of what Joseph Conrad described as "necessary illusions"--which are the barriers men build against
nothingness and futility. I mean by this that historians cannot avoid describing the early public schools as beneficiaries
of the eighteenth-century faith. After all, that faith was the
source of the world's best educational hope at the time the
common school arguments were being refined. It was a
glorious faith, an absurd faith, and we still talk in its terms.
Yet I believe that the imaginative artists of America, most
of them tragic in their perception, presented a thousand in-
timations that the faith was groundless, that the country's
very rise to world preeminence caused a falling away of the
dream.

Because our artists saw all this, I have thought their
presentations important in the shaping of perspectives in the
past, just as I have thought them important for the occasions
they offer to engage imaginatively in the felt life of America.
Melville, Hawthorne, Mark Twain, and the rest did not write
explicitly about education; but they did make possible intensified perceptions of American experience, the continuing experience of individualism contending with conformities, freedom with organization, altruism with greed, elitism with
equality--the village with "the territory ahead," the green
hills of homeland with the dangerous sea.

Most of all, they made possible an intensified perception of the fallibility of men and the limitations which define
the human career. Educational historians have seldom paid

heed to matters like these; but, it seems to me, they urgently need to be conceived.

At this moment of time, when the teacher cannot even be sure of the support of his own locality, when he can offer no child assurance of identity or a meaningful future role, I think that history of education can become significant if, in addition to stirring the teacher to interpret, to order, and to seek out meaning, it also makes it possible for him to confront the human condition and to take his stance as a teacher who is a human being with respect to the indifference of the sky. It is out of such confrontations that dignity emerges, courage and a kind of gaiety. This may be, in the last analysis, how one moves--by means of history--to a larger, more plentiful life.

MARGARET GILLETT

5.   FOUNDATION OR FRILL?[*]

While ordinary   mortals have always been assured of
those two inevitables, death and taxes, teacher trainees of
the last several decades have been harnessed to three--
death, taxes, and History of Education.   Untold thousands of
students have, perforce, taken courses which some enjoyed,
others loathed; some learned from, others lived through;
some thought enlightening, others burdensome; some found
lively, insightful, even entertaining, others found dull, dull,
dull.

History of Education has, without a doubt, become an
entrenched part of twentieth-century teacher-education programs (a bread-and-butter course, as I once heard it described).   Yet it has not been accepted with all good grace.
It has long been under attack from students who detest it or
who want it modified, and from "Methods" staff who covet-
ously eye its sometimes-generous time allocations and think
these could be used for more practical purposes.   It has
been defended, of course, by its teachers plus some administrators and other faculty members on the grounds that an
understanding of the past is essential to a thinking, cultured,
"professional" teacher.   So the argument has simmered along
for years; History of Education is a basic foundation for
teacher preparation/History of Education is an unnecessary
frill.

Because of the current upheaval on campus, when all
sacred cows are up for slaughter, this perennial question
needs to be examined once more.

---

*Education (Toronto: W. J. Gage) Vol. 8, No. 4 (1970),
pp. 29-37.   Reprinted with permission.

First, The Good News

According to supporters like Luella Cole, History of Education provides the young teacher with "a treasure trove of the world's best thoughts about education for well over two thousand years."[1] This cultural heritage, so runs the argument, is intrinsically valuable as a liberal component in the teacher's education. This is enormously important in a world that is becoming increasingly dehumanized. Teachers are concerned with people and with ideas. They are not, or they should not be, merely robots in a techno-cratic wasteland. Their preparation should include more than courses in methods, classroom management, and ma-nipulation of visual aids. The History of Education compo-nent is one reason why we can legitimately talk about "teacher education" rather than "teacher training." It is recognition that we are preparing professionals with a broad understanding of their field and not just turning out function-aries to fill occupational slots. Parallels may be found in other professional disciplines. Indeed, courses in the His-tory of Medicine, the History of Scientific Ideas, and the like are increasing. They provide for intellectual satisfac-tion and a kind of flexibility that is best suited to this rapid-ly changing era.

Furthermore, History of Education is not only a prestige, "liberal" subject, it is useful. We cannot make progress by ignoring history, and there is no reason why education should be condemened to repeat the past. Through the study of the history of Education we can see what others have done, we can borrow from them, and we can profit from their mistakes. We can also glean an appreciation of movements, trends, and cycles so that we have some notion of what to expect from the future. The student can learn the truth of Whitehead's statement:

> In the history of education, the most striking phe-nomenon is that schools of learning, which at one epoch are alive with a ferment of genius, in a succeeding generation exhibit merely pedantry and routine.[2]

In this study, the student can see something of the process of educational developments, gain a clearer perspective on cur-rent events and issues, and get a better notion of "where he's at."

It is a tired misconception to think of History of Education as dealing only with the classical Greeks. Courses are becoming increasingly relevant to the Canadian student as more Canadian courses are developed, and more Canadian books, journals, and historical research findings are available. One need only look at the recent Royal Commissions on Education to see how contemporary Canadian reformers have recognized that knowledge of the history of education is essential to an understanding of any province's present situation and a prerequisite for devising plans for future development. Quebec's Parent Report[3] is a prime example of the application of a knowledge of history to the solving of contemporary problems.

Even people who want immediate results have found practical value in History of Education. Young teachers have reported finding the substance of their courses helpful in their daily classroom work. Last year a student admitted rescuing himself from a predicament during practice-teaching by recounting, to a suddenly-assigned class, something of the medieval universities, the town-and-gown wars, and the early manifestations of student power--all of which he had learned from a History of Education lecture. Another reported she found the textbook helpful for background in her own history lessons. A third claimed that the insights he gained from History of Education were more helpful than ephemeral "tricks of the trade"! Some students have rated History of Education as the most illuminating course of their university career.

The value of History of Education to the teacher as a person is incalculable. It may not be as readily apparent, perhaps, as the usefulness of "how-to-do-it" courses, but as the understandings of History of Education are more general, so are they more lasting. The broad sweep of events, the flow of ideas, the confrontation with great educational innovators stimulate and enrich. Even when details have dissolved, a worthwhile residue remains. From this cultural lode, the modern teacher, who more and more is participating in planning for curricular innovation, structural change, modification of roles and responsibilities, can draw new ideas or fresh arrangements of the old. History of Education, Janus-like, looks both backward and forward.

Now for the Bad News

The value of History of Education certainly is incalculable. It cannot be measured. The claims made for it cannot be substantiated. There is no real evidence that History of Education endows the student with "culture," increases his understanding, broadens his appreciation of the past, or prepares him for the future. The argument that it does these things sounds as if it were based on a long-exploded faculty theory of learning, or just wishful thinking. Traditionalists simply assume that courses of this type lend grace and culture. They do not really know this to be the case.

Time is so limited in contemporary teacher-preparation programs that the unessentials have to go. A realistic set of priorities must be established. It may be nice for future teachers to hear about Plato, or Comenius, or monitorial schools, but it is downright urgent that they know about current research in learning, how to teach reading, how to introduce sets, how to stimulate interest, how to organize groups, how to handle raw data, how to use instructional media, when to talk, and when to be silent. History of Education provides no help with any of these.

It is not an appropriate foundation for a modern participant in the educational enterprise. It is only a frill, an old-fashioned furbelow, retained for reasons of sentimentality, tradition, apathy, and vested interests. Students do not want or need to know about the past; they want and need to know the present and future. They want and need to know about the child; they want to acquire the skills that will help the child develop to his full potential. In a word, History of Education is irrelevant.

And the argument can be carried even further than this. Course evaluations have shown that History of Education is frequently detested or despised. For proof, consult James D. Koerner's The Miseducation of American Teachers.[4] And even traditionalists must agree that you cannot make a person "cultured" against his will and you cannot force "intellectual appreciation" upon him.

Indeed, History of Education is worse than irrelevant, worse than useless. It undermines the whole program. It makes malcontents. Education students on the whole are not

notoriously radical, but they are frequently critical and dis-
gruntled.   This malaise is "History of Education Fever."
Students cannot see the purpose of this course; they find its
so-called "broad sweep" superficial, and its frequent eclectic nature intellectually unsatisfying. This is one of the conclusions James B. Conant came to in The Education of
American Teachers:

> In general, ... I would advise the elimination of
> such eclectic courses, for not only are they usu-
> ally worthless, but they give education departments
> a bad name. I have rarely talked with students of
> school teachers who had good words to say for an
> eclectic foundations course. Perhaps the kindest
> word used to describe most of these courses was
> pathetic. [5]

Nor, as Conant and others have noted, is it just the
nature of the material that is at fault; it is the quality of
the instructors involved.   They are so often ill-prepared for
the momentous task of transmitting the pedagogic cultural
heritage and, being swamped by the substance of the course,
take refuge in recitations of dates, names, and "-isms."
They lack imagination in presentation, their lectures are
mere condensations of any textbook other than the ones assigned their class, and their pious chatter about "progress"
and "understanding of the educational process" is hollow to
the point of hypocrisy.   It is no wonder that the students are
overwhelmed by an avalanche of dry facts, that they are
bored and embittered by the dreary way this useless information is delivered.

Now What?

The arguments against History of Education are formidable indeed.   How pleasant to be able to dismiss them
with a terse "poppycock!" and go back to teaching about the
"Five Herbartian Steps." It is far too late for this.   Professional honesty and the rising crescendo of student dissent
make us grant the complaints at least the status of half-
truths.   And it is cold comfort to the Historians of Education that critics like Koerner and Conant (or Mayer, or
Bestor, or Neatby) were not just attacking "foundations"
courses, they condemned all Education courses.   Koerner
claims that all of them

deserve the ill-repute that has always been accorded them by members of the academic faculty,
by teachers themselves, and by the general public.
Most Education courses are vague, insipid, time-
wasting adumbrations of the obvious and probably
irrelevant to academic teaching. [6]

History of Education is damned with the rest.   Still,
if you read Conant carefully, you will see that even he recognizes that History of Education courses can contribute to
the professional education of the teacher.   "The crucial question," he says, "is how they are taught and by whom." [7]

Whether or not all the criticism of History of Education is well-founded, there is enough of it, and it is loud
enough, to challenge the complacency of History of Education
instructors.   If their courses are to remain in the teacher-
preparation curricula, some changes are inevitable.   While
there is no one ideal course to which everyone should aspire,
there seem to be in general several things required.

NEEDED: A Concern for Methods of Instruction

It is not unusual for Historians of Education to have
disdain for "methods" courses and, perhaps by an extension
of this, they appear to have little interest in their own methods of teaching.   This may be something they have in common with instructors in the "academic" departments but Historians of Education, as professional teachers helping to prepare professional teachers, must share the responsibility for
providing models of good teaching.   Unless they do, the
charge of hyprocrisy will stick.

Without doubt, many History of Education instructors
are committed to improving the way they teach.   Methods of
instruction in the foundation subjects are among the central
concerns of the vigorous new American Educational Studies
Association (President, 1969-70, R. Freeman Butts, author
of A Cultural History of Western Education).   History of
Education Quarterly carried a lively correspondence as a result of a letter to the editor which began: "For as many
years as I can remember every student 'course satisfaction'
report I have come across has relegated history of education
to Dante's nth hell ..." (Fall, 1966).

Since all students are usually required to take History

of Education, classes tend to be large, the student/teacher ratio high, and so the standard method has remained the lecture. It is fashionable and easy to malign the lecture but, as anyone who has heard someone like Barbara Ward can testify, the lecture does not have to be dull. However, the very setting of a lecture almost inevitably puts the lecturer into unconscious competition with a TV performer-- and that is a competition in which relatively few academics, in any discipline, can hope to survive. If the instructor in History of Education cannot escape the lecture, he can still make it vital, he can still permit and encourage questions, he can still set it up as a model of its own genre.

NEEDED: A Sense of Drama, a Sense of Humor, a Sense of Relevance

Anyone who, year after year, goes through the same old chronological series of events must surely be bored himself and cannot help but bore his students. Instructors in the History of Education should surely recall that, at least as far back as Cicero, thinkers agreed that solemn asses did not make the best teachers. For example, there is no need to be pious about the Reformation. It can be shown to have a dynamic relationship to the current social revolution --as might be suggested in a lecture entitled "The Reformation: A Period of Protest--or Martin Luther was no WASP." Even those far-off Greeks and Romans can be related to the current scene. The phenomenon of cultural borrowing and cultural colonialism in the Greco-Roman world can be examined in the light of the contemporary Canadian-U.S. situation and the text for that day could be Al Purdy's The New Romans. [8]

None of it need be dull.

NEEDED: Variety of Class Format

This is one area where change is visible. If a survey were taken across Canada, it would probably reveal that more and more conferences, tutorials, and seminar groups are being introduced into History of Education courses. Discussions are not rare, but what of dramatizations and role-playing? How often do instructors use recordings like "Poitier Meets Plato" with its splendid jazz background or Robert M. Hutchins on "The Promise of Education"?

Team teaching has been tried, though not always with
success. Programs have been developed around films. Series of guest speakers have been brought in as discussion
leaders, again with mixed results. Individual meetings with
the instructor, though not commonly built into the formal
course requirements and not always feasible, have produced
favorable responses. These and other variants of student/
instructor contact could be explored so that charges of tra-
ditionalism in course form and aloofness of professor can be
dispelled.

There is still room for improvement.

NEEDED: Selectivity in Surveys, Optional Course Offerings

It is impossible to teach the entire cultural/peda-
gogic history of mankind in a survey course that meets for
a few hours each week and is part of a heavy course load.
If students are not to be overwhelmed, material for survey
courses has to be selected with care. At Western Ontario,
for example, attempts have been made to solve this problem
by starting, not with the Greeks, but with seventeenth-cen-
tury Canada. Another solution, now being tried at Toronto
and elsewhere, is to set up a number of half-courses, each
dealing with specialized periods, issues, or areas. This
enables students to choose in accordance with their individual interests, allows for flexibility, and gives a degree of
freedom while still making the course requirement equivalent to a full course.

The scope and demands of any programs have to be
realistic.

NEEDED: New Forms of Assignments, New Ways to Test

Reliance on the traditional term paper and the essay
exam as measures of student achievement is passé--for
History of Education as for other courses. The term paper
can be valuable, but it is frequently little more than a scis-
sors-and-paste job with words, and the greatest intellectual
effort lies in the detective work done by the instructor recalling or tracing unacknowledged quotes. A colleague has
just sent me a paper submitted at an Australian university
on the educational implications of changing sex roles in contemporary society. It is fluent and sophisticated, with a

bibliography of ten items.   But he perceived there should
have been eleven references, recognizing the missing one as
a relatively obscure (from an Australian student's point of
view) Canadian periodical--the McGill Journal of Education.
Without benefit of quotes, the student's paper begins: "Occasionally there appears a social phenomenon so broadly expressed, so repeatedly presented as to require no specific
documentation ..." A paper by Dr. F. R. Wake of Carleton
University in the McGill Journal of Education (Fall, 1968)
begins: "Occasionally there appears a social phenomenon
..." Large chunks of such striking similarities occur
throughout.

Blatant as it is, this case is by no means unique,
nor is the temptation to plagiarism the only argument against
the term paper.   However, Historians of Education have
tended to keep it on, presumably, because it is so "academically respectable." Variety and imagination are needed
here, too--freely-chosen projects, annotated bibliographies,
play/dialogue writing, film-making, or even cryptic cross-
word puzzles with History of Education clues are among the
possible alternatives.   Similarly, the conventional final exam
--essay or objective--can be modified or replaced.

Whatever you do, make it worthwhile--even tough.
One student, who apparently enjoyed a course in the History
of Education, detected that her "prof.'s secret formula was
to get his students to do all the work." She recommended,
"Pile on worthwhile assignments and students will find out
for themselves what's relevant and what's not."

Further suggestions are in order.

NEEDED: People Who Know Their Stuff

To say that we need well-prepared teachers with a
command of their material that goes beyond last year's lecture notes seems so obvious and so easy.   But where to
find them? Conant suggests the academic History departments.   This rather simplistic solution implies that all professors in History departments (or any other department,
for that matter) know how to teach.   This is debatable--
some surely do, some do not; while a case can be made for
the claim that the alleged decline in the Humanities, including History, may be attributed to a methodological breakdown.

On the other hand, the employment practices in some Colleges of Education have also rested on shaky assumptions. Because History of Education is a large, compulsory course, it has often been assigned to instructors who happened to be available, whether or not they had special training or interest. Their expertness is thus hardly guaranteed. Meanwhile, as Mordecai Richler points out in an essay on teachers, other people "who hustle out in the cold, whether we play hockey, sell insurance, or write books, must continue to produce if we want to get paid. No goals, no NHL contract. No sales, no job. Bad books, no publishers."[9] However, application of this principle to academic life leads to confrontation with academic freedom, tenure, and the vexed question, "What is an effective teacher?"

There is no simple answer, except perhaps continual self-appraisal.

NEEDED: Clinics at Conferences

Many instructors in the History of Education, along with their colleagues in other areas, get an annual "shot in the arm" at professional conferences. Yet everyone knows that conferences are "horse-trading" centres, social gatherings, and places where papers are read with little opportunity for any "conferring." Yet football coaches, who really do have to improve their methods because their output can be measured in touchdowns, attend not conferences but clinics. Perhaps conference organizers can borrow from the coaches, dispense with some of the papers, and introduce clinics in course construction and methods of instruction. With a modified micro-teaching technique, they could offer examples of ways in which selected History of Education topics might be treated, while allowing for discussion of these methods and for friendly criticism.

Clinics could easily become the most dynamic part of any conference.

So What?   So This:

History of Education does not have to be revered as a foundation nor written off as a frill. Its place in teacher-education can be justified, even if the reasons advanced are

more intrinsic than instrumental. It should not be dismissed lightly. It can serve an important function in teacher-
education, which is too often seen as a derived, remote,
second-hand affair. After all, it is said, student-teachers
are being taught to teach someone else. In this view, the
ultimate concern is not the student in college, but the child
in school. Those who support History of Education tend to
reject this concept. They recognize the importance of the
student-teachers themselves, and are interested in furthering their intellectual development, enlarging their knowledge,
and increasing their all-round professional competence. History of Education is thus not peripheral. Taught well, it
can both humanize and help legitimatize teacher-education
as an academic endeavor.

Notes

1. Luella Cole, A History of Education: Socrates to Mon-
        tessori (New York: Holt, Rinehart and Winston,
        1950).
2. Alfred North Whitehead, The Aims of Education (New
        York: New American Library, 1949), p. 13.
3. Report of the Royal Commission of Inquiry into Educa-
        tion in the Province of Quebec (Quebec: Queen's
        Printer, 1964-66).
4. James D. Koerner, The Miseducation of American
        Teachers (Baltimore: Penguin Books, 1965).
5. James B. Conant, The Education of American Teachers
        (New York: McGraw-Hill, 1963), p. 127.
6. Koerner. Op. cit., p. 56.
7. Conant. Op. cit., p. 129.
8. Al Purdy, ed. The New Romans: Candid Canadian
        Opinion of the U.S. (Edmonton: M. G. Hurtig,
        1968).
9. Mordecai Richler, "The Writer as Teacher," McGill
        Journal of Education, Vol. IV, No. 2 (Fall, 1969),
        p. 189.

THEODORE BRAMELD

6. OPERATING WITH ANTHROPOLOGICAL CONCEPTS IN THE RESEARCH AND PRACTICE OF EDUCATION

I

Opportunities, through anthropology, to enrich educational experience in its manifold dimensions are vastly wider and deeper than have thus far been explored. Nevertheless, such opportunities, especially those emerging within scarcely two decades, have already begun to prove their own extraordinary usefulness. My purpose is to review only those adventures in anthropology with which I have been personally involved, and to limit even these to methodological considerations rather than to substantive derivations.

One further personal word seem appropriate. My discovery of anthropology in any intensive way occurred some years after primary concentration in philosophy, and my first prolonged effort was to draw these two disciplines closer together by means of a third: education.[1] Subsequent research interrelating all three fields has continued to build upon the theoretical foundations earlier laid. These foundations are largely presupposed here and no doubt accordingly disclose certain predilections of my own which deviate, I hope fruitfully, from concerns more typical of formally trained anthropologists. Yet, throughout, I have tried to benefit by their own powerful impact upon my work.

I shall first concentrate upon two research field studies overseas, and then consider three different academic ventures in this country. It is my hope that others interested in anthropological-educational-philosophical developments will benefit by, while improving upon, these interdisciplinary efforts.

II

The first research study occupied the better part of

three years in Puerto Rico, the second about a year and
one-half in Japan.[2] In both studies, informal as well as
formal education has been regarded as a central agency of
cultural transmission, modification, and innovation in complex variations.   Still more broadly, education has been defined as an ubiquitous process of culture expressed through
the human capacity to learn and to teach--that is, to encul-
turate.   Philosophy, too, is viewed in cultural terms:
again both informally and formally, it is defined as the supreme symbolic expression of those beliefs and other manifestations of cultural experience that are most pervasive to
and meaningful of a way of life, however "primitive" or
however "civilized" that way may seem.

In both Puerto Rico and Japan, interpretation was
channelled through three broad, interrelated categories of
culture: order (spatio-temporal patterns and structures);
process (dynamics of socio-evolutionary change through ac-
culturation and other key instruments); and goals (particularly, value-orientations).   In both cultures, too, educational institutions and activities were constantly approached in
the context of other major ones--political, religious, economic, recreational, familial--with frequent awareness of
their overlappings, not only with one another but with the
organizing categories of order, process, and goals.

Two major clusters of informants became the principal sources of data in both studies--the one, panels of
"grassroots" citizens; the other, panels of top-level leaders.
Those "from the bottom up" consisted of spokesmen representing the several cultural institutions just mentioned.
With due regard for education, it was always important to
include teachers, students, administrators, and parents.
Those "from the top down" likewise represented institutions
of culture--thus they included politicians, businessmen, labor leaders, artists, educators, and others.   Methods of
investigation were flexible and open-ended, although more so
in the Japanese than the Puerto Rican study.   "Participant
observation" as well as "observant participation" were primary, and hence included a wide range of involvement in,
for example, political, religious, recreational, as well as
educational activities.

To recapitulate very briefly, the core of grassroots
informants in Puerto Rico totalled twenty, both men and
women, ranging widely in economic status, schooling, religious affiliation, and other characteristics.   (Three of

these were high school students.) In Japan, grassroots informants totalled forty, but only fifteen of these were the
chief resources of this investigator. The other twenty-five
were interviewed by two close Japanese associates. The
entire panel of forty, however, again represented a cross-
section of local citizens, and in all cases the data of all
three interviewers were shared in detail. Moreover, the
leader panels in Puerto Rico and Japan each consisted of
sixteen informants; these were not primarily residents of the
selected local communities but held high positions in the
country, some of great prestige. Each interview on both
levels, whether "above" or "below," occupied everywhere
from one to nine or ten hours, the total of interviews per
informant averaging about seven. These interviews occurred in many different locales: homes, offices, hotels,
beaches, bars, schools, boats--wherever it was most comfortable to converse freely. Hours devoted exclusively to
interviews totalled several hundred in each of the two cultures.

The intent of establishing both "upper" and "lower"
panels was, of course, to provide counterbalancing perspectives, looking toward a more syncretic interpretation than
either one alone could provide. Also, for purposes of further comparison, and in accordance especially with the
pluralistic theory of Julian H. Steward,[3] three grassroots
communities were carefully selected for comparison in
Puerto Rico, and two in Japan.

III

This skeleton of our research programs must now be
supplemented by reviewing some of the less orthodox means
employed to carry through both studies. Let us note several.

One was the method of selecting informants. Proceeding from the premise (this, of course, carried profound
philosophic implications) that ordinary people can exercise
good judgments if they are given fair opportunity to do so,
the majority of grassroots informants were chosen, not primarily by the researcher, but by representative groups.
After preliminary acquaintance with local leaders such as
principals and mayors from whom formal approval of the
study was elicited, several meetings were held in every
participating grassroots community. Groups of local citizens

gathered in homes, schools, or neighborhood centers where
the purposes and methods of our study were simply explained and clarified by the investigator.   Each group was
then invited to select one spokesman in whom it had confidence but who would also be expected to speak critically,
openly, and always confidentially about the role--tasks, problems, and aims--of his respective group.   Sometimes such
meetings occupied several hours of friendly discussion.
Student organizations and PTAs, for example, took their responsibility very seriously.   On several occasions spokesmen were chosen after a process of nomination that termi-
nated in secret ballots.

Not all grassroots informants proved equally effective,
of course.   A minority in both studies were hand-picked by
local leaders who, for one reason or another, did not care
to follow the participative process of selection.   (These se-
lectees often proved less productive than the others.)   Moreover, the two top-level panels of leaders were chosen entirely by academic sponsoring committees who had previously agreed to serve as study advisors, all prospective leader-
informants being visited beforehand to provide an opportunity
for them to accept or reject our invitation in view of the
substantial time and responsibility required.   On the whole,
however, the value of these democratic and cooperative procedures was demonstrated by the generosity, earnestness,
and frankness of our panelists--many of whom became our
friends, some intimately so.   This consequence was surely
due in part to the fact that they were chosen, not by a
stranger eager to promote his own research, but by fellow
citizens to whom informants felt their share of obligation,
and perhaps a certain pride in being selected to represent
their groups.

Such attitudes became, in turn, another distinctive
feature of our methodology.   I refer to the attempt to enlist
our grassroots communities in the planning and implementation of our own work, and thus to encourage greater awareness in the same local problems and concerns that we ourselves were trying to clarify and sharpen.   Thus, while we
entered these communities with definite theoretical and practical objectives, criticisms and modifications were also invited that could improve upon our own expectations--an invitation that often bore fruit at the same time that it encouraged dialogue and mutual respect.   Still further, our fellow
participants were frequently assured that they would be provided with our findings and interpretations, the hope being

expressed that the latter might prove beneficial to their efforts to improve upon their own respective communities.
These "feedbacks" have since occurred, but again with varying evidence of effectiveness.

In any case, it was during such involvements that the
concept of "anthropotherapy," which had been formulated
earlier, [4] crystallized more clearly.   By this is meant,
somewhat analogously with psychotherapy, the effort of a selected culture or subculture to engage in prolonged, cooperative examination of its own malfunctionings, looking toward
their possible reduction, again cooperatively.   Obviously,
the concept is by no means entirely unique.   It does, however, fuse a number of partial ideas in applied anthropology.
It also invites a fresh view of the potentially creative role
of education as a participative, indeed anthropotherapeutic,
agent of cultural renewal.

In the two studies here being exemplified, one could
hardly claim that this role was carried very far.   But the
procedures, already noted, of informant selection and of cooperative research planning, plus several deliberate attempts
to assist our grassroots communities in reducing their own
tensions (juvenile delinquency was one), warrant our confidence that the approach is capable of further elaboration and
implementation.   Observant participation seems unusually
germane as a companion concept of anthropotherapy.

IV

Further aspects of the Puerto Rican and Japanese
studies attempted to complement and correct in part the
"subjective" and "impressionistic" interpretations derived
from our focal anthropological method of extended interviews.
Although the "objective" instruments thus provided were of
secondary importance, they did afford still another perspective not only upon the comparisons between top-level and
lower-level panels of informants, but upon the comparisons
among our several grassroots communities.   Indeed, when
all three forms of comparison are considered together, one
may, I trust, justifiably include both field studies under the
rubric of "comparative education" itself.

In both Puerto Rico and Japan, objective data were
derived from conventional "sociological surveys" of the
grassroots communities, which provided such common infor-

mation as family size, occupation, and education. Also, a lengthy questionnaire was submitted in Puerto Rico to the three superintendents of schools representing the three grassroots communities; this probed their evaluative agreements and disagreements concerning all features of educational programs and policies, utilizing the organizing categories of order, process, and goals as equally applicable to school subcultures.

A more ambitious, although still subordinate, instrument was developed and applied to Japanese culture in terms of value-orientations. Although much less sophisticated in design, this project was inspired by the Kluckhohn-Strodtbeck work on variations in value orientations. [5] Nevertheless, our own model is, I believe, equally deserving of further experimentation--in fact, it has already been adapted in a form appropriate to American social-studies teachers of a large-scale research program conducted by the New England Educational Assessment Project, in which the author has served as consultant. [6]

Both the Japanese and American models are simple. Sets of items portraying imaginary situations are presented to the respondent, in which he is asked to select one of three alternative choices of value. These are termed the Innovative (I), Moderative (M), and Transmissive (T). Several of the items deal directly with education in Japan; all of them do so in America. Here is but one example:

> The PTA of Takashima junior high school holds a meeting to discuss the teaching of Japanese traditional arts, such as the tea ceremony and calligraphy. Three teachers present a panel discussion:
>
> A. The first teacher urges much more class time to study these traditional arts.
> B. The second teacher insists that the present tasks of Japan are much more important to study than these traditional arts.
> C. The third teacher argues that the children need a little of both but not too much of either. [7]

This I-M-T model, as it may be called, has proved beneficial not only in comparing and checking against our abundant, qualitative anthropological evidence concerning

value-orientations in Japan, but it was administered both to
the leader panel and to a random sample of citizens in the
wider municipalities adjoining our two grassroots communities.   The evidence thus obtained was especially relevant to
our overall interpretation of cultural goals--the third primary category, it will be remembered, of anthropology-
philosophy-education viewed holistically.

                                    V

        We now return from overseas in order to consider
three further attempts to put anthropological ideas to work
in education at home.

        For some years, my graduate students in education,
regardless of their specializations, have been introduced
to the importance of anthropology in the professional preparation of teachers.   One such introduction has been through
"cultural foundations of education," which is confined largely
to theoretical developments, utilizing related philosophic resources.   Even in this course, however, students are expected to begin operating with concepts through individual or
group projects that take them out of the classroom.   These
are exemplified more fully below.

        The second approach to professional education is il-
lustrated by another graduate course: "education and culture
in Japan."   Here the principal justification is that most students in education, through no fault of their own, disclose
an appalling ignorance of Asian civilization.   One modest
course is no adequate corrective, certainly.   Nevertheless,
it is better than nothing, especially when opportunities are
provided both to benefit by the framework already exemplified and to provide limited field as well as academic experiences, even in so provincial a cultural environment as New
England.

        This approach is afforded by a number of privileges.
Visits are expected to the finest collection of Japanese art
outside the mother country (in the Boston Museum of Fine
Arts), where students approach the collection with critical
discernment of cultural influences.   Visits are also required
to a Zen Buddhist center in Cambridge, where students participate in a service of meditation.   Attendance at the national convention of the Association for Asian Studies is highly selective and interpretive, not merely reportorial.   At-

tendance at a public celebration of the American branch of
the Buddhist political-educational organization, Sokagakkai,
has invited comparable cultural reactions. Within the course
itself, students are exposed both to films and to visiting experts from Japan. The entire course is therefore interdisciplinary also, although anthropology is once more the gal-
vanizing discipline.

The third and concluding attempt exposes students to
the elementary operation of key concepts by means of simple,
first-hand contact with the profusion of nearby subcultures.
By limiting enrollment to those of relevant background, it
has proved practicable to spend well over half of the total
time of a semester outside the classroom. Sometimes students form teams of three to six, sometimes the entire
group joins together. In any case, advance planning by way
of historical and current background in the selected subculture to be approached, contact with local resource persons,
and role-playing of interviews in order to test out the applicability of selected concepts to anticipated situations, are
among the preparatory steps.

The field trips themselves extend from half a day to
a full week, depending upon student enthusiasm and avail-
ability of preferred subcultures. Some of the latter are
within the abundant, although still much anthropologically
neglected, area of metropolitan Boston. Others are within
an hour or two by car. Still others require overnight and
airplane trips. In all cases, enrollees understand that field
experiences are required. Examples have included exposure
to nearby black and Puerto Rican ghettos; to Italian, Armen-
ian, Greek, Jewish, Finnish, Rumanian, Portuguese, and
other ethnic neighborhoods throughout New England; to a
"pure Yankee" town in southern Massachusetts; to the remarkable Amish communities of Pennsylvania; to American
Indian clusters in Massachusetts and Maine; to a lumberjack
camp of northern New Hampshire; to homosexual and prosti-
tution spots in Boston (aided by a social science-trained
plainclothes detective); to French-Canadian communities nearby as well as to the city of Quebec; to a women's prison
(aided this time by a criminologist); and to Puerto Rico itself. During the last of these trips, students were prepared
to search for changes discernible since completion of my
own study. Each participant chose a different focus according to his interest, such as politics, folk music, the family,
and consumer cooperatives. [8]

In every case, students have been directed to search
for implications in education as this relates to the respective subculture. Also, upon returning from each trek,
"feedback" sessions in the form of discussions and interpretive reports are typical.

VI

In none of these graduate courses are firm generalizations of scientific validity permitted. It is therefore important to re-emphasize that field experiences are not intended to emulate those of professional anthropologists.
Such emulation is, of course, impossible without a great
deal of additional training or without prolonged immersion
in the culture or subculture selected for involvement. The
intent of our own field experiences is a much more humble
one: to introduce professional educators to some of the
techniques by which anthropology approaches, examines, and
interprets cultural experience, with particular regard for
that important feature of such experience known as education.

To indicate a little more definitely how students are
asked to perform when they venture forth as subgroups, they
have been provided with the following "Guidelines for Field
Projects":

> The purpose of the field projects is to give oppor-
> tunity for direct practice in the use of anthropo-
> logical tools, with special concern for the cultural
> context of education. Since the projects are nec-
> essarily limited, their success depends upon care-
> ful preplanning so that the best advantage may be
> taken of the brief time involved. Here are some
> suggestions that may be of value:
>
> 1. Confine the scope of the project to the utiliza-
>   tion of a very few of the major tools--for ex-
>   ample, acculturation, vertical order, goals,
>   focus, nativism. Possibly only one such tool
>   might become the central interest, depending
>   upon the nature of the subculture you have
>   chosen.
>
> 2. Learn as much as possible about the selected
>   subculture before you become directly involved.

This requires tracing down reliable background sources, which may be suggested by your contact people. For example, if you are planning to work with an ethnic group, you should be able to locate published books, pamphlets, newspapers, etc., dealing with that group.

3. Try to plan several meetings, if possible, in the chosen subculture. These may be planned in rough sequence aiming at increasing involvement. For example, an initial meeting could well occur between your team as a whole and representatives of the subculture for preliminary briefing. This should be followed by meetings with individual informants, preferably between only one or two members of your team and those individuals. Such personal contact encourages greater frankness and security. Meetings in private homes are especially good because people feel more secure in familiar environments, and you are also able to observe these environments.

4. Pre-plan what you wish to discuss, but allow flexibility. Let one topic lead freely to another. It is better not to take notes at the outset (although as soon as possible after every meeting you should jot down what you learned). When you have established some rapport, then ask if you may take notes (or possibly even use a tape recorder). But assure all informants that they will not be identified in any report to the class. In this sense, all interviews should be treated as confidential.

5. If you can arrange it, try to be invited to some event (e.g. a social gathering or church service) where you can observe something of the life of your subculture. Even better, try to become a "participant observer" where you share in some event at the same time that you are trying to interpret anthropologically what you see. Record your observations as soon afterward as possible.

6. Your aim should always be to deepen your un-understanding gradually. Normally, the kind of

questions asked at the outset are much less
personal than the kind that might be asked after becoming acquainted.

7. Do not use questionnaires except as subsidiary
    devices.

8. Share your data with other group members as
    often as you can so that you can benefit by
    any suggestions they may have before proceed-
    ing to the next stage.

9. It is not your business, of course, to argue
    or disagree with any informant. To convince
    your hosts that you are genuinely interested
    in the subculture and wish to learn about it
    with an attitude of respect--this is essential
    to any kind of effective cooperation.

10. Try to bring your project around to education.
    For example, your interviews may draw out
    the attitude of informants toward the question
    of the school as a cultural change agent. [9]

Permit me to close with a statement which pertains
almost equally well to the research studies outlined above
as to the immersion in theory and practice introduced on
the academic level:

....field work cannot always be stretched even to
six months. Shall we then, if less time is available, rule out any attempt to do research at all?
Clearly the answer is "no." Anthropology is not
an exact science and it is still undergoing rapid
development. In every project, the significant
question is not: "What can the investigator
achieve according to ideal standards?" Rather it
is: "What can he hope to achieve within the limits of his resources?" If he accomplishes his
aim, he will claim no less and no more than his
evidence and his guiding theory allow. [10]

Notes

1. Theodore Brameld, Cultural Foundations of Education--
    An Interdisciplinary Exploration (New York: Harper

and Row, 1957).   For a briefer work utilized with undergraduates, cf. Theodore Brameld, <u>The Use of Explosive Ideas in Education: Culture, Class, and Evolution</u> (Pittsburgh: University of Pittsburgh Press, 1965).

2. Theodore Brameld, <u>The Remaking of a Culture: Life and Education in Puerto Rico</u> (New York: Harper and Row, 1959); and <u>Japan: Culture, Education and Change in Two Communities</u> (New York: Holt, Rinehart and Winston, 1968).

3. Julian H. Steward, <u>Theory of Culture Change</u> (Urbana: University of Illinois Press, 1955).

4. Theodore Brameld, "Anthropotherapy--Toward Theory and Practice," <u>Human Organization</u>, Vol. 24, No. 4, 1965, pp. 288-293.

5. Florence Kluckhohn and Fred L. Strodtbeck, <u>Variations in Value Orientations</u> (Evanston: Row, Peterson & Co., 1961).

6. Further information may be obtained from Thomas Dodge, New England Educational Assessment Project, State Department of Education, Montpelier, Vermont.

7. Cf.   Brameld, <u>Japan,</u> op. cit., pp. 280-293.

8. Cf.   Theodore Brameld, ed., "A Venture in Educational Anthropology: Puerto Rico as a Laboratory," <u>Journal of Education</u>, Vol. 150, No. 2, 1967, pp. 3-56.

9. Ibid., pp. 4-5.

10. Brameld, <u>The Remaking of a Culture</u>, op. cit., p. 427.

LEONARD MARSH

7. GENERIC AND SPECIFIC CONTRIBUTIONS OF SOCIOLOGY TO TEACHER EDUCATION *

Starting-Points

1.   Today's multi-dimensional world of revolution requires an awareness of sociology.

2.   Sociology does not have all the answers (but it
does have some).   Education inherently demands many disciplines and must always be part science, part art, part craft.

3.   This paper is confined of necessity to Founda-
tions--specifically, to relations between history, philosophy
and sociology as aids to the teacher's basic education.   The
issue here is the teacher's view of his world, as distinct
from the practice of his craft.

4.   Sociology badly taught will be as useless as any
other discipline.

5.   In the present ferment, neither Foundations nor
Methods can escape reappraisal nor, for that matter, can the
best way to cross-fertilize Foundations and Methods avoid re-
evaluation.   There is also need for critical appraisal of the
balance of sociology and psychology in "method" applications
(e.g., counseling, reading disabilities, programs for "disadvantaged" children, the functioning of "open schools," sub-
cultural factors in "motivation," and so forth).   These must
be kept in mind, but cannot be developed here.

*Adapted from Proceedings of the Fifth Annual Canadian Con-
ference of the Foundations of Education, University of Calgary, May 1968, pp. 101-108.

Why Sociology at all?

1.   The social context of education is now predominant.   The world has moved, e.g., from elitism to democracy; from colonialism to nation-states; from peasant cultures to mass communications.   All these arise from, and
generate, social forces which must be understood as such.

2.   Social differentials are vital dimensions in most
countries and communities (including the giant cities, now of
unprecedented importance).   Unitary conceptions of "society"
are inadequate, even intellectually dangerous.   There may
be substantial cohesion; there may be accommodation, compromise, assimilation; there may be conflict.   The degree
and the causes of these social trends and forces must be at
least part of the conceptual vocabulary.

3.   The cultural and subcultural matrix of every person is as basic as human biology or body chemistry.   It is
presently not so understood, nor taught as such.   The ubiquity of the term "individual" is partly at fault.   But even
discussions of quantitative groups and classifications (population, income groups, etc.) are sometimes also sterile, or
they may be weighted with misleading assumptions.

4.   The learning process is bound up with all of the
above.   The dynamics of socialization (including such things
as the function and impact of parents, siblings, early "life
space," social class, "life styles," relations with friends,
teachers, groups of all kinds) are vital for all schools.
They affect educability as well as motivation; they may be
adverse as well as developmental.   Of course, psychology,
psychiatry, social work, anthropology, and other disciplines
make contributions here; but knowledge of the social environment and its social dynamics is fundamental.   Sociological
"role and status" concepts are indispensable, from kindergarten to university and the many worlds of work.

The generic contributions of sociology to teacher education derive from the above.   However, it is imperative
to recognize there are three kinds of sociology:

> Theoretical: Both "grand theory," in the tradition of
> Durkheim, Spencer and the like, as well as "middle
> theories" such as those dealing with primary and sec-
> ondary groups, role and status theory.   Here, the

closest links are to philosophy.

Empirical studies: This form of sociology has become the vogue and is the most directly concerned
with contemporary issues. It constantly raises questions of the proper interpretation of research and may
become fragmented because of the specific nature of
many research projects.

Applied sociology: Examples of this have multiplied:
some are now firmly established (e. g. , town planning), others are still innovatory (e. g. , social medicine).

Since education is normative as well as "scientific,"
teachers must understand all three kinds of sociology. But
sociology, like all the other social sciences, is in an equiv-
ocal position. For teachers, the crucial directive is to understand the forces which determine or inhibit the formation
of social policy.

Some Specifics

The following specific contributions from sociology
can, and should, be made to teacher education:

1. Concepts which permit understanding as well as
the linkage of otherwise isolated facts. For example, social role and its relation to personality development, responsibility, views of authority; family types and their relation to socialization; social classes and their variants in
ethnocentricity, views of community, educational images and
aspirations, the relativity of "division of labor" applied to
nations and the world.

2. Vocabulary of analysis and comprehension--per-
mitting the semantic obstacles of "individual," "man," "society," to give way to, or at least be habitually translated
into families, parents, children, adolescents, youth groups,
clubs, gangs, churches, trade unions, political parties, factories, offices, cabinets, executive hierarchies, bureaucracies.

3. Documentary materials to supplement history and
geography in Social Studies. The culture concept is now
ubiquitous but depends vitally on examples, national, local,

regional, subcultural and deviant.

4. Concepts, documentation (including mass-media opinions and attitudes), and research findings on the analysis of communities. "Community," like "individual," must be emancipated from abstraction. Teachers and people need to understand the wide gamut from nations to neighborhoods and school districts; also the mass-society aspects of cities and conurbations and the non-communities of slums, suburbs, or unplanned housing developments.

5. Analyses of the school system--There are a dozen phases of this, some familiar, others only recently being subjected to research: group analysis (sociograms, subcultures, etc.), socialization impacts of "streaming" and selection, role analysis of teaching functions, teacher and administrator hierarchies, patterns of school-community relations and other pedagogic roles and relationships.

6. Contemporary issues of educational opportunity--Surveys of the total educational picture raise social policy questions about retention, drop-out, selection, counseling, technical training, relation of the curriculum to work and to leisure; specialized vs. general instruction in primary and secondary grades, and so forth.

7. Minority groups, including the poor and the "culturally disadvantaged"--as children or pupils, but also as adults (parents, citizens, voters), and as social classes. Poverty is old stuff to sociology: it helped to generate social work, social security provisions, housing programs and, more recently, community development in the undeveloped countries of the world. But poverty has been "rediscovered" in North America. Its linkages with racial discrimination, farm and rural decline, stranded regional areas, educational finance inadequacies and the like have made it a priority issue in social, political and educational policy. Some of its subject-matter is social economics. A growing number of studies, however, makes it clear that educational sociology here is a new and provocative dimension in the traditional corpus of educational theory.

8. The mass-media (not just television, but newspapers, magazines, films and the rest). Their ubiquity as well as their widely diverse range of taste and involvement make serious sociology imperative. The media are the most formidable competitor of formal education--teaching may be

reinforced, or destroyed by them.   Not only individual
teachers, but the teaching profession as a whole, must be
equipped to analyze, discriminate, and formulate views on
public policy, because the mass-media represent informal
"education."

       9.   Contradiction and conflict in contemporary life.
International technical assistance programs have made culture conflict a realistic issue.   The new perspectives of
French Canada, for example, make it an essential subject
for Canadian children.   But a much more subtle yet ever-
present phenomenon exists among "our own" cultures--the
parallel existence of contradictory beliefs.   This area has
been greatly developed since Lynd's Middletown, Ogburn's
culture lag, Galbraith's "conventional wisdom," Goffman's
"front-door" and "back-door" images.   Psychiatry is relevant, but needs to be balanced with understanding of folklore, advertising, the "arrested" socialization of regional
and frontier isolation.   The so-called "generation gap" (actually there are several gaps) is a current popular recognition.   The "two cultures" (humanistic and scientific) of
Snow, with the constructive possibility of the social sciences
as a bridge, is a matter of direct educational concern.   Varieties of alienation, "anomie," student rebellion and protest movements are further indications of this contemporary
reality.   All of them, not being confined to the poor, are
of much greater imporance than the social pathology (crime,
slums, etc.) which was the earliest excursion of sociology.
Social pathology, indeed, must be examined on a much wider
canvas to include questions such as racial prejudice, the
causes of totalitarian regimes, varieties of conservatism and
fundamentalism.

       Clearly, these are half-a-dozen separate areas of
study rather than one.   They have been listed together to
stress the point that irrationality (as well as communication
failures) must be spelled out, discussed, and analyzed.
While much of it sounds distasteful, there is no intention
here of presenting a solely pessimistic view.   Modern democracy faces enormous challenges but constructive citizenship
will not be generated unless it is both realistic and informed.
Teachers and secondary schools have been widely blamed for
inculcating a bland, optimistic, and consensus-type of outlook.   Current events all over the world surely make it
clear that conflict, no less than sex, must be dealt with in
schools and society as a fact of life.

Avenues of Reconciliation or Integration

The dangers of relying on history alone are: (a) there may be completely inadequate understanding of social stratification and its relation to power structure and social development; (b) unwillingness to make judgments on contemporary events or at least insufficient training of students on how to do so.

The dangers of relying on philosophy alone, especially educational philosophy, are: (a) the assumption of homogeneity in society (e.g., the elitist who is not concerned with, or does not understand lower classes and the poor, their sub-cultural limitations or different motivations); (b) the abstraction of "the individual," especially when opposed to the abstraction "society"; (c) the assumption of rationality! Sociology, like anthropology, must struggle hard to understand the long history of irrationalities in the heritage of all civilizations--by no means excluding "our own."

Of course, there would be dangers in relying solely on sociology, especially empirical sociology and especially if it is badly taught. This is somewhat hypothetical at present, however. History and philosophy are firmly entrenched in the teaching curriculum, as is psychology. Sociology is not, though interest studies and texts are all growing rapidly. The realistic issue is how to redress the balance. Here are some of the avenues which are worth considering, though they are not necessarily equal:

1. Assurance that the Education instructor gets some sociology (or anthropology, or political science) in his own undergraduate or graduate work.

2. If the teacher has already studied sociology, encouragement for him or her to get also some social history, some philosophy and desirably, relevant English literature. In other words, include curriculum objectives which promote sociology as a generic component.

3. Graduate programs in Foundations that will remedy preceding gaps or over-specialization--a generic Foundations degree. For many academics today, because competence is equated with specialization, this could be an obdurate sticking-point.

4. Revisions of the current curriculum offerings in student-teacher programs (interpretation, discussion, cross-fertilization programs instead of simple options). Shortage of sociologists able or willing to work in Education may well be the practical barrier though there is growing evidence of change here.

5. Preparation of new texts and materials for school teaching. This is now an active movement in the United States and it is gaining attention in Britain. Canadian schools need not only sociological components, but Canadian materials. It is important to note that this should not be confined to Social Studies. The wider cultural and educational opportunities of "English literature" can be easily forgotten. For the sociologist-educator, "English" teaching invites development.

6. In-service and refresher courses for teachers of all grades. These are really the most relevant and practical, provided that administrative barriers can be broken down to build them into school schedules and the work-loads of both teachers and Education Faculties. They need not be in Foundations subjects per se and they might include "Using Social Sciences Materials" or courses on "Contemporary Social Issues," "The Sociology of Canada" and the like. To mature learners, sociology must be taught as a "stimulus subject," open-ended--it must be doctrinaire.

Conclusion

Perhaps it remains to be emphasized, in conclusion, that this summary of the educational uses of sociology refers to potentials. Of course, there are treatments of sociological concepts, especially the classical ones (e.g. "structure" and "function") which seem to reinforce conformity or élitism; on the other hand, there are plenty of contemporary treatments directed to stimulating the "sociological imagination." The crucial subject of socialization can be seen as a straitjacket process cramping everyone into the accepted cultural mold or as a basic series of parental, environmental, educational, and group influences of both positive and negative character. After all, education itself, sociologically analyzed, can be liberating or restrictive! To take another prime example, the literature on social stratification includes, on the one hand, articles suggesting that social class, that unpleasant Old World heritage, has disappeared

there is all the writing from multiple sources on the rich
and the poor, on racial and cultural tensions and conflicts,
and much of this is on a world scale. The task of the
teacher is to present the multiple dimensions of modern society, and the sociological elements in the several alternatives of policy which now face the citizens of all countries.
Obviously, it is far more mind-stretching if these are presented internationally. Today's child should not only "be
aware of other cultures," he should know the successes as
well as the failures of U.N. Agencies, he should understand
not only the "culture shock" faced by U.S.A.I.D. workers,
but be able to question the areas in which he may be "culture bound" himself.

An exacting and difficult task for the already harassed
teacher? Of course. But is this unique to sociology? History or geography, with their great potentials, can be exciting or despairingly dull. And let not the academic bogey of
"value judgments" deter us. Is the physicist or the physical teacher so secure in his "purely objective" discipline,
in a world threatened with atomic weapons, to say nothing
of the present problem of the accumulation of radio-active
wastes? The inescapability of normative elements in all
education has surely been demonstrated once and for all in
the thinking revolution which has occurred, in only a few
years, in relation to all the sciences concerned with ecology
and, one could add, the social sciences, with the "new
looks" at zero-population-growth and the inadequacy of the
G.N.P!

Teaching is an art, however scientific it may, and
should, strive to be. But sociology, whose subject-matter
is humanity itself, must be intelligently conscious of differentials and, in consequence, of the controversial areas. As
an aid to fundamental education in the troubled world of the
1970's it is at the least helpful, at its best an essential.

PHILIP H. PHENIX

8. PHILOSOPHY AND EDUCATION*

The successful ordering of society ... depends on
the growth of integrative understanding, along with the advance of specialized inquiries.   There are two ways in
which the curriculum of education may provide for such integration.   The first, and by far the predominant, approach
may be designated that of plural sequential exposure.   The
student is exposed to one more or less specialized pursuit
after another, in successive subjects or courses, with little
attempt to relate the various subjects to each other within
a comprehensive perspective.   It is assumed that some integrity of understanding will result from the fact that it is
one and the same person who studies the various special
subjects.   Still, no deliberate effort is made to assist the
student in putting the various pieces of his education together.

The other way of educating for integral understanding is to teach with the deliberate intention of showing the
interrelations among the specialized pursuits.   Such instruction constitutes true general education, in contrast to the
sequence of specialized experiences.   The guiding principles
and culminating perspectives in such a program of general
education define the domain of philosophy synoptically conceived.   From this perspective, to modify Dewey's dictum,
philosophy is the theory of general education.   It is the discipline in which the relevance of knowledge, in all its varieties, to the human career as a whole is investigated and
set forth.

The need for general understanding in contemporary
specialized civilization is becoming increasingly clear, and

---

*From "Philosophy and Education: A Synoptic View," in
Philosophy and Education.   Toronto: Ontario Institute for
Studies in Education, Monograph no. 3, 1967, p. 119.
Reprinted with permission.

219

the ineffectiveness of unrelated intellectual differentiations
is abundantly manifest. Buckminster Fuller, recently com-
menting on the prospects for humanity, pointed out that
overspecialization leads to extinction, since it prevents effective adaptation to unexpected circumstances. He added
that the computer is now making human specialization obsolete, and he drew the following conclusions for education:
"Displaced as a specialist, man is now being forced to become preoccupied exclusively with integrative patterning considerations. This means an epochal reorientation. All the
educational systems from now on must forsake specialization
and cultivate powerful generalization. Everybody will be
taught to be comprehensivists. Fortunately, that will come
naturally because man is born to be comprehensive. It is
his most unique biological characteristic."[1]

While I doubt that we need go so far as to forsake
specialization in education, it seems clear that social and
intellectual advances do require the development of the capacity for powerful generalization. This task is essentially
philosophical. The goal of comprehensive understanding
will not be achieved simply by juxtaposing separate specialized disciplines. It requires a different quality of thinking
that is integrative in nature. The deliberate cultivation of
this integral perspective is the most distinctive task of the
philosopher, though he shares in this work with generalists
in other disciplines.

Note

1. "Notes on the Future: The Prospect for Humanity."
Saturday Review, August 29, 1964, p. 183.

CHRISTOPHER J. LUCAS

9. THE DEMISE OF EDUCATIONAL PHILOSOPHY*

At a time when the virtues and shortcomings of American education arouse unprecedented debate it is curious that so little consideration is given to basic philosophical assumptions. Slightly over a decade ago, Paul Woodring was one of the first to note the apparent decline of educational philosophy in this country.[1] Professional educators and the general public alike, he alleged, have ceased to give proper attention to philosophical problems underlying education. Consequently, we make curricular decisions on an ad hoc basis without regard to the objectives of the schools, our purposes are ambiguous, and we fail to discriminate between the trivial and the profound or even to recognize that we must do so. Having pleaded for a "more knowledgeable and sophisticated view of the philosophic issues in education," Woodring concluded that educational philosophy in America is moribund.

Developments in the past decade have more than vindicated his harsh judgment. Interest in the philosophical dimensions of educational concerns is virtually nonexistent. Educational philosophy as a discipline has not simply declined in influence; it has died. With the exception of a coterie of professional educational philosophers who have a vested interest in keeping the patient respiring, the vast majority of educators are indifferent to its fate. The pronouncements of educational philosophers meet with impressive public indifference, and intellectual excitement among educators is generated elsewhere. The cutting edge of inquiry has passed to more prestigious disciplines. Few look to the philosophers for news or enlightenment when confronting educational dilemmas.

------

*The School Review (University of Chicago), Vol. 79 (Feb. 1971), pp. 269-77. Reprinted with the permission of the University of Chicago Press and the author.

Despite Justice Holmes's dictum that theory is the most practical thing in the world, many educators have shown an endemic aversion in this country to anything smacking of the theoretical. Primary blame for the decline of interest in educational philosophy should rest with its practitioners, not the public or the educational "Establishment." A coroner's inquest might suggest three reasons for its demise. First, philosophers have never been able to reach agreement on what their field is or what functions it ought to perform in the service of education. Second, courses in the subject too often have been taught poorly, following approaches both atavistic and vestigial. Third, philosophical theorists have not addressed themselves to the issues which concern educators. The most influential contributions to discussion of contemporary education have come from other quarters. Worse yet, educational philosophers have not seemed to notice or care.

The writings of present-day educatinal theorists are in frequent disagreement concerning the nature of philosophy of education. So much heat and so little light have been generated out of the vast literature on this subject that it has almost become an insider's joke in the area. Dewey initiated the debate in his 1916 Democracy and Education with the claim that philosophy is the general theory of education. His view provoked immediate controversy, and the academic professionals have been arguing ever since. One camp holds that educational philosophy is an autonomous discipline with its own conceptual tools, modes of inquiry, and defining set of questions. It is related to, but not a part of, general philosophy. The other camp insists on the inseparability of educational philosophy and general philosophy, arguing that any truly basic discussion of education leads rather quickly to the perennial themes of philosophical investigation.

Failing to achieve consensus on what educational philosophy is, its practitioners, as might be expected, disagree on what they should be doing. All parties agree that philosophizing about education is concerned with general philosophy and with educational practice, but nobody seems clear as to what the relationships are. Everyone tacitly concedes, however, that philosophers will proceed handily with their work despite an absence of agreement about the nature of the activities. Unhappily, they spend a disproportionate amount of time and effort discussing how they should philosophize and precious little on philosophizing itself.

Functional Options

George Newsome suggests that philosophers have essentially two functional options. [2] First, they can play the role of moral prophets, establish evaluative criteria for educational processes, and prescribe attitudes and practices. They may make moral judgments, more or less ex cathedra, in criticizing or recommending the larger purposes of the schools. This has been the traditional view of the philosopher's role, although some allege that today's philosophers will find it difficult to pose as ethical experts. Any claim to a special monopoly on moral wisdom is likely to elicit more suspicion than support. But for those who hold to this view of the philosopher's job, the imperative is clear: a philosophical scrutiny of the inherent logic of each subject studied in the school in light of the ends it serves and, more generally, the underlying rationale for formal education itself in terms of its broad aims or objectives. Dewey's notion of educational theory as a reflective viewing of the means and ends of education as a unity falls in this venerable tradition.

A second option for philosophizing entails the morally neutral analysis of pedagogical concepts. The educational philosopher's job is to explain the meanings of the terms educators use, to define the logical characteristics of any discussions about education. Philosopher Newsome explains why this shift in emphasis has taken place:

> Philosophy in the 'grand manner' in education is rapidly becoming suspect. Progressive Education is a dead movement and dying issue. Dewey is no longer regarded as the high priest of philosophy of education. Indeed, there appear to be no more priests at all. Philosophy of education seems to be shifting from interest in doctrines, movements, and personalities to interest in concepts and their logical status in the language of the discipline. [3]

A third major approach to educational philosophy combines synthetic system building--philosophy done in the "grand manner"--and analysis of the language of education. Beside the analysis of terms, an attempt is made to comment on large, pervasive "problems of men." The philosopher seeks to clarify what is said in educational discourse while still offering a "vision" for education as a whole.

These distinctions among possible functions for the educational philosopher may seem obscure to the layman. And so they are sometimes. The point is, philosophers have been baffled in trying to explain how philosophy can "direct" or "guide" educational practice. Some still struggle with the problem. Others conclude that philosophy's questions have nothing to do with classroom problems and turn to other matters. The difference emerges in the ways philosophers organize courses in the subject matter.

Teaching Strategies

For years, the prevailing strategy for teaching educational philosophy has been what one might term the "derivative" approach. Typically, a range of philosophical schools is presented to the student, neatly labeled idealism, realism, pragmatism, neo-Thomism, existentialism, and so on. The basic concepts and precepts of each are given in summary fashion. The student learns to compare the basal assumptions in each philosophic system. The differing theories of knowledge, of value, of man, and of human society associated with the various positions are scrutinized. Then, the implications for education are drawn out. And so the student rummages through the philosophical department store, selecting merchandise to fit. The pious hope is that the customer will find something attractive and depart outfitted with a "name brand" educational philosophy to be worn as occasion demands. A variation on this theme is the "great minds" approach, where a number of classics in educational philosophy--ancient or modern--are selected and students asked to catalog the answers they propose to educational problems.

All of this is likely to create an aura of unreality in the student's mind. He senses that particular classroom problems bear little connection to the lofty generalizations handed down by philosophers. The distinct impression given is that philosophy is fine as moral uplift or window dressing but of scant value in confronting specific pedagogical difficulties. A student is likely to conclude that philosophy consists of profound ambiguities and obscure wisdom. Were he a bit more sophisticated, the student would also realize that philosophical systems are not alternative structures addressed to the same set of questions and yielding equivalent answers of the same order. In scope and emphasis, existentialism, for example, is not the same kind of animal as pragmatism.

Worse yet, the entire business of deducing educational implications from a philosophic perspective is suspect. As Oak-
land University's dean of the School of Education phrases it,
"Nothing could be less useful than to imbue the student with
the comforting delusion that once you have settled on a few
axiomatic beliefs you can, by a series of syllogisms, arrive
at curriculum, methodology, school organization, and the
like."[4] One can only wonder how many educators have been
alienated from philosophical reflection in education because
they were misled by a course in educational philosophy to
accept such a delusion--only to have it shattered when practical reality intruded.

Yet another teaching strategy reflects the critical
temper of modern analytic philosophy. Some hold that philosophy's task has been so altered by empirical science that
its function now is to develop methods which lead to the clarification of educational confusions. The chief method is linguistic analysis, by which theorists determine whether problems are empirical and hence subjects for scientific investigation, or are merely verbal problems, or simply pseudo-
problems arising from a misuse of language. The job of a
course in educational philosophy is to introduce the student
to the conceptual tools with which such analyses are undertaken. If it is successful, this approach counteracts the habit of some educators of answering fundamental questions with
superficialities or clichés. Philosophical analysis can show
up the fuzzy concepts, the faddish slogans and poorly defined
terms that abound in educational circles. Terms like
"teaching" and "learning," for example, are ripe for analytical scrutiny. Do we know what they mean and do we mean
what we say when we employ these and similar common
ideas? Is the old controversy between those who urge more
"liberal" courses in the curriculum and those who want
"technical" courses simply a function of semantic confusion?

The philosophical analysis of meanings is a highly
technical, exhausting, and often inconclusive business. Some
skeptics will question whether the pressing issues in contemporary education require this kind of analysis. Does debate between those who oppose and those who favor introducing more classroom hardware, say teaching machines, hinge
on differences of definition? What about the conflict over
school segregation, compensatory instruction, or alienated
youth? Or do the great issues spring from a clash of social
ends and incompatible values, as Dewey used to maintain?
"When philosophy, for one reason or another, has run dry,"

one critic alleged, "when it has ceased to have anything to
say, or fears to have anything to say, it turns inward upon itself, and proposes as a self-sufficient task, to analyze
the meanings of terms ... When [this] becomes identified
with philosophy, it seems to me to have been transmuted
into a device for repressing philosophical questions."5 One
corollary of an end of ideology in this country and an end
of God in theology may be an end of philosophy, including
philosophical theory in education.

The real tragedy of the demise of educational philosophy is that it was unnecessary. Were its practitioners
willing to forsake their traditional categories of thought and
internecine quarrels, there is no scarcity of tasks to perform. Decisions in education can be made on a random
basis, go by default, or be made in a coherent, systematic
way. Educators cry for a body of comprehensive, reliable
generalizations as a framework for the formulation and appraisal of educational policy. If prospective teachers were
invited to investigate systematically the assumptions underlying educational controversy in terms of various comprehensive schemes of values, the eventual results in classrooms
might be far-reaching indeed. Because we have no basis
for adjudicating conflicting demands on the school, we have
no way of knowing what is important. Hence, everything is
important--we must do everything.

In a heterogeneous, pluralistic society, educators
need not agree; philosophic consensus is neither possible nor
necessary. But diversity of persuasion does not excuse educators from acquiring some philosophically grounded convictions about their lifework. It seems unlikely, though, that
they will get them from philosophers.

If educational philosophy is to become functional once
again, addressing itself to the contemporary dilemmas of
education, some basic shifts in conception and strategy are
going to be necessary. We do not presume to stipulate a
set of Procrustean criteria, but we suggest the following as
fruitful ways for philosophers to become more relevant.

The Practice of Philosophy as an Applied Process of Inquiry

Instead of focusing on the products of philosophical re-
flection--for example, cataloging the doctrines of Plato, Dewey, and so on--philosophical theorists might better empha-

size the process of asking philosophical questions about education. Raymond Houghton writes: "The screaming cry of the approaching 21st century is that education is that which transpires after the last fitful burp of the computer."[6] Here is an open invitation to inquire about how the educational process is being described. What sort of claim is this? To what important aspects of teaching and learning does this statement draw attention, and what sorts of assumptions are being made? Somewhere, the disucssion has to result in an idea, a challenge, or an imperative meaningful to the educator.

Beginning with Live Issues and Concerns

What interests philosophers does not necessarily animate educators. Judging from the technical literature, the academic discipline of educational philosophy has no raison d'être of its own. The professionals may make cursory reference to education, but by and large, their problems are strictly derived from general philosophy. A "cult of irrelevancy" emerges, claiming that true philosophical discourse cannot be tied to practical needs. Yet the theme of the philosophical gadfly speaking to social issues has an ancient lineage going back to Socrates. In education, interest has shifted from philosophers like Horne, Adler, and Hutchins to critics drawing inspiration from the social sciences. Some, like Hentoff, Kozol, or Holt, are concerned with the depersonalizing aspects of the bureaucratic school.[7] Others, Friedenberg and Goodman among them, indict the schools as they criticize the larger social structure of American society. These theorists are as provocative as they are relevant. Should not educational philosophers be likewise concerned with issues such as alienation and dehumanization, the impact of educational technology, or student and teacher activism? It may be that a philosophical examination will lead quickly to the most recondite considerations. But initially, discussion ought to begin with a live issue and then ascend to higher ground instead of reversing this procedure, that is, proceeding from abstruse generalizations to more specific problems. Too frequently, philosophers never get back to the dilemmas perplexing educators.

The Imperative of Responsible Partisanship

What little we know about the mechanics of demo-

cratic decision-making suggests that educational philosophers
will be listened to when they provide a position to which
educators can react. Since provoking discussion is usually
more important than analyzing it to death, the shibboleth of
objective neutrality in philosophical matters needs to be
abandoned. One would hope the philosopher of education is
uniquely qualified to present a partisan position. He may
wish to exhibit the range of alternatives in a given situation.
But finally, his discussion ought to terminate with a recom-
mendation--about curriculum, school organization, instruction, or whatever. It is significant to note that those few
philosophical theorists whose voices have been heard in the
market place of ideas inevitably do espouse a position. In
an age that eschews commitment in favor of moral neutrality, the greatest service the philosopher can render is to
provide intellectual leadership. Although his views may not
find acceptance, educational controversy will be informed by
a measure of the philosophical insight it so sorely requires.

One might still hope that philosophy of education can
be resuscitated to speak to the pressing controversies of today's education. Failing this, any mourners at its grave-
side will soon hasten past without regret.

Notes

1. Paul Woodring, "The Decline of Educational Philosophy,"
     Phi Delta Kappan 40, no. 1 (October 1958), 6-10.
2. George L. Newsome, Jr., "Educational Knowledge and
     Philosophy of Education," Educational Theory 17,
     no. 1 (January 1967), 48-55.
3. Newsome, p. 55.
4. Laszlo J. Hetenyi, "Philosophy of Education in the Un-
     dergraduate Curriculum," Educational Theory 18,
     no. 1 (Winter 1968), 55.
5. Lewis S. Feuer, "The Aims of a Philosophy of Educa-
     tion," Harvard Educational Review 26, no. 2
     (Spring 1956), 113.
6. Raymond W. Houghton, "The Focus of Humanism and
     the Teacher," in Humanizing Education: The Per-
     son in the Process, ed. by Robert R. Leeper
     (Washington, D.C.: Association for Supervision
     and Curriculum Development, National Education
     Association, 1967), p. 59.
7. Harold W. Sobel, "The New Wave of Educational Literature,"
     Phi Delta Kappan 50, no. 2 (October 1968), 109-11.

N. C. BHATTACHARYA

10. PHILOSOPHY, EDUCATION, AND TEACHER EDUCATION*

In discussing the role and value of philosophical investigation in education, two basic points must be borne in mind. R. S. Peters said somewhere that the field of education is a "philosophical slum." In no area of human activity is there more linguistic confusion and fallacious thinking than in the field of education. This is partly due to the complexity of the activities themselves, but also in part due to the professional educator's firm reliance on poorly understood slogans and unrelated snippets of research as the overall educational panacea. And, secondly, we should be able to see, though I admit that it is not always an easy thing in the face of partisan claims, that philosophical analysis of language is not mere wordmongering. It is indeed relevant to the understanding of the substantive problem of human life.

It can be argued that the difference between a careful formulation of an educational "value" or "end," and the clarification of the meaning of the term or terms by means of which the "value" or "end" in question is expressed, is by no means a fundamental one. However, the latter--i.e., the clarification of the meaning of terms used in conventional educational discourse--has been found to be a more thorough and fruitful method of approaching the difficult questions of educational aim and practice. Once we have a clear understanding of the concepts and the logic of discourse involved, the problem of choice is certainly less difficult.

The problem of choice is important. There is, as we know, considerable difference of opinion among contemporary philosophers as to the nature and function of philosophy, and among philosophers of education as to the content and use of philosophy of education. However, one thing seems to be pretty clear: if philosophy of education is to remain

---

*Teacher Education (University of Toronto), Spring 1971, pp. 32-4. Reprinted with permission.

an integral element in teacher preparation programmes, it must have a purpose. In other words, the work of the philosopher of education, or the business of philosophical clarification generally, must have some relevance to professional practice in education. This relevance, as has been explained by many, cannot be direct; the philosopher of education cannot legislate for the practitioner. But his work of clarification and examination must exhibit the range of reasonable and desirable choices confronting educators in their professional work. That an act of choice in many matters related to education will also require some warrants of empirical investigation goes without saying; but much will depend on the educator's understanding of the issues involved and on his conception of what is "reasonable" and "desirable" in any given situation within his field of operation. This is, in fact, another way of saying that teachers must learn to think for themselves.

A Philosophical Slum?

Philosophy of education, in any form, has never been a popular subject with teachers-in-training or with teachers generally. As Rupert C. Lodge wrote more than fifteen years ago:

> Systematic thinking they find hard to follow. Abstract reasoning leaves them untouched. An inspiring address on the beauty and spiritual significance of teaching as a life-work, they applaud-- is it not a recognized morale-builder? Indeed, will they not expect something of the sort to be featured on their convention programmes? But among themselves, they are convinced that anything savouring of 'general issues' is of no practical use in their day-to-day work. 'Philosophy cuts no ice and bakes no bread.' [1]

In the last decade or so, introduction of the analytic philosophy of education has in fact made very little difference in the appreciation of philosophy's potential contribution for teachers. In rating the value of their professional courses, teachers-in-training often put philosophy of education pretty low on the list. The vast majority of education undergraduates, geared as they are primarily to the "practical," find philosophy of education courses "too theoretical" --by which they mean "useless." Many curriculum and

method instructors, on their part, find it almost painful that
some people on the faculty's payroll should even try to analyze and question the established values and currently popular boosters they have so dutifully delivered to their students.
In other words, contemporary philosophy of education has so
far made very little impact on the professional discourse on
education or on the programmes of teacher education.

The reasons for this are many, but part of the problem lies in the way philosophy of education has been and still
is taught in schools and faculties of education. The subject
is usually presented as a separate and self-contained course
with practically little or no bearing on what else is done in
teacher preparation. The methods and results of philosophical analysis are not brought to bear upon the diverse talk of
educational goals, curriculum theory, methods of teaching,
cognitive development, objectives of social studies, creativity,
freedom, measurement, etc., etc. Thus, in teacher education programmes philosophy of education plays only a minor,
compartmentalized, and narrow role; it is just one other
course in a mass of courses. But if we agree that linguistic clarity and logical accuracy are basic to clear understanding and sound decision-making, then philosophy as a
method of achieving these objectives should play a much big-
ger role in teacher education.

However, it must be realized that within the time
available to student teachers it is quite impossible to study
an adequate number of courses in philosophy of education
alone that might cover all important areas of their professional preparation. One should also remember that philosophers of education themselves may lack special competence
in some of them. The answer to these practical difficulties,
as it seems to me, lies in decompartmentalizing the role
and function of philosophy of education in teacher education.
While a general course in philosophy of education may be retained for student teachers, their work in such other areas
as curriculum, method, evaluation, and administration must
include consideration of philosophical questions that are relevant to those areas. If this implies that instructors of
teaching subjects in colleges and universities, and the
teachers-in-training themselves must be turned into mean-
ing-oriented philosophers in their respective areas of specialization and preparation, that is what we must strive for.
This may not be easy to achieve, but nothing worthwhile is
easy.

There are signs that professional philosophers in increasing number have come to recognize that the field of education is after all worthy of their philosophical steel.   If in Peters' phrase they are clearing the slum, professional educators in every area must take note of it.   And as things are, this will be good for a start.

Note

1.   Rupert C. Lodge, "The Essence of Philosophy of Education," Educational Theory, Vol. III (October, 1953), p. 353.

EDMUND J. KING

11.   COMPARATIVE STUDIES OF EDUCATION[*]

In considering comparative education not too long ago,
one would think only of teachers.   Even if thinking of teachers now, one has to bear in mind not only the imparting of
information during a period of initial preparation but also the
probability of in-service review, and the pursuit of some intellectual or pedagogical interests far beyond the level once
considered appropriate to intending teachers.   Thus it is not
simply a matter of a curricular subject for the first teacher's
certificate (or for a first degree in the United States which
mainly serves pedagogical purposes).   All countries are now
providing a more advanced first qualification for the abler
teachers--degrees in place of certificates, and a higher intellectual content in any case.

Moreover, the teacher is seldom thought of only as
part of school personnel.   The teacher is much involved in
the activities of the modern world.   Its challenge increasingly requires a comparative attitude of mind and the continuous appraisal by international comparison of whatever is done
domestically.   The growth of consumer world and a sense of
growing civic responsibility make teachers answerable not only to their local authorities or to their own parent-teacher
association but also to a much wider public.   Their con-
sciences are more sensitive too.

A richer and more mature approach to comparative
studies of education is also demanded by alterations in the
composition of those who come to study it.   Throughout the
world there is constant concern to induce married women and
those who have graduated in non-pedagogical subjects to take
up teaching.   Moreover, the idea of international service has
induced many would-be teachers to spend one or more years

*From Comparative Studies and Educational Decision.   Lon-
don: Methuen, 1968, pp. 138-39.   Reprinted with permission.

233

abroad in low-income countries during the early part of their
lives. Such people returning to teaching want something
rather different from the fare of the undergraduate or
teacher-in-training once familiar. The general increase in
sophistication, both social and intellectual, demands much
more of any comparative study of education than would once
have sufficed. The inclusion in comparative study of sociologists, area study experts, and similar well-qualified
people also enhances the considerations just outlined.

The general climate of uncertainty may be a Socratic
beginning of wisdom. Yet such initiation to wisdom needs
Socratic midwifery. Information about experimental work,
or about systematic research, in these days requires the intelligent and co-operative participation of teachers and students on all fronts--and also of administrators. We cannot
bear too much freedom. In any case, freedom is not isolation. Systematic and institutionalised communication as referred to in this book is needed for the diffusion of innovation, and for incorporating all responsible citizens and professions in the innovatory process. The constituent parts of
modern knowledge are widely diffused, and inevitably require
some co-ordinating process. The uncertain meaning of much
research news (at least with reference to its social implications) necessarily demands a provisional and comparative
attitude of mind. Education is now being charged, as no instrument has been charged before, with the task of shaping
the future--at a time of greater uncertainty about the terms
of reference and about the instrumentation of that purpose.
Comparative studies are the very essence of the continuing
enquiry that modern education is seen to be, with no false
divisions between research and experiment, between teacher
and learner. Only in this way can a continuous decision-
making process be established. For in educational decisions relevant to the modern world no one stands alone, and
no one alone can take thought for himself, much less the
others.

SAUL B. ROBINSOHN

12. THE RELEVANCE OF COMPARATIVE
EDUCATION FOR TEACHER TRAINING*

1. Needs and Possibilities

Unlike the pastor in the well-known American story who preached about sin and, in the concise account of one listener, "was against it," the galaxy of comparatists mustered by the organizers of this conference to speak about comparative education in teacher training are all "for it." I am also for it, but I do not think that the need, let alone the possibility, of including comparative education courses in the regular programmes of pre-service teacher education is quite self-evident. The case will have to be made out in some detail.

Criticism of current institutions for teacher training has been levelled--with varying accents in different places-- at the lack of educational relevance or, alternatively, of scholarly quality of studies in the subjects of instruction (this need not concern us here), at the inadequacy and primitiveness of method courses, at the redundancy and lack of intellectual rigour in the foundation studies. Effects of such training, it is argued, quickly give way to the conventions, the "practical experience" and the folklore of an established craft, thus diminishing the chances of a critical and innovative attitude on the teacher's part and of genuine professional standing. In consequence, reform plans aim at improving the training for professional competence, at creating opportunities to form critical attitudes vis-à-vis the practices of the prevailing system and to foster awareness of its social and political problems.

A plea to include the systematic study of comparative

*Reprinted, with permission, from <u>Proceedings of the First World Congress of Comparative Education Societies</u>. Ottawa: The Congress, 1970.

education in the regular training curriculum will therefore
have to show what specific contributions such studies are
expected to make with respect to the practical competence
and to the critical awareness of the future teacher.   There
is no reason why, in justifying curriculum content for teacher
education, we should be less demanding than in developing
curricula for other phases of schooling.   Claims on the
training syllabus come from many parts of that wide field
called, or not, the discipline of education, including the very
just demand for an integrated programme of theory and practice.   If we are asking for a permanent place for comparative education we should be able to show

- that it employs an intellectually rigorous method af-
  fording useful explanations of educational phenomena,

- that, moreover, the claims usually made for comparative education--that it accords "perspective", that it
  engenders sensitivity for the relative range of national experience etc., --really amount to a theoretical understanding, through cross-cultural comparison, of
  education as a system,

- that we really have here that integrating approach
  which, as is often said, leads to an understanding of
  the politics of education and, consequently, to political alertness and a reforming attitude,

- that, finally, the cross-cultural study of education is
  of practical value, both in an applicative sense--the
  critical use of a repertory of devices and solutions--
  and in an interpretive sense--an improved orientation
  in the wide field of educational institutions and practices.

We may call these four aspects the relevance of method and
of theory, the political and the practical relevance.

2.   Relevance of Method

     It is well known that through comparative analysis we
wish to arrive at general explanations of relationships between educational phenomena and those of other dimensions
of society, making use of the wide variability of an intercultural field.   On the basis of this uncontroversial postulate it
has been contended that, as an honest scientific method, com-

parison will have to be subjected to the strict rules of the
various forms of multivariate statistical analysis, that methodological "eclecticism" is at the bottom of the "identity
crisis" of comparative method, and that it is only by strictly adhering to pure scientism that we can, through comparative education, teach our students "a systematic method."
Now, I must resist here the temptation to step out into the
wondrous land of general methodological discussion and shall
limit my argument to the context of teacher training.   And
in this context I am sure that there are other sectors of a
training programme, no less essential than comparative education, through which the elements of strictly enforced research and statistical analysis can be imparted.   (Which is
certainly not to say that the latter is not an important aspect of C.E.).   The characteristic contribution however of
the comparative method is, I submit, rather that synthesis
of complementary modes of insight which has been called
the "scholarly amalgam of history and the social sciences,"
the combination of hermeneutic interpretation, statistical analysis and hypothetico-logical construction (the "imaginary
experiment").   Comparison challenges the imaginative faculties of empathy and, at the same time, exercises competencies of disciplined reasoning and systematic generalization.   It is thus not only methodologically "eclectic" (if you
wish to call it that, why not?), but also inter-disciplinary
in its scope.   Its introduction into the curriculum of teacher
education could fill the place of the history of education--
though I hold no brief to disinherit that subject--and at the
same time open up an avenue to the other social sciences.

     What about "Education in Other Lands" (Auslandspäda-
gogik)?   Is there any place left for the native "comparative
argument," for the imaginary and real "educational tourism?"
I shall come back to this later, when I speak of "practical
relevance."   On principle however I should say this: If we
are to foster a critical attitude, this must begin with the ex-
actness of analysis and argumentation in our own field.
There is, to be sure, in the employment of comparative
method a place for description, as well as for analysis and
interpretation; its functions are of a heuristic as well as of
a generalizing, a predictive and a speculative kind.   But an
improved teacher training programme can no more afford
the vagaries of uncritical "cultural borrowing" than it can
retain the caprices of psychological folklore.

     Which brings me to my last point on "method."   We
have reason to mistrust operational reductionism which sub-

jects criteria of theoretical and practical relevance to those
of methodological purity.   The barrenness of much of the
work of psychologists for educational practice--and theory!
--bears this out.   Similarly, in comparative education, we
must beware of formulating our questions and of reducing
research design to fit operational requirements at the price
of theoretically satisfying interpretations and practical guidance.   If this is true of research, a fortiori should it be
applied to the education of teachers.

The request to include some research experience in
our teacher training curriculum is, I believe, well founded.
Such experience is expected to foster critical and experimental attitudes toward prevailing practices and to prepare
the future teacher for later co-operation with educational research, both as a consumer, as it were, and as a partner.
Comparative education seems to be well suited to such an
exemplary task.   The very pluralism of its methods makes
it possible for the variety of intellectual inclinations and of
aptitudes which must be expected among student teachers to
be challenged, and for a wide field of subjects to be investigated.

3.   Relevance of Theory

The none too useful discussions on the question
whether or not Education is a "discipline" have at least
shown that, whatever its dependence on the contributions of
a family of cognate, connected disciplines--a feature which
it has in common with other instances of disciplined professional knowledge, --Education has its tasks in applying such
contributions to a specific practical domain, thus lending it
coherent conceptual structure, and in formulating general
theories about its institutions and its processes.   The field
of education has offered strong resistance to theory-building,
a fact which has sometimes--wrongly, I think--been attributed to the incompetence of its professors.   Quite apart
from the undeniable fact that other domains of social action
have--so far, and for good reason--not been much more successful, we seem to be faced in this case with an exception-
ally intricate matrix of influences and dependences with so-
called "molar" problems of values and cause-effect relationships, strongly determined by cultural parameters.   Evidently, this employed in its heuristic function, can, to begin
with, place the institutions and processes within a conceptual model, being aided in identifying structural-functional char-

acteristics by a great variety of particular systems. For
the future teacher this may be an almost unique opportunity
to clarify and, at the same time, question his educational
categories and notions. Examples are hardly needed, but
take, just for one, the concept of "achievement" and its relations, say, to variables of ability on the one hand and of
needs and aspirations on the other. Relate this concept to
Swedish pragmatism, American ideals of specialization,
Marxist theory of personality growth, Japanese achievement
orientation; then--only then--speak of "achievement" and the
conditions leading to it. Or take the concept of "differentiation." I know of no better way to lend it more clarity and
distinctiveness than to investigate its different functions in
different educational systems. In fact, an application of
this notion in an analysis of the Soviet system for instance
can prove a key to a realistic understanding of the system
itself. The clarification of such concepts and categories is
of course a prerequisite for any methodical, theoretically
valid work.

Let us go one step further. I think that there is one
particular aspect of educational theory, the exploration of
which by comparative analysis can be of special benefit in
teacher training--the aspect of the development of an educational system. It is here where those middle-range theories
can be formulated that are the proper domain of comparative
investigation. Call it "change," "reform" or "modernization," we want--and the future teacher certainly wants--an
insight into the dynamics of the system. You will notice
that I do not speak of "innovation," since, while research of
innovation aims at identifying the conditions under which occur the initiation, the management and the diffusion of particular devices for an improved function of certain details
within a system, I speak here of the impulses, the discussion, the formation of consensus and decision leading up to
the reform of a complex system. Some researchers consider the concentration on innovation of methodological advantage. Perhaps they are right. I regard the more complex task just sketched as the proper assignment of comparison which is to arrive at a kind of "field theory," at a con-
ditional-genetic explanation of educational processes within a
larger societal field and thus to add the dynamic dimension
to mere structural-functional analysis of a system. Perhaps
we are thus echoing--in a somewhat more sophisticated and
more modest fashion, I hope--the claims of the early comparatists who spoke of arriving, through their new method,
at a "science of education ..."

You may have noticed that I have come close to identifying one aspect of comparative education with comparative
politics. Quite so. We are dealing with a problem area
where both subsystems, the political and the educational,
overlap and which, incidentally, has attracted the special attention of certain political scientists in recent years. Like
them, we are interested in aspirations and in their articulation, in commitments, resources and pressures and in their
conversion into a political decision, in change, and, indeed,
reform. The focus of our interest is of course different,
ours being the substance of education. In fact, those of us
who have devised their work round the concept of "International Development Education" are, methodologically and
thematically, working in both spheres--comparative education and politics. (By the way, the ambiguity of the very
term "development education" with its triple connotation, the
personal, the historical and the technical, does not make for
particular clarity.)

Let it be marked however that, while comparative education is especially interested in the dynamics of educational policy--an interest which we should introduce into the
programmes of teacher training--we must never lose sight
of the immanent character of the specific educational aims
and of the complex instruments which serve them. An exclusive preoccupation with one set of parameters tends to
produce a lopsided view on the overall development which we
wish to study, as witnessed by certain conclusions of the
economics of education and by certain so-called trend analyses. Only too frequently do such analyses fail to take account of the wide range of adjustments of an educational system and of its institutions to new economic, political, social
conditions and ignore the influence of "determinants" rooted
in ideology, cultural traditions, practical convention. Comparative education should give its students an opportunity of
understanding educational development within this wide and
variable range. This will equip them only the better for
their practical political tasks.

4.   Political Relevance

It is not just a matter of understanding the politics
of education. A most important question is whether in the
curriculum of teacher education provisions can be made to
foster attitudes of an active political commitment on the
part of the future teacher. Teachers, individually and in

many instances collectively, in their professional organizations, have shown a measure of abstention from involvement
in the great controversies of educational policy that has often been interpreted as a want of self-reliance and autonomy
and has consequently impaired their professional standing.

Why will comparative education help them to amend
this lack of "engagement?" Because the study of a wide
variety of experiences and practices helps, I think, to overcome parochialism, conventionalism and routine. The quick-
sand pace of educational development since the end of the
last world war and the need to reformulate educational policies have led to a realization of this possibility. Parlia-
mentary and other advisory bodies in many countries have
included comparative studies and surveys in their reports
and recommendations and have thus broadened the horizon
of the politician and of the educational administrator. Members of the profession most intimately concerned should not
lag behind. However, this is as yet a rather unsophisti-
cated, if correct, way of looking at the issue. The matter
may be more serious than that. The teacher may be in
danger of being relegated to the periphery of social development, if he clings to the conventions of accustomed and
well-established educational instruments and practices.
Through the study of educational developments in other systems he may become aware of existing or of imminent crises in his own. Thus, to mention just a few examples,
comparative studies of student revolt or of his not-so-silent
partners in out-of-school education or of the educational
problems of the suffering masses at the urban periphery--
may well lure him out of the complacency or at least the
seclusion of what has largely been, if not a universally respected, at least a protected professional group. (I realize
that there are considerable differences in this respect in
the conditions of countries represented at this conference.)

What I am really driving at is, I suppose, nothing
less than a sense of solidarity to be engendered by a study
of the universal and common socio-educational problems
within a highly developed and expanding industrial society.
Study and communication can lead to empathy, empathy, in
turn, to sympathy and solidarity. If this sounds, as well
it may, unduly idealistic or utopian, I will just remind you
of the connections between education and utopianism in general, and, indeed, between utopia and comparative education in particular ...

Whether feelings of solidarity will lead to active commitment and co-operation, within a national system and beyond, will partly depend on the intensity of relevant educational experiences offered.   Other speakers will, I presume,
speak about international exchange and other forms of organized experience abroad.   My own concern is with the effect
of a systematic study of common problems in a universal
perspective, undertaken--whatever the resources and oppor-
tunities--under the aspect of their relevance to the future
teacher's own problems and personal commitment.

In the communist east there is little doubt about such
practical effects of comparative education in teacher training.   As the representative of a discipline, at once analytic
and "prognostic"--so the argument runs--the comparatist
asks "what could be", "why is it not so?", "how is it possible that it will be so?".   Thus, through generalizing from
the aggregated experience of "progressive" education and
from a critical analysis of "state monopolistic" educational
practice, "objectively founded blue-prints for reform" will
be generated.   An insight into the trends and basic regularities of educational development gained in this manner
will raise the quality and the effectivenss of the teacher's
work.   A way of arguing in favour of comparative education
for teacher training which, if somewhat naive, is straightforward.   It raises the question of practical relevance which
we must now consider.

5.   Practical Relevance

The dividing line between what is here called "political" and "practical" relevance is of course uncertain.
Let us consider the concept which seems prevalent in comparative law as an instance of a practical--or pragmatic--
approach to cross-cultural comparison.   The characteristic
uses of comparison in this field are: (1) regarding the various systems as an "arsenal" of possible solutions to common problems;   (2) looking for functional equivalences in a
quickly contracting field of international relations and inter-
dependences.   Having myself rejected the naive usage of
"cultural borrowing," the uncritical "comparative argument"
in the beginning of my remarks, I yet see no reason to
depreciate a cautious use of intercultural transposition altogether.   Here too any rigid purism is quite impractical and
untenable.   Experience in a wider field shows, first of all,
"what is possible" and must then lead to a closer examina-

tion of the particular circumstances. Why not study in this
manner, say, forms of student participation in secondary
schools or the requirements of polytechnic education in "post-
industrial" society or alternative organizations of teacher
training or the use of language laboratories in foreign language instruction. In fact, the simple study of international experiences may sometimes be a more effective way to
break the tenacity of a professional subculture than subtle
scientific enlightenment. Industry all over the world has a
good deal to teach in this respect.

The case for this kind of comparative study becomes
particularly evident with regard to former colonial areas.
The need to escape, to a degree, one single metropolitan influence is obvious and will be well served by a rather comprehensive survey of alternative systems.

Finally, if a strong interlacing of theory and practice
has been demanded for teacher training, in order to improve
the relevance of theory on the one hand, and to promote a
critical approach to conventional practice on the other, this
is valid for comparative education as well. One speaks of
a "fruitful tension" between pragmatic orientation and scholarly insight. Take the case of curriculum development as
one instance of growing teacher participation in educational
planning--regardless of the relative influence of teachers in
shaping major educational policy. A comparative study of
curricula over a wide range of educational systems is likely
to yield information about a great variety of alternative solutions under similar circumstances and to stimulate the imagination to produce new ones. Such comparative study has
been an explicit part of the preparations for curriculum revision in some countries of Eastern Europe. Eventually, a
sharpened perception of the peculiar culture--and system-
bound curriculum variables, as well as of the recurring patterns of curriculum construction, may well result in more
sophisticated conceptual and theoretical models of curriculum
development.

These then are the objectives of the study of comparative education within the teacher training programme:

    a heightened awareness of educational problems and,
    hopefully, an ensuing readiness to engage in political
    action for their solution,

competence in dealing with educational matter with a measure of methodical refinement (without undue technicality) and with a pretension to theoretical consistence,

better preparation for responsible choice among the alternatives of day-to-day practice.   A large order, is it not?

FLOYD G. ROBINSON

13. THE CONTRIBUTION OF EDUCATIONAL PSYCHOLOGY TO TEACHER TRAINING*

In the limited time at my disposal I want to look at the following four questions:

a)   What is the intent of educational psychology?
b)   To what extent is this intent realized in current textbooks?
c)   What might be done to improve the content of educational psychology?
d)   What experiences should be planned for the teacher in training which go beyond subjecting him to improved content?

Before turning to these major questions, I should like to raise some preliminary issues, mainly in the hope of establishing an appropriate mental set for the conference. To begin with, I think we should keep in mind that the problem of introducing an appropriate educational psychology component into teacher training is part of the much larger task of bringing psychological knowledge to bear upon educational decision making in general. I believe that two unfortunate consequences will follow any attempt to isolate the problem of teacher training. The lesser evil is that we tend to pad our courses with information the classroom teacher cannot use, because the action proposed lies for the most part outside his domain of decision making. For example, theories of cognitive development might deal with when a child is ready to learn particular concepts and thus with how curriculum content should be spaced out over the grade structure, but the decision as to which concepts should be taught at which grade level is generally made by the curriculum developer rather than by the teacher. Similarly, while educational psychology has many useful things to say about practice, the

---

*Speech presented at Conference sponsored by Ontario Institute for Studies in Education, April 1968.

245

existing degrees of freedom for constructing practice schedules are almost determined by the author of the reading
text, the arithmetic text, or spelling text.   It might be interesting, in fact, to speculate upon the extent to which
such devices as programmed instruction, educational television, and the explicit teaching procedures derived from
task analysis either eliminate independent teacher behavior
altogether or enmesh him so tightly in a network of specific procedural directions that the teacher's knowledge of
educational psychology could hardly be a significant variable
affecting student learning.

The fact that we give teachers knowledge which is
relatively useless to them may be of no great importance.
The second consequence of treating teacher education in isolation, however, is that we easily forget that the failure of
both psychology and educational psychology to make an impact at those levels of decision making where the real character and substance of public education is decided will mean
that our intervention in teacher education may have only a
peripheral effect; indeed, I will conclude my paper by arguing that until some substantial changes are made in the
expectations that exist at these higher decision-making levels, the defeat of whatever inventive methodology might be
devised with the help of educational psychology is fairly assured in advance.

Some documentation of our failure to influence high-
level decision making can be had by looking at the field of
mathematics education.   More than a decade ago when the
first wave of the mathematics revolution rocked our traditional viewpoint, it was hoped that an opportunity had arisen
to inject psychological insights into educational practice via
the new curricula.   Many efforts were made to bring psychologists and mathematicians together to achieve that end;
the results, however, were disastrous as far as psychology
was concerned, for mathematicians rapidly concluded that
psychologists had little to tell them.   In my opinion the current attitude of mathematicians and mathematics methodologists toward the likely contribution of educational psychology is best epitomized by the prestigious Cambridge Report
on Goals for School Mathematics, which dismissed Piaget
with the simple assertion that his theoretical and experimental work had no relevance for the major reform of
mathematics education which they were proposing.

Mathematicians, then, have proceeded to take mat-

ters into their own hands, have completely dominated the
thinking that lies behind new programs in secondary school
mathematics, and in many cases are even exercising critical influence on the programs designed for elementary
school children.   In pontificating on the appropriateness of
different levels of abstraction at different ages, on the
proper sequencing of ideas, and on appropriate methods of
presentation, the mathematicians have become the acting educational psychologists in the mathematics field.   Moreover,
since mathematicians and other university subject-matter
specialists have the upper hand in instituting curriculum reform and in influencing the educational hierarchy, their active disdain for the educational psychologist is likely to have
important implications for teacher training.   For example,
while many of the proposed reforms of educational psychology call for an exapansion of its offerings in teacher-training programs, I suggest it would be more realistic to believe that while opportunities in that direction may be created by increasing the length of teacher-training programs,
the additional time made available will be usurped by subject-matter specialists who are determined that teachers in
training will receive more instruction in their substantive
fields.   As an example of the trend in local events I would
point out that in Ontario, a province blessed by both strong
psychology and educational psychology communities, we have
recently established a Master of Arts in Teaching (MAT) degree in mathematics, the precursor of general developments
in this field.   In the midst of talk of expanding educational
psychology offerings it is interesting to note that the typical
course pattern for the MAT consists of four courses in
graduate-level mathematics and one course in educational
theory, and that the latter requirement need not be educational psychology or any of its near relatives (measurement,
curriculum development, research, and the like).   It is
clear then that the prestigious elements of the mathematics
education community conceive of the master teacher as a
person who has no need for the insights of educational psychology.   The major implication I draw from the preceding
observations, aside from the need to tone down our expectations, is that any plan for the reform of educational psychology in teacher education must take into account the existing
power structure in educational decision making.   I will return later in my paper to this question.

The Intent of Educational Psychology
Programs in Teacher-Training Institutions

What is it that educational psychology is trying to
do? Judging from the textbooks and writings of those who
express themselves coherently on the subject, I believe it
is the intention that educational psychology should attempt
to create a kind of input-output model. According to this
conception, the "output" would be a class of variables comprising those outcomes which are considered to be the
school's responsibility. The "inputs" represent a class of
psychological variables--or variables linked to mediating
psychological variables--known to be causally linked to the
desired behavioral outcomes, and whose manipulation or
accommodation lies within the school's power. While this
abbreviated statement leaves a few "tag-ends," such an input-output conception is clearly visible in our writing efforts. Thus, we explicitly categorize behavioral outcomes
in such terms as concept learning, generalization learning,
problem solving, creativity, and the like. Moreover, the
bulk of our text is concerned with empirical evidence and
logical argument linking a great variety of cognitive, affective, social, situational, and task variables to these outcomes. And to varying degrees, different authors attempt
to formulate a set of unifying ideas that allow some economy
in predicting, explaining, or simply organizing the vast multitude of potential relationships.

When we intervene in teacher training we assume that
the teacher will be able to superimpose this input-output
mesh upon his classroom decision making and that, as a result, decisions will be reached which--as the common word-
ing goes--"will optimize or maximize the product," the latter being some function of output variables. I think it unfortunate that this rather facile assumption has never been
scrutinized by detailed analysis. It seems to me that we
must possess an infinite amount of uncertainty as to what
the optimum program might be, or even what the optimum
individual choice will be, in a particular situation; and that
the application of any empirically derived generalization--
which is capable of reducing uncertainty by a finite amount
--will still leave us mightily uncertain. The only conclusion I can come to in this respect is that we had best cease
speaking of the maximum or the optimum when referring to
procedures that might be concocted for classroom use on
the basis of educational psychology. More realistically, one

could probably demonstrate that the assignment of the values
of input variables on the basis of an empirically derived
generalization will produce a positive probability of increasing the value of some well-defined output function over that
produced by the assignment of the values normally made by
a teacher whose intuitive generalizations disagreed with empirically derived ones.

I am, then, prepared to believe--on purely logical
grounds--that educational psychology can have some positive
influence on decision making, although I cannot accept the
facetious platitudes on the benefits to be derived from our
field which are advanced largely by questionable analogy by
our spokesmen and textbook writers. But even my more
modest formulation of the benefits to be conferred requires
that the essence of our discipline, the propositions or generalizations that we formulate, must meet certain requirements. My list of requirements is as follows:

a) The generalization has to be incorporable into the
    cognitive structure that is activated by the teacher
    while operating in the classroom. In other words,
    the concepts and variables contained in it must have
    meaning for the teacher to the point where their val-
    ues or exemplars can be unequivocally identified.
b) The generalization has to suggest manipulations of
    input variables or methods of accommodating input
    variables over which the teacher has some control.
c) The generalization has to suggest manipulations that
    the teacher would not ordinarily arrive at by simple
    inspection of the situation or by more profound intui-
    tion.
d) The generalization has to be valid, that is, has to
    possess some uncertainty-reducing potential in an ob-
    jective sense.

From this point on I shall refer to generalizations
meeting these criteria simply as being "potentially useful"
generalizations.

The Educational Psychology Literature

Given that our intent is to create an input-output system with the hope that it will improve educational decision
making, and having laid down certain conditions for generalizations which might be useful in this respect, we must next

ask to what extent this intent is realized in our current
textbooks. Since I should not want any particular author to
take umbrage at my remarks, let me state that the quota-
tions I shall be citing are not from authors presented at
this meeting; moreover, to avoid embarrassment in other
quarters I have paraphrased liberally. Perhaps it would
make everyone feel better if I were to say that the deficiencies I will report are those I first discovered in my
own recent attempts to write an educational psychology textbook; as a matter of honesty, however, I must record that
comparative reading suggests that these faults are fairly
widespread.

Undoubtedly part of our difficulty in formulating useful generalizations in educational psychology can be traced
to the fact that while we borrow many of our concepts from
academic psychology, we exhibit a curious approach-avoid-
ance tendency toward that discipline. On the one hand, we
are attracted by its power to confer respectability upon our
work; on the other hand, we are anxious to take our audience somewhat into account. The typical compromise
reached in dealing with the concepts of psychology is to di-
lute their definitions into language thought aura congenial
to the teacher's ear. The result is that even the most rigorously defined concepts acquire a gratuitous auro of ambiguity in the translation. For example, the common definition of a positive reinforcer as "a stimulus whose presentation strengthens the response which it follows" remains
ambiguous because the word "strengthens" is undefined and
exceedingly misleading. Not many would attempt to improve
on this definition by defining "strengthen" in terms of the
probability of a response and by indicating how this probability is to be measured. If we begin this far from the
accurate definition of a concept that is capable of clarity,
it is understandable that as we engage intrinsically vaguer
terms like "motivation," "personality," "need," "problem,"
or "ability," the informality of our language increases to
the point where it is difficult to see how the student can
emerge with a clear concept. Such beginnings augur an unfortunate ending, for from fuzzy concepts one can surely
generate only chaotic generalizations.

The substance of the generalization itself introduces
a second problem. I think the typical approach of the educational psychology textbook writer might be described as
an eclectic one, in that he grasps hold of established psychological theory or hypotheses resulting from laboratory

studies and uses these as the basis of hypotheses or inferences as to what will happen in what he regards as an analogous educational situation.   No doubt this approach will
keep educational psychology abreast with the advance of psychological knowledge in general and has the further advantages that it is both interesting and comfortable for the
writer and lecturer.   I think, for example, that it is attractive to many minimally qualified instructors because a
one-lecture-stand on Berlyne's theory of transformational
thinking or on operant conditioning, in addition to generating
the interest that accrues to any plausible idea on first encounter, does not allow time for perceptive students to collect their thoughts sufficiently to ask embarrasing questions.

However the eclectic-translative approach suffers
from what appear to be sizeable weaknesses.   The most
dangerous one is that at least some of the extrapolations
appear to be invalid because the assumed analogous situations in the classroom are simply not analogous.   We all
say that the phenomena of the classroom are of a different
order of complexity than the phenomena of the psychological
laboratory and that one cannot indiscriminately extrapolate
from the simple to the complex.   Yet, apparently our conviction does not travel with this assertion.   For we seem
to persist in citing the interference theory of forgetting with
its implications of the inevitability of retroactive inhibition,
the operant conditioning view that explicit refinforcements
ought to be built into instructional materials, or the Thorn-
dike-Skinner view that aversive simulation is generally in-
effective and should be avoided as a classroom motivational
device.   Yet the tenability of such generalizations when examined in terms of the actual complexity of the learning
of an organized body of knowledge and of the sophisticated
motivations operating in the school setting, seem highly
questionable and can hardly be thought to have a positive
influence on classroom decision making.

Another tendency inherent in the loose structure of
an eclectic approach is that of our backing ourselves into
elaborate tautologies.   For example, many writers--during
the rapid review of learning theory--define a positive reinforcer as the stimulus that strengthens the response it
follows.   Fifty pages later, in the discussion of motivation,
these writers can be found advising teachers that if they
want a particular behavior to recur they should make sure
that an appropriate positive reinforcement follows the desired response.   Putting these statements together, the

teacher has now been informed that to make behavior recur
he must provide something which will strengthen it, that is,
make it more likely to recur. Somehow this does not seem
very helpful.

Typically, our writing is not sufficiently sustained to
carry us all the way to complex tautology, and we stop at
mere meaningless generalization. For example, we say
that "authoritarian teachers tend to depress pupils' creativity"--and we leave both "authoritarian" and "creativity" undefined. These faults of tautology and meaninglessness cannot,
of course, be entirely attributed to the eclectic-translative
approach. We are in danger of them whenever, starting off
in a great conceptual confusion, we inch toward generalization with little more than syntax as a restraining influence,
coming back at last upon ourselves in the dense verbal fog.

Not all our generalizations are fuzzy, however; many
are clear enough but stand at a great distance from any suggested or implied action. Such, for example, are detailed
data--including graphs and charts--on the relative height and
broad-jumping abilities of boys and girls at various ages,
on the distribution of socioeconomic classes in particular
towns, on the improvement of maze learning with practice,
or on the forgetting of nonsense syllables over varying periods of time. I suppose one might argue that by understanding such relationships the teacher acquires a firmer
grasp of the phenomena of education; and yet, no manipulable variable being in evidence, I find it difficult to believe
that any of these statements would figure very prominently
in the improvement of the educational product.

Of course it would be unfair to assert that all educational psychology consists of nothing more than erroneous,
tautologous, vague, or inconsequential generalizations. In
fact, a good part of the writing is merely descriptive and
when this is done accurately--as for example in elaborating
a system of behavioral outcomes or describing a particularly relevant experiment--the product can have some value.
Moreover, some of the generalizations offered do seem to
meet the criteria of potential usefulness cited in an earlier
section. And yet I feel that my bland descriptions have not
really captured the "unreal" impression of the prose in this
field. To do this, one must make two excursions: first by
sampling intact sections of writing rather than isolated generalizations, and second by proceeding to those remarkable
statements which conclude our labors.

As to the first excursion, the stringing together of a series of undefined terms and vague generalizations of the type previously described reaches its most ludicrous extreme in the numerous five-page summaries of Piaget's theory, the last part of which typically begins in somewhat the following fashion:

> In the stage of "formal" operations, beginning somewhere in the 11-15 age group, the child acquires the ability to undertake "combinatorial," "hypothetical deductive," and "if-then" thinking. At this stage the child is no longer bounded by the "empirical givens" but can hypothesize and is capable of "thinking about thinking." ...

This account is typically larded with further undefined terms (curiously set in quotation marks as if this practice somehow explained their meaning) and several incomprehensible passages from Piaget himself. Such small snatches as I have been able to understand strike me as being extremely misleading and I find it difficult to believe that the teacher can profit much from them.

Our second excursion is to travel to the back of the chapter where, having now defined concepts and formulated generalizations, the textbook writer must take the last desperate step and attempt to offer the teacher some straightforward advice on how to manipulate input variables. Here I feel educational psychology sinks to levels of banality unmatched in any other scientific or professional writing. "The teacher," we announce with a straight face, "must keep in mind that her pupils are individuals, each with his own unique pattern of abilities." Other good advice is that the teacher should remember that "not all pupils are motivated toward school work," and that "the child should move at the pace determined by his abilities." Frankly, I think this is as patronizing and insulting as it would be to inform a neophyte physicist that "objects generally fall downward, other things being equal," or the medical student that "patients are not always as sick as they think they are."

In summary, it seems to me that educational psychology, as represented by the texts we put into the hands of teachers in training, moves through the progressive errors of defining its concepts poorly, fashioning generalizations by an uninhibited translation of psychological theory into the educational situation, and abstracting from these

generalizations some pitiful caricature of good advice. By
the time we have finished one of these wretched essays I
think we know in that region of our soul not contaminated
by the poisons of rationalization that, having written at enormous length, we have said very little of any real value to
the teacher. The impression that experienced teachers take
from our writing, if I might cite a response from a course
evaluation, is that "after a bold initial sally in which educational psychologists cite the importance of a particular topic,
they retreat from the phenomenon as it is found in the classroom with frightening acceleration, resorting in the final
stages to covering their tracks with desperately spiraling
verbal gymnastics."

Reforming the Educational Psychology Text

        I believe it will be worthwhile to attempt to reform
the educational psychology text because, aside from what
may happen in a few advanced experimental programs--and
despite the fanciful speculations that we shall no doubt hear
during the next two days--what the typical teacher is likely
to know about our discipline for a considerable period in the
future will be what is contained between the covers of a
text, coupled with such folksy elaborations as may be offered by a none-too-well-qualified instructor. Such reform
will not be an easy task, since texts are oriented toward a
large commercial market that seems to impose its own conditions for approval. Surely, only a belief that the market
place demands complete coverage could induce us to range
so widely over the cognitive, affective, and motor domains;
to add to this, miniature courses in statistics and evaluation,
and, finally, to season the work well with liberal extrac-
tions from learning theory, developmental psychology, and
personality theory.

        We were terribly fearful of leaving anything out; yet
common sense dictates that coverage must be narrowed if
our writing is to acquire any depth. And with less coverage
perhaps we can make some inroads on the problem of vague
terminology. No writer can emerge with a universally accepted and for-all-times definition of "problem solving," but
he should be expected to be consistent in the use of this
term throughout his tome and to distinguish it from "creativity" or "discovery" if he uses the last two terms.

        But a bigger step forward will come, in my opinion,

when we are able to wean ourselves from the eclectic-translative approach that characterizes contemporary educational psychology. Although it can be interesting, its net effect is like shining a number of small colored lights on a vast dark object: there are points of brilliance here and there, but the total structure of the object and the relationship of its parts remain invisible. It would be preferable, I believe, if we started by setting out the categories of behaviors we are interested in producing in public education, and by adhering doggedly to the phenomena defined by these categories as they exist in the classroom. For example, believing that problem solving is an appropriate educational goal, let us analyze the characteristics of problems as they exist in the context of complex bodies of knowledge taught in school; let us define some reasonable criteria for setting off problems from lower orders of behavioral outcomes; and let us exemplify how strategies can be devised to lead students to independent solution of classes of such problems. By all means let us draw upon laboratory psychology where it is appropriate, but an immense difference in utility results from making the classroom phenomena the focal point of our discussion or from wandering vaguely through Einstellung effects, the two-pendulum problem, "after-the-fact" habit family analyses of problem solving, Dewey's five stages, and a host of other miscellanea.

And where, as is usually the case, definitive empirical evidence is lacking, I would not hesitate to speculate on the basis of analysis and deduction from a set of theoretical constructs; such approaches are, after all, luxuries unavailable to the harried teacher, and their application may well cast a good deal of light on classroom learning. Of several instances that might be cited, I would think that much of the impressive success of task analysis in recent years can be attributed to the power of reasoning unfettered by psychological dogma. Thus Piaget's theory argues that children will not ferret out the cause-effect relationships in natural phenomena until their mental operations form the complex structure characteristic of the formal stage of thinking: task analysis, abetted by straightforward reasoning, suggests that Piaget has read too much into the problem and that the child can, given a small amount of training, produce acceptable solutions at much younger ages. Although no hard data appear to be available, I think that the task analysis conclusion should be entered as a relevant educational hypothesis and guide to the teacher's action.

Beyond the Textbook

One might thus envisage an educational psychology
text of the future which would contain a number of useful
generalizations, either empirically derived or speculative,
bearing on classroom learning and organized around the central concepts of the nature of the learner and the learning
process. Since I might be challenged to produce such entities, I would say that generalizations concerning the efficacy of advance organizers, or the distinctive kinds of
stimulus support (dependence upon empirical props) required
by children at different stages of cognitive development, or
the differential relationship of arousal--manifested by drive
level, emotion or anxiety--to performance of simple, as opposed to complex, tasks all satisfy my criterion of potential usefulness and can be incorporated into a larger idea-
tional structure.

The preceding are potentially useful generalizations,
but they are not likely to be used by the individual classroom teacher.   The difficulty is that they are indeed generalizations across tasks, personality types, motivational
states and--most important--subject-matter areas.   They
are not ready for incorporation into the teacher's decision-
making structure without further working down, at least to
the level of his particular subject-matter field.   One can
understand well enough the general principle of organizers,
but it takes a good deal of further initiative and invention
actually to construct an organizer for an algebra passage,
or to discern the proper placement, level of generality,
and method of incorporation of a series of organizers into
an algebra course.

Now, while we intimate in our educational psychology textbooks that the teacher ought to do this working down
--or do "applied research" as we say--we cannot realistically expect this to happen.   The teacher will not do it even if
he has the time, because the teacher's decision-making
schema| are completely pre-empted by the ultraspecific pro-
cedural rules of the methodologist who, not content to speak
of trends, general relationships, or suggestions, tells the
teacher which book to buy, how to teach specific lessons,
how much homework to assign, how to take it up, what to
write on the board, what to put on the bulletin board, and
so on.   Moreover, these specific procedural rules are reinforced by observation, practice teaching, and written ex-

aminations. It is not surprising, then, that these strictures
tend to be prepotent from the moment a teacher steps into
the class and that the teacher finds they will work well
enough--at least up to whatever ambiguous standard he may
be able to fashion, given no training in evaluation. Furthermore the teacher--particularly in his early years--is in a
high-anxiety situation, a state which does not lend itself to
that more extended reflection that draws upon remote rules
and peripheral knowledge. Thus an initial pre-potency, en-
ergized by a high-drive level and lack of opportunity for
critical assessment, causes the methodological rules to con-
geal rapidly into fixed habits, while the airy generalizations
of educational psychology travel the way of all unused ideas.

The previous paragraphs suggest the direction of my
proposed solution. In view of the prevailing power structure in education, and for the reasons previously cited, it
seems to me that during the next few years the "enlightened"
methodologist will provide the best hope for educational psychology to make an impact through teacher training (as opposed to contributions at higher levels). It is in the framework of inventive methodology that the potentially useful generalizations of educational psychology, mixed with other ingredients, jell into detailed procedural rules for developing
specific kinds of behavior in the school setting. This is not
to say that methodology will ever be a derivative of psychology, for the former is still largely an inventive process and
seems likely to remain so. How educational psychology contributes to the process of methodological invention will vary
from case to case; sometimes it may suggest a procedure
directly; more often, however, it may merely act as a set
of logical and empirical constraints upon otherwise free-
wheeling hypothesizing about procedures.

Perhaps my view of the ultimate relationship between
educational psychology and methodology is too much colored
by personal experience. For some years (as a classroom
teacher) I labored to no great avail to inculcate in my students the ability to solve the kinds of geometry problems to
which we were all subjected in our high-school days. Even
though I was unsuccessful, I expect I would have gone on for
thirty years with the procedural rules taught in the methodology courses, had I not been diverted by the enticements
of graduate study. Anyway, I came back to the problem
many years later and worked out a strategy that seems to
allow much younger children to cope with these logical exercises, even to the point of handling "originals" (that is,

problems they have not seen before). When embroiled in
the kind of discussion which underlies this conference, I
have often reflected on the contribution of educational psychology to this small personal triumph in methodological
invention. For the most part, this success was largely a
matter of having time to analyze what appeared to be the
component tasks in the class of problems and to ask myself
in respect to each task, "How can I get around the difficulties that kids seem to have here?" I had no conscious
experience of the generalizations of educational psychology
suggesting a solution, but possibly these generalizations
were active in whatever internal-combusion chamber creative fires burn. And when ideas came forth, such principles
frequently allowed a rapid assessment of practical potential.
"Perhaps I should have the children explicitly verbalize a
rule for proceeding from a fact to be proved to a class of
propositions which would establish this fact," I would say
to myself. "Ah yes," I would answer, "this is consistent
with the general efficacy of verbal rules in steering the
child's mental operation through tasks with a higher order
of perceptual complexity." And so the internal conversation went, some internal process (possibly aided by psychological principles) throwing up suggestions; a critical faculty
dissecting and evaluating them in the light of known relationships.

My proposal that we should make our move through
the methodologist is at considerable odds with such solutions
as:

a) Core courses in academic psychology surrounded by
   satellite courses stressing application;
b) Educational psychologists combining in team fashion
   to acquaint teachers with their basic research interests;
c) Educational psychologists attempting to make application to subject-matter areas themselves.

The first two approaches seem appropriate to graduate instruction in educational psychology, but I would reject all
three for teacher-training programs because, in general,
neither psychologists nor educational psychologists are prepared to keep up with the rapid changes underway in the substantive fields now taught in our schools--and therefore they
are not in a position to make imaginative application. On the
other hand, I think we can safely assume that the methodologist, if he so wished, is quite capable of assimilating in

relatively short order the essential substance of our discipline.

An alliance with methodologists is just the beginning
step, however. I agree with proposals that the teacher in
training needs some kind of behavioral laboratory experience, my reasoning being that the procedural rules obtained
from inventive methodology need strengthening through practice until they are at operational strength prior to the time
the teacher enters the classroom. No doubt the practice-
teaching experience--now largely an exercise in observing
and practicing specific methodological rules--could be used
to better advantage. For example, if the instructor in the
educational psychology course is talking about categories of
behavioral outcomes and the methodologist is illustrating
these in the teacher's substantive field, then the teacher
himself should be instructed to identify and classify those
activities observed in an ongoing lesson. Again, if the educational psychologist explains the theory of organizers and
the methodologist examines their application to a subject-
matter field, then the teacher should be required to design
and use one in his actual teaching. Much can be done in
that way to give the teacher some experience in applying
educational psychology principles.

However I would also advocate exercises in behavioral change which employ much smaller groups of children,
perhaps even one child. The typical classroom teacher is
so harried, and so far removed from the possibility of close
observation and the precise control of the child's behavior,
that he actually learns little about learning from his experience. For this and other reasons he is susceptible to the
many myths about learning which permeate professional
thinking, one of the most pernicious being that the present
limitations on what the child learns in school can be safely
attributed to the operation of some kind of natural law of
development. Every teacher should have the experience of
identifying some bheavioral goal presently thought difficult
or impossible for a child to attain, of performing a task
analysis to reveal component skills, of attempting to teach
these skills, and of evaluating the results; if the outcome
were successful--as it would be with careful selection--the
teacher would go into the classroom with a healthy respect
for the potential of the child and a valuable impatience with
the limitations of mass education.

Not all such "lab" experiences need be of this dra-

matic kind.   I have found that requiring experienced teachers
to teach a concept to children of different age levels, while
carefully observing both the kind and quality of props required to do so, fixed the essential attributes of stages of
cognitive development in their minds far more precisely and
permanently than reams of printed discourse.   I would add,
too, that the results of these exercises in attempting to produce specified behavioral goals should figure prominently in
the training institution's decision as to when the neophyte
should be allowed to assume independent status in the classroom.   I expect that the suggestion that the teacher should
not be granted a certificate until he demonstrates he can
change behavior will sound abrasive in the ears of more
genteel teacher educators, but it seems reasonable counsel
nonetheless.

        Effecting a liaison with inventive methodologists will
not be an easy task, but not for the reason that they are
a breed limited in number, nor even because they presently
despise us.   The chief obstacle is that there is little incen-
tive at the moment to improve methodology--other than
changing the content with which it deals--because the present methodology is quite capable of accomplishing the low-
level behavioral goals we have set in education.   By way of
analogy, I would think that the typical group of children in
today's schools could be compared to a group of runners
jogging around a track who are required merely to keep pace
with a slow-moving mechanical rabbit.   If the traner's
methods are 20 percent less efficient than they might be,
then the student may have to expend roughly 20 percent more
effort, but he will have no trouble keeping up to the modest
standard.   The point is that efficient methodology becomes
critical (insofar as achievement is concerned) only at the
point of maximum effort, and we are far away from this
point at the moment.

        What I have just said may be thought a negative view.
Let me, then, express the ultranegative view.   For some
time a private hypothesis has been pressing inward upon my
consciousness--supported by personal observation--that certain attitudes are so ingrained in educators that the methodologist will be subjected to ridicule, scorn, and abuse in direct proportion to his inventiveness, that is, in direct proportion to his ability to produce behavior change over and above
that now produced by the school.   Although I am tempted to
speak of other people's experience here, certain matters of
delicacy do not permit it, so that I will continue my account

of my own limited personal experience. Having worked
out a method for getting children aged eight to ten to solve
problems that most students in the age group 14-16 found
difficult, thus making a methodological improvement of the
order of approximately 200 percent on my scale, I was
naturally ready to accept the plaudits and homage of teachers
who were, I supposed, awaiting this beneficence.   Alas, no
commendation was forthcoming, but rather--if I might appeal to literary sources--curses, both loud and deep. Typical reaction of teachers when told of these results were:
"I think it is monstrous to force logical thinking on imma-
ture minds;" "All you will succeed in doing is warping the
child's mind;" and this--which particularly grieves me--
"What right have you to play God?" It is easy to single
out the romantic naturalists, the embryological model theorists, the humanistic psychologists, or the Summerhillians
as the official spokesmen for such viewpoints, but I think
there is a kind of ambivalence in most of us about the desirability of producing, via external control, dramatic
changes in the behavior of a normal child.

At long last I have come back, not entirely in circular fashion I hope, to the point from which I started.   In
my view, until we are able to change the expectation of
senior educational decision makers and significant elements
of the public, to enlist not only their support but also their
demand for our inventive methodologies, the creator of such
methodology must be prepared to be something of a martyr.
Some may be willing to do this, but although I once felt I
might have made some modest contribution to mathematics
instruction, I am too thin-skinned to endure sustained criticism, or even the interminable hassle that invariably arises
from conferences of this kind between those who believe
that inventive methodology means, in the final analysis, that
one must be prepared to shape the child's behavior toward
well-defined goals and those who would have few external
controls, permitting the child to develop according to his
own "needs" and "nature." Thus, frustrated in the public
sphere, I have retreated into retirement where at least I
can try out my methods on my own children, imbibe the
fermented juices of Niagara District grapes, and write paro-
dies on educational practices and personalities.   And if all
attempts at honest employment fail, I can always make my
living as a professor of educational psychology.

"... we should keep in mind that the problem of
introducing an appropriate educational psychology component

into teacher training is part of the much larger task of
bringing psychological knowledge to bear upon educational
decision making in general."

PART III

NEW DIRECTIONS

MARGARET GILLETT

INTRODUCTION

The Canadian essayist and humorist, Stephen Leacock, writes of an impetuous horseman who races out of his home, swiftly mounts his steed, and rides off in all directions simultaneously. Foundation Studies could perhaps be following this fabulous cavalier. There are so many ways Foundation Studies can go into the future and we seem to be riding so many of them all at once. The possibilities range from the virtual extinction of Foundations to their proliferation or to their reappearance in many new and cross-bred guises.

Where Shall We Bury the Foundations?

The demise of Foundation Studies might be brought about from two divergent directions: from changes instituted, on the one hand by the practically-oriented reformers, and on the other by the academically-oriented. In the first case, the argument will be made that Foundation Studies should be discontinued simply because the curriculum cannot possibly accommodate all that the modern teacher needs to know, not even if basic teacher preparation programs are lengthened to five years, as is being advocated in some quarters. It is said to be a simple question of practical priorities. It is more important for the student teacher to have command of a body of knowledge and to learn techniques of classroom management, to understand child development and something of group dynamics, and to study the special needs of ethnic groups, inner city schools or other specific problems he is likely to encounter in his early years of teaching. With this kind of rationale, and in spite of the sort of arguments set forth in Part II, it is to be expected that "new" teacher preparation curricula will be developed with no Foundations allocation, or perhaps a mere token. The University of Guam,[1] for example, in its 1970-72 catalog lists only one Foundation course. This is an option called "Foundations of Education" which carried three credits (out of a degree total of 124) to-

ward the Bachelor of Education and is limited to seniors
who have the consent of the instructor. Another possibility
is that, if the teacher preparation curricula are made very
flexible in response to demands for freedom of choice,
Foundation Studies courses might wither away for lack of
customers. They might thus stay on the books for a while,
but only as dead letters because practically-minded students
do not choose to sign up. This may tend to happen even in
new patterns of teacher preparation which hope to humanize
the program. It will be interesting to see the fate of Foundation Studies in schemes such as the University of Florida's
New Elementary Program which abolished courses and regularly scheduled classes, replacing them with individual study
and small discussion groups. Foundation Studies are still
available, along with work usually treated in methods, curriculum, and testing courses, in the "substantive panel"
where the students have wide latitude of choices.[2]

Other new patterns of teacher education may involve
so much restructuring that Foundation Studies as such will
ostensibly disappear. One proposal, described as an "Integrated Teacher Education Program,"[3] seeks to rationalize
the entire operation. It is based on a task analysis of
teaching and involves provision for assessment of performance following training, demands that teacher education no
longer be the responsibility of the universities but of the
whole educational system, that graduates of this task-ana-
lytical approach to instruction be treated as a cadre group
and remain in close touch with the training institution.
Foundation Studies are apparently ignored in this kind of
proposal--at least there is no specific provision for them.
They may not necessarily be excluded when details were
worked out, but from the behavioristic thrust of the argument and the language of the proposal--"performance,"
"training," "instruction," and the like--it is not likely that
Foundations would be central to this kind of scheme.

This approach appears to be spreading quickly from
the proposal stage toward implementation. Thus, under the
rubrics of "competency based" or "performance based"
training, New York State has gone ahead with a scheme to
take teacher preparation away from the universities and
place it in "centers" where it will be "the performance that
counts." Competency based programs, which seem to be
rousing zealot support in pockets of reformism from East
coast to West, constitute a real and present danger to the
apparently "non-performing" Foundation Studies.

        The academically-oriented threat to Foundation Stud-
ies is perhaps not so much a threat to the studies themselves as to the professors. This kind of reorganization
would continue to give a place to the history of education,
philosophy of education, sociology of education and so on,
but that place would be in the academic departments in the
College of Arts rather than in the professional College of
Education. Conant and other "outside" reformers have recommended this change to legitimize Foundation courses by
bringing them into the mainstream of the humanities or social sciences where they could be taught by specialist scholars rather than educationists. Some educationists, who
still suffer from the inferiority complex of long-term second-
class academic citizenship and who speak of "academic" departments in hushed tones, also support this idea. Others,
of course, deny the dichotomy between "scholars" and "educationists" and see the need for keeping the educational emphasis in the Foundations by presenting the courses in a
scholarly way in the Colleges of Education. They also note
that other special forms of history have been under similar
pressure. History of Science, for example, is sometimes
located in History Departments, sometimes in Science--
both of which are academic. [4] However, both locations appear to have certain advantages and disadvantages that can
cause unhappiness for both professors and students. Which
arrangement makes for the best education has not yet been
finally determined.

        While this pedagogic issue thus remains unresolved,
some apologists for the status quo consider that the threat
of the abolition of Foundations Departments in favor of the
parallel departments in Arts is politically unreal, simply
because Education is generally such a numerically strong
college. Nevertheless, the closure of the Department of
Education at Johns Hopkins in 1971 shows that the improb-
able can happen--leaving the uneasy feeling that if a whole
program can go, Foundations courses of "questionable" worth
certainly might disappear.

        In spite of these gloomy forebodings, it is not yet
time to write the obituary for Foundation Studies. Indeed,
wedding invitations might be more in order as we have multiple marriages among the disciplines. In spite of pressures and complaints both within and without the field, there
are many people in Foundations with clear and positive suggestions for revitalization. Their exhortations are not based
on fear, but hope, and they give considerable zest and ex-

citement to the debate. There are calls, for example, for
"perspectives and purposes in foundational studies to become embracive and majestic."[5] "Embracive" and "majestic" are just two of the interesting developmental possibilities for Foundations, as changes occur in personnel,
methodologies, and subject matter.

The New People

        To think about changes in Foundation Studies is first
to think about the people involved. If we assume that Foundation Studies professors have the usual strengths and weaknesses of other human beings, that, like professors in other
areas, some of them are "good" at their work, some "poor,"
some are enthusiastic and committed, others mere function-
aries; and if, on top of all this, we recognize the dangers
of generalizing about thousands of highly schooled individuals, we might still join with Paul Nash's sweeping statement
(in the following paper) that "The whole role of the professor of foundations of education will have to change." It
seems indisputable that differences in the professor, his activities and his attitudes, are fundamental requirements for
venturing far into the future. Nash goes on to say of him:

                He will have to spend at least as much time in the
                schools as in the library. His classroom will
                have to be an epitome of the ideas and values he
                expresses. The time so often misspent in attempt-
                ing to gain respectability according to academic
                canons that are themselves gross anachronisms
                can be put to much better use. He should become
                a broker between the university and the schools,
                playing a unique communication role by being in
                touch with currents of opinion, need, experiment,
                and discovery in both. Above all, he should be
                the one who is most concerned with the complex
                relations between practice and theory with the dif-
                ficult task of enriching each with the other.

        This is a call for action that will not unseat the Foun-
dations professor, but will simply get him moving. It does
not suggest that he abandon theory, only that he enrich it
with relevance. The notion of his being a broker between
the university and the schools does not mean that the Foundations professor will have to be assigned to practice teaching supervision (something he probably hates because he feels

inadequate for that task), but opens wonderful possibilities.
Envision the Foundations professor holding his seminars,
not in the college, but in the schools with both student-
teachers and practicing teachers participating, discussing issues on the spot, grappling with questions of value in the
place where priorities are actually being established, "hack-
ing it" in the hurly burly of argument and open skepticism.
This may take courage.   But how salutary!

Nash opens the way for a détente between the competency based performers and the Foundations theorists.   He
shows that the latter are not against change, recognizes
that in the future more teacher education is likely to take
place in the schools and indicates that Foundations professors can and will be there where the action is.   It thus
seems tragically ironic that Nash's own Foundations department at Boston University is one of those being abolished by
a "new broom" president.

The Foundations professor of the future may have to
make a number of accommodations to the new realities, to
situations where his courses are no longer compulsory and
where he has to compete for his share of the declining enrollment.   Perhaps one of the hardest things he will have to
do is to learn not to be paternalistic.   Just because he himself has discovered the value of Foundation Studies and is
utterly convinced, he cannot impose his convictions upon the
young.   His dejà vu approach--I have been there before and,
despite what you think now, I can assure you that you will
find Foundation Studies to be of vital importance to your
teaching career--is passé.   It is unacceptable to the young.

One alternative might be for Foundations professors
to do what they have applauded in the schools since the
Progressive era--show more concern for the student.   The
plea for more feeling applies to them as much as to the
grade teacher.   Yet the reason so many Foundations courses
seem to be sterile, despite the academic qualifications and
the conscientiousness of the professors, is that they are so
often taught with the text, or the course, or the discipline
foremost.   The gulf between reason and emotion is perpetuated and this again is, at least in part, a product of the illusion that academic respectability lies in rigorous, no-non-
sense treatment that has a logical rather than a psychological base.   Among the assumptions that Nash makes as he
considers the future place of humanistic and behavioral studies in teacher education are that "feelings are part of the

human personality, that they are important determinants of
human thoughts, values, acts, and decisions, that they can
be influenced, refined, and modified, that they are of legitimate concern to educators." His inference is that feelings
can appropriately be included in a program of teacher education. This is not a banal conclusion. Consider that some
of the Woodstock generation are now in Foundation Studies
courses; if they are to be reached, their emotions cannot be
ignored. Old impersonal attitudes, old techniques will have
to be revamped.

The New Methodologies

Significant changes in Foundation Studies are currently under discussion among theoreticians, even if they have
not yet found their way to the college classroom. Many of
these are based on developments in methodologies--the conceptual changes derived from the methodological developments within the various contributing disciplines as well as
the pedagogic changes derived from the "revolution" in instructional methodology in general.

In the last few years, history of education, for example, has taken a lot of criticism. Attacks on the superficial historiography of historians of education were mounted
with some vehemence by Bernard Bailyn and others. Bailyn
complained about the development of spurious history of education by people who were not historians but educational
missionaries who "with great virtuosity ... drew up what
became the patristic literature of a powerful academic ec-
clesia,"[6] and who flourished in "almost total isolation from
the major influences and shaping minds of twentieth-century
historigoraphy."[7] He indicated that improvement would only
be possible when the self-engrossed, missionary concerns
were replaced by a broader definition of education and a different notion of historical relevance, a view that saw the
history of education not simply as the progress of pedagogy,
but as the full process by which culture is transmitted. In
an issue of Daedalus devoted to History, John Talbott pointed out some of the ways which a "new" history of education
may go. He agreed that a new concept of this interrelation-
ship of education and society has to be explored and much
that has been taken for granted must be examined critically.
The example he gave--the relationship of literacy to devel-
opment--was a crucial one. He called for more precise research into the history of education: "Research into who

actually got educated will lend a good deal more precision
to statements about the historical role of education in the
promotion of social mobility."[8] He wanted to know: "What
have been the social and political consequences of the paradoxical principle of the career open to talent, which holds
that everyone should have equal chance to become unequal."[9]
He recognized that establishing cause/effect relationships
between education and changes in other sections of society--
for example, the unexpected political consequences of educational change--are difficult to isolate, but most rewarding.
He also recognized the need for a new, precise historiography to replace the old Whig "progressive" view.

More criticism of the old methodology is discovered
in Colin Greer's The Great School Legend: A Revisionist
Interpretation of American Public Education. Greer asserts
that, "The assumption that extended schooling promotes
greater academic achievement or social mobility is ... entirely fallacious."[10] But he is at some pains to attack other revisionists, Bernard Bailyn and Lawrence Cremin.
Which goes to show that there is still plenty of life in the
historiography of education and it is highly probable that the
vigor of the critics will continue to keep the field in motion.
Thus, we can safely join with Edgar Bruce Wesley, author
of "Lo, the Poor History of Education" when he later concludes "I should change my title ... to 'Hail, the Flourishing History of Education'."[11]

R. Freeman Butts has joined the quest for new methodologies. In a paper included here, he notes that in the
past two decades, when half the world has come to political
independence, the enormous gap between the old nations
and the new has not only underscored human interdependence,
it has also shown that economic and social disparity is basically educational disparity. Historians in the U.S. and elsewhere have seen that the post-war revolutions required a
basic reinterpretation of the writing of history. The new
situation demanded that historians "confront the crisis point
which such social changes produce" and, according to Professor Butts, it is this kind of revision in historical scholarship that must provide the setting for reconstruction in the
history of education. Also, the "new" history of education
must have a conceptual framework that "will be suitable not
only for answering historical questions but will draw upon
the insights and germinating ideas to be gleaned from the
fundamental study of social change in related social sciences."

Butts also sees the need to relate historical generalization to the broad social problems, which are the concern
of other social sciences, in so far as they try to deal with
the major questions of the world. From a search of social
science literature, he identifies three recurring themes of
great relevance for the historical study of education: comparative analysis, international impact, social change. And
he arrives at a theory of modernization which can provide
the intellectual underpinnings--or as one historian phrased it,
"the central grouping concerns"--for research, writing, and
teaching in the history of education.

Both the contemporary call for strengthening the disciplinary bases of Foundation Studies and the demand for interdisciplinary approaches are evident in Professor Butts'
paper. The case for interdisciplinary approaches is encountered again and again in current writings on Foundation
Studies, sometimes espoused with a view to glean insights
from diverse disciplines, sometimes with a more specific,
action-type goal. The Teachers College, Columbia University Institute of Philosophy and Politics of Education (established in 1965 under the direction of Lawrence Cremin) offers a wide-ranging program of research in history, philosophy and social sciences as they affect educational theory and
policy making. The Institute's five major investigations in
1971 were all interdisciplinary: 1. studies of the socio-
economic correlates of metropolitan education; 2. studies of
cosmopolitanism and nationalism in nineteenth-century pedagogy; 3. studies of problems of ideology in theories and
practice of formal and informal education; 4. studies of the
development of American education; 5. studies of educational policy-making at the local level.

The name of the Institute itself and the nature of
these projects may well point to new directions for many
other institutions and individual researchers in Foundations.
Harold Noah and Max Eckstein, directors of the studies of
the socio-economic correlates in metropolitan education,
have brought new vigor to interdisciplinary, cross-national
research. Their writings even have the rare and valuable
quality of humor. Their book, Toward a Science of Comparative Education, is a significant signpost for comparative
educators of the future. In their view, clearer aims when
doing research and more precise criteria after the research
has been completed will point the way toward "an influential,
intellectually cogent, and elegant science of comparative education."[12] Andreas Kazamias, in a paper included here, al-

so manages to make the methodology of comparative education both lively and entertaining. He questions the "scientific" approach, bemoans the instrumental uses to which the
study of education has been put, and calls for a paradigm
that will look at education in relation to the individual rather
than to society.

Yet another interdisciplinary approach to Foundations
has been put forward by James W. Wagener. Wagener recommends that Foundations courses should deal with the phenomenon of knowledge, indeed, that knowledge should be the
basis of Foundation Studies.   Thus, the philosopher, sociologist, historian, psychologist would all make the rule of
knowledge the focus of their attentions. He argues, in a
paper reproduced here, that the knowledge revolution and
the symbiosis between knowledge and society require a re-
ordering of teacher preparation.   He notes that the need is
not so much for the arithmetic teacher to prepare the future
engineer to fit into a set vocation as it is to explore how
arithmetic and other modes of quantification make a new
conceptual world which the engineer will share in creating.
In this view, the Foundations area should take as the target
of analysis the configuration of knowledge as it defines and
reshapes both the learner and his environment.

The dimensions of interdisciplinary research related
to the Foundations of Education seem infinite.   If Foundations professors follow the advice of Martin Levit, they will
consider an inquiry oriented approach, the purpose of which
is not to describe or prescribe roles and rules that do or
should exist, but rather to evaluate critically "sets of educational roles and rules and the criteria used to accept or
reject them."[13]   This view conceives Foundations professors as actively contributing to the improvement of educational policies and practices.   It also results in a consideration of the multiple, interlocking sets of dependency relationships between systems of objects, properties, and events.
Levit suggests how inquiry must take note of the significant
connections between domains formerly considered unrelated,
areas such as culture, biochemistry and individual choice.
He notes that there is no such thing as a really closed system; neither is there a bifurcation of "individual" and "society," so that the need is for inquiry to take into account
the comprehensiveness and inter-connectibility of systems.

The systems approach has other proponents.   A
brief statement by Herbert K. Heger, included here, is an

attempt to develop an ecological systems approach to teacher education. It is based on the recognition that all people
live and work within a total environmental system and within particular sub-systems, so that their actions and decisions can reverberate from sub-system to sub-system, and
even to the total system. This concept applied to the Social Foundations could lead to the development of a technique that would "increase curricular congruence." Such a
technique might involve the use of simulation and field experience as well as the development of hypotheses about the
dynamic forces at play within the model.

These kinds of ideas are more fully developed in
Moses Stambler's paper, "A Systems Approach Model for a
Disciplined Organization of a Social Foundations of Education Course," also included in this Part. Stambler recognizes the futility and the wastage involved in many Foundation Studies courses which consume enormous amounts of
fragmented material without the use of disciplined analysis
that would make the information transferable and applicable
to the school scene. He also believes that attempts to organize material through the social science disciplines often
result in syntheses that are not only limited but also anachronistic. He describes in some detail a system which
would enable Foundation Studies professors to think through
nodal problems so that a logical, consistent and coherent
organization for their courses can be designed.

The methodology and concerns of futurology also hold
potential for the "new" Foundations. The accelerating pace
of change outmodes information, techniques, ideas, even
language. All Foundations professors, even the most conservative, are, by the very nature of their profession, preparing for the future--they are preparing future teachers
who will teach future generations who will live and work in
the 21st century. Serious interest in understanding and con-
trolling the future is widespread--not just among the astrol-
ogers or palm and teacup readers, not just among mystics
or visionaries, not just among "original" intellectuals like
Lewis Mumford or Buckminster Fuller or Marshall McLuhan, but also among everyday social scientists. Their work
with Delphi techniques and other modes of prediction is already used by educational administrators and their ideas are
filtering down with surprising rapidity. Thus, books like
Future Shock command long-term stands on the best-seller
list. In this work we find the call:

It is no longer sufficient for Johnny to understand
the past. It is not even enough for him to understand the present, for the here-and-now environment will soon vanish. Johnny must learn to anticipate the directions and rate of change. He
must, to put it technically, learn to make repeated, probabilistic increasingly long-range assumptions about the future. And so must Johnny's
teachers. [14]

It is gratifying to note that educators have not waited
for this kind of directive before taking action. New kinds of
future-oriented Education programs are already taking shape.
At Teachers College, Columbia University, for example,
there is recognition that:

In addition to having competence in such customary
fields as administration, facilities planning, and
personnel management, the new educational leader
will have to be well grounded in sociology, economics, and political science. He or she, must be
able to utilize sophisticated methods of analysis,
for it becomes increasingly clear that no process
or system of education is universally applicable.
Tomorrow's educators will find assignments not
only in schools or other traditional institutions.
They will work also in government, in the community, in industry, in voluntary enterprises--in
short, wherever people seek to learn and wherever
educational influences can assist human development. [15]

Among the specific ways designed to fulfill these goals is
the three-year doctoral Program of Educational Leadership,
through which students participate in revolving internships in
government, educational industry, school administration, and
the like. Their courses, which cut right across depart-
mental boundaries, include work in the humanities, political
sciences, sociology and economics, as well as professional
specialities. They also involve training in technological
areas such as computer simulation and situational analysis,
sophisticated tools for helping observers record and evaluate
what actually happens in situations of human interaction.

Programs involving complex, experimental techniques
and research methodologies at present are largely, but not
exclusively, restricted to the graduate level. In the future,

they will be incorporated with increasing frequency into regular teacher preparation programs, but already new instructional methodologies are becoming part of the Foundations
scene.   The whole spectrum of innovations in technological
aids, materials, organization of classes, and emphases on
learning experiences rather than teaching techniques is open
to the Foundations professor.   In practice, some may still
cling to the book as the proper method and mode of communication and perhaps they need to be reminded that even as
classic a text as Cubberly's history of education had an accompanying set of slides.   All the contemporary counter-
parts--film, videotape, computers, cassettes and the rest--
do not need to be enumerated here but perhaps it should be
noted that a particularly useful source of analysis and criticism of education and society is available in the Canadian
Broadcasting Corporation's Learning Systems tapes.   With
these, seminar groups or individual students can hear people
like Illich, McLuhan or Goodman, whose voices may stimulate much more than their printed words.

The current debate over the role and efficacy of
Foundations Studies along with vocal student protests should
stir many into a re-examination of their methods and a realization that professor-dominated lectures are not acceptable
to the products of the child-centered school--or to the tax-
payers.   It may be an epoch, or it may be a phase, but we
seem to live in a time when God and the teacher may both
be dead.   Certainly, paternalistic pedagogy is passé.   Increased flexibility in Foundations classes is surely necessary; hopefully, it is also inevitable.   The School of Education at the University of Massachusetts may have set a precedent in 1971 by modularizing its course structure, thus
permitting great variation in the treatment of Foundation
Studies as well as the other components of the teacher education program.   Modules, a manifestation of the trend towards "adhocracy," lend themselves to intensive if brief
treatment of current issues or traditional topics.   Workshops,
field work, encounter and shadow techniques, simulation
games can all become accepted parts of the Foundations
repetoire.   Techniques may be borrowed from the humanities
as well as the social sciences--thus, there seems to be a
growing interest in the use of literature in Foundations
courses.   For example, the role of the teacher in novels,
plays, films and television continues to gather attention.[16]

It is obvious that these changes in classroom procedures are not necessarily or inherently "good."   They can be

abused, they can be as boring as note taking, or as arid as
a list of dates. They can fragment and they can generate
activity without reflection. But, when coupled with the new
research interests and the new methodologies derived from
the contributing disciplines, they have potential to revitalize
Foundation Studies. New life may also come to Foundations
from an expansion of their scope through the emergence of
new fields of study or through the application of different
"old" ones to the problems of education. Consider how old
is the notion behind "Philosophizing--A Radical Proposal for
Teacher Training," in this Part!

The "New" Studies

        The question of definition of the Foundation Studies
has been dealt with extensively in the Introduction to Part I
and is touched upon in a number of other papers in this
collection. It has been noted that Foundation Studies were
long recognized as four: History of Education, Philosophy
of Education, Comparative Education, and Psychology of
Education. Sociology has been gathered in in recent decades, while Psychology has tended to separate itself as an
independent discipline. International Education has become
recognized as distinct from Comparative and, as educators
have become more deeply involved with the cultural complexities of their field, anthropology, political science, economics have been brought into the fold of Foundation Studies.
Religion, too, is sometimes included as one of the Foundations. This broad range of contributing disciplines drawn
from the humanities, social sciences and behavioral sciences has not stopped expanding. The future of Foundation
Studies is likely to be one of still broadened scope.

        While this expansion may appear healthy, we have
learned in the last few years not to accept growth as an un-
alloyed good. The new interests may potentially infuse
more contemporary relevance but they may fragment the
Foundation Studies still more and intensify the debate about
the viability of Foundations. They may challenge, even
threaten, the older studies and they will certainly compete
with them for time, dollars, and students. However, they
are coming.

        One of the areas that bids fair to win a more gener-
ally recognized place in the Foundational Studies is the Aesthetics of Education. It is true that aesthetics as a field of

study is not new; it can be traced back, if not to Aristotle, at least two hundred years to the work of the German philosopher, Alexander Baumgarten, but Aesthetics of Education is not yet widely taught on this continent. It is already firmly established at the University of Illinois where a new doctoral program, within the Department of History and Philosophy of Education, was set up in 1971. Ralph A. Smith, of the University of Illinois and founding editor of the Journal of Aesthetic Education, has contributed a paper to this Part explaining the nature and role of Aesthetic Education in teacher preparation. His rationale depends on both the growth of the study of aesthetics, itself, and on the special character of the demands of our emerging leisure society. The new society will be one in which social arrangements, including institutional forms of education, will be justified increasingly in terms of aesthetic experiences and values. Smith argues that Aesthetic Education, like the other Foundational Studies, provides knowledge for the interpretation of problems rather than application for their solution. The perspective it provides may not be a sufficient condition for solving practical problems, but it is a necessary one since interpretation determines the direction in which thought and action will proceed. Aesthetic Education makes a fundamental contribution to the understanding of the theoretical issues underlying educational activities and provides the kinds of insights which characterize the professional worker in a complex field such as education.

     The aesthetic dimension is also part of the growing concern for environmental education. As the schools are charged more and more with the task of engendering respect for the natural environment, so teacher education will have to accommodate this new responsibility. Thus, another new direction for Foundation Studies to explore is environmental studies. A summary of relationship between Foundation Studies and environmental studies is found in Edward Weisse's brief statement, while a more extended treatment appears in Margaret Gillett's "The Ecology of Education"--both of which are reproduced in this Part.

     Concerns of this sort are obviously stimulated by current socio-political controversies, but they are far more than temporary excitements or passing fads. They recognize forms of human needs that have been overlooked in the onrush of technology: the need for space, the need for quiet, the need for beauty. They are based on a worldview in harmony with Schweitzer's "reverence for life" and,

since they are involved with both values and process, they
are vital rather than static.   They may draw their data and
concepts from established fields such as the now-fashionable
ecology or the somewhat neglected discipline of geography.
The issue of school busing, for example, can be re-inter-
preted in the light of spatial dynamics, or the question of
curriculum in terms of wastage and pollution.   New perspectives on many old political, economic, or human problems might emerge with the development of a new interdisciplinary discipline such as "Ecography."[17] This has been
identified as a study of facts and values which describe and
control man's interaction with his habitat and as a disciplinary beachhead in what appears to be a critical no-man's
land between the two cultures of science.   Whether or not
ecography achieves the disciplinary status of an academic
department, it has an enormous potential contribution for
the Foundations of Education.

As an extension of this kind of interest in natural
and physical environments, and as an outcome of current
emphasis on the wholeness of human nature and the desirability of unified development, it is possible that Foundations of Education might be extended to include biological
studies.   The case for biological studies, their inter-con-
nection with moral questions and their foundational role in
teacher preparation might also be made.   Biological studies,
which would provide a disciplinary base for discussion of issues such as sex education or racial discrimination, may
not readily win wide acceptance in traditional Foundations
departments, yet they may be welcomed as segments of
Foundations courses, just as urban studies, black studies
and women's studies have been.   Modularization will make
this easier.

Some degree of resistance may also be encountered
toward "The Future of Education" as a serious, substantive
course of study.   Yet reputable scholars have produced a
significant body of literature that deserves, even demands,
systematic, critical analysis by the teacher of the future.
The Future of Education might have a number of different
intellectual bases--for example, Buckminster Fuller's "com-
prensive anticipatory design science" or Robert Specht's
view that the responsibility of the scholar is to recognize issues which are likely to become important in the future,
rather than to divine the future.[18]   And there would be no
dearth of materials for study[19]--not only actuarial figures
and statistical projections, but all the utopias and anti-

utopias in literature, from The Republic to Walden II and
Beyond Freedom and Dignity; the proceedings of the many
conferences on "Education for the 70's," "Teacher Education for the 70's," "Towards 2000" and others stimulated
by the turn of the decade or the upcoming millenium; the
World Future Society's reports, its journal, The Futurist,
its bibliographies and lists of films; research prepared for
gatherings such as the American Anthropological Association's symposium on Cultural Futurology (1970); and, above
all, the speculations of imaginative educators who are not
afraid to confront the new temporal dimension.   Futurists
such as Alvin Toffler point out that at present, the children in our schools are focussed backward rather than forward; they are given courses in history but then time comes
racing to a halt.   Toffler claims that there is no good reason why the future should be banned from the schools, why
courses in the possibilities and probabilities of the future
should not be explored, just as we now explore and recon-
struct the historical and archeological past.

   "The Future of Education" as a Foundational Study is
not pure fantasy, but it will deal with neither received nor
empirically validated truths.   It will, of course, be highly
speculative and may lead to a new realm of "Meta-Educa-
tion" or, to follow a model from science, to "Trans-Educa-
tion."   The Director of the Oak Ridge National Laboratory
points the way:

> Many of the issues that lie at the interface be-
> tween science and politics involve questions that
> can be stated in scientific terms but are in prin-
> ciple beyond the proficiency of science to answer.
> In a recent paper in Minerva, I proposed the term
> 'trans-scientific' for such questions.   For example,
> the biological effect on humans of very low level
> radiation (or of other physical insult, for that mat-
> ter) will probably never be fully ascertained,
> simply because of the huge number of animals re-
> quired to demonstrate an unequivocal effect.   Esti-
> mates of extremely unlikely events (such as a seri-
> ous reactor accident) can never be made with any-
> thing like the scientific validity that one can apply
> to estimates of events for which there are abun-
> dant statistics.[20]

He also notes that in current attempts to weigh the benefits
of technology against its risks, the protagonists are asking

for the impossible--namely, scientific answers to questions
that are trans-scientific. In matters of science, the scientist can bring his expertise to bear to establish scientific
truth; in matters of trans-science, he can, at most, help
delineate where science ends and trans-science begins.
Education faces similar problems. The scientific educator
may help establish scientific truths through accepted scientific methods; the trans-educator, like the trans-scientist,
will seek wisdom (rather than truth) through new procedures
which are adjudicative and political and that will involve
(even welcome) participation from the uninitiated public.

Another controversial new approach, one with Marx-
ian overtones, is suggested in the paper by Wayne Urban on
Social Foundations, included in this Part. Urban takes his
point of departure from two important Foundation Studies
models, namely the programs at Teachers College, Columbia University and at the University of Illinois. According
to his analysis, the first of these emphasized ideologies and
ideals, while the second was based on W. O. Stanley's methodological principle of authority. Urban, drawing upon the
ideas of C. Wright Mills, recommends using the theory of
bureaucracy and recognizing teachers and their organizations
as the agencies of future educational reform. Bureaucracy
and teachers' organizations, generally overlooked in the past,
demand more prominence in the Foundations courses of the
future.

The papers assembled here do not represent all the
possible new directions in which Foundation Studies may develop. They do not necessarily even present a coherent
pattern, nor do they make pat predictions. Hopefully, however, they suggest the wealth of possibilities that exist for
the development of the field. But lest innovation and expansion should get out of hand, we end with a warning from
Patricia Mills entitled, "Which Way is Up? Some Caution-
ary Notes to Model Builders in Teacher Education." Nevertheless, the possibilities for revised attitudes, experimental
methodologies, inputs from new disciplines, and innovative
teaching techniques are all here for the Foundations professor to choose and use. It has been said that in the practical, rapidly-changing world of Business Administration, experience is no longer more valuable than training. It has
been stated that the half-life of the engineer does not need
to flicker out before in the face of technological advances if
he is not taught engineering as it was done yesterday, but
is given the proper foundations. If this is to hold true for

education, Foundation Studies professors must be among
those who provide ideas for the future and who protect the
entire educational endeavor from obsolescence.

Notes

1. A U.S. institution which began in 1952 as a teacher-
    training school, was accredited as a degree grant-
    ing college in 1965, and became a university with
    graduate offerings in 1968.
2. See, A. W. Coombs, et al., Florida Studies in the
    Helping Professions. Social Science Monograph
    No. 37. Gainesville: University of Florida Press,
    1969; and Robert Blume, "Humanizing Teacher
    Education," Phi Delta Kappan, March 1971, pp.
    411-15.
3. John Macdonald, The Discernible Teacher. Ottawa:
    Canadian Teacher's Federation, 1970. See es-
    pecially pp. 1-21.
4. For a discussion of this problem see Thomas S. Kuhn,
    "The Relations Between History and History of
    Science," Daedalus, Spring 1971, pp. 271-304.
5. Martin Levit, "The Study of Education," mimeographed
    paper, prepared for the National Standing Confer-
    ence on Humanistic and Behavioral Studies in Edu-
    cation, April 1971, p. 191.
6. Bernard Bailyn, Education in the Forming of Ameri-
    can Society: Needs and Opportunities for Re-
    search. Chapel Hill: University of North Caro-
    lina Press, 1966, p. 8.
7. Ibid., p. 9.
8. John E. Talbott, "The History of Education," Daedalus,
    Winter 1971, pp. 133-50.
9. Ibid.
10. Colin Greer, The Great School Legend: A Reconstruc-
    tionist Interpretation of American Public Educa-
    tion. New York: Basic Books, 1972, p. 109.
11. Edgar Bruce Wesley, "Lo, the Poor History of Educa-
    tion," History of Education Quarterly, Vol. IX
    No. 3 (Fall 1969), p. 342.
12. Harold J. Noah and Max A. Eckstein, Toward a Sci-
    ence of Comparative Education. New York: The
    Macmillan Company, 1969.
13. Martin Levit, op. cit., p. 6.
14. Alvin Toffler, Future Shock. New York: Bantam
    Books, 1971, p. 403.

15. "New Leaders for Tomorrow's Education," Perspectives in Education. Teachers College, Columbia University, Winter 1971, pp. 5-6.

16. See, for example, John Farrell, "The Teacher Image in Fiction," McGill Journal of Education, Vol. V No. 2 (Fall 1970), pp. 121-32. An ongoing report of new programs and experiments in Foundations courses may be found in the Newsletter of the American Educational Studies Association, edited by Cole S. Brembeck of Michigan State University.

17. See Everett M. Hafner, "Toward a New Discipline for the Seventies: Ecography," Ecotactics. New York: Simon and Schuster, 1970, pp. 211-19.

18. See Buckminster Fuller, Education Automation. Carbondale: Southern Illinois University Press, 1962; and Werner Z. Hirsch et al., Inventing Education for the Future. San Francisco: Chandler Publishing Co., 1967.

19. Harold G. and June Grant Shane, in a paper called "Forecast for the Seventies" in Today's Education (Washington: N.E.A., January 1969), reported having studied about 400 published and unpublished articles and books dealing with educational projections and conjectures for the remainder of the twentieth century. See also "Courses in Futuristics Grow in Number and Variety," The Futurist, August 1972, pp. 158-60.

20. Alvin M. Weinberg, "Science and Trans-Science," Science, Vol. 177, No. 4045 (21 July 1972), p. 211.

PAUL NASH

1. THE MAJOR PURPOSES OF HUMANISTIC AND BHAVIORAL STUDIES IN TEACHER EDUCATION*

I have assumed that my task has been to reflect on what should be the major purposes of humanistic and be-havioral studies in teacher education. As I did this, I be-gan to fantasize: what would it be like if there were no humanistic or behavioral studies in programs of teacher edu-cation? Should we be worse off? Would the teachers in training be worse off? And would the children they teach suffer? There can be little doubt that we professors of Foundations of Education would suffer, at least in the short run, for we would have to find alternative ways of making an honest or dishonest living, perhaps by going back to teach the school children whose needs and abilities we discuss with such easy authority. But that might eventually be a salutary experience both for us and for our students. As for the teachers and their students, I am not aware of any evidence that demonstrates the value of humanistic and be-havioral studies in the lives of those who undergo them and of those whom they teach.

Two pictures came strongly to my mind during my fantasy. One was of my own teaching in elementary and secondary slum schools in London after World War II. I remember that many of my colleagues were products of the post-war Emergency Teacher Training Program, which pro-vided six months' training for mature people, many of whom had not even completed high school but who had tried other occupations and now wished to move into teaching. In my recollection, these briefly and minimally trained men and women were almost invariably the liveliest, most interest-ing, most committed, and most effective teachers in the school, often making their graduate colleagues look dull and

---

*Prepared for the working conference of the National Standing Conference on Humanistic and Behavioral Studies in Educa-tion, AACTE, Washington, D.C., April 14-15, 1971.

heavy by comparison.

The other picture that came to my mind was of the
large number of doctoral students in education that I have observed and come to know as they have slowly passed through
their programs at universities with which I have been associated. As these students build up credits towards their doctorates, the credits appear to pile on top of them, weighing
them down. The students become more morose, dull, and
stupid as time passes and they approach their appropriately
named terminal degree. By "stupid," I mean that they appear to become increasingly unwilling to take decisions and
responsibility, to make up their own minds, to trust their
judgments, or to be in touch with their own reactions, feelings, or convictions.

What this fantasy said to me was that I should be justified in refusing to take for granted that anything that at
present goes on in institutions of teacher education is of self
evident value, either to those who experience it or to those
whose lives they will affect. Given this stance, I began to
think not in terms of what teacher education is, what purpose it now serves, what external and institutional pressures
it now responds to, what traditions and thought patterns it
brings to the present, but rather in terms of what needs and
desires I perceive as being paramount in children I meet and
talk with, in my own students who are teachers or preparing
to be teachers, and, not least, in myself. These needs and
desires stem from one's inner dynamics as they interact with
contemporary social forces.

In a preliminary view of this analysis, I see the needs
and desires of all three constituents as falling into three
parts. We seem to be asking for help in learning how to
feel, learning how to think, and learning how to act. I suggest, therefore, that an analysis of the purposes of humanistic and behavioral studies in teacher education might be made
under these three rubrics.

I

First, let me make clear that this threefold division
is made merely for purposes of easier handling. It implies
no clear or distinct separation between any of the categories.
On the contrary, it will be a vital part of my case not only
that the three categories are overlapping and interpenetrating

but also that their operations crucially affect and influence one another in ways that should be at the heart of our educational concern.

My argument rests on the assumption that feelings are part of the human personality, that they are important determinants of human thoughts, values, acts, and decisions, that they can be influenced, refined, and modified, that they are of legitimate concern to educators, and on the inference that they can be appropriately included in a program of teacher education.

When I listen to young people, in an attempt to assess what are their strongest needs and desires, a number of recurrent themes come through, themes that evoke strong responses in my own emotional life. These themes manifest themselves in two characteristic ways: a feeling of oppression, of being stifled or being prevented from satisfying a need or fulfilling a desire; and a feeling of hope or aspiration, often utopian or fantastic, about what life might be like. A typical theme is that of feeling purposeless, drifting, not sure where you are going or even where you want to go. In helping students to explore their own feelings of oppression, I have found this mood of purposelessness to be the commonest manifestation. They want to feel more sure of their own values. To achieve this, they feel a need first to know more about themselves. Still not sure who they are, and hence what they might choose to become , they feel unable to get out of the bind of respecting and pleasing only others, never themselves. This oppression is experienced as a feeling of dehumanization, or depersonalization. They want strongly to feel more fully human but do not know how to go about it; and they feel incapable of helping others to grow in this way until they have made some significant progress themselves. Hence, they often feel panic at the prospect of entering teaching as phony pretenders.

Another characteristic theme is the feeling of being isolated. Not only young but also many middle-aged people among the population of students and teachers I am speaking about hunger for a significant experience of community. They feel this lack as one of the most oppressive qualities of their lives. At a deep level they feel drawn towards their fellows and long for an experience of intimacy and communion. But their personal histories, their education, and their perceptions of social and economic demands keep them apart.

In circumstances of great warmth, security, approval, and support, they are able to make some tentative advances towards one another. But, given a somewhat more threatening or uncertain environment, they are easily trapped into a mutually fearful, competitive stance. Their old upbringing and training then induce them to seek to win, to beat, to exploit, to manipulate. These old forms of behavior are then further reinforced by the university's mechanisms of grading, testing, examining, and so on.

Thus isolated, they experience another feeling that emerges as a characteristic theme, that is, alienation. An increasing number of teachers and prospective teachers appear to feel alienated from mainstream American values and attitudes. They are outraged when they observe the blindness, indifference, or even condonation with which the majority of the American people permit a small group to profit through the destruction of the culture, the economy and the ecology of ancient civilizations, and through the depredation of the cities and natural environment of the United States. Their outrage is felt as a slow burning anger and yet it is mute and despairing, for another of their characteristic feelings is of impotence.

Although many of these students feel that many things are terribly wrong with their society and fear for the future that faces the children they will teach, they feel largely powerless to do anything significant to save either themselves or their children. In this, they are reflecting a wider malaise in our society. Many people seem to have lost faith in themselves as important, functioning persons and hence it is hard for them to conceive that ordinary people can effect significant change. For this reason they look for leadership to political salesmen, to gurus, to fashionable writers, even to professors of education. It is only when we ourselves become one of those to whom others look for leadership that we realize how appallingly dangerous are the feelings of impotence that render them so easily frightened, led, and deceived.

Most poignant of all these characteristic themes is the feeling of being anesthetized, the feeling of being unable to feel. Many people with whom I talk find their oppression in an experience of the vicariousness of life. Everything is indirect, once removed, fuzzy, opaque. The illustrations range from the bland anonymity of supermarket food to the technological vicariousness of the American bomber crew dropping high explosive and napalm on Vietnamese peasants whom they never see. American business has mastered the art of creating desire and, when we reach out to satisfy it, putting in our hand an intermediate product for which we have no use. Advertising parades an unending sequence of beautiful young women, apparently for my pleasure, but when I move to consummate the arrangement I discover that all that is available is the bottle of beer or package of ciga- rettes or automobile that the young woman is selling. By being constantly immersed in a polluted ocean of this deceit, by living constantly under the stress of this stimulus-re- sponse-substitute-no satisfaction game, we come to distrust our feelings and the guidance they might give us.

When measured against these perceived needs, ex- pressed through feelings of oppression and the desires that are often the reverse side of that oppression, teacher educa- tion in this country does not strike me as a particularly rele- vant, important, or humane activity. Rather, it appears most often to be merely another aspect of the oppressions that these people feel. It usually either ignores feeling or treats it as something to be controlled or transcended. The civilized person is often presented as one who has success- fully expunged or controlled all expression of spontaneous feeling, especially inconvenient or threatening ones like anger, hostility, physical affection, or intimacy. Teacher education programs seem largely unemancipated from the notion of a mind/body dualism; they are vulnerable to the tryanny of pseudo objectivity; they are often guilty of inappropriate uses of scientific method; they are apt to overemphasize the cog- nitive dimension of learning, especially when it is abstracted from personal experience; and they rarely work as a con- structive force in counteracting the experience of personal disintegrity that is such a characteristic product of formal education.

In place of these characteristic manifestations of a domesticating education I should like to see the purposes of humanistic and behavioral studies purified in the light of the genuine needs and desires of contemporary students and teachers. This will necessitate, in the first place, consid- erable emphasis on unlearning. Before most of the students I encounter are able to move forward they must be helped to unlearn many of the habits and assumptions they bring with them. In particular, I refer to their typical marks of do- mestication: their habits of subordination, obedience, wait- ing, following, and accepting domination and oppression with

resigned patience.   They need to unlearn their habitual mistrust of their own feelings, reactions, and intuitions.

Then we can go forward into these experiences that
can build self trust, self respect, refinement of and sensitivity to feelings--one's own and others'.   For this purpose
all studies can be used, but we need to be much more imaginative and experimental in exploring the uses of the humanities, the arts, religion, and human relations.   One of
the major revolutions needed in teacher education concerns
the role of psychology.   In the first place, we need to liberate teacher education programs from their present domination by psychology, thus allowing the field to be nurtured
by the many other ways of studying educational problems
(not only the philosophical, historical, and sociological, but
also the economic, political, aesthetic, comparative, literary, anthropological, and religious) that are at present
grossly underutilized.   Secondly, we need to liberate psychology itself from its quantitative and reductionist strait
jacket.   This will involve giving greater attention to psychiatry, existential and humanistic psychology, social and community psychology, gestalt psychotherapy, and the whole
realm of the unconscious as a major element in the study of
education.   The miserably thin, quantitative pablum that is
fed to students of education in the name of psychology is a
caricature of what it could and should be.

Most of all, the dimension of feeling can be explored
and developed through the field of human relations.   Sensitivity training is both fashionable and much abused.   It is
being widely introduced, is popular with students, and is often practiced by incompetent leaders and advocated by fanati-
cal missionaries.   But we would do well not to be misled
into errors of policy judgment by its failings.   For this is
without doubt a tool with tremendous power for good, as
well as with corresponding dangers.   And the fact that
people respond to its invitations in enormous numbers should
warn us that, whatever the quality of the experience they obtain, the existence of an undeniable need is remarkably
demonstrated.   This need is what I have been adumbrating
in this section: the restoration of feeling to a respected and
significant place in human life and education.

The strongest indictment that could be made of contemporary programs of humanistic and behavioral studies in
teacher education is one that I lack the proof to substantiate
but that I suspect may be true or largely true.   It is that

these studies make not the slightest different to what the
trained teacher does either in the classroom or in everyday
life. To the extent that this is true, I believe that it is because these studies purport to be intellectual but are merely
irrelevant. They are irrelevant because they touch neither
the personal feeling level at one end nor the commitment to
action level at the other. A genuinely effective program of
studies must help the student to do all three: to get in touch
with his feelings and to trust his gut preferences; to conceptualize from these beginnings in forms that can be tested
against public standards; and to translate these feelings and
conceptualizations into value positions that will ensue in consistent action. But we must start the process with respect
for the domain of feeling. This means that these studies
must stem from the students' direct experiences, must be
felt by them to be both real and important, and must lead to
an experientially grounded understanding of the self and others. In practice, this becomes a process of problematizing
personal, existential situations. This stage leads naturally
to a consideration of learning how to think. But because of
the integration of feeling with conceptualizing, our thinking
processes will no longer be at the mercy of unexamined emotional drives.

II

I have suggested that a second major purpose of humanistic and behavioral studies in teacher education is to
help students to learn how to think. This is a sufficently
ambiguous injunction to need explication. Let me relate this
to my remarks about the restoration of the dimension of feeling to education. It can be inferred, I trust, from what I
have already said, that matters will not be improved if we
merely topple intellectualism from its narrow perch and put
feeling in place of thinking or body in place of mind. The
expression of feeling does not itself lead to new insight or
transferable learning. For this to happen, feelings need to
be conceptually clarified and understood in relation to one's
own life and to the needs and demands of others.

Moreover, the substitution of feeling for thinking
would do nothing to relieve the dichotomies I have already
criticized. What is needed, rather, is to help students gain
understanding of the separation of feeling, thought, and action, of the harmful consequences of this separation, and of
ways in which human wholeness can be restored. There is

a great need in teacher education, as in education generally,
for a primitivization of perception and feeling, a descent to
a deeper level of unconscious stirring and spontaneous emotion.   But this should be encouraged not in order that we
can wallow at that level (although we should not ignore the
danger of premature return) but in order to use the fruits
of that primitivization to feed the imagination and then har-
ness it in the cause of richer conceptualization and more
potent action.   It is regression in the service of greater integrity.

Thinking of a sort is not absent from current programs in teacher education.   But that thinking is of the
crudest and lowest form.   Largely memorization, simple
organization, and reproduction, it encourages and develops
qualities like obedience, docility, passivity, reactiveness,
and spectatorship.   It is not surprising that students experiencing such programs subsequently teach in ways that
develop similar qualities in their pupils.   Instead, learning
how to think should involve primarily a growing confidence
in one's own intellectual processes, in one's own intuitions,
reflections, findings, personal knowledge, and commitments.
It should result in increased intellectual autonomy and less
derivative thinking.   Success in this endeavor can be measured by the degree to which students of education begin to
forsake their customary passive, non-initiating, non-partici-
pating intellectual behavior for a more pro-active, initiating,
participating style.

We must examine not only the forms and styles of
thinking that are encouraged by educational studies but also
the content of that thinking.   The most promising direction
for change would be to encourage students to think more
about their own first-hand experiences and feelings, for the
cardinal problem is to learn to relate practical experience
to theoretical understanding.   Our students should become
bridge builders between life in the classroom and life outside, both for themselves and later for their own students.
Not a small part of the difficulty in achieving this lies in
the fact that professors of education consistently teach that
learning is more vividly, functionally, and permanently
gained when it is based upon first-hand experience and has
existential relevance for the learner, and equally consistently ignore this teaching in their own pedagogical practice.

When we begin to develop this greater intellectual
autonomy and respect for one's own experiential insights

among students of education, then we can hope to raise the
generation of teacher-skeptics that we need. Teachers
should be skeptics not in the more recent sense of evaders
of commitment but in the original sense of incurable askers
of questions, being aware that no answer ever exhausts the
richness and complexity of reality. In particular, teachers
should be askers of questions that lead to new forms of thinking about teaching and learning. It is not enough for us to
train people to do more efficiently what is already being
done: we must educate them to create new concepts about
the nature and purpose of education. To continue what is being done is to sentence ourselves to live with conventional notions that are condemned, more swiftly than ever before, to
anachronism and irrelevance. Teachers and students should
engage in raising questions about every assumption upon which
education operates: they should ask why schools need buildings, why administrators need schools, why teachers need administrators, why learners need teachers, why education
needs schooling, and other similar and dissimilar questions.

Our greatest enemy is the unreflective momentum that
carries us all comfortably forward in familiar and unexamined
ways. Our thinking, therefore, should be primarily about the
purposes and consequences of what we do. As teachers, we
should be constantly asking "why" questions, not only about
things like grading procedures and the subjects we teach, but
about the overall impact and meaning of our very presence in
the classroom. Thence, perhaps, we and the teachers who
study with us can learn to become lifelong students of teaching.

How can these purposes be achieved in teacher education? Let us look breifly at the program in humanistic behavioral studies for some tentative illustrations. A problem
immediately arises. Since one learns to become more pro-
active, initiating, and participating in part by successfully
practicing these forms of behavior, it follows that programs
of educational studies should not be completely pre-planned.
Students should be involved actively in the collaborative designing, planning, and executing of the program, the learning
process, and the evaluation procedures. This means that it
would be inconsistent for me to lay down dogmatically my
plan for a program of studies. However, since my notion of
collaboration leaves an important place for faculty initiative
and participation, I feel free to offer some of my own preferences, acknowledging that these would in practice have to be
tempered and modified in the light of the actual situation fac-

ing me and the response or initiative of the students.

Overall, my intent would be to help the student to engage in reflection and dialogue on his feelings and experiences, with a view to the development of concepts, generalizations, evaluations, and applications.   As an educational
practitioner, the student is going to spend much of his professional life trying to make sense of his experiences, trying
to organize them and generalize about them in order to understand them, and then trying to act or decide wisely in the
light of this understanding.   His program of educational studies should reflect this expected pattern of professional life.
It should start by immersing him in personally relevant, non-
trivial experiences.   There should be significant clinical experience from the first year, as in the best medical schools
today.

This clinical approach should merge into a study of
significant problems.   The so-called disciplines that make up
the foundations of education will probably be retained, since
established interests in education are hard to dislodge, but
we should try to reduce the educational dysfunctionality of
their imperialist ambitions, jurisdictional obsessions, and
restrictive tone.   For the student tends to approach the study
of a discipline acceptingly and passively.   His relation to it
is that of a more or less entertained audience.   In order to
begin to be an active learner he must become dissatisfied.
Problems provide this possibility because of their openness,
their incompleteness, and their unsolved nature.   Since they
await solution, they invite the student to themselves as a creative participant.   Their difficulties present a challenge that
compels the student to face himself, his resources, goals,
standards of evaluation, and willingness to commit himself
to a position.   When he tackles a problem seriously, he becomes an agent of change, and his decisions affect both himself and society.   Thus the study of problems has within itself the possibility of both individual and social regeneration.
Various disciplines, their data, methods, and insights, can
be used in the study of problems but the disciplines must be
demythologized and demystified and restored to their rightful
and useful role as temporary vehicles, to be picked up and
dropped as convenient, rather than as permanent penitenti-
aries whose prisoners and guards spend much of their energies agonizing over the limits of their jurisdiction.

The dangers of the discipline approach lie not only
in the difficulty of breaking down the barriers between them

and thus letting the breezes of innovative and imaginative
thinking to blow through, but also in the temptation for the
instructor to allow the content to be determined by his own
research and theoretical bias rather than by the personal/
professional needs of the students.   When an instructor in
foundations of education teaches as if his students were planning to follow the same career as himself, he runs the risk
of having them merely write off his offerings as irrelevant
theorizing with no bearing on their practical problems.
Such pseudo-scholarly behavior is as much responsible for
anti-intellectualism in this country as are hard hats.

     Students who are to be educational practitioners need
to develop the ability to conceptualize about educational problems that seem important to them, to be skeptical about common sense and conventional solutions, to analyze, assess,
and use relevant research findings, and to formulate significant questions and hypotheses of their own.   They should also
become aware of the difference between a problem and a
mystery, of the dimensions and limitations of human power,
and of the necessity for living gracefully with that which cannot be changed.

     In order to become skillful and creative agents of so-
cial and educational change these students need to learn how
to operate in and create the kind of atmosphere where such
change can best occur.   Here again, skills, methods, and
insights from the field of human relations can be invaluable.
From this source much can be learned about the nature of
interdependent learning and about the gains that accrue from
supportive, noncompetitive, collaborative modes of relating.
The students can also learn that the group atmosphere that
best motivates people to learn to think creatively is one in
which there is much real listening, openness, trust, constructive feedback, and free speculation; in which people feel
free to think metaphorically, analogically, and absurdly; in
which there is great tolerance of fantasy, ambiguity, and new
ideas; in which people explicitly give each other credit for
their contributions, and point out the strengths and good
points in even crazy sounding notions; in which everyone
builds on what has gone before rather than knocking down
and starting afresh; and in which, instead of some winning
(those whose ideas prevail) and some losing (those whose
ideas are rejected), all win, because ideas are built upon
others' ideas and everyone feels he has a stake in the final
outcome.

But even creative conceptualizing is not sufficient as a goal of educational studies. Just as a focus on feeling can become a form of self indulgence, so a focus on thinking can become a kind of academic game. In order to skirt these dangers, feeling and thinking must be integrally related not only to each other but also to appropriate action. A successful program of educational studies will lead the student to a commitment to social, cultural, and educational change that will appear to him as the appropriate outcome of his self exploration and his conceptualizing. Not any action will receive his commitment but only that which grows out of his deeply felt and rationally examined values. Thus those studies that emphasize value clarification should have a central role in teacher education.

III

The principal failure in teacher education is the failure to ask why. We do not question with sufficient vigor why we do what we do. As a corollary, the most important task we can accomplish is to help teachers develop a clear sense of purpose. There is a great difference between knowing how to teach (which tends to provide short term success and the repetition thereafter of the successful formula) and being a student of education (which means being continuously involved in a reappraisal of one's actions, values, and purposes). Our programs of teacher education are, on the whole, better designed for the former than for the latter.

The third major purpose of humanistic and behavioral studies in teacher education, then, should be to develop the ability to relate the affective, cognitive, and conative in an integrated way. This will involve giving much more attention to problems of the will to act, decision making, value clarification, freedom and authority, and the quality of life. Perhaps professors are not well equipped to help others do this, for we seem to find it difficult to distinguish between rhetoric and reality, often appearing to believe that once a thing has been said or written it has also been done. A clear example lies in the history of progressive education. If one were to judge from written histories, one would think that the public schools of this country were revolutionized by Dewey's ideas in the first half of the twentieth century. But when one goes into the schools, he realizes that the authors of these books gathered their data in the

archives rather than in the schools. Similarly, professors
of education often appear to believe that it is enough for
them to advocate progressive pedagogy: it is not necessary
for them also to practice it. I am inclined to believe that
the relationship between theory and practice in education in
this country is represented not so much by a time lag, as
is often maintained, as by a complementarity: that is, the
theory becomes a substitute for the practice. It is rather
like listening to a sermon on Sunday. After hearing some
revolutionary educational rhetoric from one of our band of
hellfire entertainers and nodding our heads in agreement,
we all feel better and return to our jobs on Monday to do
the same thing as before.

     In order to make it more difficult to indulge in this
complacent inertia, programs of educational studies should
include a more searching examination of the prevailing values underlying characteristic behavior in American education. These should be measured against both the values that
each student pays lip service to and those that his behavior
manifests. We should assess the extent to which the idols
of the market place dominate American society and education: the values of competition, exploitation, manipulation,
control, selling oneself, buying others, gaining "contacts,"
winning "friends," using people as commodities. And we
should estimate what room there is for the values of humane living: cooperation, love, intimacy, equality, authen-
ticity, genuineness, openness, wholeness. There should be
in our program a re-examination of the model of man that
dominates conventional educational practice. The educational practitioner has a normative model (explicit or assumed)
of the educated person towards which he works: we should
help him to make his realization of this model clearer and
to judge how closely it corresponds to his examined values.

     Such an examination may well reveal to him that
many "problems" in American life and education, such as
the so-called racial problem, are not really problems in a
strict sense since they cannot be "solved" within the context
of the prevailing value system. Minor ameliorations may be
made and some of the grossest abuses can be reduced, but
there can be no real solution. The so-called racial problem cannot be solved because our value system (actual rather than ideal) pits men in individual competition with one another. It also insists that all must strive for success.
But the structure of society ensures that not all can succeed.
Many must fail according to prevailing standards and this

leads to widespread frustration, which emerges in scape-
goating and other repressive mechanisms. Blacks (or some
substitute for them) are necessary to American society as
failures, drop-outs, also-rans. When society believes in
the survival of the fittest there can be no "fit" without also
the "unfit." Blacks play the latter role for us, hence making success possible for others. We could not afford to
solve this problem, for it would threaten our basic values.

Nevertheless, many revolutions are already under way
in our society, as in the rest of the world, and as a result
many parts of our educational structure (including practices,
institutions, and values) are rapidly becoming maladaptive
and dysfunctional. Educational studies should make students
into educational revolutionaries. That is, they should not
only become dissatisfied with things as they are but they
should also become equipped with the experience, knowledge,
and skill to live in a revolutionary world and to help guide
the direction that revolution will take.

In aiding the student of education to learn how to act
in an integrated, consistent way, one of the major tasks is
to help him to be himself in a world that is trying hard to
make him everyone else. It is to be hoped that the process
of value clarification will enable him to see that success in
conventional terms is success defined by others, in ignorance and carelessness of his own unique needs and possibilities. There is another, self defined notion of success,
which involves him in the never-ending task of self discovery,
with the goal of establishing his own life style. With success in this endeavor, he can then break down the artificial
barriers between the personal and the professional. He can
perceive, for example, that there can be no so-called "professional ethics" distinct from his personal ethics. Then his
feelings and concepts will begin to emerge integrally through
his values, choices, and acts.

Clearly, for some of these things to come about,
there will have to be other changes in the pattern of humanistic and behavioral studies in teacher education. The whole
role of the professor of foundations of education will have to
change. He will have to spend at least as much time in the
schools as in the library. His classroom will have to be an
epitome of the ideas and values he expresses. The time so
often misspent in attempting to gain respectability according
to academic canons that are themselves gross anachronisms
can be put to much better use. He should become a broker

between the university and the schools, playing a unique communication role by being in touch with currents of opinion, need, experiment, and discovery in both. Above all, he should be the one who is most concerned with the complex relations between practice and theory and with the difficult task of enriching each with the other.

Furthermore, he should be working to dissolve the harmful dichotomy between the humanities and the behavioral sciences. Not only should both dimensions be found in every student's program, but both ways of looking at the world should inform the attack on every educational problem. Through the behavioral sciences the student can be helped to look at the world as it is, to encounter the impersonal demands made by the world, to respect intellect and cognition, to acknowledge the world of others, to envision civilization, and to meet the outside world as it moves towards him. But to end there is to leave the picture no more than half done. For through the humanities the student can be helped to look at the world as he would like it to be, to encounter the demands of his own personal wishes, to respect his fantasies, feelings, preferences, and values, and to meet the world from inside himself as he moves outwards to encounter others. At the present time, we fail to get maximum power from either approach because we use them in isolation from each other and do not benefit from their mutual strengthening.

Hence, the program in educational studies should include as a central focus the opportunity for the student to gain understanding of the nature of man, to study alternative models of the educated person, and to create his own model, not only from the materials of past and present, from history and science, but also from deep and careful introspection into his own personal past and present, the causes of his dehumanization and the sources of his hope. It is important that those who will become teachers be presented with alternative models of teaching because in their own student experiences they have been exposed for so long to so many bad models. Without an enlarged vision of human potentiality they will tend, under the stress of everyday pressures, to teach the way they were taught.

Even given these richer models of human possibility, however, teachers will quickly become discouraged and disillusioned unless we can also provide them with some of the human relations and organizational skills needed to bring

about the institutional changes required to permit these alternative human patterns to develop. Teachers usually lack
the experience, knowledge, and skill required to be effective
change agents, either in the classroom or in the wider institutional, community, and societal dimensions of education.
The program in educational studies should give high priority
to these needs. Means of bringing about educational change
should be systematically examined. Students should have
practice in effecting change in a specific location, perhaps
in the university itself, through the development of curricula,
the formulation of educational policy, and the gaining and responsible use of knowledge and power.

Similarly, since in this post-bureaucratic age they are
going to have to be able to bring about change by working
collaboratively with others in group situations, their program
should be conducted in such a way as to foster the skills of
collaborative planning, goal setting, and the conducting of
courses and programs. It should make available sensitivity
training and emphasize knowledge of group processes. One
of the ways in which we have kept teachers relatively powerless has been to teach them as if they were lonely scholars
preparing for a life of professional isolation in closed classrooms. Isolated people are easily controlled.

The dimension of values should infuse every stage of
the educational program. Evaluation should be constant and
pervasive. Although we could profitably dispense with most
of the grading that goes on in education, we need more evaluation of our processes and performance, especially in the
forms of self evaluation and honest feedback. The program
should provide frequent opportunities for students to engage,
in collaboration with fellow students and faculty, in the evaluation of their own behavior and performance, of the program, and of the faculty.

When all this has been said, however, it remains
true that our best efforts at pre-service education are puny.
If the teacher does not remain a continuous student of education throughout his career, our work is virtually worthless.
But it is much to expect from a teacher working in an unfavorable environment. It is necessary for teacher education
to continue day after day in every school. This would be
materially facilitated if we could end the unfortunate dichotomy between teaching and administration. There is no good
reason why every administrator should not teach, nor why
every teacher should not carry some administrative duties.

If the principal became again the head teacher he could be a key person in the necessary program of continuous in-service teacher education. But he would need help from the resources of the university. This is where the professors of foundations of education could play a vital role, providing support in the form of research data, human relations skills, consultation, and specialized knowledge. It is to be hoped that they would also represent in their persons models of the humane integration of feeling, thinking, and acting.

R. FREEMAN BUTTS

2. RECONSTRUCTION IN FOUNDATION STUDIES*

The revival of interest in the foundations of education
during the past half dozen years is a heartening sign of vitality and pertinence in the professional preparation of
teachers.[1] Not only has there been a rash of newly published books for use in foundations courses, but the professional educational societies most concerned have been holding joint consultations which have resulted in the formation
of A Standing Conference on the Humanistic and Behavioral
Studies in Teacher Education. This is a dramatic reversal
of the two-decade trend toward specialized and discrete interest in the particular foundational fields. The seven organizations are the History of Education Society, the Philosophy of Education Society, the John Dewey Society, the Society of Professors of Education, the American Association
of Colleges for Teacher Education, and the American Educational Studies Association. The last named society, formed
in 1968, has elicited remarkably widespread interest because
one of its explicit purposes is to try to improve the general
courses in the foundations of education. Its journal, Educational Studies, is entirely devoted to book reviews in the several foundations fields.

In a paper prepared for the first meeting of the Standing Conference of the seven societies in April, 1971, Martin
Levit struck the notes I would like to stress in this article:

... Foundational studies should be focused on the
critical, comparative and comprehensive evaluation

---

*The substance of this paper was originally delivered as the
keynote address at the annual conference on the Association
for Teacher Education in Africa, held at Makerere University, Kampala, Uganda, March 29, 1971. It is to be published in a forthcoming issue of Educational Theory and is
reprinted here with the permission of Dr. Butts and the Editor of Educational Theory.

of socio-educational policies.

> ... no discipline is able to validate its truth-
> claims by its own resources.... no discipline con-
> tains or is connected with enough warranted prem-
> ises to make, by itself, justified recommendations
> for educational policies and programs.

> Because this is so, we stand in great need of
> more comprehensive and interconnected perspec-
> tives as a foundation for more rational educational
> policies ...

> ... Thus, educational policy and national policy
> and, increasingly, the policies of nations must be
> developed together. Long range perspectives, em-
> bracive ideals, and the powerful cultural and ideo-
> logical forces that now shape education must be
> kept together in mind. [2]

I would like to underline Levit's stress on the need
for a conceptual framework in the foundations studies that
will cross the boundaries of the disciplinary lines and that
will cross the borders of national lines. Foundational theory
must not only be policy-oriented, it must be interdisciplinary
and international as well. Indeed, the problem of teaching
the foundational subjects is today a world-wide problem.
In a recent survey made by the Commonwealth Secretariat
in London, William A. Dodd says:

> ... of all the aspects of the curriculum for teacher
> education [in the developing countries] it is that
> which relates to the social role of the future
> teacher which receives the most attention. [3]

Especially is this concern agitating the professional
educators of the English-speaking black universities of Africa. [4] The nineteen member institutions of the Association
for Teacher Education in Africa have launched a major effort to reform the teacher education curriculum of their universities and training colleges, and they have decided to begin with the foundations studies.

Each discipline, as Martin Levit says, is bound to be
partial or limited in its approach, whereas the problems of
education and of society are basically indivisible except for
intellectual diagnosis and study. Thus the more specialized

and limited each discipline becomes, the greater is the necessity to try to see the interrelationships among the subject matters of the disciplinary fields, and the more important it is to try to reintegrate for purposes of judgment and
action.   The problems of the world's societies and of education will not be solved within the framework of any one
discipline or field of knowledge.   The problems to be solved
are situational; they require judgment, generalization, and
application of knowledge from a variety of sources.   The
greater the specialization of knowledge, the greater the need
for generality, integration, and interdisciplinary study.

The ultimate goal of foundational study is normative
and judgmental; it is the effort to solve problems, improve
policy and practice, and move in desired educational and
social directions.   To arrive at improved judgments we not
only need to be grounded as securely as possible in the objective, empirical, and disciplined methods of analysis that
the scholarly fields of knowledge can provide, but we must
also face the fact that education is integrally involved in the
deepest social concerns of society and culture.   Education
is often involved in the crises points, the turmoil, the conflict, and the controversy that swirl around the process of
social and cultural change.   Thus the knowledge we require
is policy-oriented knowledge, knowledge that is relevant to
those deepest social concerns that affect education.   But
that knowledge, I repeat, must be as objective, as valid, as
reliable as the canons of scientific and rational thought can
make it.

Even if you agree with these generalizations, there
are formidable tasks ahead: the matter of selection of
problems to be included in the curriculum, the bringing together of applicable knowledge that is relevant to the problems, and the teaching and learning required to achieve
some kind of common orientation among teachers and a common medium of discourse among educational specialists.
What they should have in common is a general framework
of ideas concerning the role of education in the processes
of social and cultural change, and an understanding of and
commitment to the general direction in which social change
should go.

The foundational task in the various societies of the
world is thus nothing less than the use of disciplined knowledge to understand and evaluate the most fundamental social
and cultural problems of those societies, the direction the

societies are moving, and the role that education should
play in that movement.   If the year 1971 means anything in
the realm of teacher education, it should have made it clear
that foundational studies cannot be provincial nor narrowly
national in perspective.   The international system was being fundamentally reordered as Britain moved to join Western Europe, China moved into the United Nations, and India
moved to assert herself in Asia.   The education of teachers,
whether in Africa, the Americas, Europe, or Asia, could
no longer afford to be exclusively nation-oriented or inward-
looking, if indeed it ever could be.

Three common approaches to teaching the foundations
studies are:

(1) through study of one or more of the generally accepted foundational disciplines, the history of education,
philosophy of education, educational psychology, comparative
education, educational sociology;

(2) through direct study of certain fundamental social
and cultural problems and their bearings on education, e. g.,
industrial urbanization, national economic development, pollution of the environment, the role of civil and military
bureaucracies, conflict among religious, linguistic, or racial
groups; and

(3) through the study of basic issues in education,
e. g., centralization vs. decentralization in educational control, achieving equality of educational opportunity, the educated unemployed, the external examination and certification
system, stress on scientific training vs. the humanities.

Approaching the foundational study through the several disciplines has the undoubted merit that it can achieve a
depth of understanding in a single field of knowledge and
provide the methodological tools for thinking about education
and society in a particular way, historical, philosophical,
psychological, sociological.   But the trouble is that the more
successful the disciplinary approach is in the eyes of the
scholar the less useful it may be for the non-specialist student.   The disciplinary specialist needs a conceptual framework to guide the selection of instructional materials that
will be relevant to the interplay between education and society.

Approaching foundational study through the other ave-

nues, social problems or educational issues, has the immediate advantage of greater relevance for the common
problems facing educators, but the danger is that the study
may be superficial and shallow, with too little depth of real
knowledge as the basis for making judgments or enlisting
commitment for reform.   If a problem approach is used,
the most valid scholarly knowledge of the several disciplines
must be relied upon, but this too requires a well-formulated
framework of thought to serve as a principle of selection
for instructional materials to be plumbed from the depths of
the disciplines.

Now I would like to give a specific example of what
I mean by a conceptual framework that might be a guide
through this enormously complex but extremely important
matter.   My framework grows out of many years of experience at Teachers College, Columbia University, in teaching
integrated foundations courses dealing with social problems
and educational issues, as well as disciplinary courses in
the history of education.   In recent years I have been trying to reinterpret and rewrite the history of education in the
light of new developments in the world of scholarly disciplines as well as in the world of social and educational problems. [5]   My experience in the field of history may be sug-
gestive of a similar process that might well be going forward in the other foundations fields, and I hope may set forward the task of cooperative reconstruction in the foundations
studies as the touchstones of reform in teacher education.

The need for basic reinterpretation in the history of
education has arisen from a number of momentous developments of the past two decades.   I put at the top of the list
the world-wide national revolutions in the course of which
more than half the world came to political independence.
This portentous fact has dramatized the enormous and omi-
nous gap in economic and social development between the
older nations and the newer nations and at the same time
has underscored their mutual interdependence.   Above all,
it has demonstrated that one of the basic reasons for the
vast disparity between traditional and modern nations is the
disparity in education.   Much of my argument flows from
this elemental and fundamental watershed in human history
that followed World War II.   The revolution in the world of
nations has mandated a basic reinterpretation in the writing
of history. [6]

I have long argued that the history of education

should be married to general history and to intellectual history, that it should relate the history of education to the history of society and thought.   So I gravitate to the revisionism that leads to problem-oriented world history and the history of civilization, not to the revisionism that preached social neutrality and accommodation that marked so much of the revisionist movement in American history in the 1950s and 1960s.

Another trend in historical scholarship requisite for the "new" history of education is the need for a conceptual framework that will draw upon the insights and germinating ideas to be gleaned from the fundamental study of social change in related social sciences.   Conceptual schematizations or "central grouping symbols" like industrialization and urbanization, or imperialism and nationalism, enable the historian to formulate generalizations that are more inclusive as well as more explicit and precise than the historian's usual descriptive generalizations. [7]

A particularly significant company of social scientists in the fields of political science, economics, sociology, and anthropology have been devoting themselves in the past decade and a half to several recurring themes of special relevance for the historical study of education in relation to social change.

Comparative analysis has had an important revival in all of the social sciences,   resulting in cross-cultural studies of family, social class stratification, bureaucracy, empires, elites, organization theory, economic development, political systems, whole societies, and whole civilizations.   There is increasing concern with discovering uniformities and regularities as well as differences among societies and cultures. Education has shared in this upswing of interest in comparative analysis in the form of an outpouring of studies in comparative education.   And comparative history has begun to attract the attention of historians to a significant degree. [8]

An "international" theme also runs strongly in the recent theoretical and empirical literature of the social sciences.   This points to the importance of the interconnectedness and linkages among societies and cultures, the cross-cultural contacts, the intercultural influences, diffusion and interdependence, transfer of ideas and institutions, international impacts of one society upon another.   Whatever else the external influence has been, it has been a catalyst of

innovation and social change throughout history, whether between ancient Mesopotamia and Egypt, India and China, Islam
and much of Asia and Africa, or the West and the rest of
the world.[9]

I come then to the theoretical framework which seems
to me to bring together the most urgent social concerns of
our time with the new scholarship in the disciplines of social
knowledge and with the foundational problems of education.
It provides a conceptual link between educators in different
countries of the world as they face some of their most urgent common tasks. This framework is the interdisciplinary
study of the modernization process and the role that education should play as traditional societies either seek or are
impelled to transform themselves into modern societies.
The process of modernization provides a principle of selection for materials to be included in the foundational study of
education, a study that can link the education of teachers in
modern societies with that in traditional societies.

The crucial point is that those societies which first
modernized themselves had a head start in achieving the social power that modern knowledge bestows. The fundamental
role that organized education played in the production of
knowledge and its dissemination gave it a strategic place in
the modernization process when it first appeared in the West
from the sixteenth century onwards, especially in England
and France. It plays a role no less important in the societies that have only lately entered upon active modernization.
It may very well be a different role from that which education played in the first modernizing societies, as indeed the
process of modernization itself is different today from what
it was in past times.

The first modernizing societies became "reference
societies" or models which others emulated or borrowed
from, whether willingly or not. External factors have been
powerful influences in inducing modernizing social change in
one country after another.[10] And education has been right
in the middle of the process. But we are now all caught up
in the world-wide tide of the process whether we like or not,
and whether we are members of highly modern societies, or
moderately modern, or scarcely modern.

Now to bring this argument to a head, let me simply
list ever so briefly the social and cultural problems facing
modernizing societies which I have formulated in the course

of my reexamination of the history of education. I have
tried to put these in terms that are pertinent both to the
more highly developed modern societies and to the less developed traditional societies. This is not to say that the
problems are the same in all societies, but I believe they
are recognizably comparable in the setting of transformation
from tradition to modernity. I shall then turn to the characteristic trends of modern education which distinguish it
from a traditional education, recognizing that in the nature
of the case there are few if any instances of a wholly modern or a wholly traditional education. The "modernity of
tradition" is a common phenomenon; and most educational
systems, like most societies, reflect a mixture of both.

I have tailored my topical headings to give a visual
picture of the whole schema of the foundations of education
on one sheet despite the violence this does to scholarly sensibilities. Figure 1 shows the ABCs of the Foundations of
Education from the perspective of the discipline of history:

A. Social and Cultural Problems of Modernizing So-
cieties
B. Issue-Laden Trends of Modern Education
C. Humanistic and Behavioral Disciplines

Beginning at the lower right hand corner, the foundation block is built as follows:

A. Social and Cultural Problems of Modernizing Societies

1. Nation-building and National Development

A basic feature of modernizing societies is the mobilizing and centralizing power of the nation-state in relation to
the other institutions of society. The process of rationaliz-
ing political authority into a single integrated policy to coordinate the centrifugal particularisms of local or regional
groups has been one of the most difficult yet characteristic
aspects of the modernization process from the sixteenth century to the present. Among the major agencies that have
promoted nation-building are highly organized administrative
and military bureaucracies, differentiated political structures
designed to channelize legislative, executive, and judicial
functions, and large scale educational systems. Organized
education has recruited leaders and socialized the populace
to the general political system and has provided professional

Figure 1
The ABCs of the Foundations of Education

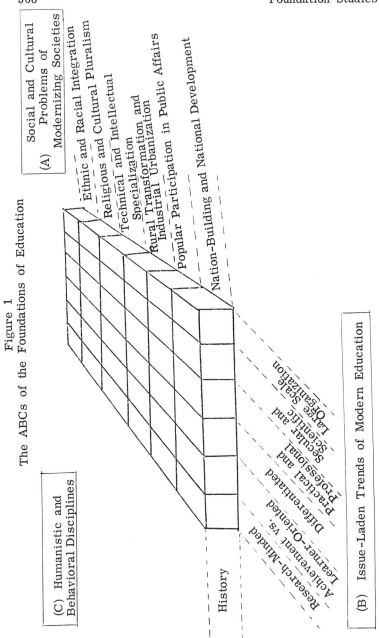

(A) Social and Cultural Problems of Modernizing Societies

Ethnic and Racial Integration
Religious and Cultural Pluralism
Technical and Intellectual Specialization
Rural Transformation and Industrial Urbanization
Popular Participation in Public Affairs
Nation-Building and National Development

(C) Humanistic and Behavioral Disciplines

(B) Issue-Laden Trends of Modern Education

Research-Minded vs. Achievement-Oriented
Learner-Oriented
Differentiated
Practical and Professional
Secular and Scientific
Large Scale Organization

History

training for those who manage the manifold institutions of a
modern nation-state. The more modern the society, the
greater the capacity of the political system to influence the
whole range of social and economc affairs of the society.
A pervasive dilemma of the modern world is that while this
characteristic of modernization (nation-building) constantly
threatens to pit one nation against another and to disrupt the
peace of the world, still other marks of modernity (industrial urbanization and technical specialization) tend to produce or require a growing interdependence among nations.
Education is torn by the same dilemma--how to contribute
to a nation's development and at the same time promote international comity?

2. Popular Participation in Public Affairs

A second characteristic of modernizing societies is
the increasing involvement of larger and larger numbers of
people in political, economic, and social affairs.   Histori-
cally, this trend was vastly accelerated by the democratic
revolutions that swept Europe and America in the later
eighteenth century, Latin America in the nineteenth century,
and Africa and Asia in the twentieth centuries.   Whether
the form of government be consitutional monarchy, representative democracy, socialism, communism or fascism,
mass participation has become a means of mobilizing the
populace into greater group efforts on behalf of the society.
The entire political spectrum from left to right now pays
more attention to the power of the people than ever before,
even if this is limited to mass demonstrations, political
rallies, or 99.9% affirmative elections.   Whether based on
the proletariat, the peasants, the army, the middle classes,
or a ruling elite, whether there is only one or several in
competition, the political party has become one of the distinctive institutional aspects of a modern society.   Mass
participation has not only basically changed access to education but in large measure has been made possible by mass
education.

3. Rural Transformation and Industrial Urbanization

More often taken as an attribute of modernization
than any other characteristic is the shift from an agrarianate
society to a citified society; from agriculture and other primary means of production to commerce, the market, and
machine production in factory and city.   These trends are
related to the industrialization or commercialization of ag-

riculture itself, as well as to the growth of industrial urbanism, so that the rural transformation, if not actually preceding industrialization, at least has accompanied it. The application of science and technology to both the rural and urban sectors developed with accelerating speed after the first industrial revolutions in Britain and France; it characterized the rapid economic developments of Germany and the United States in the nineteenth century, and Russia and Japan in the twentieth. The magnet of industrial urbanization continues to attract more and more people, until its "field" now literally covers the world despite the convulsive threats to an urban way of life posed by ecological imbalance, pollution, and all their attendant problems. And education seems to be intimately related to the speed and scope of the process, wherever it has taken place, either as a pre-condition or as a post-condition.

4. Technical and Intellectual Specialization

Modern societies are peculiarly the inheritors of the scientific revolution, initiated in the sixteenth and seventeenth centuries, accelerating in the eighteenth and nineteenth centuries, and exploding in the twentieth century. Not only does this secular lamp of knowledge, lit so brightly by the European Enlightenment, apply to the physical and natural sciences themselves but to the humanities, the social sciences, and the arts as well. The "rational organization of knowledge for practical purposes," which is Emmanuel G. Mesthene's succinct definition of technology,[11] applies to much more than simply industrialization. It applies to the technical means of achieving concrete goals by interdependent spcialization, a process whereby Denmark modernized its agricultural base without becoming a large scale power-mechanized industrial society. Marshall Hodgson uses the unlovely word "technicalization" to refer to this "condition of rationally calculative (and hence innovative) technical specialization."[12] The "increasingly inclusive and interdependent nexus of technical specialism" has enabled invention and new discoveries in knowledge to increase at a geometric rate of progression. And modern education has contributed to and been deeply affected by technical specialism. An irony of the different stages of modernization is that while many students in the United States have become alienated from education for technical specialism, the educators of less modern nations are sedulously promoting education for technology as a prime means to modernization.

5. Religious Freedom and Cultural Pluralism

This heading points not so much to a universal characteristic of a modern society as to the widespread tensions
that characterize most societies that are involved in the turmoil of modernization. Religious beliefs and practices, the
value patterns of homogeneous cultural groups, their distinctive literature, music, and art, and especially their language loyalties, all have deep traditional roots that may be
threatened by the modernizing sweep of nation-building, industrial urbanization, and the spread of secular knowledge.
Within the early modernizing nations, the tensions between
religious fervor, religious freedom, and established churches
played predominant roles in their national development.
Some moved to religious tolerance, others to various forms
of separation of church and state. In some later modernizing nations religious groups have been suppressed or strictly controlled. Nearly everywhere old nations and new have
had to face the restiveness, the clamor, the turbulence of
groups who feel their identity threatened by the trend to
modernity. Schools and educational institutions have been
thoroughly bound up in the dual drive, on the one hand to
build national secular unity, and on the other to permit or
encourage the diversity that would enable individuals and
groups to live in dignity, security, and freedom. What is
legitimate freedom to one group, however, may be viewed
as threatening separation and divisiveness by another. The
terribly complicated problem related to the languages of instruction in schools and universities is only one phase of
this issue.

6. Ethnic and Racial Integration

Of all the problems associated with the tension between social integration and unity on one side and diversity,
pluralism, or separatism on the other side, the most difficult may be those that revolve about ethnic and racial differences. When these factors are linked with religion, language, regional, or generational loyalties, the explosive confrontations may make the modernization process almost un-
bearable. Some would-be nations have faltered, or foundered, or even split asunder over these issues. Others have
managed to survive by uneasy truces or by violent repres-
sion of the subjected groups, whether they be minorities or
majorities in the total population. The historical reminders
of the slave trade and the slavery institutions of the seventeenth, eighteenth, and nineteenth centuries, the massive

ethnic migrations of the nineteenth century, the imperial
and colonial systems and their demise in the nineteenth and
twentieth centuries, and the present drives for integration
or for separatism continue to plague the larger part of the
world, as they have since the modern era began. And education has been a deeply involved party to the problem, both
negatively when it withholds its benefits from some groups
on ethnic or racial grounds, and positively when it provides
a necessary means of achieving equality and independence.
No more important issue faces the educators of heterogeneous societies that would become modern.

B. Issue-laden Trends of Modern Education

A pervasive characteristic of modernizing societies
has been a remarkable faith in the efficacy of massive educational endeavor. Mass education is not only distinctive of
modernity but it carries its own freight of problems into a
modernizing society. I mention six trends which illustrate
the issues raised when education itself sets out to become
modern.

1. Large-scale Organization and State Systems

By and large the nation-states have taken major responsibility for providing popular education in modern societies. The trend has been toward free, compulsory, and universal elementary education, widespread secondary education,
and expanding higher education. To bring these levels into
some sort of integrated system, educational bureaucracies
have been organized to coordinate the increasingly complicated system and to relate it to the other administrative
structures of the state. A pervasive issue is whether the
structure should be disjunctive or integrative. A disjunctive
system sets up separate institutions for different groups in
the population: racial or ethnic groups, religious groups,
language groups, social classes, occupations, academic aptitudes, or intelligence levels. An integrative system tends
to deal with such differences, if at all, within common
schools open horizontally to all such groups and open verti-
cally right up to post-secondary institutions for many, if not
the majority, of youth and young adults. And, curiously,
just as the traditional societies that aspire to modernize are
seeking to expand their systems of organized education, the
cry goes up in the most modern nations that the school is
dead and that society ought to be deschooled.

2. Secular and Scientific Curriculum

The curriculum in modern educational systems is increasingly secular and scientific in character. This trend poses the issue whether a relative decline in religious studies and in humanities is a good thing in relation to the rise of scientific and technical studies. Joseph Elder of the University of Wisconsin even goes so far as to say that a secular education is the essence of modernity:

> ... I shall define 'modernity' as corresponding to 'secular education,' that type of education endorsing the establishment of objectifiable evidence for proof of phenomena in opposition to the type of education that endorses tradition or faith as the basis for proof of phenomena. [13]

3. Practical and Professional Service

The demand that educational studies at all levels be more useful and more practical for social purposes as well as for the individual development of students has been a major theme of the "modernists" versus the "ancients" since the European Renaissance, and especially since the seventeenth century. The original purposes of the medieval universities were largely professional; the early humanists were professional teachers and public officials; the educational "reformers" up to the twentieth century have been more likely to be preaching practicality and social usefulness than not. The "defensive modernizers" in the nineteenth and twentieth centuries borrowed heavily from the West's technical and scientific and professional education. The debates over whether colonial education should have been practical or academic have not ceased in post-colonial times. What kind of education is most suitable for rapid modernization now agitates nearly all nations alike.

4. Differentiated and Diversified Institutions

In contrast to the relatively homogeneous types of formal education provided in traditional, narrowly limited educational systems, a modern system is characterized by an increasing differentiation and specialization of offerings. Education has taken on more and more of the specific functions which had formerly been performed by family and kinship circles, communities, churches, apprenticeships, and the like. The growing functional specificity in political and

economic affairs and consequent specialization of training
are basic characteristics of a modern society which a modern education supports.   Some modernizing societies have
tended to set up separate single-purpose educational institutions that are specialized and highly selective for distinct
clienteles (separate academic schools, technical schools,
trade schools, teacher training schools, etc.).   Others have
tended to lump together their diversified offerings into multi-
purpose or comprehensive institutions, especially at the secondary and higher levels.   These different approaches have
elicited enormous debate as to which type of institution provides the greater range for individual choice, opportunity for
occupational mobility, and contribution to national development.

5. Achievement-oriented Pedagogy
    versus Learner-oriented Pedagogy

         Modern education has constantly been under pressure
to face in at least two directions at the same time.   On one
hand, achievement is viewed as the goal of pedagogy.   It is
widely agreed that in a modern society, social roles and
positions should be allocated on the basis of merit and the
competence actually achieved by the individual rather than to
assign them on the basis of family, kinship, social class,
race, or ethnic origin.   When large-scale systems of education began to replace a few schools for a small ruling class,
the achievement goal led to the use of external examinations
at virtually every level of the educational system.   It also
led to public certification of graduates by awarding credentials attesting to their competence to perform professional
duties or hold public offices.   Note once again that while
middle class radical students have recently become disaf-
fected from "credentialing," the desire of the disadvantaged
to acquire the credentials as an aid to a better job seems
to be stronger than ever.

         On the other hand, it has recurringly been argued
that a single-minded stress on the achievement of a predetermined subject matter by students in spite of their backgrounds, talents, and interest stifles the real purposes of
education.   Spokesmen for learner-oriented pedagogy from
Plato to Piaget, or from Democritus to Dewey, or Socrates
to Silberman, have tried to elevate attention to the nature
of the learner and his active role in the learning process.
How difficult it is to strike a balance between these two differently oriented types of pedagogy and to unite them in a

viable functioning dyad is revealed by the recurring cycles
of critics who find the pedagogy too soft and then too restrictive, too loose and then too formal, too progressive and
then too joyless, too informal and then too intellectual.

6. Research-mindedness

The latest to arrive but by no means the least important or controversial characteristic of a modern education
is the deliberate effort to advance knowledge by disciplined
inquiry and research. Whether the research enterprise is
designed to stress pure research or applied research, the-
ory-oriented research or field-oriented research, "conclu-
sion-oriented inquiry" or "decision-oriented inquiry," the
search for new truth has revolutionized the role of education
in modern society. It has meant that England could be the
first nation to industrialize in the eighteenth century with
relatively little help from the traditional university organizations, but ever since that time universities and higher technical institutions have played a larger and larger role in the
development of theory, the application of theory to practice,
and the production of new knowledge as well as the transmittal of old. The creating and organizing of valid and reliable knowledge are now recognized as a prime function of
a modern educational system. Without such an enterprise
a society that hopes to modernize itself is greatly handicapped. And of particular importance in developing a modern system of education is the research enterprise that focuses directly upon education itself, upon the processes of
human growth and development and learning, the processes
of teaching, administration, and organization, and the role
of education as a social and socializing institution.

I have come at last full circle to the foundations
studies and their focus upon the linkage of education and society. As you can see in Figure 2, the totality of the foundations studies is made up of the interpenetration or inter-
section of (A) the social and cultural problems of modernizing societies, (B) the issue-laden trends of modern education, and (C) the scholarly knowledge of the relevant humanistic and behavioral disciplines. I include the following disciplined methods of analysis and judgment: history, philosophy, psychology, sociology, anthropology, political science,
economics, and comparative and international studies. We
may enter the domain of teaching or research in the foundation fields through any one of the portals A, B, or C, but
we should always try to relate our own particular paths to

Figure 2

The ABCs of the Foundations of Education

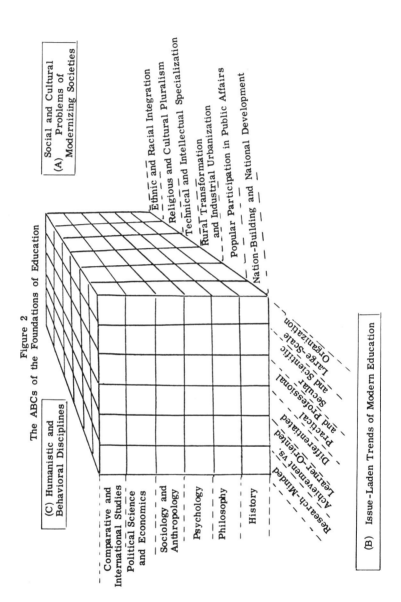

(A) Social and Cultural Problems of Modernizing Societies

- Ethnic and Racial Integration
- Religious and Cultural Pluralism
- Technical and Intellectual Specialization
- Rural Transformation and Industrial Urbanization
- Popular Participation in Public Affairs
- Nation-Building and National Development

(C) Humanistic and Behavioral Disciplines

- Comparative and International Studies
- Political Science and Economics
- Sociology and Anthropology
- Psychology
- Philosophy
- History

(B) Issue-Laden Trends of Modern Education

- Research-Minded vs. Achievement-Oriented
- Learner-Oriented vs. Differentiated
- Practical and Professional
- Secular and Scientific
- Large-Scale Organization

to the terrain of the larger field. How best to do this is
the task before us.

I hope we can begin in earnest to fit the various
pieces of the foundations fields together. Each of the contributing disciplines has a part to play in the "critical, comparative, and comprehensive evaluation of socio-educational
policies." Each will have, I hope, a pardonable belief that
its contribution is particularly important, but I would also
hope there is little insistence on pride of place. In his
presidential address to the American Historical Association,
John K. Fairbank stated his belief that history has a special
assignment for the 1970s:

> Many of us are trying to take a next step: to move
> from an integrated European-American history to
> an intercultural and interconnected world history.
> But this is not an easy step to take. It cannot be
> taken merely by area specialists, intent on the
> uniqueness of their areas, but only by historians
> able to steer their way across the 360-degree
> ocean of human experience. Historians who try
> this must be part social scientists ...[14]

So far, I agree with Fairbank, and I believe that his
argument applies as fully to the history of education as to
history in general. But then Fairbank drops into a common
academic failing when he finishes that last sentence:

> Historians who try this must be part social sci-
> entists, though in the end the social sciences can
> provide only bits and pieces, and historians must
> put the picture together.

Now that spoils it for me. Historians are just as
prone to deal with unrelated bits and pieces as any others.
In fact that is my basic criticism of too many foundations
studies in teacher education: they are all too likely to consist of scattered bits and pieces.

That is why I believe that the members of the international fraternity in the foundations of education, with their
combined resources in the humanistic and behavioral studies
and their varied experiences in professional education, could
make such a great contribution to the reform of teacher education and to education at large, if they would but gather
up the bits and pieces of the foundational fields and "put the
picture together."

Notes

1. See, for example, R. N. Anderson, et al., Foundation
   Disciplines and the Study of Education. Toronto:
   Macmillan of Canada, 1968; W. O. Stanley, "The
   Social Foundations Subjects in the Professional Edu-
   cation of Teachers" in Educational Theory, vol.18,
   Summer 1968, pp. 224-236; James Shields, "So-
   cial Foundations of Education: Trends and Texts"
   in Teachers College Record, vol. 70, October,
   1968, pp. 77-87; R. Freeman Butts, "Charting
   Our Position on the Way to ..." in Teachers College Record, vol. 70, March 1969, pp. 479-493;
   "What Are the Foundational Questions?", Teachers
   College Record, vol. 71, December, 1969, pp.
   179-224; and the successive issues of Educational
   Studies; a Journal of Book Reviews in the Foundations of Education published since the Fall of 1970
   by the American Educational Studies Association.
2.   Martin Levit, "An Inquiry Approach for Foundational
     Studies" in AACTE Bulletin, American Association
     of Colleges for Teacher Education, Washington,
     D.C., vol. 24, May-June, 1971, p. 1.
3.   W. A. Dodd, Teacher Education in the Developing Coun-
     tries of the Commonwealth; A Survey of Recent
     Trends.   London: Commonwealth Secretariat,
     1970.
4.   See, for example, Kenya Institute of Education, New
     Directions in Teacher Education. Nairobi: East
     Africa Publishing House, 1969; R. B. Renes, Teach-
     er Training at Butimba; a Case Study in Tanzania.
     Groningen: Walters-Noordhoff Publishing, 1970;
     and P. C. C. Evans (ed.), Report of the Sixth An-
     nual Conference of the Afro-Anglo-American Pro-
     gramme. Oxford: Alden Press, 1968.
5.   See forthcoming The Education of the West; a Forma-
     tive Chapter in the History of Civilization, to be
     published by McGraw-Hill Book Co., New York,
     early in 1973.
6.   See, for example, C. Vann Woodward, "The Age of Re-
     interpretation" in American Historical Review, vol.
     65, October, 1960; and John K. Fairbank, "Assign-
     ment for the 70's" in American Historical Review,
     vol. 74, February, 1969.

7. See H. Stuart Hughes, "The Historian and the Social
    Scientist" in American Historical Review, vol. 65,
    October, 1960; Werner J. Cahnman and Alvin Bos-
    koff (eds.), Sociology and History; Theory and Re-
    search. New York: Free Press, 1964; Edward
    H. Saveth (ed.), American History and the Social
    Sciences. New York: Free Press, 1964; and
    John Higham, et al., History. Englewood Cliffs,
    N.J.: Prentice-Hall, 1965.
8. C. E. Black, The Dynamics of Modernization; a Study
    in Comparative History. New York: Harper &
    Row, 1966; and C. Vann Woodward (ed.), The
    Comparative Approach in American History. New
    York: Basic Books, 1968.
9. See, for example, William H. McNeill, The Rise of
    the West. Chicago: University of Chicago Press,
    1966; and R. Freeman Butts, "Civilization-build-
    ing and the Modernization Process: A Framework
    for the Reinterpretation of the History of Educa-
    tion" in History of Education Quarterly, Summer,
    1967, pp. 147-174.
10. Reinhard Bendix, "Tradition and Modernity Reconsid-
    ered" in Comparative Studies in Society and His-
    tory, vol. 9, April, 1967, pp. 330 ff.
11. Harvard University Program on Technology and Society,
    Fourth Annual Report, 1967-1968, Cambridge,
    Mass.
12. Marshall Hodgson, "The Great Western Transmutation"
    in Chicago Today, vol. 4, Autumn, 1967, p. 50.
13. Joseph W. Elder, "Brahmins in an Industrial Setting:
    a Case Study" in William B. Hamilton (ed.), The
    Transfer of Institutions. Durham, N.C.: Duke
    University Press, 1964, p. 141 (n).
14. Fairbank, "Assignment for the 70's" in American His-
    torical Review, vol. 74, February, 1969, p. 871.

JAMES W. WAGENER

3. A NEW ROLE FOR FOUNDATIONS COURSES
IN TEACHER EDUCATION*

Do foundations courses have a role in emerging patterns of professional teacher education?   As presently
viewed and conducted, probably not.

What constitutes a foundation is more than an academic question.   Curriculum committees, deans, and accrediting agencies are sometimes less than appreciative of
the rationale for inclusion of these courses in professional
sequences.   Students, queried about their place and meaning,
are often hard pressed for an answer beyond their personal
like or dislike of the course, the teacher, or the materials
used.   Representative syllabi reflect a potpourri of approaches and content that does little to reassure the skeptic.

Trends in Foundations Offerings

What are some of the answers given to the question
of the role and scope of these courses?   The first is, Let
liberal arts do the job the foundations departments have been
trying to do.   Teachers colleges have a right to expect that
teacher candidates have an adequate general education.   Let
the history of education be taught as a branch of intellectual
history in the history department; professional historians are
not likely to turn didactic nor to bias their considerations in
the way foundations teachers might.   Sociology of education
should be taught in the sociology department, for obvious
reasons.   Philosophy of history, art, and religion are taught
in the philosophy department, why not philosophy of education?

There is much to commend this arrangement.   The

*The Journal of Teacher Education, Vol. XXI, No. 4 (Winter
1970), pp. 489-93. Reprinted with permission.

major question centers on the nature of the liberal education acquired in many colleges and universities.   As William Arrowsmith has argued,[1] liberal education, as currently practiced, does not liberate any more than teacher education sequences equip to teach.   An undergraduate taking a history course, for example, seldom finishes it with any sense of the sweep of his subject; instead, he is subjected to a junior version of a graduate course.   History or philosophy of education taught in this way under the aegis of liberal arts is ill suited to the future teacher's needs.

A second move some universities have made is to promote joint appointments of faculty between the college of education and other colleges.   A joint professor in philosophy and education is equipped to analyze the language or practices of education in a more telling manner than his generalist colleague.   The same is true of the anthropologist, the sociologist, the historian, or the economist; educational activity is analyzed through modes of inquiry appropriate to the parent disciplines.   An added benefit of the joint professorship plan is the strengthening of educational research.   If research in education is to become more sophisticated, the academicians of the mature disciplines need to take a decisive role in research design and effort.   Joint appointments are one means of achieving this end; a drawback to this strategy, however, is that joint professorships perpetuate research in keeping with the interests and styles of the parent disciplines rather than the less tidy needs of schools and teachers.   Happily, the two interests coincide some of the time, but a respectable marriage between the two is unlikely.

A third effort being made to rejuvenate foundations departments is to specialize them.   This move is not without precedent, since foundations in the past have been tuned to such matters as international, comparative, and ethnic education.   A major topic today is urban education, and some foundations departments have incorporated this into course offerings.   The black studies impetus has also figured in the present educational mix.   Another concentration has been educational policy and the policymaking function at all institutional levels, which has often in the past been decided by narrowly trained administrators whose values were molded on a business rather than an educational model.

The push for relevance reflected in these decisions is commendable.   Trading promising new functions for old ones that have lost their focus is a healthy sign.   At the same time, a law school does not trade jurisprudence for international law, even though the latter may seem more relevant at the moment than the former; the function of jurisprudence permeates international law even though its substance may need to be radically recast.

A fourth answer is the academic study of education, distinct from the preparation of educational practitioners but a prerequisite to professional courses. A prototype of this is political science: political science departments are not primarily concerned with training politicians as practitioners but in developing a substantive body of theory and information. Similarly, in the academic study of education, concern is for a descriptive treatment of the academic establishment. Tools of analysis are principally those of the social sciences. If the analyst attempts a comprehensive examination, he may resort to a cybernetic model of systems operation; if he attempts to plot more limited problems, he is likely to do sociography (in John R. Seeley's phrase), a description that is usually idiographic. Quantification is the descriptive doorway and manageability the cramped but secure workroom in which the analyst labors. The methodological limitation, however, is not the only soft spot in this approach; the limitation of focus is equally restrictive. The institutional expression of teaching and learning is a relevant research field, but that it is the sole subject matter of education is debatable.

An Alternate Proposal

The thesis of this paper is that foundation courses should deal with the phenomenon of knowledge, which here means the configuration of noetic claims made at any given time. The configuration or shape of knowledge is not the substance of those claims: facts, ideas, information, data. Nor can it be reduced to the structure of knowledge or modes of analyzing knowledge, although these are important considerations for this view. The shape of knowledge refers rather to meta-knowledge or knowledge about knowledge. As succinctly stated by Walter J. Ong:

> Growth of knowledge soon produces growth in knowledge about knowledge, its constitution, and its history, for knowledge is of itself reflective. Given time, it will try to explain not only the world but itself more and more. [2]

Two aspects of today's culture seem to justify exploring this direction. The first, and more obvious, is the knowledge revolution. [3] The exponential growth and overlapping of fields of knowledge and the meteoric rise of research and development as an influence on educational practice are aspects of the revolution catalogued by Bell and others. The first two items lead one to despair of knowing all there is to be known in a single field of knowledge. Aristotle's dictum for separating scientific proficiency in a subject from educational acquaintance with all subjects becomes wishful thinking. If one is stymied by the abundance, he is equally frustrated by the absence of any epistemic common frame that offers order.

A second cultural factor is a symbiosis between knowledge and society. The knowledge revolution forces the question of how knowledge is shaping society rather than the older question of how it fits present expectations or how it can be used by society. Relevance is turned upside down; the learning society is a different subject with a different starting point from that of the business society. The geneticist, Theodosius Dobzhansky, voiced this enigma in his contention that as we change what we know about the world we change the world we know. This alteration shifts the view of educational foundations as reflecting the already formed conceptual world to the view of their reflecting the impact of knowledge on the knower as his conceptual world is altered.

The need today is not so much for the arithmetic teacher to prepare the future engineer to fit into a set vocation in society as it is to explore how arithmetic (and other modes of quantification) are making a new conceptual world that the engineer will share in creating. The librarian's old question was, What resources (books, tapes, visuals, etc.) are needed to make this library adequate? The new questions may be, What forms of information storage and retrieval is the present state of knowledge forcing us to? What kind of learning resources center is knowlege demanding?

The Copernican revolution in knowledge (from society being served by knowledge to the kind of social arrangements made necessary by knowledge itself) cannot be facilitated merely by updating methods courses in strategies of instruction. It requires additionally a conceptual reorientation in how the new knowledge shapes the knower and his intellectual universe; this is a fitting task for foundations courses.

Already the communications revolution is recasting methods courses in colleges of education. The cultural revolution of our time is leaving its mark on the subject areas; the zoology department of the University of Tennessee, for example, is offering this year for the first time a course in biology and human affairs. That the knowledge revolution will influence foundations offerings in the years ahead does not seem an inflated claim.

How is such an approach to be facilitated? The first prerequisite is that new offerings cross traditional disciplinary lines. The philosopher, the historian, the psychologist, and the sociologist have contributions to make; but (and this is a second prerequisite) the locus of their work is the role of knowledge rather than an academic specialty. The psychologist will examine the relationship of knowledge to the knower--not just learning theory but how the knower in all dimensions is molded by what he knows. The philosopher will look at the constitution of knowledge, not just in formal but also in the relationship of quantification and qualification to the noetic task. The historian's concern will be the history of knowledge. This differs from intellectual history in that the intellectual historian is concerned with tracing the impact of the substance of an idea (vox populi, for example), on men and their times; the knowledge historian, on the other hand, is interested in the impact of forms of knowledge on previous epochs. Similarly, the sociologist goes beyond sociology of knowledge to examine what alternatives the social placement of new knowledge makes possible.

It is apparent from even a cursory look at these components that the foundations area, thus conceived, does not take society, the public school movement, or the school as an institution as its target of analysis. Rather it takes the configuration of knowledge as it defines the learner and his environment and considers the alternatives open to him for shaping this environment.

This perspective seems to avoid the pitfalls of past efforts as well as some of the limitations of present trends. The knowledge of knowledge approach is the direct opposite of theoretical imperialism, which tries to draw implications for educating from experimentalism, realism, behaviorism, or some other system (a questionable effort on several counts).[4] It does not foist limited methodologies of inquiry upon the study of education; it is not a cataloguing of research findings into a compendium of claims based on hard data; it does not aim at a synoptic view of current theories and practices from a supposedly objective standpoint as the repertoire from which the teacher puts together his own theory of education. Neither is it a dialectical dance between varying positions, each standing as a corrective to the former, nor another stab at an overarching conceptual system (a metaphysics of education).

Knowledge of knowledge does not begin with a method, a system of ideas, or an encyclopedia of research findings, nor does it start with an institution, current society, or the teacher's vocation. It begins with the phenomenon of knowledge and attempts to articulate its shape, its relationship to the knower and his conceptual world. For the past century, in this country, knowledge has served society. The situation has changed: knowledge is now becoming the shaping agent of society. Teachers must come to terms with this in ways that may not now be visible. Facilitating this transition is a relevant foundations task.

Notes

1. Arrowsmith, William. "The Future of Teaching," The Public Interest; Winter 1967, pp. 53-67.
2. Ong, W. J., editor. Knowledge and the Future of Man: An International Symposium. New York: Schuster, 1968, p. 8.
3. Bell, Daniel. The Reforming of General Education: The Columbia College Experience in Its National Setting. New York: Columbia University Press, 1966, pp. 73-87.
4. Burnett, Joe R. "Some Observations on the Logical Implications of Philosophic Theory for Educational Theory and Practice." Proceedings of the Fourteenth Annual Meeting, Philosophy of Education Society. Lawrence: University of Kansas Press, 1958, pp. 51-57.

RALPH A. SMITH

4. EDUCATIONAL AESTHETICS TODAY*

Introduction

I am somewhat reluctant to think of "educational aesthetics" as a "new direction" in educational studies, not only because talk about newness is too easy, but also because
educational aesthetics in my understanding of it is simply
reflection about the educational significance of a certain variety of experience--aesthetic experience--and such reflecting has been going on for some time, at least since Plato
and as recently as any number of articles and books published in this century. What is perhaps novel in the present situation is a cultural trend that makes aesthetic objects
and events accessible to large numbers of people, a situation which has had the effect of stimulating aesthetic interests generally, including the curiosity of educational theorists. This cultural trend, moreover, is doubtless a consequence of the evolution of industrial society into a post-in-
dustrial era. That is to say, there had to be both sufficient
wealth and leisure available, or the promise of such, before greater thought and attention could be given to cultural
activities. Indeed, it is the opinion of some social theorists
that we are in fact experiencing a "third American revolution," the distinguishing mark of which is the unprecedented
cultural consumption of the middle class.[1] It also seems to
be the case that cultivation of aesthetic sensitivity is believed by some to be an antidote to the alleged dehumanizing tendencies of modern technology and science, a belief
incidentally that runs counter to another view occasionally
expressed, viz., that far from the arts being inherently
civilizing, there may rather be a covert relation between
aesthetic experience and inhumanity. To this list should
probably be added the motives of career- and profession-
building; in a mass society everything, including aesthetic
education, will eventually be organized. Readers can per-

---

*Prepared especially for this volume.

haps think of still other factors which account for the emergence of aesthetic interests, but that the arts can on the
one hand be held to civilize and on the other to desensitize
is sufficient to indicate that there is work for an educational
aesthetics. Where, however, does one get bearings on the
pertinent issues and topics? A customary place to begin is
with the literature, and this unspectacular suggestion will be
followed here.

The Literature of Aesthetic Education

Since space limitations do not permit extended discussions of the key topics and sources in the theory of aesthetic education, I must rest content merely with passing
reference, leaving it to the reader to follow up items in the
discussion and bibliography as his interest dictates. My acquaintance with the literature, apart from my own inquiries,
derives from having received an invitation to assemble a collection of readings consisting of key topics and sources in
aesthetic education which were identified in the Philosophy of
Education Project at the University of Illinois. [2] This literature was arranged under a variety of topical headings and
my organization ultimately included such subdivisions as historic ideas of aesthetic education, aims, curriculum design
and validation, and teaching-learning. In my estimation, the
key orienting essay in this literature is Harry S. Broudy's
"Some Duties of a Theory of Educational Aesthetics," published in Educational Theory in 1951. [3] It marked, I think
it is correct to say, renewed concern on the part of contemporary educational theorists with the problems of aesthetic education. And it is the contention of this essay that since
1951 a significant theoretical literature of aesthetic education
has appeared. It is this literature, moreover, which, I think,
educational theorists have in mind when they talk about the
foundations of aesthetic education. In the following I will
pass in review Broudy's list of relevant types of problems
which theorists in his opinion needed to address themselves
to, indicating along the way recent discussions which touch
on these same problem areas. Finally, I will suggest some
additional duties in light of recent events and scholarship.

A Brief Progress Report: 1951-1971

In 1951 Broudy believed that theorists should address
themselves to four theoretical tasks: (1) explaining the na-

ture of aesthetic experience; (2) accounting for the peripheral status of aesthetic education in the schools; (3) justifying aesthetic education; and (4) explaining both the nature of
value judgments and the discrepancy between persons' ready
acceptance of popular forms of art and their general inept-
ness in dealing with serious or demanding art. Broudy's
own interpretation of aesthetic education in the 1951 article
rested on showing how the aesthetic experience of fine art,
which expresses the meaning of the more complex and subtle
modes of human experience, helps an individual in his quest
for the good life. The justification for aesthetic education,
he believed, could appeal to a variety of purported benefits,
such as the development of creative dispositions, mental
health, and the enrichment of experience. The case for formal instruction derived from the untutored tastes of individuals and the failure of our culture generally (for a number of
historical reasons--e.g., religious fundamentalism and pragmatic, frontier mentality) to reinforce the taste for serious
art. Broudy's aim in the "Duties" essay was not to present
a comprehensive theory of educational aesthetics; it was only
to illustrate the sorts of things that should go into one.
Still, the kernel of Broudy's later educational aesthetics is
contained in this article, and the refinement of his ideas can
be progressively traced in a number of important papers and
books published since 1951.[4] Moreover, as director of the
previously mentioned Philosophy of Education Project, Broudy
was responsible for having brought together in convenient
form the basic topics and sources of philosophy of education
which, again, involved identifying the principal theoretical
literature of aesthetic education. He has thus continued to
be a leading theoretician of educational aesthetics and the
impetus for developing foundational studies in aesthetic education owes much to his efforts and encouragement.

Having said this, special mention must be made of
the work of Thomas Munro who, as long-time curator of education at the Cleveland Museum of Art and editor of the
Journal of Aesthetics and Art Criticism, has certainly made
theoretical contributions to educational aesthetics. His collection of essays in Art Education: Its Philosophy and Psychology[5] amply attests to this. Such contributions notwithstanding, Munro's scholarly status rests more on such publications as The Arts and Their Interrelations, Evolution in
the Arts and Style and Form in the Arts[6]--works in the domain of pure aesthetics--than it does on his distinctively educational writings. The principal thrust of his career can also be discerned in his devotion to building the American So-

ciety of Aesthetics, a learned society. Nonetheless, Munro's achievements are singular and belong in any reference to the modern literature of educational aesthetics. But other work, in addition to that of Broudy and Munro, has been proceeding apace.

Aesthetic Experience

With regard to clarifying the nature of aesthetic experience, the period since 1951 has been particularly fruitful one. The concept has been intensively analyzed and the structure of such experience is now much better understood. Pertinent in this connection are a number of writers, but I shall restrict reference here to the work of the American philosopher, Monroe C. Beardsley, and the English theorist, Harold Osborne, both of whom, to be sure, are not educational theorists in the sense in which this term is generally used. Their work, however, has pedagogical import and both have written for educational publications.

Granting some variations in detail and emphasis, Beardsley's and Osborne's conceptions of aesthetic experience involve a number of characteristics which indicate how aesthetic experience is marked off (not, to be sure, neatly and sharply) from other types of experience.

Beardsley thinks that aesthetic experience has approximately five characteristics:

> 1. It involves attention to a portion of a phenomenally objective field, either sensuous (such as the colors in a painting) or intentional (such as the events in a novel), and to its elements and internal relationships....
>
> 2. It involves an awareness of form, i.e., relationships among the elements of the phenomenal field, especially (but not exclusively) relationships of similarity/contrast and serial order. More specifically, it involves perceiving the phenomenal field as a stratified design, in which a complex appears to possess a certain unity just because of the relationships among the parts of which it is (or appears to have been) composed.
>
> 3. It involves an awareness of regional quality--

by which I mean simple qualities of complexes,
and especially (but not exclusively) those qualities
that are described by words taken over metaphorically from human contexts. (...[e.g.] beauty,
elegance, grace, dignity, frivolity, irony, wit).

4.   It is characterized by a fairly high degree of
unity, in comparison with ordinary everyday experiences.   Unity has two distinguishable parts:
Coherence and completeness.   An aesthetic experience is unusually coherent, in that the various
perceptions, feelings, inferences, recognitions,
memories, desires, etc., that occur in the course
of its development (and not all of these kinds of
mental state need occur) have a character of be-
longing or fitting together or succeeding one another with continuity.   An aesthetic experience is
unusually complete, in that the experience marks
itself off fairly definitely from other experiences--
both from contemporaneous items of awareness
that do not belong to it and from experiences that
precede and follow it.

5.   It is intrinsically gratifying, or, in other words,
brings with it both a continuing enjoyment that is
felt as part of the development of the experience,
and a final satisfaction or fulfillment that may
linger after the experience has ended. [7]

It should be noted that although the five factors mentioned by Beardsley are interrelated, they can be interpreted as combining two major aspects: the phenomenally objective, or the object of the experience; and the phenomenally subjective, or what the experience feels like to the subject having it.   Thus when the somewhat ambiguous expression "quality of experience" is used, it is helpful to know
which pole, the objective or subjective, or perhaps both, is
intended.

Osborne's eight-point treatment may be summarized
as follows:

1.   Whatever is perceived aesthetically is abstracted
in attention from the environmental system and is thus
framed for attention.

2.   Implicit in this isolation for attention is that the

percipient does not, during the aesthetic experience, conceptualize or think discursively about the object.

   3.   In aesthetic apprehension, the object is perceived
as a complex structure whose parts do not stand independently of the structure but are articulated to perception only
as parts of that structure.

   4.   Because practical and other interests are held
in abeyance, aesthetic experience has its own characteristic
emotional color: serenity and detachment.   Furthermore, it
is an outward-directed activity leading to absorption in an
object, not an inward dwelling on moods.

   5.   Aesthetic contemplation fixes attention upon the
presented object in a process of increasing awareness of
that object in perception, to the exclusion of meditative mus-
ings and plays of the imagination.

   6.   During the process of experiencing an object
aesthetically, the question of its real existence is irrelevant,
for aesthetic contemplation is concerned with appearance.

   7.   Absorption in the object during aesthetic contemplation does not reach the point where ego-consciousness
disappears; rather, it allows the object to assume heightened
reality and vividness.

   8.   Though anything at all may be experienced aesthetically, not all things are capable of sustaining attention in
the aesthetic mode.   However, "Works of art are aesthetic
objects specifically designed or particularly adapted to favor
prolonged and repeated activity of aesthetic percipience."[8]

   Osborne's account underlines at least three features
of aesthetic experience worth remarking.   The subject should
fix his attention primarily on appearance and while doing so
distance practical and other nonaesthetic interests; that is,
he should refrain not only from distinctively discursive thinking but also from idle musing and isiosyncratic flits of imagination.   Second, aesthetic gratification is qualified: it is
often a serene, detached sort of pleasure.   And finally, Osborne is emphatic that works of art are preferred objects in
aesthetic percipience.

   Regarding the possible benefits of aesthetic experience, Beardsley, in a convenient summary, has suggested

that high-grade aesthetic experience may provide a moral
equivalent for violence, satisfy man's need for excitement
and novelty, quiet destructive impulses, achieve clarification
and integration of conflicts within the self, refine perception
and discrimination, cultivate emotional relations, improve
mental health, develop cognitive, imaginative, and sympathetic powers, and provide an ideal for human life, though
it need not do all of these things, nor do them simultaneously, for all persons. [9] For Osborne, though he would not deny
the possibility of some of these benefits, it is sufficient, and
he refers to Herbert Read in illustration, that aesthetic percipience provides a significant counterpoise to the dominant
spirit of scientific rationality.

Justification and Aims

Noteworthy as an attempt to justify aesthetic education, or at least "qualitative education," is the work of a
group of educational theorists who since the 1950s have been
attempting to develop the germ of an idea in the later philosophical writings of John Dewey. I refer to the writings of
Francis Villemain, Nathaniel Champlin, David W. Ecker, and
Elliot W. Eisner. [10] The central contention of these writers
is that the goal of arts study is the development of qualitative intelligence, a habit of mind which is cultivated by non-
scientific, qualitative problem-solving. In Ecker's formulation of it, qualitative problem solving (as it unfolds in the activity of the artist) consists of: (a) presented relationships;
(b) substantive mediation; (c) determination of pervasive control; (d) qualitative prescription; (e) experimental exploration;
and (f) conclusion, or total quality. Ecker concludes that
"qualitative problem-solving is a mediation in which qualitative relations as means are ordered to desired qualitative
ends. Thus to choose qualitative ends is to achieve an artistic problem. Whenever qualitative problems are sought,
pointed out to others, or solved, therein do we have artistic
endeavor--art and art education." [11]

In other writings Ecker has attempted to show how
qualitative controls also function in the basic processes of
teaching and learning. [12] He has further collaborated with E.
F. Kaelin to advance a conception of aesthetic education from
the point of view of phenomenological aesthetics which has resulted in two important articles, one a survey of research in
aesthetic education, [13] and another which suggests new paradigms for educational research in the arts. [14]

Kaelin's several systematic articles on aesthetic education, again from the point of view of phenomenology,
stress the importance of providing guidance in the art of
making aesthetic judgments which, when properly understood
and expressed, result in intensified and clarified experiences
as well as a number of other social benefits.   For example,
in "Aesthetic Education: A Role for Aesthetics Proper,"
Kaelin holds that learning to make contextual aesthetic judgments of artistic significance (contextuality being a major
feature of aesthetic judgments) helps to produce a type of
personality no society can afford to be without.   Indeed it is
even thought that scientific enterprise itself can find fulfillment in the development of aesthetic consciousness: "Science
for science's sake, without any application to the problems
of men, is as empty a catchword as art for art's sake.
Both activities are meaningful to the degree they enrich the
lives of men.   This they can do only by remaining true to
their intrinsic purposes: science to uncover the truth, and
art to present the quality of a lived experience in a perceptual context."[15]

Some of the extra-aesthetic benefits that could conceivably result from aesthetic instruction have also been persuasively articulated by Iredell Jenkins, particularly in his
notions regarding the ways aesthetic education can contribute
to moral refinement.   Like many theorists, Jenkins reduces
the complexity of human experience to prominent moments
or dimensions of consciousness--what he calls the cognitive,
the affective, and the aesthetic.   Regarding the functions performed by these moments of experience, Jenkins writes:

> First, these moments are present throughout con-
> sciousness: every experienced occasion has its
> aesthetic, cognitive, and affective aspects.   Second,
> these moments are of coordinate value and signifi-
> cance; no one of them has priority of any sort over
> the others.   In a very great deal of experience,
> these elements do not separate out, and we do not
> become aware of them as distinct.   Rather things
> are given to us in experience as fully three-dimen-
> sional and as a synthesis of these moments.   But
> there are a sufficient number of experienced occa-
> sions when one of these perspectives becomes domi-
> nant and subordinates the others, though these are
> always present.   Then our awareness and concern
> are concentrated on one aspect of things, experi-
> ence takes on a distinctive coloring and we push

our acquaintaince with things in a specific direction.
If the aesthetic component dominates, our attention
is centered on the 'particularity' of things; it is their
assertion of their individual existence and character
that holds our interest, so we are led to regard things
from their own point of view and to explore them on
their own terms.   When the cognitive component is
dominant, our attention centers on the 'connectedness'
of things; it is the similarities and regularities that
run among them that hold our interest, so we are led
to regard things as items in an abstract schema and to
explore the patterns of order and connection that bind
them together.   When the affective component dominates, our attention centers on the 'import' of things;
it is their immediate impact upon us and their avail-
ability to our uses that fills our concern, so we are
led to regard things from the perspective of our
selves and to explore the possibilities and the threats
that they offer us and the ways in which these can be
manipulated so as to serve our own purposes.

It is in these terms that I would explain the aesthetic life, from the most transient and spontaneous encounters with particularity to the most carefully contrived and highly sophisticated works of
art in which particularity is finally clarified and
embodied. [16]

Jenkins further believes, on good grounds it would
seem, that men tend to be influenced by things which are experienced with heightened concern and interest, and since
works of art, both good and bad, are invariably so experienced, they are especially significant in affecting people's
attitudes and values, that is, their notions about the true,
the good, and the beautiful.   Aesthetic education is thus in-
escapably implicated with moral education and just as the
harmful consequences of pseudo-science and pseudo-technology
are held in check by professional criticism and official regu-
lation, so some control, Jenkins thinks, should be asserted
over the possibly harmful consequences of pseudo-art,
though not necessarily by official fiat.   To discourage the
creation of pseudo-art Jenkins believes that "society must
acknowledge in the aesthetic domain the same two fundamental obligations it accepts in the cognitive and affective domains: to assure that good art is available and that men
are cultivated to appreciate it. "[17]

The belief that the experience of art helps to shape individual morality could also be said to be the principal emphasis of the writings on literature education by Maxine Greene and James L. Jarrett. In a number of interesting variations on a theme these writers have posed human understanding and self-knowledge as important outcomes of literary encounters. By virtue of imaginative identification with the fictive characters of literature, sensitive readers gain insight into human nature. Literature in particular, Greene thinks, has a special capacity to invoke the feeling of what it is like to be alive at a certain moment of time, the experience of which for the reader can point the way beyond stereotypes and conventional modes of being.[18] Jarrett, on the other hand, has emphasized the role literary dramatic devices play in inducing readers to set aside the attitude of the casual onlooker in ordinary life.[19]

In this connection--that is, with regard to the role of the dramatic in human experience--the writings of Albert William Levi are of special significance. In a number of important volumes Levi has charted the typography of the humanistic complex (the locus of the Imagination), which he contrasts with the scientific chain of meaning (the locus of the Understanding). Characteristic of the humanistic complex are such notions as reality and appearance, illusion, destiny and human purpose, fate and fortune, drama and the dramatic event, and tragedy and peace; whereas the scientific chain of meaning deals more with the problem of error, true and false propositions, causality, prediction and scientific law, chance, fact, competition, biological growth, and the stasis or equilibrium of systems.[20] Levi accepts, then, C. P. Snow's notion of two cultures but believes that the distinction rests fundamentally in a conception of mind that because of divergent interests and aims triggers radically different mental faculties.

R. A. and C. M. Smith have also surveyed the justification question, and after explaining Beardsley's useful distinction between intrinsic and inherent value, suggest three important outcomes that could accrue from aesthetic education: (1) a distinctive type of enjoyment; (2) a distinctive type of perceptual content; and (3) a distinctive kind of knowledge.[21]

There are then quite a number of ways to justify aesthetic education, and the list could easily be expanded, as F. E. Sparshott has patiently done in "The Unity of Aesthetic

Education. "[22]

Curriculum

In 1951 Broudy could only discuss the duties of a theory of educational aesthetics; there was little systematic
work in aesthetic education to review. Now there is something to talk about, for the 1960s witnessed both the appearance of new schemata for curriculum in aesthetic education
and some attempts to implement curriculum ideas (although
the ideas implemented were not always those formulated by
educational theorists).

For curriculum schemata proposed by educational
theorists, e.g., Philip Phenix, Harry S. Broudy, and others,
there is a good summary by D. K. Wheeler in the April
1970 issue of the Journal of Aesthetic Education,[23] a special issue devoted to curriculum in aesthetic education. The
Autumn 1966 issue of Studies in Art Education[24] should also
be consulted, as should a publication of the Music Educators
National Conference, Toward an Aesthetic Education.[25] This
latter contains a lengthy essay and bibliography by R. A.
Smith on the philosophical literature of aesthetic education
on which this essay has drawn. Descriptions of actual cur-
riculum-building in the arts may be found in Bennett Reimer's
Philosophy of Music Education,[26] Elliott W. Eisner's Educating Artistic Vision,[27] and in the publications of CEMREL
(the Central Midwestern Regional Educational Laboratory),[28]
whose work in aesthetic education at the elementary level is
currently the most ambitious. The work of the Educational
Research Council of America (Cleveland) in the area of elementary school humanities instruction has also been on a
fairly large scale.

Many of the curriculum schemata advanced in the
1960s, as Wheeler points out, emphasized the importance of
content and were heavily influenced by recent scholarship on
the structure of knowledge. Some problems involved in basing literature curricula on the concept of structure are carefully analyzed by Alan Purves, who ultimately opts for a notion of structure that resides in the nature of a sensitive
reader's response to literature,[29] a topic on which, with
Victoria Rippere, he has done original research.[30] English
or literature education, however, owing doubtless to its
strong traditions and high cognitive content, has not been as
receptive to aesthetic emphases as have art and music edu-

cation, even though much of the modern tradition of literary
criticism can be construed as underlining the importance of
formal (aesthetic) readings of various kinds of literature.
A good impression of the diverse positions in contemporary
English studies may be found in The Uses of English by
Herbert J. Muller, a report on the Anglo-American conference in English education held at Dartmouth College. [31]
State departments of education have also been preparing
guidelines and materials for the arts and humanities, but as
one moves into the area of "humanities education" the emphasis varies considerably from curricula with strong aesthetic biases to others with almost none at all, the preference being rather for great ideas, cultural epochs, American studies, social studies and, in some instances, even the
natural sciences. A task for an educational aesthetics in
this connection is clarifying the meaning and uses of the
terms "aesthetic" and "humanistic," or at least indicating
the problems of definition at issue.

     It should be noted that practically all of the forego-
ing references interpret aesthetic education as in some way
concerned with the study and appreciation of the arts. Distinctive in the philosophical literature, and deserving of
more attention than it has received, is the work of Donald
Arnstine, especially his Philosophy of Education: Schooling
and Learning. [32]

     Arnstine's carefully constructed philosophy of educa-
tion rests on two key notions: disposition and discrepancy.
If a disposition is a proneness "to do and feel certain things
in situations of certain sorts," then learning, Arnstine believes, can be defined as "the acquisition of dispositions,
along with related knowledge, skills, habits, and attitudes."
The acquisition of dispositions, moreover, and this is the
heart of Arnstine's thesis, involves the notion of discrepancy, that is, the difference between what learners expect
to see in situations and what they actually see. The task
of the teacher thus becomes that of skillfully devising discrepancy situations which promote learning. Arnstine also
analyzes the important role of affect, positive and negative,
in the learning act. Important for a theory of educational
aesthetics is Arnstine's belief that aesthetic experience is
one of the major types of discrepancy situations and that
under proper conditions the felt quality of the experience of
perceiving the formal pattern of a work of art is the same
as the experience of listening to a good lecture (on any subject). Arnstine's effort is further valuable for his syste-

matic use of diverse theoretical materials, psychological as
well as philosophical, in building his philosophy.

In a provocative essay Kenneth Conklin has also attempted to indicate the prevalence of aesthetic perception
and experience in contexts not ordinarily mentioned in aesthetic discussions. Using the ideas of Michael Polanyi and
the writings of mathematicians, Conklin builds an argument,
perhaps too uncautiously, which leads to such assertions as
"mathematical discovery is an aesthetic experience of the
most profound kind" and that "following a single proof or
studying a whole branch of mathematics provides an aesthetic experience closely similar to that of reading a novel
or seeing a play .... "[33]

Arnstine's and Conklin's ideas actually belong to a
category of literature which has appeared only sporadically,
a type of writing which attempts to draw illuminating parallels or to develop significant analogies between distinctively
aesthetic enterprise (in the arts) and other educational activities, or which attempts to construe a great deal of educational activity itself as inherently aesthetic. An earlier
essay in this category was Max Black's "Education as Art
and Discipline, "[34] and the essays (on play, style, intention,
imagination, feeling, etc.) in R. A. Smith's Aesthetic Concepts and Education are in a similar vein. [35]

At this point special mention should be made of two
major British theorists, Herbert Read and L. A. Reid, and
some younger writers. So far as his writings on aesthetic
education are concerned, Herbert Read stressed the importance of creative aesthetic activities for young children and
believed that the method of all education should be the method of art, by which he generally meant arranging situations
which encouraged pupils to create and intuit form in a variety of situations. In this respect, all subjects, including
the sciences, needed to cultivate the processes of expression found in artistic creation. But Read's writings on education, something less than systematic, do not suggest a
coherent set of educational practices, [36] and in the opinion
of one of his more thoughtful critics his career is less noteworthy for its contributions to aesthetic or educational theory
than it is for its persistently humane protest against the dehumanizing tendencies of modern technology. [37]

The same cannot be said of L. A. Reid whose writings, though ranging less widely than Herbert Read's, are

more unified and of direct relevance to aesthetic education.
His culminating work, Meaning in the Arts,[38] sets forth a
complex and subtle concept of meaning which is intended to
characterize the nature of aesthetic knowing and at the same
time clear up some difficulties in the influential aesthetic
system of Susanne Langer.   For Reid, meaning in the arts
is not so much expressed meaning as it is "embodied"
meaning, and such meaning is properly understood only
through aesthetic experience.   Embodied meaning, however,
and this is central to Reid's thesis, is felt import, accessible only through feeling.   But feeling can be thought of as
cognitive (in a special way) and, consequently, the apprehension of the meaning of a work of art qualifies as a cognitive
act, or as a form of knowing ("indwelling" knowledge, as
Reid also calls it).   It is this latter claim that enables Reid
to make a strong case for the arts in liberal education.

      The idea of the arts as one of the basic ways of
knowing, or "forms of understanding," has also been advanced by some younger British and Australian scholars
whose interests are in general educational theory and not exclusively the arts or aesthetic education.   In this connection
an exchange between P. H. Hirst and Walter Gribble in Educational Philosophy and Theory should be read.[39]   At issue
between Hirst and Gribble is whether it is art itself (Hirst)
or criticism (Gribble) that is the aesthetic form of understanding.   The curriculum consequences of an educational
commitment to teaching forms of understanding may be found
in R. F. Dearden's The Philosophy of Primary Education.[40]

Teaching-Learning

      The theoretical literature of educational aesthetics
since 1951 has been heavily weighted on aims, justification,
and curriculum; less attention has been devoted to teaching
and learning strategies, an understandable imbalance during
a period in which an area of study is undergoing conceptualization.   Of the literature devoted to teaching-learning, that
containing discussions of aesthetic judgment and criticism is
of interest here.

      One of the more pedagogically useful interpretations
of criticism is contained in Beardsley's Aesthetics: Problems in the Philosophy of Criticism.[41]   Beardsley breaks
down critical statements about aesthetic objects into cognitive,
moral, and aesthetic judgments, the latter consisting of ref-

erences to genetic, objective, and affective aspects of aesthetic situations, of which objective aspects (the qualities of
unity, complexity, and intensity possessed by aesthetic objects) are aesthetically most relevant; that is, they are the
qualities which make works of art good or bad as art.
Beardsley's classification of critical statements is derived
from a careful examination of the many sorts of things which
critics themselves say about works of art, and a knowledge
of his writings could go a long way toward clarifying this
thorny area for educators.

        That aesthetic objects and works of art can be evalu-
ated in a variety of ways, some more aesthetically defensible than others, does not entail, obviously, a major emphasis on evaluative criticism in aesthetic education.   And indeed, systematic, deliberative judgment is but one attitude
that may be taken up toward works of art.   Also relevant to
our commerce with works of art, as Harold Osborne points
out in "Taste and Judgment in the Arts,"[42] are the attitudes
of liking and discriminating appreciation in which, to be
sure, there is an element of judgment, but judgment is not
the major aim and enters into appreciation only tacitly.
Now, there are certainly limitations to the attitude of liking
if it be taken as the ideal outcome of aesthetic instruction,
but discriminating appreciation, or percipience as Osborne
calls the art of appreciation, has some noteworthy parallels
with social intercourse.   In both our aesthetic commerce
with works of art and in our relation with people the goal is
not so much judgment and evaluation as it is the expansion
of awareness and the enrichment of personality, of the world
of aesthetic qualities in the case of works of art and of human nature in the case of persons, which is not to say that
works of art are denied the capacity to provide insight into
human nature or that persons are devoid of aesthetic qualities.   It all depends on the work of art, the attitudes taken
up toward it, and the ways people present themselves to others.   Osborne suggests that efforts to resolve the famed
antinomy of judgment (i. e., aesthetic judgment seems to be
both subjective and objective) which has plagued philosophical aesthetics since Kant may then be directed toward solving a pseudo-problem.   Rather the task is to sharpen an understanding of the different types of attitude that can be taken
toward works of art--the attitudes of taste, discriminating
appreciation, and deliberate appraisal.   Osborne concludes:

            If from the widest purview of the task of the edu-
        cator is to help and guide others in the lifelong

business of equipping themselves to live in the
world of men, refining their sensibilities and improving the delicacy and range of their apprehen-
sions, then in the narrower field of aesthetic education the goal may not absurdly be represented as
the provision of guidance and help to those who are
interested in equipping themselves to live and move
in the world of art, mingling with its inhabitants
as persons of sensitivity and tact.   Insight and
percipience stand a man in better stead than erudi-
tion, though learning in its proper place is never
to be despised.   Friendships will be formed and
the educator must realize that these will always
display an element of arbitrariness, can never be
reduced to reason and rule: the important thing is
that they should be formed on the basis of discriminating perceptivity and not from the superficial purblindness of perceptual obtuseness.   Over
a wider range a man will progressively achieve a
system of appraisals in which his personality will
be corroborated as a lens reflecting from his own
angle and within the confines of his natural endow-
ment the universal norm of human concsiousness
as such.   In this field the educator must realize
that appreciation is a cognitive skill, the deliberate
exercise of a faculty of trained percipience, not
merely a response of unregulated and capricious
emotion. [43]

Another point made by Osborne, that criticism is a
species of persuasive writing, is well understood by Brian
S. Crittenden, whose essay, "Persuasian: Aesthetic Argument and the Language of Teaching," is perhaps the most
systematic account of this aspect of language in the philosophical literature of education[44] Crittenden argues that aesthetic criticism is inherently persuasive and that, with a
variegated repertoire of techniques and methods, critics attempt, in a rational spirit, to persuade others that a painting or other work of art is properly seen or understood in
a certain way.   Crittenden's educational consequence is that
teaching too has important persuasive elements, that teaching has in other words an important aesthetic-like character
irrespective of the domain of instruction.   He writes:

... the educator is involved in initiating others into a distinctive style of life characterized by specific values, attitudes, and ways of proceeding.

Because he is convinced that this style of life is
worthwhile and because one of its distinguishing
preferences is for reasonable rather than arbitrary choice, part of his task as an educator is
to persuade rationally those being initiated to see
the whole life style and to choose it as such. No
doubt an educator may use various kinds of argument in this process of rational persuasion, such
as examining the consequences of being or not being educated. In the end, however, I believe he
is forced back to depicting as fully as possible the
characteristic features of the life style of the educated mand and to comparing and contrasting it
with alternative styles. It is thus finally a form
of aesthetic or critical argument--a judgment not
about means but about the total pattern which the
component elements form. At this most fundamental level, the norms of rational persuasion for
the educator are essentially those of aesthetic
argument.... [45]

Some New Duties of an Educational Aesthetics

Educational Policy, Schooling and Deschooling, Alternative
Education, Free Schools, Open Schools, Etc.

The above notions are lumped together for they comprise a cluster of issues and problems which derive from
the rediscovery that schools are not the exclusive locus of
teaching and learning and that educational policy-making, often made with public schools in mind, now must take into
account a variety of other agencies. Indeed, as anyone
reading this volume knows, policy proposals for education
today range from conventional prescriptions for the public
schools to schemes for getting rid of schools altogether.
At issue for a theory of educational aesthetics is who makes
policy for aesthetic education, for whom, and by what mandate?

Consider, for example, a view being advanced which
holds that practically all of society educates, not only teachers in schools but parents, peers, doctors, dentists, journalists, wardens, union officials, and many others. The
work of education is thus to be assumed by all of the major
institutions of society. Schools are but one agency which
educates and they, it is repeatedly said, are not doing very

well. [46] Indeed the dynamic may well have passed, say, to television. Accordingly, a need is expressed for "alternative" ways of providing education. Now "alternative education" falls within the purview of an educational aesthetics so far as it involves aesthetic activity, and as a point in fact numerous proposals for alternative education rest on aesthetic or quasi-aesthetic presuppositions. For example, in some notions of "open education" (the rebirth, purportedly, of progressive education), not only are the arts held to be ideal materials for integrating all learning in the curriculum, there seems to be in addition a special penchant for "movement" and "drama," and photographs of open classrooms invariably reveal a preference for children expressing themselves. I have examined the concept of art and aesthetic enterprise involved in at least one conception of open education and will not repeat my observations here, [47] only my conclusion that the illustrations and rhetoric used distorted the complex nature of art and aesthetic enterprise.

One could wish then for more of the informed and balanced educational reporting displayed by Barbara Leondar in her study of the arts in alternative schools. [48] Educated in literary studies and educational theory, and with no apparent axe to grind, Leondar read the literature and visited numerous alternative schools and programs to discover how the arts fare. She is wary, to be sure, of generalization, given the idiosyncrasies and brief life of so many of these ventures, but the thrust of her remarks is clear. She concluded that although enthusiasm and vitality can be discerned in isolated instances, and while achievement, especially in the crafts and occasionally in writing, is sometimes high, there is also what she calls an "alternative tyranny," in that freedom, individuality, and diversity (the holy trinity of alternative education) are all too often purchased at the price of discipline, commitment, and purpose, not to say contemplation and privacy. Indeed, she says, there seems to be little appreciation for the "silence, exile, and cunning" which Joyce took to be the conditions of art. Neither student nor adult life in such schools, she reports, has aesthetic or intellectual focus and the restless psychological tempo of the students invariably prevails. Further, while it is true that the experience of visiting artists and performing groups is often not lost on such programs, the image of a knowledgeable and talented instructor, even an artist-in-residence, providing a model of sustained work and dedication is generally anathema. Students who occasionally wish to withdraw from the group, perhaps to sketch or write, commit social

indiscretions. Leondar questions, therefore, whether
wretched teaching and the substitution of indifference, dis-
order, and distraction for school schedules, formal instruction, and authority is much of an improvement. Still further, there is little effort, even in places where Leondar observed noteworthy work, to assess the methods alternative
educators use, with the consequence that there is no systematic information being compiled about what works and what
doesn't. Still, the arts do find a hospitable home in alternative education, even if at this time such education seems to
be providing confirmation for those who by virtue of common
sense or past personal experience anticipated the consequences
of freedom without restraint, work without discipline, activity without purpose. But an educational aesthetics will
not reject a priori aesthetic experiments wherever they occur. More than once in history the shape of the future has,
in retrospect, been observable in the margins and periph-
eries of the conventional and the established, and alternative
education may yet inject new life into the formal curriculum.

But to return to the original point: an educational
aesthetics, in light of a new educational policy-making complex, will continually ask who makes policy for whom and
by what criteria, and it will point out that policy-making
will be repetitive and noncumulative, when it is not simply
axe-grinding, if not informed by a common critical literature.[49] An educational aesthetics will help delineate that
literature, use it judiciously, and hold others responsible
for a knowledge of it.

Behavioral Objectives, Accountability, Competency-Based Instruction, Career Education, Etc.

The above notions, all relatively new labels (if not
new ideas) in the last decade or so, are also discussed together for they too involve issues which it is the duty of a
theory of educational aesthetics to clarify.

What, for example, is the meaning of "accountability"
in aesthetic education? There can be no simple answer to
this question, for the term means different things depending
on the interests and motives of its user. A popular understanding of the term has it implying the demonstrated
achievement by schools of pre-specified learning objectives;
those, as the current jargon goes, which have been stated
in precise behavioral terms. This meaning of accountability

has recently been linked to the further expectation that learning outcomes should be relevant to the future work of the
schools' clients.   This seems to be one of the objectives of
"career education."   That is to say, students should be enrolled in schools which from bottom to top prepare students
for realistic initiation into the world of work.   Thus does
the net of issues expand as one notion gets associated with
another in the world of educational policy talk.   The issues,
however, are not without theoretical interest, can have tan-
gible consequences, and thus need careful study.   For example, from the judgment that schools are not performing
according to stated intent, i.e., are not achieving specified
objectives, it is but a short step to the cutback of funds and
even the firing of the "incompetents" responsible.   Converse-
ly, evidence of successful achievement of stated objectives
ensures the steady flow of funds in probably increased
amounts.

It is clear that the model influencing talk about accountability is a technological one derived from business
management and military and space systems of operations,
and the net effect is an attempt to impose technological form
on educational activity. [50]   Should educators accept and cooperate with such efforts?   Or should they say "Cease and
desist?"   Indeed can educational activity take a technological impress?   Is it tractable enough?   That many educators
are confused and often don't know what to think about accountability and related notions is a sign that analysis is
needed.

Except for certain didactic purposes (and such purposes need not be unimportant)--for example, the straightforward imparting of knowledge and its learning--a technological model is quite crude and overly simple when applied
to the complicated enterprise of educating individuals.   In
education in a democratic society the task is as much to
provide conditions for the orderly arbitration of conflict
among competing educational philosophies of education as it
is to design a "product" or pre-specified set of learning outcomes, and then gear up operations which will efficiently and
economically deliver the stipulated output.   The causal relations between "inputs" and "outputs" in teaching and learning,
moreover, are still imperfectly understood; tacit learnings
and experience, and, as it were, tacit ignorance, continue
to bewitch the theorist in search of scientific explanations
of learning. [51]   Moreover, there is something inappropriate
in wanting to cast education in a technological mold, espe-

cially in the aesthetic domain.   Some of the more difficult
activities of human experience not only defy precise specification, but one has the feeling that two modes of thought
and organization, the technological and the educational, are
being joined which don't go together.   Who says they don't
go together?   One answer, which is still accepted in some
instances, is that those who have carefully and systematically studied the issues have at least earned a right to talk
about appropriateness and inappropriateness.   So far as a
theory of educational aesthetics is concerned the major task
is deciding what kind of talk is reasonable and appropriate
regarding the specification and achievement of learning outcomes.   It must be admitted that if aesthetic instruction is
distinctive, then some specification of outcome is justifiable.

     To begin one might appeal first to a principle of suf-
ficient complexity, and second to the rule that one should
not expect more from schooling than it can realistically attain.   First, the principle of sufficient complexity.   As indicated, knowing what is prerequisite to what in teaching
and learning is not well understood.   Just exactly or precisely what a person needs to know, for example, in order
to perceive intelligently and sensitively something new or
novel in the world of art cannot be pre-specified to any
great extent.   Special milieu, personal experience, and education will affect persons in diverse ways.   Considerable
knowledge about the history of art, for instance, was used
by the late Erwin Panofsky to illuminate the character of
the new medium of film in a way few film specialists themselves have been able to do. [52]   Does it follow that a knowledge of Christian iconography, mosaic technique, and the
evolution of graphic styles are prerequisite to film appreciation, or even the Panofsky essay for that matter?   Arthur
Danto, moreover, has argued that "a sense of an artworld,"
that is, a generous knowledge of the theory and history of
art, is conditional to the perception of the new in art (his
example was the Tenth Street Abstractionists in New York
City). [53]   Doubtless this is true in some sense.   But who
would be rash enough to state precisely the essential ingredients of an "artworld"?   The ultimate intellectual components (and then only for the visual arts) might be the fifteen volumes of the McGraw-Hill Encyclopedia of World Art
and all subsequent editions, and even that impressive project has gaps.   There must then be a wise simplification of
the knowledge and skills believed relevant to the cultivation
of aesthetic sensitivity, and as Dewey pointed out long ago,
the logical organization of knowledge in the disciplines is

not necessarily the best pedagogical organization. It is thus
general ideas and topics, general ways of proceeding, or dispositions to act in certain ways which seem appropriate candidates for specification in aesthetic education, in contrast
to long and detailed lists of content, skills, and tasks. This
may seem obvious but the way some aesthetic educators
themselves have eagerly taken up the role of engineer and
specification expert suggest otherwise.

As to the rule that more should not be promised than
can be delivered, perhaps all that it is necessary to say is
that the world does not always cooperate with pedagogical in-
tentions. So far as the schools are concerned, even the environment within them may be hostile to teaching and learning, and socio-economic level, peer culture, and political
conflict (professional and community) may further combine to
thwart expectations. Perhaps schools and teachers involved
with aesthetic education can be held accountable, i.e., are
being responsible, if they can point to defensible intellectual
content, knowledgeable and well-educated teachers, and a
genuine effort to promote aesthetic literacy. But neither
schools nor teachers should expect learners to demonstrate
high degrees of aesthetic sensitivity, nor should schools generally be held directly responsible for the quality of life.
Such outcomes are much too global and beyond the potentiali-
ties of the schools to achieve.

Some Other Duties

There are two other duties which I will simply mention, hoping that others will be moved to give them the attention they need.

First is an emerging "great debate," intimated earlier,
which turns on the question whether the arts, and especially
literature, inherently civilize or whether the arts are more
mischievous than beneficial to mankind. The Arnoldian tradition in literature studies has been most pointedly questioned
by George Steiner in an essay "To Civilize Our Gentleman,"[54]
and Jacques Barzun and Lionel Trilling, among others, have
reinforced Steiner's skepticism.[55] The assumptions underlying the tradition and the challenge to it, since the situation
seems to mark one of those polar shifts in cultural temperament, deserve scrutiny as aesthetic educational literature invariably assumes the beneficent view of art's function.

Second, there is what might be called "the attack on objectivity" controversy within both art and science. On one level is the kind of attack on "the myth of objective consciousness" made by Theodore Roszak, [56] which any number of other similar volumes have inserted as a plank in the "new politics."

On another level is the kind of attack on objectivity discussed by Israel Scheffler in Science and Subjectivity, where one is jolted--at least an aesthetic educator ought to be somewhat jolted--into the realization that a way of talking generally thought reserved for the aesthetic domain is also appropriate, according to some writers, for the scientific domain. Thus critics of scientific objectivity point out, in effect, that there is no disputing scientific paradigms rationally, that science is something of a matter of paradigm taste, that scientific knowledge is noncumulative, that objectivity, in short, is a will-o'-the-wisp. A theory of educational aesthetics has the duty to stay apprised of such controversies for it is clear that they may ultimately alter in fundamental ways the manner in which curriculum is conceived and justified. The recent work of Nelson Goodman[58] in the area of symbol systems further suggests that certain aspects of instruction in the arts and sciences may have more in common than is usually assumed.

Concluding Remarks

The essays and books sampled in this essay collectively convey something of the progress in the field of educational aesthetics since Broudy's 1951 "Duties" article. Work in building this literature has been aided by the appearance of the Journal of Aesthetic Education, which started publishing in 1966. The purpose of JAE is not only to promote and disseminate a literature of educational aesthetics but also to keep critical tabs on it. For, like so much educational enterprise today, writings on the arts and aesthetic education get published but are not subjected to sufficient scrutiny. Numerous scholars from parent disciplines, from philosophy and the social and behavioral sciences, have aided JAE in its venture, thus helping to bridge professional domains the distance between which has often handicapped educational progress.

The duties of an educational aesthetics are, of course, perennial, and the bibliography will change as new theorists enter the field and new programs and practices are implemented. It is hoped that this essay, especially the references, will facilitate future work.

Notes

1. Arthur J. Vidich and Joseph Bensman, The New American Society: The Revolution of the Middle Class (Chicago: Quadrangle Books, 1971).

2. Harry S. Broudy et al., Philosophy of Education: An Organization of Topics and Selected Sources (Urbana: University of Illinois Press, 1967), and Supplement, 1969. The collection of readings I assembled has been published by the University of Illinois Press, Urbana, under the title Aesthetics and Problems of Education (1971). Several of the references in this essay are reprinted in this volume.

3. Vol. 1, No. 3 (November 1951), 190-98.

4. E. G., Building a Philosophy of Education (Englewood Cliffs, N. J.: Prentice-Hall, Inc., 1954; revised 1961); Democracy and Excellence in American Secondary Education, written with B. Othanel Smith and Joe R. Burnett (Chicago: Rand McNally & Co., 1964); "The Structure of Knowledge in the Arts," first printed in Stanley Elam, ed., Education and the Structure of Knowledge (Chicago: Rand McNally & Co., 1964, pp. 75-106; reprinted in R. A. Smith, ed., Aesthetics and Criticism in Art Education (Chicago: Rand McNally & Co., 1966), pp. 23-45; and most recently Enlightened Cherishing: An Essay on Aesthetic Education (Urbana: University of Illinois Press, 1972), in which the ideas of aesthetic experience and contemplation are interpreted within a conceptual scheme that places emphasis on the functions performed in human culture by aesthetic images and their generative force the creative imagination.

5. New York: The Liberal Arts Press, 1956.

6. Revised edition (Cleveland: The Press of Case Western Reserve University, 1967); Cleveland: Cleve-

land Museum of Art, n. d.; Cleveland: The Press
of Case Western Reserve University.

7.   "Aesthetic Theory and Educational Theory," in R. A.
     Smith, ed., Aesthetic Concepts and Education
     (Urbana: University of Illinois Press, 1971), pp.
     9-10.

8.   The Art of Appreciation (New York: Oxford Univer-
     sity Press, 1970), pp. 27-37.

9.   Monroe C. Beardsley, Aesthetics: Problems in the
     Philosophy of Criticism (New York: Harcourt,
     Brace & World, Inc., 1958), pp. 574-76.

10. See the references in Ecker's "Some Inadequate Doc-
     trines in Art Education and a Proposed Resolu-
     tion," Studies in Art Education, Vol. 5, No. 1
     (Fall 1963), 77-80.   Two recent articles by Ville-
     main and Champlin are: Villemain, "Toward a
     Conception of Aesthetic Education," Studies in Art
     Education, Vol. 8, No. 1 (Autumn 1966), 23-32,
     and Champlin, "Education and Aesthetic Method,"
     Journal of Aesthetic Education, Vol. 4, No. 2
     (April 1970), 65-85.   Eisner's views are contained
     in Educating Artistic Vision (New York: Macmil-
     lan Co., 1972).   It should be noted that there are
     two versions of the qualitative thesis: noncognitive
     (Ecker) and cognitive (Eisner).   It may also be
     the case that some of these writers are now pur-
     suing more independent paths.

11. "The Artistic Process as Qualitative Problem Solving,"
     Journal of Aesthetics and Art Criticism, Vol. 21,
     No. 3 (Spring 1963), 289.

12. "Some Problems of Art Education: A Methodological
     Definition," in E. L. Mattil, A Seminar in Art
     Education for Research and Curriculum Develop-
     ment (University Park: The Pennsylvania State
     University, 1966), pp. 24-57.

13. David W. Ecker, Thomas J. Johnson, and Eugene F.
     Kaelin, "Aesthetic Inquiry," Review of Educational
     Research, Vol. 39, No. 5 (December 1969), 577-
     92.

14. David W. Ecker and Eugene F. Kaelin, "The Limits of Aesthetic Inquiry: A Guide to Educational Research," in Philosophical Redirection of Educational Research, The National Society for the Study of Education Seventy-first Yearbook, Part I (Chicago: University of Chicago Press, 1972), Chap. 11.

15. Journal of Aesthetic Education, Vol. 2, No. 2 (April 1968), 64. See also Kaelin's monograph An Existential-Phenomenological Account of Aesthetic Education (University Park: The Pennsylvania State University, 1968).

16. "Aesthetic Education and Moral Refine," Journal of Aesthetic Education, Vol. 2, No. 3 (July 1968), 184-85. See also Jenkin's Art and the Human Enterprise (Cambridge: Harvard University Press, 1958).

17. Ibid., p. 193.

18. "Literature and Human Understanding," Journal of Aesthetic Education, Vol. 2, No. 4 (October 1968), 11-22. See also Greene's "Real Toads and Imaginary Gardens," Teachers College Record, Vol. 66, No. 5 (February 1965), 416-24.

19. "Coming to Know Persons, Including Oneself," The Monist, Vol. 52, No. 1 (January 1968), 81-103.

20. Philosophy, Literature, and the Imagination (Bloomington: Indiana University Press, 1962), p. 47. See also Humanism and Politics (Bloomington: Indiana University Press, 1969), and The Humanities Today (Bloomington: Indiana University Press, 1970).

21. "Justifying Aesthetic Education," Journal of Aesthetic Education, Vol. 4, No. 2 (April 1970), 49.

22. Journal of Aesthetic Education, Vol. 2, No. 2 (April 1968), 9-21.

23. "Aesthetic Education and Curriculum," 87-108.

24. Vol. 8, No. 1.

25. Washington, D. C. , 1971.

26. Englewood Cliffs, N. J. :   Prentice-Hall, Inc. , 1970.

27. Op. cit.

28. See e. g. , Stanley Madeja and Harry T. Kelly, "A Cur-
    riculum Development Model for Aesthetic Educa-
    tion," Journal of Aesthetic Education, Vol. 4, No.
    2 (April 1970), 53-63.

29. "Structure and Sequence in Literature Study, A Second
    Look, " Journal of Aesthetic Education, Vol. 3,
    No. 2 (April 1969), 103-17.

30. Elements of Writing About a Literary Work: A Study
    of Response to Literature (Champaign, Ill. :   Na-
    tional Council of Teachers of English, 1968).

31. Bloomington: Indiana University Press, 1967.

32. New York: Harper and Row, 1967.

33. "The Aesthetic Dimension of Education in the Abstract
    Disciplines, " Journal of Aesthetic Education, Vol.
    4, No. 3 (July 1970), 21-36.

34. Ethics, Vol. 54, No. 4 (July 1944), 290-94.

35. Urbana: University of Illinois Press, 1971.

36. Read's two principal educational works are Education
    Through Art, 3rd edition (New York: Pantheon
    Books, 1958) and The Redemption of the Robot:
    My Encounter with Education Through Art (New
    York: Simon and Schuster, 1966).

37. Michael J. Parsons, "Herbert Read on Education, "
    Journal of Aesthetic Education, Vol. 3, No. 4
    (October 1969), 27-49.   See also, in the same is-
    sue, John Keel's "Herbert Read in Education
    Through Art, " 47-58.   Keel has written a number
    of sympathetic articles on Read.

38. London: George Allen & Unwin and New York: Hu-
    manities Press, 1969.   Also see his "Knowledge,
    Morals, and Aesthetic Education, " Journal of Aes-

thetic Education, Vol. 2, No. 3 (July 1968), 41-
54.

39. See James Gribble, "Forms of Knowledge," Education-
     al Philosophy and Theory, Vol. 2, No. 1 (May
     1970), 3-14, and Hirst's response, "Literature,
     Criticism, and the Forms of Knowledge," EPT,
     Vol. 3, No. 1 (April 1971), 11-18. It was Hirst's
     influential essay "Liberal Education and the Nature
     of Knowledge" (in R. D. Archambault, ed., Philo-
     sophical Analysis and Education [London: Rout-
     ledge and Kegan Paul, 1965]) that initiated the dis-
     cussion.

40. London: Routledge & Kegan Paul, and New York:
     Humanities Press, 1968, esp. chap. 4.

41. Op. cit. See also Beardsley's "The Classification of
     Critical Reasons," Journal of Aesthetic Education,
     Vol. 2, No. 3 (July 1968), 55-63, and The Possi-
     bility of Criticism (Detroit: Wayne State Univer-
     sity Press, 1970).

42. Journal of Aesthetic Education, Vol. 5, No. 4 (October
     1971), 13-28.

43. Ibid., 28.

44. In R. A. Smith, ed., Aesthetic Concepts and Education,
     op. cit.

45. Ibid., p. 154.

46. This view, which has roots in the classical era, has
     been recently expressed in chapter two of Charles
     E. Silberman's Crisis in the Classroom (New
     York: Random House, 1970). Also see Lawrence
     A. Cremin's The Genius of American Education
     (New York: Random House, 1965), a volume which
     strongly influenced many of Silberman's ideas about
     education.

47. R. A. Smith, "Silberman and the British on Aesthetic
     Enterprise, I, II," Journal of Aesthetic Education,
     Vol. 6, Nos. 3, 4 (July, October, 1972), 5-10,
     (in press).

48. "The Arts in Alternative Schools: Some Observations, "
    Journal of Aesthetic Education, Vol. 5, No. 1
    (January 1971), 75-91.

49. See James E. McClellan, Toward an Effective Critique
    of American Education (New York: J.B. Lippin-
    cott, 1968), p. 315.

50. I have discussed this briefly in my "An Educator's
    View of Industrial and Educational Growth, " The
    Educational Forum, Vol. 35, No. 1 (November
    1970), pp. 15-23.

51. See Harry S. Broudy, "Tacit Knowing and Aesthetic
    Education, " in R. A. Smith, ed. , Aesthetic Con-
    cepts and Education, op. cit. , pp. 77-106, and
    Cyril Burt, "Personal Knowledge, Art, and the
    Humanities, " Journal of Aesthetic Education, Vol.
    3, No. 2 (April 1969), 29-46.

52. "Style and Medium in the Motion Pictures, " in Morris
    Weitz, ed. , Problems in Aesthetics, 2nd edition
    (New York: The Macmillan Co. , 1970), pp. 663-79.

53. "The Artworld, " Journal of Philosophy, Vol. 61, No.
    19 (October 15, 1964), 571-84.

54. George Steiner, Language and Silence (New York:
    Atheneum, 1967), p. 61.

55. Jacques Barzun, The House of Intellect (New York:
    Harper, 1959), p. 17, and Lionel Trilling, Beyond
    Culture (New York: Viking Press, 1965), pp. xvi-xvii.

56. The Making of a Counter Culture (New York: Double-
    day & Co. , 1969), chap. 7.

57. Indianapolis: The Bobbs-Merrill Co. , Inc. , 1967.

58. Languages of Art: An Approach to a Theory of Sym-
    bols (Indianapolis: The Bobbs-Merrill Co. , 1968).

EDWARD WEISSE

5. ENVIRONMENTAL STUDIES IN EDUCATIONAL FOUNDATIONS[*]

As educational studies re-evaluate the structure upon which they are built, one finds interaction taking place among the traditional foundations--i.e., historical, philosophical, psychological, and social foundations--and an emerging, integrated new foundation coined environmental studies. Environmental studies is the meeting place of the historical, philosophical, psychological, and social foundations. If the aim of foundations is to give the aspiring teacher insights into the teaching-learning act, then it appears that the prospective teacher would benefit from an approach that integrates the foundational studies.

The change to the new approach would have as some basic goals the following: (1) developing a sensitivity to environment; (2) discovering relationships between environment and sense perception; (3) discovering the force of methodology and personhood as environmental conditioners; (4) probing the relationships of the new technologies to environmental manipulation; and (5) seeking out dimensions of the learning environments that explode beyond the traditional walls of classrooms. In all probability, these basic goals would serve as foundational integrators.

The historical, philosophical, psychological, and cultural bases for world events are interrelated; to treat a traditional foundation as isolate is to misrepresent. The interrelationships and environments of the classroom are interfoundational and need to be treated as total rather than segments of the whole. If the teacher in tomorrow's school is to be effective in carrying out the cultural and psychological needs of society, he must become sensitive to the totality of

---

*American Educational Studies Association, Newsletter, Vol. I, No. 1 (May 1969), p. 3. Reprinted by permission of the author.

his environment.   This sensitivity leads to a new emphasis
in basic education studies--an emphasis on environmental
studies!

MOSES STAMBLER

6. A SYSTEMS APPROACH MODEL FOR A DISCIPLINED ORGANIZATION OF A SOCIAL FOUNDATIONS OF EDUCATION COURSE[*]

I. The Problem

The expansion of mass communication and the information increase that mark our modern society require a major shift in the general aims and methods of education. In response to these rapid technological and social changes, we should be moving from a model of education viewed as acquiring information and memorizing facts to a view of education providing transferable skills and models of inquiry tools.

The social foundations of education course is particularly in need of this re-direction because of its heavy reliance on the insights of the social sciences and humanities without the explicit utilization of disciplined transferable ways to analyze the social and human scene. In most cases, the social foundations course has become dependent on an enormous amount of fragmented material without an internal logic or discipline for enabling the teacher to sort out and utilize this material. At some institutions, social foundations of education courses have turned into amorphous, directionless courses representing little of a disciplined approach and serving as a catch-all for whatever theory seems to be in the ascendency or whatever "discipline power" predominates.

The social foundations of education course poses many difficulties of organization for the teacher and serious problems of significance and relevance for the students. What often emerges are bits and pieces of information and

*Proceedings of the Second Annual Meeting of the American Educational Studies Association, Chicago: 1970, pp. 5-17. Reprinted with the permission of the author.

values put together in an eclectic fashion for students to
pick and choose as they go along.   Even commendable attempts to organize the material along the lines of social
science disciplines often result in a synthesis and perspective on educational problems frequently limited to an anachronistic point of time and place on a rapidly changing
educational landscape.

It is my contention that we who teach the social foundations courses have a responsibility to think our key problems through in some form of structured communication
with one another in order to develop some type of logical
and coherent organization for our discipline.   We owe this
to our students, many of whom have difficulty recalling significant courses they took; we owe this to the profession,
which is requiring teachers of broader perspective and understanding of the educational field for involvement in vital
professional decision-making; and we owe this to ourselves.
We are at a disadvantage because few of us teaching this
course majored in social foundations of education for our
doctorates, intensifying the problem that exists with an already amorphous "discipline."   We do, however, have the
advantage of being in a sufficiently flexible position to develop and structure a content and process for our discipline
without the traditional constraints of forgotten "truths," and
archaic organizational patterns.   We, the social foundations
teachers, are in a good position to think our discipline
through, and chart our course based on logical consistency
and current-relevant insights.

II.   Definition of a "System"

I have titled my article, "A Systems Approach for a
Disciplined Organization of a Social Foundations of Education Course," and feel that a brief explanation should be
given of how I use the term "system."   There are many
different definitions for this term and committed purists,
from engineers to audio-visual specialists, can often be seen
and heard in the war of definitions that mark this terminology.   The systems approach used in my course is based on
the assumption that there is need for an organized investigation of the manner a society educates its citizens.   This
approach also suggests how that process can be modified to
meet our needs more effectively and efficiently.   Using a
systems approach, we view our educational operation not as
piecemeal and fragmented but as an organic system with com-

ponents that interact and affect each other's performance.
This is particularly useful because the educational system
is a dynamic organic whole and if one wishes to critically
analyze and prescribe innovations, one should view it on the
basis of a unified system of relationships between key components. Changes or innovation in some key components of
our educational system may well require or bring far reaching changes and adjustments in other components of the system.

It is neither possible nor necessary to have complete
knowledge of every detail and component in the educational
system, nor are we able to measure and mathematically express all of the operations involved. Neither can we control all the variables in the system. The key to proper analysis understanding and limited control is to select vital
components in the system, and access points for innovation.

In organizing the component parts of our educational
system, four distinct operational functions can be discerned.
First the specific "mission" of this system in our societal
structure (essentially socialization and innovation) and the
specific enabling objectives we develop for this broader
"mission." Second, we also can discern an "input" category
consisting of the various key elements of our societal context, which serve as constraints or guides for the objectives
we formulate and try to implement. These "inputs" can
serve as a "reality daemons" helping us define the options
for courses of action. Third, we can formulate a "strategy"
category which operates as the vehicle or means we use to
achieve our objectives. Fourth, we can formulate a testing
operation which functions to check on the efficiency and effectiveness of our educational organization and helps suggest
necessary modifications. Throughout each of these operational functions there also should be adequate feed-back and
measurement to help us modify our goals and strategies and
make our system more effective while it is still in operation.

This four-fold division does not preclude moving an
aspect of a particular component to a different operational
function. Realistically too, assignment of a component to
one of the operational units rather than to another necessarily includes a value judgment as to its major role on the
broader education scene. The systems approach I use for
my courses in Social Foundations is based on this definition
of a system and its sub-division into the previously men-

tioned four functional operations.

III.   The Approaches Used in My Courses of Social
       Foundations of Education

   A.   Course Mission and Objectives

       Our first area of concern is the course "mission"
and the enabling objectives.   The "basic mission" of this
course is the service to our society and our students as individuals through providing continuity and socialization, as
well as adaptive innovation.   Realistically, this course
stresses achievable "enabling" objectives consistent with the
"basic mission."   These are:

1.   Information
     Organize information into usable and functional form;
2.   Process
     Learn the process for analyzing an educational system;
3.   Relevance
     Develop content and process which is functional and
meaningful in terms of the student's "real world" experience;
4.   Transferability
     Organize content and perceptions for maximum trans-
ferability and continuous learning;
5.   Decision-Making
     Develop perception and knowledge for professional
choice of priorities in educational decision-making;
6.   Empathy
     Develop a concern and interest for the parties in-
volved in the educational process.

   B.   Course Inputs

       Our second area of concern is that of significant in-
puts of a social and technological nature.   These influence
what one should teach, how to teach, and realistically affect the choice of enabling objectives.   I have listed six
areas of significant input but recognize full well that other
components, including previously designated objectives might
well fit into this category.   "Questions" are guides to questions I have posed to aid in reaching decision on what and
how to teach.   "Input reality" refers to significant features
of the broader environment that guide my choice of content
and process.

1. INFORMATION
    Questions
    1. What types and quantities of information are available and how do these affect the choice of what should be taught?
    2. What is the significance of the information explosion and inundation of data for our decision on what and how to teach?

    Input Reality
    Innundation of information; lateral transmission of knowledge; bombardment of multi-media

2. "PACE OF CHANGE"
    Questions
    1. What is the impact of the rapid pace of innovation and change on the choice of what and how to teach?
    2. What principles are operative in the process of change?

    Input Reality
    Very rapid change; learning today might require "unlearning" tomorrow--stress on adaptation

3. "STUDENTS"
    Questions
    1. What is the relevance of the types of commitment our students have developed, for our decision on what and how to teach?

    Input Reality
    Need to develop functional perception of educational organization; seeking commitment and identity; "doing one's thing," wish to be involved in decision-making process.

4. "TEACHERS"
    Questions
    1. What is the relevance of the increased decision-making role of teachers for our decision on what and how to teach?

    Input Reality
    Increasingly called upon as educational decision-makers.

5. "SUBJECT DISCIPLINE"
    Questions
    1. What is the content and process of the discipline
        that is to be taught?
    2. What is the relevance of this educational disci-
        pline for our decision on what and how to teach?

    Input Reality
    Broad, vague; little traditional disciplined structure.

6. "SOCIETY"
    Questions
    1. What developments or trends in the social area
        are relevant for our decision on what and how to
        teach?

    Input Reality
    Pressures for equalizing educational opportunity;
    race, urbanization and manpower needs; innovation
    to protect continuity.

    C. Course Strategies

         The third area of concern is that of strategies.
These should be carefully developed on the basis of objectives and input, and should be internally balanced to secure
a maximum achievement of desirable objectives. Key questions that might be asked in the development of relevant
strategies are:

--On the basis of "significant inputs" and objectives for this
  course, what strategies might prove most effective for
  teaching this course?

--In what way and to what degree will these strategies affect our inputs and objectives?

--In what way and to what degree will these strategies affect each other?

Based upon my answers to these questions, I have developed
the following major strategies for use with my courses:

         1. Use of my edited book of readings as the corner-
stone for this course. This book, A Systems Approach to Social Foundations of American Education, New York, MSS
Educational Publications (19 East 48th Street), (Dec.) 1969,

618 p. , provides a disciplined systems model for the course.
I have organized this book on the basis of
a. a broad Unit Divisions of major systems operations
    and sub-divisions for the major component sub-cate-
    gories. This provides a simulated model enabling
    students to transfer the analytic and critical skills
    and perceptions from the classroom to the changing
    "real world." The book provides a three-fold pattern
    of organization. Unit I deals with delineating the
    variables in a society that can be significant factors
    in defining and determining the goals of education.
    In Unit II, the readings are concerned with those
    strategies which are or can be used for moving to-
    wards the goals of education. In Unit III, for read-
    ings suggest evaluation of strategies and structures
    on the basis of proficiency tests and problem solving
    criteria. Naturally, the three units are not independ-
    ent and should feed-back and modify priorities and
    choices both within each unit and among the units.
    In this way any change in composition of significant
    variables would affect the entire system.

b. This book contains over eighty up-to-date charts,
    graphs, and meaningful statistics for testing hypothe-
    ses, developing generalizations and using inquiry
    skills. It also consists of relevant selections of re-
    cently published articles (most from 1968-1969) deal-
    ing with the current educational scene and sufficient-
    ly involving to "turn students on."

c. There are persistent questions preceding each chap-
    ter, which have been designed to develop a systemat-
    ic understanding of the organization and functioning of
    American education. This understanding should in-
    clude developing an awareness of the interrelationship
    of the component parts of the system. The questions
    for each unit and each chapter are organized to rein-
    force a model of descriptive, analytical and prescrip-
    tive skills. They also provide persistent transfer-
    able questions and modes of inquiry that students can
    utilize with the increasingly available information out-
    side of a classroom situation. The following ques-
    tions have been developed as achieving the above ob-
    jectives:

Graphic Model of Operational Functions and
Component Part for Social Foundations of Education

UNIT I

UNIT II

UNIT III

Introduction--An Overview of Systems

Ch. 1 A Systems Approach to Education

Societal Input as Defining Goals of Education

Ch. 2 Political Context: Impact of Federalism

Ch. 3 Philosophical Context

Ch. 4 Historical Context

Ch. 5 Socio-Economic Context: Racial Problems

Ch. 6 Socio-Economic Context: Problems of Urbanization, Class, Decentralization, and Student Rebellion

Strategies for Securing Goals

Ch. 7 Levels of Educational Organization

Ch. 8 Methods

Ch. 9 Curriculum

Ch. 10 Teachers

Measurement of Goal Achievement Through Output

Ch. 11 Tests and Measurements

Ch. 11 Tests and Measurements

Ch. 12 Effectiveness

A Systems Approach to Social Foundations of American Education, New York, MSS Educational Publishing Co., 1969, p. 111.

(Ch. 1-A) Systems Approach to Education
1. What is a "systems approach" to education?
2. What is the relevancy of a systems approach for understanding, modifying or changing American Education?
3. Why is the relevancy of this approach for educational planning in America?

(Unit 1)--Societal Input as Defining the Goals of Education
Persistent Questions
1. In what way and to what degree do the various input factors interact with each other to affect the definition of American educational goals?
2. In what way and to what degree do these various input factors affect the strategies currently used in American education?
3. What are the currently accepted goals of American education? What is the relevance of these goals for modifications of American education?
4. What social conditions have influenced the formulation of these goals?
5. In your opinion, what should be the main goals of American education?

(Ch. 2)--Political Context: Impact of Federalism
1. What have been the negative and positive impacts of the political system on the goals and strategies of American education?
2. What changes, if any, should be made in the Federal system to aid in improving American education? Why?

(Ch. 3)--Philosophical Context
1. What major philosophical positions are significant for understanding American education?
2. How do these affect the goals of American education?
3. Which philosophical approaches do you find most suitable for developing an effective educational system?

(Ch. 4)--Historical Context
1. In what way and to what degree are historical experiences influencing current educational goals?
2. Which American historical experiences are relevant for understanding current educational problems?
3. Which current experiences of American education

might well prove significant for historians in the
future?

(Ch. 5)--Socio-Economic Context: Racial Problems
    1. In what way and to what degree are racial is-
        sues affecting current goals of American educa-
        tion?
    2. Should these issues loom as important factors
        for deciding on educational goals? Why? or
        Why not?
    3. What changes are taking place in the significance
        of these issues? Why?

(Ch. 6)--Socio-Economic Context: Problems of Urbaniza-
        tion, Class, Decentralization and Student Rebellion
    1. In what way and to what degree are the following
        issues affecting the goals of American education?
        a. urbanization
        b. class
        c. student pressures
    2. Should these issues be permitted to have this ef-
        fect on educational goals? Why? or Why not?
    3. What should be the educational response to these
        issues?

(Unit II)--Strategies for Securing Goals
    Persistent Questions
    1. In what way and to what degree do the various
        strategies used affect each other?
    2. What is the general relationship between the
        goals and strategies of American education?
    3. What strategies are currently being used to
        reach designated goals?
    4. What is the long range significance of using
        these strategies to reach our goals?
    5. What changes should be made in our goals?
        Strategies?
    6. In what way and to what degree are each of the
        strategies, levels and types of educational or-
        ganization, methods, curriculum, and teachers
        being affected by changes in the: political con-
        text, philosophical context, historical context
        and socio-economic context?

(Ch. 7)--Levels of Educational Organization
    1. In what way and to what degree do the different
        levels of American education help to reach the

goals of American education?
2. In what way and to what degree do the different types of educational organization contribute to making education more effective?
3. What should we do to improve our educational organization? Why?

(Ch. 8)--Methods
1. What methods are being used to help achieve the goals of American education? Why?
2. Are the above methods suitable?
3. What methods would you suggest using? Why?

(Ch. 9)--Curriculum
1. What types of curricula are being used to help achieve the goals of American education? Why?
2. Are the above curricula suitable?
3. What types of curricula would you suggest using? Why?

(Ch. 10)--Teachers
1. In what way and to what degree are teachers effectively utilized for achieving educational goals?
2. What changes are taking place in teacher education programs? What additional changes should be made?
3. In what way and to what degree are the goals of teachers and the profession compatible or incompatible with the goals of American education? Suggested changes?

(Unit III)--Measurement of Goal Achievement Through Output
(Ch. 11)--Tests and Measurements
1. What types of measurement techniques have we developed to ascertain whether or not we are moving toward our educational goals?
2. What major trends are evident in educational tests and measurements?
3. Are the measurement techniques and devices adequate for evaluating our degree of success in moving toward the goals? What additional measures should be taken? Why?

(Ch. 12)--Effectiveness
1. How effective is our educational system in reaching the goals?
2. What is the significance of our success or

failure?

3. How should we change our strategies to increase our effectiveness?

4. How and to what degree should we modify the goals we originally set?

5. How and to what degree should we try and influence our social context and to improve our effectiveness?

6. How and to what degree would modifying our tests and measurements improve our effectiveness?

Course Strategies (cont.)

d. Films play a major part in dramatizing issues and expanding the perceptive reference frame of students. In this course, I avoid the stilted traditional education productions and stress the TV documentaries and exciting films such as: "Meet Comrade Student," "The Way It Is," "Summerhill," "The Coleman Report," and 21st Century films. These films, and others of this quality, are strategies designed to bring the outside world into the classroom.

e. Emphasis can be placed on the strategy of small group discussion even with classes as large as one hundred students. The key to effective small group discussion is a common experience of significant readings for the session and well phrased discussion questions. Meaningful interaction is further stimulated with role playing on the basis of articles read, and utilization of simulation techniques.

f. Students also read the education page of the Sunday New York Times on a weekly basis. In class the articles are placed into appropriate categories and the issues are related to other readings and experiences. This strategy is a significant means of continuous revitalization of the course through the use of current case study or illustrative material. I also Xerox and distribute pertinent newspaper and periodical material.

D. Course Tests and Measurements

The fourth and last area of concern is tests and measurements. There is a clear need of measurement criteria to check out the internal consistency and design logic of the developed model, and to evaluate the level of performance and the success in reaching our objectives. Questions that might aid in developing measurement criteria are:

--What measurements should be developed to determine our degree of success in reaching course objectives?

--At what points should they be instituted?

--What do our measured results indicate about necessary course revision of our objectives, input, and appropriate strategies?

--How should these be implemented?

Although I utilize a number of different feed-back paths, I must admit that these are not adequate for a truly effective systems approach. Much work still needs to be done in this area. The major means of testing and measuring with this course are the following:

1. Students are required to classify articles from external sources into course categories. I consider ability to categorize on the basis of a model, a significant first step for students to deal with the mass of information available. A second step is to bring into play a mode of inquiry, hypotheses, generalizations and perceptions that are related to this category of information.

2. Students are required to write a term paper using the same model that has been developed in the course. This helps reinforce the course organization. Their success in this area indicates to me the degree to which they have been able to transfer the course model to an area of their own interest and concern.

3. The final exam in this course is based on the persistent questions which preceded chapter readings. Student answers to test questions are also expected to incorporate information and insights from films,

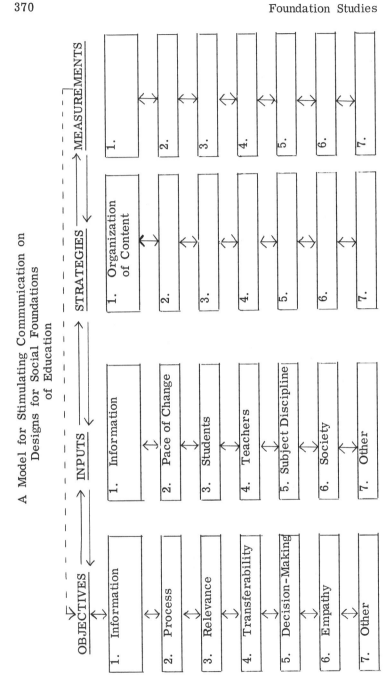

A Model for Stimulating Communication on
Designs for Social Foundations
of Education

OBJECTIVES → INPUTS → STRATEGIES → MEASUREMENTS

OBJECTIVES	INPUTS	STRATEGIES	MEASUREMENTS
1. Information	1. Information	1. Organization of Content	1.
2. Process	2. Pace of Change	2.	2.
3. Relevance	3. Students	3.	3.
4. Transferability	4. Teachers	4.	4.
5. Decision-Making	5. Subject Discipline	5.	5.
6. Empathy	6. Society	6.	6.
7. Other	7. Other	7.	7.

class discussions and other sources as well.

4. Course feed-back sheets are handed out at the end
    of each semester for detailed categorized feed-back
    from students on the content and strategies of the
    course. Naturally, they do not sign their names.
    Their replies have proven most helpful in retaining
    a functional dimension and innovative structure to
    this course.

5. A number of students have contacted me two or
    three years after taking this course to indicate the
    transferable value of the organization and its useful-
    ness in their continued professional growth.

IV. Utilization of a Model as a Basis for Increased Communication

Based upon my experiences with this course, I would
like to propose a general but tentative model of categories
to enable those of us involved in teaching this course to
systematically communicate and develop an outline for a social foundations discipline. It is likely that use of this design model might very well lead us to develop a number of
different types of organization because I'm certain that there
isn't any one model course that will meet the objectives and
perceptions of everyone. I do, however, hope that the following abstract I used to develop a systems organization of
my Social Foundations of Education Course, stimulates dialogue and hastens the day when we as a profession can develop a more disciplined approach to our subject area.

V. Conclusion

The education of teachers, despite many valuable
innovations, still requires extensive vitalization and modernization. This can be aided by educationally sound and current modes of perception, as well as appropriate psychological and logical organization. The designing of effective
courses in the Social Foundations of Education presents an
opportunity to develop and implement a relevant first step.
If we succeed, the course can also provide a guide and
challenge for modernizing other aspects of teacher education
programs. We have the means and capability of turning an
otherwise fragmented experience into a vital learning situation and it is my hope that we will accept the responsibility.

HERBERT K. HEGER

7. AN ECOLOGICAL SYSTEMS APPROACH
TO TEACHER EDUCATION

Increasingly, efforts are being made to apply the
principles of ecology and general systems theory to curriculum development; yet, teacher education programs have rarely, if at all, been conceptualized in this framework. This
article is a beginning attempt to develop an Ecological Systems Approach (ESA) for certain aspects of the teacher education curriculum.

General education for teachers needs to provide more
than minimum literacy in the several disciplines; it also needs
to provide the teacher with the ability to translate the cultural heritage of man into forms useful in the megolopolis.
This relevancy is especially important in the teacher's professional role, for every teacher is partly responsible for
the general education of his students. Therefore, the general education of teachers should be the vital concern of teacher
educators.

The Ecological Systems Approach is an attempt to provide congruence between the teacher education curriculum and
social reality by including three of the most important new
ways of thinking about and dealing with problems: Kimball's
concept of social interdependence,[1] von Bertalanffy's approach
to general systems theory,[2] and the well-established principles of ecology. The changes in problem-solving techniques
that these concepts provide are as dramatic as a shift from
algebra to calculus. As a society, we are moving from static solutions of social equations to the study of social dynamics, the identification of variables and the projection of alternatives. We are studying total systems. No longer do we
automatically shoot the coyote that is eating our chickens;
instead, we first investigate the consequences of our actions.

*The Journal of Teacher Education, Vol. XX, No. 2 (Summer
1969), pp. 158-59. Reprinted with permission.

Although productive citizens still need an understanding of acts, concepts, and the structure of knowledge, the new demands of society require mastery of the concepts of (1) interdependence, (2) interaction, (3) dynamics, (4) balance, and (5) resource allocation as they relate to the systems concept. These factors are present in all systems, whether natural or artificial. All people live and work within the total environmental system and within particular subsystems. Their decisions affect their subsystem and all other members of that system; some also affect other subsystems, and even the total environment. Hence, people must anticipate the impact of their decisions.

The ESA technique would increase curricular-societal congruence by developing systemic problem-solving skills through the use of simulation techniques with real and hypothetical systems; field experiences would be emphasized where appropriate. A typical ESA module would be carried out by an interdisciplinary team of students whose task would be to collect data about the system under study, develop a structural schema of the system, identify external links in the case of open systems, and develop hypotheses about the dynamic forces within the model. The completed model would be compared with social reality and evaluated in terms of accuracy by experts in the particular field. For example, if the task had been to study the effects upon the housing system of a community of razing two ghetto blocks, the project would be climaxed by an examination of the real community situation.

Although the ESA technique could be implemented directly into the public school curriculum, a first application in teacher education would permit future expansion of the approach through graduates of an ESA program, thereby reducing the problems of adequate in-service education for the new curriculum.

Notes

1. Kimball, Solon T. "Culture, Class, and Educational Congruency." Educational Requirements for the 1970's: An Interdisciplinary Approach. (Edited by Stanley S. Elam and W. P. McLure.) New York: Praeger, 1967. pp. 6-26.
2. von Bertalanffy, Ludwig. "General System Theory." Main Currents in Modern Thought, Vol. 11, No. 75; 1955.

MARGARET GILLETT

8. THE ECOLOGY OF EDUCATION*

Introduction

In the very first year of the 1970s, virtually every responsible newspaper, journal, and TV station in North America devoted time and space to topics dealing with environmental conditions; politicians campaigned on anti-pollution tickets; students across the U. S. and Canada staged an "Earth Day" in honor of natural resources; public indignation was aroused at the spectacle of ruined beaches and threatened fish and marine bird life; resolutions to clean up and beautify the country appeared before legislatures; and state governments sponsored "Green-Up Days." Ecology, hitherto the semiprivate preserve of conservationists, the once-arcane interest of biologists, suddenly became a major social and political issue. Ordinary people became deeply concerned about the balance of forces in nature, the harmony and interconnectedness of mankind with the animal kingdom, the earth's surface, and even outer space. They became agitated at the enormity of the desolation, dislocation, and irreparable damage our species had wrought. They petitioned and they picketed in defense of open spaces, vanishing wildlife, clean air, and pure water. They had a cause.

On the face of it, the environment controversy does not seem to have a direct bearing on education. Schools, after all, are not factories. They do not spew out smoke to befoul the air we breathe or produce mercury to contaminate the water we drink. They do not leave chemical residues on the food we eat or litter the earth with debris. Or do they? If your principal entered your classroom and accused you, the teacher, of the social crime of pollution, you would say, "Ridiculous!" There may be a few papers on the floor, may-

*Reprinted with permission from Dwight W. Allen and Eli Seifman, eds., The Teacher's Handbook. Chicago: Scott, Foresman & Co., 1971, pp. 746-54.

be even some gum or orange peel, but that hardly constitutes pollution.   You may be working in a rural or an urban
school which is indisputably derelict, which is, in plain un-
varnished language, not "underprivileged," but simply a
slum.   However, if you teach in an average school, it will
probably be relatively well cared for, relatively clean, relatively neat.   Yet obviously there is more to the environment issue than the question of simple neatness.   Indeed,
the charge might be laid that the school as an institution is
both a victim and a perpetrator of pollution.   Furthermore,
the case might be made that one of the most important tasks
for contemporary teachers, philosophers, and social scientists is to consider the whole matter of the ecology of education.   To approach education from an ecological point of
view is to search for a fresh perspective and new insights.
It is to cast in modern context the perennial quest for balance, harmony, and understanding of relationships.   It may
call into question long-accepted value systems and lead away
from competitive, exploitative practices.   It is more than a
passing fad, a creation of the media; it is potentially a new
world view.

     In any event, as long as we believe that education re-
flects society and take for granted that the school is a social institution, we educators cannot ignore a question like
ecology that consumes public attention and commands public
concern.   Without doubt, both the "educational establishment"
and educational institutions have been profoundly and permanently affected by the other great issues of our times.   Issues like civil rights, violence, and the morality of war have
led to student protests, resignations of teachers and administrators, the development of new courses, modifications of the
grading and examination systems, and a multitude of minor
changes.   In the confrontations on and off the campus, commentators have talked about "the winters of discontent" and
"the long hot summers."   It is now time to consider "the
silent springs" and, in the process, to test a few metaphors.

Pollution and the School

     Critics of the North American way of life attack mass
consumption, not so much because it is inherently evil, but
because it has led inevitably, inexorably, to mountains of
waste.   The assembly lines that manufacture millions of
shiny, comfortable automobiles also produce massive grave-
yards of people and cars; the refrigerator, once used to pre-

serve food, is abandoned and becomes a death trap for a
child.   Products designed to hold refreshing drinks serve
their purpose, then become the unlovely rusting cans, the
ubiquitous bottles, the untidy metal caps that decorate highways, recreation areas, and city streets.   Energy used to
transform raw material into the goods that can help make
life civilized or transport people to places of work or pleasure escapes into the air as eye-searing, lung-destroying
smog.   Effluvia from the factories produce dying lakes; un-
consumed consumer goods create a littered landscape.

Critics of mass education observe similar happenings
in the schools.   It would not be hard to find innumerable
students or former students, whether graduates or dropouts,
who would characterize the enterprise of formal education
as one great garbage dump.   Litter is to the landscape as
much of the present curriculum is to learning.   It is not so
bad in itself--there is nothing basically wrong or even unlovely about a beer bottle--but it becomes an eyesore, a
public nuisance, even a hazard when it is misplaced.   Similarly, there is nothing inherently wrong with the content of
many traditional courses, but much of it is used, worn out,
and misplaced, in time if not in space.   Literature courses,
for example, continue to include and even to emphasize the
works of nineteenth-century writers--fine writings in their
day, but now often sadly irrelevant.   Reverence for Shake-
speare clutters the curriculum with great plays that were
written in a language and reflect a value system largely foreign to American high school students today.   There is no
question that these are great plays and that they should be
preserved, but in many classrooms they are just so much
waste.   The time spent upon them is time not spent on material that really "grabs" the young.   As citizens, we need
to spend millions picking up car hulks and reclaiming the
countryside; as educators, we need to spend millions teaching the things neglected by our preference for inert ideas and
obsolete material.

The landscape of my schooling is littered with imper-
ishables, with deathless phrases and useless items that have
stayed with me over the years.   All I can remember from
a high school history course are some rodomontade phrases
from the textbook, such as, "William Gladstone had a smile
like the silver plate on a coffin," while Robert Walpole "was
fond of the bottle and the chase; he took off his cares when
he took off his clothes; and his motto was 'Let sleeping dogs
lie.' "   Alas for British history!   What of other subjects?

Geography, perhaps? Mercifully, children are no longer required to recite stops on various rail and sea routes around
the world, but I still remember a section of a rail line in
western New South Wales, Australia ("Broken Hill, Menindie,
Ivanhoe, Condobolin, Parkes, Forbes, Orange, Blaney, Bat-
hurst ..."). I can't go any further and I can't do it back-
wards, though after thirty years I never make a mistake as
far as I go--but that line is unlikely to take me anywhere.
There are other distorted memorabilia from the classroom,
half-eroded like rusting cans, trivia on the order of the definition that states, "The equator is a menagerie lion running
around the earth," or the hymn that vows, "Gladly, the
cross-eyed bear." All of this kind of junk was collected
and inspected at regular intervals called examinations, then
left to rot.

Curriculum content is not the only thing that links the
school to the dump or relates it to other environmental problems. We also have our pedagogic smog, our erosion and
deserts, our detergents and dead fish.

Physically there may be no smog in your classroom,
but what is that heavy pall that hangs about the school and
lifts miraculously at vacation time? It seems as if the
gloom of learning persists, despite the best efforts of the
progressives to make work fun. "Learning, the educational
process, has long been associated only with the glum," observed Marshall McLuhan in 1967. "We speak of the 'serious' student."[1]

What happened to the bright-eyed, eager child who entered first grade and loved her teachers all through elementary school? Could she be the bored, slightly hostile teen-
ager who is thinking of leaving or is smoking grass to escape the tedium? What tragic erosion of interest! Why and
how did the school let (make?) this human disaster take
place? For the idealistic new teacher who really wants to
reach his students, there is perhaps nothing more forbidding
than rows of blank faces which years of monotony have
smoothed to unreceptiveness. Only with time, special attention, and a lot of care can he reclaim this desert.

It is perfectly true that we do not try to turn our students off. On the contrary, we provide counselors and advisors of many brands to help clean up individual confusion,
just as we try to "brighten" up our homes and clothes with
detergents. But the price of clean clothes--incredibly, un-

intentionally--is too often frothy lakeshores, stinking waters, dead fish. Counselors, whose role is placement of students, not displacement of dirt, may succeed in directing young people into certain channels and thus help solve immediate personal and administrative problems. Yet the long-term effects of their efforts could be as unexpected as those of "innocent" soap powders. Their ultimate function may be the anti-human typing of students, who are left to float in a hostile environment or are doomed to dead-end futures because of their assignment to predetermined categories. For example, girls are often directed, albeit with the aid of the enzymes of convention and social expectation, to courses and occupations "for women" simply because they are girls, regardless of their individual potential as human beings. The connection between the washing machine and the dead fish was a surprise to most of us; the connection between the school and the prepackaged future for the child should be no surprise at all.

Critics of the school could easily extend the metaphor indefinitely: another form of litter is obviously the ceaseless piles of notes that students take year after year or the stencils that teachers churn out endlessly; litterbugs are those "experts" who pollute the schoolscape with unintelligible jargon and tricky gimmicks; slag heaps are those locked closets filled with obsolete, dysfunctional A-V material; runoff is the "brain drain," and so forth.

From these rather devastating examples, we might conclude that all is not well with the school. In other words, the school as ecosystem is out of balance. We shall return to this idea later, but first we shall explore some other relationships between learning and the environment.

Environment and Education

The connection between environment and education has long been acknowledged, even if not fully recognized. It has recently been noted in Richard Armour's good-humored Diabolical Dictionary, where we find the following entry:

Environmental factors. These include blackboard, desk, window, door, floor, ceiling, and anything else that may affect the student favorably or unfavorably, even a tic in the teacher's left eyelid. Psychologists have recently discovered that an important part of the word 'environmental' is 'mental.' Nutritionists point out that it contains 'iron,' which is good for young, growing bodies. Experiments such as writing with black chalk on white blackboards and hiring prettier teachers may improve the learning environment. Incense and background music are also being considered. [2]

Armour's satire flicks across some of the items in the immediate classroom situation. These bear further scrutiny, and so does the whole global environment in which we try to teach and learn.

While there may be no requisitions extant ordering "black chalk for white blackboards," each year teachers make more and more requests for instructional materials of all kinds--requests which commercial firms are happy to supply or even anticipate. Each year administrators must budget for more classroom supplies; each visit of an accrediting team takes into account the number of library books and the condition of facilities; most international educational aid programs supply "hardware" as well as know-how. Instructional support material has become a multimillion-dollar business. The electronic classroom, the language lab, the science lab are a far cry from the primordial picture of Mark Hopkins and his student on their homely log. Contemporary educational requisitions cover a startling range of items from TV cameras to toilet paper. Teaching and learning become more and more dependent on things.

Yet while elaborately equipped institutions proliferate, and school design becomes a recognized specialty in architecture, there appears to be a concurrent counter-trend. Storefront schools, an important part of urban education-renewal programs, make do with minimal facilities, and in Philadelphia there is even the "school without walls," where the instructional environment is the city itself. Reform efforts like these are directed toward a return to learning and a deemphasis on the external trappings of teaching. However, the basic difficulty in directing educational change comes from the fact that the educational system does not work in isolation.

Miners in Alaska who wash away mountains in their search for gold could do so with impunity (there are plenty of mountains!) if the slush they generated did not cover the flats, kill the vegetation, and eliminate the animals that live

on it.   The mineral and the animal worlds are vitally inter-
connected.   Similarly, the educational system is bound up in
infinitely intricate and fundamental ways with other systems.
These are often very powerful--the economic system, which
pushes and pressures for more plants and books and equipment; or the political system, which decrees whether or not
a school bond issue will be floated, whether or not children
must be bussed to school; or the system of cultural values,
which determines how students perceive their environment.

"Culture and environment are so directly linked together that the quality of environment has as direct an effect on the quality of a culture as a culture, through its values, has on the values of space and resources of a civilization."[3]   This idea was recently explored in an educational
context in Montreal, Canada.   A study conducted in thirty-
two schools showed that Canadian teachers with different cultural backgrounds reacted differently toward environmental
factors as apparently objective as school buildings.[4]   French-
speaking Canadian teachers showed a higher degree of satisfaction with the spatial characteristics of their classrooms
than did their English-speaking counterparts--even though
their rooms were smaller and the space per pupil less.   The
English teachers proved more satisfied with the temperature
of their rooms, though these were on the average two degrees cooler than those of the French.   No variations were
found between French and English teachers in their appreciation of classroom lighting, but there was a significant meas-
urable difference in the light intensities.   The French rooms
were almost twice as light as the English.   Apparently Eng-
lish-Canadian teachers were more comfortable in less bright
environments, which caused the author of the study to wonder
whether this related to the fact that "the forefathers of the
English-Canadians came from a country with dull skies while
those of the French-Canadians came from a sunnier country."[5]

The late Richard Neutra, who has been called the last
of the pioneers in modern architecture, always sought to accommodate human biological, physiological, and psychological
needs.   Among other things, he realized that--for his school
buildings as for his big community projects--"bad acoustics
can lead to shouting and that calls forth an argumentative
mood."[6]   He recognized clearly the connection between the
formal learning situation and the physical environment.

One of the ways human beings have learned to deal
with their total environment is through the development of

conceptual categories which are transmitted through language.
Obviously, different languages have different words for the
same objects. This is not merely a difference in labels; it
represents a difference in outlook. To take a well-known
example, in English the words for ice and snow are limited;
on Baffin Island, however, twenty-one different terms for
ice and snow have been identified. [7] There these things constitute a significant part of the environment and affect in
many ways the daily lives of the people. The words an individual uses and the way he uses them shape both his concept of reality and his relationship to his milieu. Further,
the structural aspects of language may influence ways of
looking at the world even more than vocabularies do.
Greenlanders, for example, have a language without transitive verbs. Thus, they tend to see things happening without
specific cause. "I kill him" becomes "He dies to me."
This is a very different approach to life from that held by
speakers of European languages, where action accompanies
perception and transitive verbs give events purpose and
cause.

It is unlikely that many of us will encounter Baffin
Islanders or Greenlanders, but the peculiarities of their languages have important messages for us anyway. They can
help us to stop taking the obvious for granted and begin to
realize the wide variations in world views revealed by language study. Since language is a product of environment,
a means of experiencing it, and a tool for its control, and
since language is also the principal medium of education,
its nature and function cannot be ignored by teachers. The
limited vocabulary or strange speech patterns of the child
from the ghetto, the hills of Appalachia, or the Indian res-
ervation have significance far beyond their degree of devia-
tion from "standard" English. These differences exemplify
variations in perception of reality which condition everything
the teacher attempts to teach and everything the child attempts to learn. [8] Thus, we have an interaction that, over-
simplified, goes something like this: environment→ lan-
guage→ learning→ perception of environment.

The School as Ecosystem

This language-environment interaction is not unlike
the mineral cycle in nature, one of the two ecological processes involving interaction between the physicochemical environment and the biotic assemblage. Mineral nutrients are

incorporated into plants, which are grazed upon by herbiv-
orous creatures, which in turn are eaten by carnivorous
creatures. When the nutrient-containing protoplasm eventually decomposes, the minerals are released to the environment, where they are available for reuse. Thus we have a
cycle that goes something like this: minerals in environment → plants → herbivores → carnivores → environment.

The other major ecological process is that of energy
flow. This pattern involves the conversion of radiant energy
into chemical energy. Energy in the form of sunlight is incorporated into a producer (plant), synthesized into other
molecules and fed upon by a consumer (herbivore), which
may be fed upon by another consumer (carnivore), which in
turn may be fed upon by another carnivore consumer. In
other words, we have producer → consumer, or plant →
herbivore → carnivore → carnivore. This energy flow is
not cyclic but unidirectional--only in very rare instances do
plants eat animals. It may be equated in educational terms
with the learner's exposure to the culture of the past, his
absorption of it, and his resultant individual growth and development.

Mineral cycling and energy flow lie at the heart of
ecosystem dynamics. [9] The ecosystem is an ecological unit
comprising living and nonliving components interacting to
produce a stable system. It is the basic unit in ecology.
For example, a pond, or a lake, or a forest may be considered an ecosystem. "The principle of the ecosystem provides a unifying framework within which specialized study at
the individual, population, and community levels can be meaningfully conducted." [10] In educational terms, the school is
the unit within which specialized study of the individual pupil, student body, and school community can be meaningfully
conducted. It is a basic tenet of ecology that no organism
or ecosystem is self-sufficient; similarly, no single student
or school is self-sufficient. All ecosystems are open--which
means that energy and matter continually escape from them
during the processes of life and must be replaced if the system is to continue to function. The school, like the ecosystem, is dynamic. (Perhaps one of the consoling things for
educators in this analogy is that nature is not completely efficient and that, with every transfer of energy, there is considerable loss.)

One of the major facts about ecosystems is that they

age. They undergo succession. An aquatic ecosystem proceeds predictably to a semiterrestrial or fully terrestrial
state. This is accompanied by significant changes in structure and function, both biotic and abiotic. Some nutrients
increase or become more readily available and others are
depleted through long-term storage; dissolved oxygen tends
to be decreased, especially in deep water; electrical conduc-
tivity and thermal properties are altered. There are, of
course, corresponding changes in the life forms present.[11]
One of the undeniable truths about the school is that it ages
--the building becomes dated, as do those who teach in it,
the materials they use, and the ideas and attitudes they
transmit. As Whitehead once said, "In the history of education, the most striking phenomenon is that schools of learning, which at one epoch are alive with a ferment of genius,
in a succeeding generation exhibit merely pedantry and routine."[12]

Reviving the natural environment is a major concern
of contemporary ecologists; reforming schools is a commitment of many contemporary educators. A major aspect of
environmental pollution concerns the disposal of waste, both
biological and cultural. Some ecologists see waste as

> a resource being present in a system that is not
> adapted to it and thus constituting an unaccustomed
> stimulus ... an 'insult' to the system. These are
> stimulants or insults that may terminate some or
> initiate other biological processes, alter efficiency,
> affect species composition and structure, and in
> general thereby alter the dynamics of an ecosys-
> tem.[13]

The current student generation, with its protests about inappropriate teaching methods, remote administration, and irrelevant courses, has made it clear that our present school
system contains many "insults." As a result, the dynamics
of the school as ecosystem are in the process of being sig-
nificantly altered.

Toward an Ecology of Education

The ecological approach originates with the study of
plants and animals in nature. It recognizes the interdependence of living things on each other and on their environment.[14] Thus, to take an ecological approach toward educa-

tion would involve a return to nature. Though this would not be a new naturalism in the romantic tradition, neither would it dismiss Thoreau's statement: "I went to the woods because I wished to live deliberately, to front only the essential facts of life, and see if I could not learn what it had to teach and not, when I came to die, discover that I had not lived." To learn how to "live deliberately" should be a responsibility of mankind, a species with a unique ability to manipulate the environment. It should be the task of education to help human beings to live deliberately and to understand their relationships with each other and with their environment.

Ecology can show just how complex and unexpected, how exciting and devastating these relationships can be. Long ago, Charles Darwin pointed out an unsuspected connection between cats and clover. He found that bumblebees were indispensable for the fertilization of clover. But the number of bees depended on the number of field mice, which ate the brood that the bees reared in the ground. The number of mice depended on the number of cats. So wherever there were lots of efficient cats, the mice were less numerous, there were more bees, and the clover was more abundant. Ecologists have recently discovered an apparently far-fetched link between the use of insecticide in the United States and the impending extinction of the Bermuda petrel, one of the world's rarest birds and one that feeds at sea, visits land only to breed, and breeds only on Bermuda. Significant levels of DDT have been found in unhatched eggs and dead chicks, but the only source of the insecticide is in the petrel's oceanic feed chain, which must be contaminated by runoff from the mainland some 650 miles away. Awareness of the possibility of such unlikely relationships can help ecologists solve the problems of environment; sensitivity to the possibility of "extraordinary" relationships can help free the educator from the mechanistic expectations of "The System."

The ecological viewpoint in education may be seen as an antidote to the dehumanizing, technological, systems-analysis, input-output approaches, but it is by no means anti-scientific. Indeed, since ecology itself is the science that studies the interdependent relationship between living things and environment, an ecology of education would be expected to employ the methods of science for identifying and solving its problems. Nor is the ecological approach really inimical to technology; indeed, the "global village" concept of technological theory harmonizes perfectly with the ecological view.

It is true that, in looking to ecology for a model, we are not turning to a science that has solved all its own problems. Far from it. The fundamental issues of ecology are the complex and vexing ones that have to do with the future of mankind. To confront these problems, some ecologists are calling for a rethinking of our ideas about the total environment and for the development of a new ethic of the land. One notes:

> The roots of the crisis in which man finds himself are deep in the outlook western man, in particular, has had about the land--land as his adversary to be conquered, as his servant to be exploited for his own end, as a possession of rightful and eminent domain, and, most importantly, land of unlimited capacity. These concepts must give ground to an ecological conscience, to a love, respect, admiration, and understanding for the total ecosystem of which we are part; our course, otherwise, is one of collision, an inexorable Armageddon. [15]

Educators can join the quest for new attitudes and a search for new understanding of the relationships between the child, the teacher, the school, and all of them to the total environment. Such an approach would involve considerable intellectual flexibility and would demand interdisciplinary studies. It would not ignore specialization, but it would aim at integration. It would search for balance, harmony, continuity; it would eschew gaps. The need for this kind of approach in other areas has already been recognized.

> Every scientific discipline for the study of living organisms--bacteriology, botany, zoology, biology, anthropology--must, from its own special standpoint, develop a science of ecology--literally, "the logic of the household"--or the study of organism/ environment fields. Unfortunately, this science runs afoul of academic politics, being much too interdisciplinary for the jealous guardians of departmental boundaries. But the neglect of ecology is one of the most serious weaknesses of modern technology, and it goes hand-in-hand with our reluctance to be participating members of the whole

community of living species.[16]

Admittedly, the idea of an integrated approach to or
philosophy of education is not new.   It could doubtless be
traced back to Plato.   And the history of education is
peopled with Froebels, Montessoris, and Arnolds who, in
one way or another, would seek to don Whitehead's "seam-
less garment of knowledge."   Similarly, the ethics of an
ecology could probably be expressed in old terms.   Phrases
like "No man is an island," or "I am my brother's keeper,"
for example, epitomize the inherent values of community
and responsibility.   Nevertheless, we still need an approach
to the nature of learning, the learner, and the outcomes of
learning that is at once scientific and humane.   Such an approach would be an ecology of education.

Notes

1.   Marshall McLuhan and Quentin Fiore, The Medium
        is the Massage (New York: Bantam Books, Inc.,
        1967), p. 10.
2.   Richard Armour, A Diabolical Dictionary of Education
        (New York: The World Publishing Co., 1969),
        p. 46.
3.   Henry B. VanLoon, "Earth, Space and Human Culture,"
        American Institute of Architects Journal, August
        1963, p. 23.
4.   Vrej-Armen Artinian, "Culture and Environment: In-
        teraction in the Classroom," McGill Journal of
        Education, Fall 1970.
5.   Ibid., p. 164.
6.   Ibid.
7.   William F. Mackay, Concept Categories as Measures
        of Cultural Distance (Ste. Foy, Quebec: Interna-
        tional Center for Research on Bilingualism, 1969),
        p. 2.
8.   Cf. "It is quite an illusion to imagine that one adjusts
        to reality essentially without the use of language
        and that language is merely an incidental means
        of solving specific problems of communication or
        reflection.   For the fact of the matter is that the
        'real world' is to a large extent unconsciously
        built up on the language habits of the group" (Ed-
        ward Sapir, "The Status of Linguistics as a Sci-
        ence," 5, pp. 207-214).   This concept has been
        further elaborated and is known in linguistics as

the Sapir-Whorf hypothesis.

9. G. Edward J. Kormondy, Concepts of Ecology (Englewood Cliffs, N. J. : Prentice-Hall, Inc., 1969),
   pp. 3-4.
10. G. Edward J. Kormondy, ed., Readings in Ecology
    (Englewood Cliffs, N. J. : Prentice-Hall, Inc.,
    1965), p. 165.
11. Kormondy, Concepts of Ecology, p. 181.
12. Alfred North Whitehead, The Aims of Education (New
    York: The New American Library, Inc., 1949),
    p. 13.
13. Kormondy, Concepts of Ecology, p. 180.
14. R. E. Balch, The Ecological Viewpoint (Toronto: Can-
    adian Broadcasting Corporation), 1965.
15. Kormondy, Concepts of Ecology, p. 196.
16. Alan W. Watts, The Book (New York: P. F. Collier,
    Inc., 1966), p. 86.

ROBERT J. MULVANEY &
ROGER J. SULLIVAN

9. PHILOSOPHIZING--A RADICAL PROPOSAL FOR TEACHER TRAINING*

Two things need to be said: (1) philosophical positions are unavoidable; (2) genuine philosophizing is the only
important skill the teacher needs to learn. These two positions may sound odd or not clearly distinguished, but this is
because some typically think of philosophizing as a "neutral"
activity, however much they believe that real differences exist between philosophical positions. That this is confused is
a major point of this paper; that there are important conclusions for teacher training in this confusion is its main point.

Let us start with the first of these, the unavoidability
of philosophical positions. Clearly, the chief characteristic
of the expert in practical matters is his know-how: his ability to get done what needs to be done, and to do it well.
Few would argue with that, and most also believe that, as
our knowledge improves, it becomes more technical. So the
mark of the advanced department or college of education is
the large number of courses it offers in the various techniques. For various tasks there are various and appropriate methods and procedures, and the expert in educational
matters clearly is the person who knows the "how's" of
things.

Our beliefs about the nature of expertise in general
and of educational expertise in particular have a long and
honorable history. We can trace them to the Sophists--the
first group of professional teachers in the Western world.
They believed that, insofar as men have mastered their
world, they can set out that knowledge in rules so that they
in turn can transmit that knowledge to others. It was no
historical accident that the Sophists paid a good deal of at-

*Cutting Edge, Vol. 3 No. 1 (Fall 1971), pp. 9-11. Re-
printed with permission.

tention to grammar and to eloquence; displaying one's knowledge requires a language, and, the more specialized one's knowledge, the more technical one's language becomes.

The educational principle involved is a persuasive one: knowledge is power, and power is a matter of know-how.

Small wonder, then, that Socrates was regarded as odd when he attacked this view. His contention, briefly, was that when men give their attention so exclusively to techniques, they are bound to fail at that which is far more important--their own moral excellence.

The Sophistic defense is interesting even today: techniques, they argued, are, in modern language, 'morally neutral'. The educator passes his expertise on to his pupils, and his responsibility ends there. Men set their own goals; it is not the business of the educator to impose particular moral standards on his students. That might be the case in a totalitarian society but surely not in a democracy such as Athens!

Socrates' response was to accuse the Sophists of playing verbal games. He admitted that men do desire and seek success, but, he argued, the notion of success simply cannot be analyzed merely in terms of means. Rather, means are always means to something. It is only a pretense for educators to say that ends are no concern of theirs, for such a view already is the assumption of a fundamental philosophic contention that ends are not subject to rational and critical examination; they are all purely subjective and not within the realm of the challengeable.

The Socratic thesis is a tough one: every teacher ineluctably assumes a particular moral stance whenever he teaches, and this holds no matter how eloquently he may protest his 'professional neutrality' and the neutrality of the skills he transmits. Further, because the education of the citizens of a state is never a completely private affair, the teacher also necessarily assumes a particular political stance by the very fact that he promotes certain skills he knows will be used in particular political ways.

Thrasymachus was perhaps more honest than his fellow Sophists. He saw Socrates' point and agreed with him. But he then argued that justice and power are identical, and

good education should be a matter simply of training in
rhetoric, for that is how to produce the power politician.
(cf. The Republic, Chap. IV) Many men have been remarkably successful in using this view, but the Thrasymachean
state corrupts education and turns it into a school in propa-
ganda. To adopt it is to license both political and academic
tyranny.

Although contemporary educators may stress social
influences on the formation of goals more than most of the
Sophists, they often still tend to follow a Sophistic rather
than a Socratic approach. Some departments of education offer no courses at all in philosophy of education; some that
do, do not think them important enough to build them into
their curriculum requirements; and those that do, often provide courses that are the most boring and nihilistic in the
curriculum.

But the Socratic thesis still has not been defeated:
teachers--and teachers of teachers--ineluctably assume particular philosophic commitments when they teach. Until
those commitments are examined explicitly and thoughtfully,
they hardly can be presumed to reflect a self-consistent,
sensitive self-consciousness of what it is to engage in the
profession. Finally, the refusal to discuss those commitments with students while simultaneously shaping them in
those same commitments produces a methodology which is
more like tacit indoctrination· than genuine education--surely
not the ideal technique for a department of education nor any
university department in a politically open society!

We turn now to our second point--one to be found also in both Socrates and Dewey: the only important thing for
a teacher to learn is how to philosophize, because philosophy is the general theory of education.

This may seem like an extravagant claim--and is
surely one not shared by all philosophers, much less educators. But we take this as evidence only that Sophists can
be found almost any place--even in philosophy. Of course we
are arguing on behalf of a particular view of the philosophic
enterprise, a view which distinguishes between theory and
practice (or between pure and applied theory) but which re-
fuses to believe in a dualism of incommunicable realms of
thought and action. On this view, theory is not only the
source but the continually operative rationale and ultimate
end of practice. Practice, in turn, generates, tests, and

represents theory in concrete situations. However abstract-
ly we may formulate our theories, their meaningfulness and
truth finally depend upon the concrete situations which constitute our educational life.

The consequence is the Socratic view that philosophizing is never a merely descriptive enterprise (nor is education), so that to engage in philosophy is to undertake the
agonies of constant self-re-evaluation and of social criticism.
Both are integral to an educational program deliberately designed for long-term and not short-term gains. This means
that, while courses in philosophy surely need to consider the
content of various political and educational theories, teaching
philosophy is never merely that, if it is to localize what we
have said of the connection between theory and practice.

What we mean to say is that the form of philosophical expressions is far more basic than any particular content. What we offer is an alternative to the power rhetoric
of the Sophists, namely, the critical rhetoric of Socrates.
This is what is meant by dialogue, the willingness to evaluate positions in common, together. This method has immediate political consequences, as well as educational ones,
because it cannot support a tyranny and can serve only truly
democratic purposes. These effects are felt up and down
the spectrum of a man's social relationships--the family, the
school, the society.

This, then, is why philosophy is the only important
study: because, where it exists in this form, everything is
subject to its examination. Those who argue that the philosophic training of teachers should be "to acquaint them with
the great systems" or "to introduce them to the rigor of
analyzing a text" are those who, in the Sophistic tradition,
believe that even philosophy is essentially a 'neutral' discipline which can be taught in a 'neutral' fashion. They cannot but fail to appreciate that philosophy is not peripheral to
but at the heart of the educational enterprise.

The teacher's college which is faithful to the Socratic
view will erase any hint of despotism, encourage the presence of little Platonic academies, minimize a destructive distance between teacher and student, and eliminate those subjects which of their nature cannot tolerate examination by dialogue.

Some may see in this analysis a rationale for foreshortening the apprentice's training. On the contrary, it is precisely the rationale for arguing that the teacher is never finished with his own education, but rather even after securing his degree, constantly participates in the functioning of the school of education. Through the enlarged experience of its older participants, the school continually deepens its own conception of its function and meaning. The teacher's college will no longer find it necessary to supplement its offerings by a growing identification with the larger university. Far from it. It will become an ideal form of that university, in which young and old share their common political experiences by reference to their special social function: teaching.

ADREAS M. KAZAMIAS
with KARL SCHWARTZ

10. WOOZLES AND WIZZLES IN THE METHODOLOGY OF COMPARATIVE EDUCATION *

'Hallo!' said Piglet, 'what are you doing?'
'Hunting,' said Pooh.
'Hunting what?'
'Tracking something,' said Winnie-the-Pooh very
   mysteriously.
'Tracking what?' said Piglet, coming closer.
'That's just what I ask myself. I ask myself, What?'

In this paper we shall examine certain recent developments in two interrelated aspects of comparative education:
methodology and intellectual perspectives.[1] Specifically we
shall argue: that some well-publicized recent efforts to make
comparative education "scientific" are limited in scope and
are often based on questionable views and assumptions about
"science" and the "scientific method"; and that partly because
of the influence of other social studies, notably economics,
sociology and political science, education has been largely
treated "instrumentally," namely, as a means to analyze other spheres of social activity, and thus it has subserved the
concerns and interests of economists, sociologists, and political scientists. As such, the educational phenomena examined
of necessity have been restricted to those bearing upon the
economy, the polity, and the social system.

From "Pre-Science" to "Empirical Science"

The story of comparative education, at least since the
nineteenth century, has been told in different ways. Comparative education, it has been maintained, has moved or
evolved from impressionistic, individual unpatterned observa-

---

*Comparative Education Review, Vol. XIV, No. 3, pp. 255-
61. Reprinted with permission.

tions and reports to more organized statements, or attempts
to establish patterns; from unsystematic reporting to systematic description, analysis, and explanation; from historical-
cum-philosophical-cum-melioristic to more objective, social
scientific investigations; from unorganized, individual social
philosophies to "full-fledged organized, empirical science";[2]
from theoretical interpretative but also speculative enquiries
aiming at <u>understanding,</u> to more specific, quantified "empirical" studies aiming at control, scientific explanation, forecasting, or prediction.   Furthermore, there appears to be
an implicit assumption, in some of the histories of the field,
of inexorable progress from a pre-scientific to a scientific
stage of investigation.

        The story of comparative education described above
and the implicit assumption of scientific inevitability are
themselves open to serious criticisms, which, however, we
shall not elaborate here.   The empirical scientific phase,
still in the process of development, has been the single most
distinguishing mark of the last decade.   To put it differently,
many comparative educators have sought to make their enquiries "scientific" and establish a "science" of comparative
education.   In their minds this phase distinguishes it from
the previous "non-scientific" endeavors.

The Restricted Interpretation of Science

        Proponents of scentific comparative education have
stressed empirical techniques, procedures, and modes of
thinking.   The primary concern, according to them, ought to
be with the observable world, with empirical "facts." Observations must be used to formulate hypotheses which need to
be tested for verification or refutation.   An accumulation of
such tested hypotheses, always generated from empirical observations, provides a corpus of empirical generalizations or
a theory, which can be used for purposes of explanation, prediction, or retrodiction, as well as for generating other hypotheses.   It has been contended that to engage in this mode
of inquiry and to employ its procedures is to engage in science or is to chart the proper course of scientific comparative education.   The development of the social sciences along
such empirical lines has marked an intellectual breakthrough,
and has contributed to better understanding of the real world
and to academic respectability.   Comparative educators have
accordingly been urged to seek a similar breakthrough by
emulating the above-mentioned trends of characteristic of the
social sciences.

There are some difficulties and logical fallacies in the view of science sketched above. Here we shall try to show that at best it represents one view of science, and a limited one at that. At worst, it is no more than natural history. To be sure, it is more systematic, and, as such, it may be viewed as a salutary development. Like Piglet's and Pooh's tracks, however, cumulatively tested hypotheses or empirically tested generalizations may not lead anywhere and certainly not to scientific principles and laws. If the task of scientific studies is to establish principles and laws a more profitable approach might be to start with what T. S. Kuhn[3] and others have called paradigms.

A criticism of the recent scientific trend, therefore, is its assumption that the rules, aims and methods of science are well-established; that there is such a thing as the method of science; and that there is a universal recipe for all to follow. But as Stephen Toulmin has said:

> There is no universal recipe for all science and all scientists any more than there is for all cakes and all cooks. There is much in science which cannot be created according to set rules and methods at all. And ... even the general nature of science itself is something in a state of development....

> Science has not one aim but many, and its development has passed through many contrasted stages. It is therefore fruitless to look for a single, all-purpose 'scientific method': the growth and evolution of sceintific ideas depends on no one method, and will always call for a broad range of different enquiries. [4]

Among other things, this calls for a new interpretation of the development of comparative education as it was outlined earlier. For example, the work of the classic comparative educators, for example, Sadler, Kandel, Hans and others, cannot be described as unscientific. These writers asked different questions about education and society than many of us do today, they employed different methods and techniques, they formulated different theories, and some of them openly declared their subjectivity and ideology. They did not use experimentation, quantification, and they did not seek prediction or forecasting. This raises another question regarding the contemporary view of scientific compara-

tive education.   To what extent is the mere presence or absence of prediction or forecasting necessary for an investigation to be properly called scientific?

    The Babylonians, Toulmin reminds us, "acquired
great forecasting power" in computing celestial motions in
a "purely arithmetical way" through the pragmatic method of
trial and error.   Yet this technique was mastered without
any understanding of the "heavenly motions," that is, without
any explanatory or interpretative theory.   It had no scientific
basis.   It was "an application of science rather than the kernel of science itself."[5]   Looking at the activity of prediction
from another way, proper scientific theory, i.e., one that
possesses explanatory power need not lead to or be used for
predictions or forecasts, let alone to their verification.   Examples of such perfectly acceptable scientific theories are
those of Darwin and Marx.

    Like all empirical sciences, a special concern of sci-
entific comparative education, we are told, must be the formulation of hypotheses, defined by one source as statements
asserting presumed relations among natural phenomena.   One
form of a hypothesis would be: "As x changes, so y changes."
This statement asserts a functional relationship between two
variables; it refers to covariation, not necessarily to causal
relationships.   In the field of comparative education, for example, the variables may be political totalitarianism and
classroom authoritarianism, literacy and urbanization, educational provision and income differentials, and religion and
educational development (or in its more specific forms, Islam
and educational provision, or Catholicism and curriculum
studies.)   These hypotheses emerge or are generated from
empirical observations.   A sophisticated hypothesis must not
merely assert the existence or absence of the relationship.
It must indicate its direction, for example, "The more x
changes, the more y changes," and preferably it must be a
quantified statement of the relationship.   Examples of such
hypotheses would be: "The more totalitarian the political system, the more authoritarian the classroom"; "The more oth-
erworldly the religious beliefs, the greater the emphasis on
theoretical studies in education"; and "The lower the pupil/
teacher ratio, the higher the rate of growth of the GNP."[6]
As noted above, an accumulation of such tested hypotheses
would establish general statements analogous to the empirical
generalization "All crows are black," which can be used deductively to explain particular relationships or phenomena.
So that in the example cited above, to the question "Why in

x situation is the rate of growth of the GNP high?" an answer would be "Because we have found that where there is a low pupil/teacher ratio, the rate of growth of the GNP is high."

There is circularity, conceptual fallacies and limitations to this view of scientific inquiry. In the first place a mere statement of a relationship between two observable variables without a presentation of its theoretical basis, that is its scientific foundation, is no hypothesis but an observation analogous to "Water boils at a temperature of $100°C$." Secondly, it follows that proper hypotheses are not generated from empirical observations of variables; rather they are derived from scientific principles, laws, or paradigms. Strictly speaking, therefore, the previously mentioned hypotheses are forms of empirical generalizations, not problems or puzzles to be solved.[7] Thirdly, an empirical generalization, regardless of whether it is based on two or a million observable cases, does not constitute a scientific law or a scientific theory. It does not transcend the realm of data collection and description. As Karl Popper, Eugene Meehan, and others have suggested, one is confronted with a conceptual stumbling block when one talks about a proposition as being both "empirical" and "general," or when one concentrates on the validation or confirmation of empirical generalizations. Meehan quite rightly points out: "No amount of empirical testing could possibly establish a general proposition because it refers to the future as well as to the past, to what has not been observed as well as to what has been observed."[8] Fourthly, explanations of empirical phenomena or relations by means of empirical generalizations or empirical theory are not particularly illuminating. They are analogous to the following type: 1. "Why is this crow black?" (a particular phenomenon); 2. "Because all crows are black." (an empirical generalization). Moreover, there is an element of circularity in this type of explanation. A more illuminating and scientifically more satisfactory explanation of the crow's color would involve genetic theory, optical theory, etc. Lastly, to restrict oneself to a form of science which essentially deals with relationships between empirical facts or links one event with another is to leave unresolved the crucial problem of explanation. Noah and Eckstein acknowledge this difficulty when they state:

> Thus, to summarize the argument so far, functional statements [hypotheses] may show no more than covariation; and if they do show covariation, they

may not reveal the direction of the influence between factors; and even when the direction is
known, the mechanism of the relationship between
cause and effect may remain obscure. [9]

An explanatory system must be broad in scope and possess
generality. Concrete events must be linked to abstract conceptions and not to other events, otherwise explanations remain narrow, simplistic, and of very limited value. [10]

The Search for Paradigms

Comparative education conducted along the empirical
lines discussed above may indeed have contributed to systematic gathering of data; and in some cases it may have
helped develop sophisticated techniques of testing empirical
propositions and predicting or forecasting events. But, we
have argued, it has not developed general principles and
laws, abstract conceptions, or paradigms to make it truly
scientific. (The same could be said of other social studies
carried out along similar lines.) Partly as a result of its
correlational, covariational, or functional emphasis and partly as a result of the nature of the role assigned to hypotheses, this view of "empirical comparative education" has created a stumbling block in grappling with the critical problem
of explanation. Furthermore, this type of enquiry has lacked
the "speculative imagination"[11] believed by some to be necessary for the development of science. Interestingly, this
element characterized the previous "forces and factors" approach to comparative education, which is often summarily
dismissed as pre-science or non-science.

The Paradigmatic Interpretation of Science

It might therefore be profitable to look at the field
from a somewhat different scientific viewpoint, what may be
called the paradigmatic interpretation of science. A paradigm, according to Kuhn is an accepted model or pattern; it
is rarely an object of replication. Kuhn adds: "Like an accepted judicial decision in the common law, it is an object
for further articulation and specification under new or more
stringent conditions. ... Paradigms gain their status because
they are more successful than their competitors in solving a
few problems that the group of practitioners has come to
recognize as acute."[12] Meehan uses the term system para-

digm and defines it as "a formal logical structure, an abstract calculus that is totally unrelated to anything in the
empirical world." In addition, he continues, "The system,
as a system, says nothing whatever about empirical events;
it generates expectations within its own boundaries."[13]

The paradigmatic view of science helps us overcome
the conceptual stumbling blocks referred to above, transcend the mere accumulation of facts, establish scientific
principles, laws and theory, and provide more meaningful
explanations. Hypotheses, according to this view, are derived from an "abstract calculus" or "paradigm" not from
observable, that is, empirical variables. Hypotheses are
expectations about the "real" world, generated on the basis
of relationships in the paradigm. Their role is not to relate one empirical variable with another, that is, educational development with economic development. Rather it is to
demonstrate isomorphism between the paradigm and the observable world. On the question of explanation, the view of
science chosen here avoids the previously mentioned difficulty and limitation of explaining one empirical event by
means of another or by relying on the weight of an empirical generalization. Instead events are explained by means
of abstractions, that is by looking outside the realm of
events to be explained.

Although we have been critical of the view of science
advocated by recent and contemporary writers, we are well
aware of the difficulties and problems posed by the paradigmatic view of science. We suggest, however, that greater
concern for the search for paradigms will be a significant
step forward. Already we have some embryonic paradigms,
e.g., what may be called the prestige paradigm in Foster's
Education and Social Change in Ghana, and Coombe's system maintenance paradigm. As illustrations from other social studies, one could cite Daniel Lerner's paradigm of empathy and, of course, Marx's more formidable ones of class
conflict and alienation.

Finally, the question arises: Where should comparative educators search for paradigms? This depends on how
the field is visualized or from what intellectual perspectives
it is examined. An adequate treatment of this aspect of
comparative education is impossible within the limits of this
paper. Suffice to mention that, as I have pointed out elsewhere,[14] the study of education has been envisaged almost
exclusively in relation to society and the perspectives from

which it has been examined have been mostly those of other social studies, for example, economics, sociology, and political science. Among other things these perspectives have been restrictive in their treatment of education, and have created an imbalance in the sense that education is no longer the focus of inquiry analogous to politics and economics. In the search for educational paradigms one could profitably look at education in relation to the individual rather than to society, and at what may be called the educational culture of a system. This would mean different units of analyses and would open up new areas of investigation.

Notes

1. By methodology we mean the study of methods, i.e., the procedures used to describe, understand and explain educational phenomena, or the study of the theories that have been offered about what comparative educators are doing when they are engaged in their studies. Intellectual perspectives refers to the ways or conceptual frameworks by which education has been analyzed, investigated or approached.
2. See C. Wright Mills, The Sociological Imagination (London: Oxford University Press, 1959), p. 61.
3. Thomas S. Kuhn, The Structure of Scientific Revolutions (Chicago: Phoenix Books, 1967).
4. Stephen Toulmin, Foresight and Understanding (New York: Harper, 1963), pp. 15-17.
5. Ibid., p. 36.
6. For an excellent presentation of this viewpoint see Harold J. Noah and Max A. Eckstein, Toward a Science of Comparative Education (New York: The Macmillan Company, 1969), pp. 93 ff. and passim.
7. The idea of puzzles derived from paradigms as a characteristic of science is taken from Kuhn, op. cit., pp. 35 ff.
8. Eugene J. Meehan, Explanation in Social Science: A System Paradigm (Homewood, Illinois, The Dorsey Press, 1968), pp. 10-11.
9. Noah and Eckstein, op. cit., p. 96.
10. See Meehan, op. cit., pp. 84-88.
11. Speculative imagination, Toulmin reminds us, along with interpretation, and theory, and hence understanding characterized the Ionian approach to the science of astronomy, in contrast to the forecasting techniques of the Babylonians. See Toulmin, op. cit., pp. 29-30.

12. Kuhn, <u>op. cit.</u>, p. 23.
13. Meehan, <u>op. cit.</u>, p. 43.
14. See "Editorial," <u>Comparative Education Review</u>, 14
        (February 1970).

WAYNE J. URBAN

11. SOCIAL FOUNDATIONS:
FORWARD WITH MILLS AND MARX*

What I would like to do is to sketch out an argument
as to where I think we should go in social foundations, especially in the first course.   First, let me indicate some
bases from which my argument starts and which do not need
to be argued for extensively.   The notion of social foundations as encompassing advocacy of certain positions or pos-
tures has been admirably discussed and defended in a recent
article in Educational Studies by Mary Anne Raywid. [1]   Also,
the necessity for the interdisciplinary nature of study in the
social foundations has been convincingly established, at least
to my mind, most recently by Professor Raywid and before
that by others. [2]   Thus, the interdisciplinary focus and the
advocacy posture of both the Teachers College and the Illinois programs seem to me to still be models upon which we
can build.

My own focus will be on the modifications I would
like to see made in these earlier approaches and my reasons
for urging the modifications.   I will attempt to get at these
matters by assuming that both these earlier programs were
really seeking to establish a social and political philosophy
for the public schools and those who work in them.   This assumption enables me to analyze the earlier approaches from
the point of view of C. Wright Mills.   In a book on the philosophy of Marxism, Mills opens with a discussion of political philosophies.   He argues that political philosophies contain ideologies, ideals, and theories, and furthermore, that
they designate agencies of action to implement the ideals.
Ideologies are political positions which indicate that certain
institutions and practices are to be defended and others are
to be attacked.   Ideals are ethical principles which establish

---

*Paper presented to the American Educational Studies Associ-
ation, Washington, D.C., November 1972.   Published here
with the permission of the author.

the goals and guidelines toward which the ideologies are directed. Theories of man, society, and history indicate how
society works, where the conflicts which inhibit the ideals
and ideologies are to be located, methods of study which will
bring about a resolution of the conflicts, and the expectations that will occur from the resolution. Agencies are the
means of reform, the programs, strategies, and organiztions that will win the sought after ideals. [3]

      Both the Teachers College and the Illinois approaches,
it seems to me, failed to encompass all of the four elements
identified by Mills. The Teachers College course, Education 200F, seems to be quite strong in the numeration of
ideals and ideologies. If one looks at the various syllabi
and the two volumes of readings published specifically for
this course, he sees lengthy coverage of the western political and cultural heritage and the American democratic tradition. [4] Democracy and humanism may be said to function as
the ideals in this program and the public schools are seen
as the institution which provides the ideological fulfillment of
these ideals. Some attention is paid to a theory of society;
however, the theory gets tied up in discussion of Marxism
and the Soviet Union and seems to be searching for a compromise between Soviet Marxism and American capitalism
without really attaining one. The discussion of theory is as
often idealistic as it is analytic and it never quite seems to
get concrete enough to indicate what actions follow from the
discussion. Especially lacking is an indication of the agencies which would be responsible for the implementing of the
theoretical principles in an effort to reach the ideal goals.

      Turning to the Illinois program, we find a somewhat
similar situation. [5] Democracy remains as an ideal to be
reached and the public school still embodies the institution
which is seen as the ideological fulfillment of the ideal. The
theory in this program is somewhat refined in relation to the
earlier formulation. W. O. Stanley's methodological principle
of authority is developed after lengthy discussion of social
theory. It is the scientific method applied as a pedagogical
principle in the school and the larger society. Discussions
carried out under the principle of authority as developed by
Stanley are seen to lead to resolution of conflicts. Stanley's
theory is really a method and, as such, falls short of explaining the conflicts that exist in society. It is a good
method for solving conflicts but it cannot explain why the
method itself may not be adopted by the contending groups.
Further, the Illinois approach, like the Teachers College ap-

proach, is silent on enumerating the particular agencies of reform.

My intent is not to condemn the earlier approaches, but to try and build upon them. If what we have said up to this point is correct, the place to look for improvement is the area of theory and agency rather than ideals and ideologies. In the area of political theory, there is a concept that was being developed in the late nineteenth century and the early twentieth century which may be helpful. I am referring to the concept of bureaucracy. In another place, I have argued that George Counts, one of the founders and guiding lights of the Teachers College group, ignored the concept of bureaucracy as he developed his notions of the role of the state in a democratic society.[6] This caused him to over-estimate the reforms that would be accomplished by state intervention in the economy.

Bureaucracy, which in the above context is a theory of political administration, can also be considered as a general theory of organization.[7] Studies of educational bureaucracies have occurred frequently in the last few years. One of the conceptions resulting from most of these studies is that the increasing bureaucratization of education tends to separate the interests of teachers from those of administrators.[8] This development is seen by students of educational organization, as well as those of other forms of social organization, as a significant factor in the rise of occupational groups to positions of power, prominence, and controversy.[9] The term bureaucracy is nowhere to be found in either the Teachers College or the Illinois social foundations programs. Consequently, they have a tendency, when discussing teachers and organizations, to exhort teachers to join them or to argue why teachers should or should not join them rather than to analyze the bureaucratic conditions that are pushing teachers toward organizations.

If the analyses of bureaucracy are correct, the teacher organization may well be an agency for realizing whatever ideals and ideologies we find extant in contemporary discussions of education. If we look at contemporary approaches to social foundations, however, we find them no more acutely aware of the theory of bureaucracy and the rise of teacher organizations than were the earlier approaches. Contemporary students have much more of a base on which to build a study of bureaucratic theory and teacher organizations as agencies for the implementation of educational ideals, but they do not seem to have done so.

In support of this last contention, let us look briefly at four readers in the social foundations of education. The books in question are those by Vogel, Batchelor, and Zepper; Stoff and Schwartzberg; Linton and Nelson; and Blackington and Patterson. [10] Two of these volumes, those by Linton and Nelson and by Vogel, et al., have a section on teachers or teaching; however only one has an article on teacher organizations. One of the other volumes has no section on teachers while the final volume, that by Blackington and Patterson, mentions the professional educator in the title, devotes one section to a discussion of professionalism and another to teacher education, but contains no articles on teacher organizations. Though there are many differences in content among the four volumes, one similarity is the relative lack of attention paid to teachers and the even greater lack of attention paid to teacher organizations. Furthermore, none of the four contains any discussion of the growth of bureaucracy in education. Also, with the exception of the Vogel volume, all of the four can be characterized as being primarily involved with ideals and ideologies rather than theories and agencies, though not necessarily the same ideals and ideologies as those of the Teachers College and Illinois programs.

The neglect of teacher organizations by the Teachers College and Illinois programs seems explainable because of the relative weakness of the organizations up until the 1960s. The past decade and a half, however, has seen a tremendous increase in membership and militancy in teacher organizations. Yet, if the four volumes just mentioned are characteristic of those in social foundations generally, this movement has been ignored. Those who have made the kinds of studies that seem to relate to the theory of bureaucracy and its resulting effect on teacher organizations seem to be outside the field of social foundations. Two of the most recent studies of educational bureaucracy have been made by a sociologist of education (pure academic variety) and an educational administrator. [11] The above-mentioned sociologist is also the author of a recent study entitled Militant Professionalism. [12] The obvious question is where have we been?

The most outstanding student of teacher organizations in the past fifteen years is one who might be considered as a student of the social foundations of education. That person is Myron Lieberman, author of Education as a Profes-

sion and The Future of Public Education,[13] and numerous
articles on teacher organizations.   Lieberman received his
doctorate at the University of Illinois in the area of social
and philosophical foundations.   Close examination of Education as a Profession reveals much content that seems drawn
from the Illinois program in social foundations as well as
much, especially the detailed studies of teacher organiztions
themselves, that seems unrelated to the Illinois content.
The Future of Public Education shows Lieberman arguing for
centralization of educational control in terms not unsimilar
to those of both the Teachers College and the Illinois programs.   Again, there is much in the book that seems to be
new ground and not related to either of the earlier programs.
This is not the place to affirm or criticize Lieberman sub-
stantively, but it is appropriate to point out that he seems
to be taking a position not in conflict with the earlier approaches.   In a sense he is adding to or building on to the
earlier approaches while at the same time he is altering the
focus of those studies.   There is much less discussion of
democracy and much more attention paid to teachers themselves, teacher education, teacher organizations, and the
whole question of professionalization.

      The direction taken by Lieberman is much more in
line with what we called for earlier, a concentration on
agencies and theories rather than ideals and ideologies.
Lieberman's work has not gone totally unnoticed by those
who write social foundations textbooks, since many, including three of the four mentioned earlier, contain what I would
like to call a "token" Myron Lieberman article.   If my argument is correct, we need much more than these "tokens" in
order to bring the social foundations into touch with the realities of the American educational world.

      The textbooks mentioned earlier seem to me to be
among the best of the current lot, even though they are still
concerned with ideals and ideologies and relatively uncon-
cerned with theories and agencies or Myron Lieberman concerns.   These readers at least are still trying to conceptualize the social and educational world.   The great majority
of recent readers which claim to be "issue oriented" seem
to have abandoned even that task.   One wonders why we who
are involved with teacher training have also taken on the
task of those in the sociology departments who teach "social
problems."

      By all of this I do not mean to imply that the

Teachers College, Illinois, or Lieberman approaches are sacred, or even correct.   I do mean to imply that each and
all of them are preferable to most of what we are doing in
social foundations now if our task is to deal with a political
philosophy for the schools.   In a sense, I think we have re-
gressed, or at least gone off the track, or at any rate abandoned the task as conceived by our predecessors.

Let me offer some speculative comments on why we
have changed direction, why we do not consider the theories
and agencies that are having an impact on American teachers,
why we largely ignore teacher organizations in our work.
First, it is not academically respectable to deal with these
kinds of concerns, especially for those of us who see ourselves as historians, philosophers, sociologists, and what
all with an "interest" in education.   Second, and this is the
converse of the first, this kind of study is for administration professors and other mundane types and intellectually be-
neath social foundations people.   Third, it is not radical
chic, as are some other concerns such as the counter-cul-
ture.   Fourth, organizational study inherently hits at the middle class bias, whether conservative or liberal, which sees
social concerns in individualistic terms.   This is especially
a problem for those among us who are humanistically minded.
Fifth, this kind of study in many parts of the country--es-
pecially, though not exclusively, the South--is politically
dangerous.

Finally, I think many of us are haunted by the Ocean
Hill-Brownsville fiasco.   Again, this is not the place to debate that event but it is the place to state that serious study
of this event is in conformity with the approach suggested
herein.   By serious study I mean study which seeks to isolate the dynamics and determine the generalizability of the
events rather than label the participants as good guys or bad
guys.

I would conclude with a reference again to Teachers
College and Illinois.   Insofar as each of these groups sought
to extend the studies of Dewey, let me characterize them
philosophically as composed of pragmatists.   This allows me
to refer to a general study of social thought in America by
the sociologist T. B. Bottomore.   He argues that pragmatism
was the only case in American philosophy in which a distinctive and critical body of thought was developed.   Pragmatism's main problem as a critical philosophy was "... the
absence of any powerful social movement which might have

responded to it."[14] If social foundations is in this sense a
pragmatic study, we in the field now have a powerful social
movement in education which could respond to our concerns,
namely teacher organizations. But we have abandoned both
the pragmatic study and the organizations themselves.

Notes

1. Mary Anne Raywid, "Social Foundations Revisited,"
    Educational Studies, III, (Summer, 1972), 71-83.
2. Ibid., also see Wyne J. Urban, "Social Foundations
    and the Disciplines," Teachers College Record,
    LXXI, (December, 1969), 199-205.
3. C. Wright Mills, The Marxists (New York: Dell Pub-
    lishing, 1962), 12-13.
4. Division I: Foundations of Education, Teachers College,
    Columbia University, Readings in the Foundations
    of Education (New York: Teachers College, 1941),
    passim. I am also grateful to Professor R. Free-
    man Butts who generously provided me with sever-
    al versions of the course syllabus for Education
    200F.
5. My discussion of the Illinois program is based on my
    reading of three volumes produced by the Illinois
    group: William O. Stanley, Education and Social
    Integration (New York: Teachers College, 1953);
    William O. Stanley, Joe R. Burnett, and John R.
    Palmer, eds., Outline and Selected Readings: So-
    cial Foundations of Education (Danville, Illinois:
    Interstate Printers, 1967); and William O. Stanley,
    B. Othanel Smith, Kenneth D. Benne, and Archi-
    bald W. Anderson, eds., Social Foundations of
    Education (New York: Dryden Press, 1956).
6. Wayne J. Urban, "George Counts and the Communists:
    The Consequences of an Anti-Communist Ideology,"
    unpublished paper delivered to The Social and Po-
    litical Philosophy Interest Group, Philosophy of
    Education Society, (March 26, 1972), 8-9.
7. A lucid discussion of the various meanings and usages
    of the concept bureaucracy is found in Martin Al-
    brow, Bureaucracy (New York: Praeger Publish-
    ers, 1970).
8. For illustrations of this separation phenomenon see
    James G. Anderson, Bureaucracy in Education
    (Baltimore: Johns Hopkins, 1968), chapter 3 and
    Ronald G. Corwin, A Sociology of Education (New

York: Meredith Publishing, 1965), Chapter 10.

9. Corwin, A Sociology of Education is a contemporary
    illustration.   The functions of occupational groups
    in reaction to the division of labor, a general phe-
    nomenon which subsumes bureaucracy as its ad-
    ministrative embodiment, were discussed as early
    as 1902 by Emile Durkheim.   See The Division of
    Labor in Society (New York: Free Press, 1964),
    1-31.
10. Foundations of Education: A Social View (Albuquerque:
    University of New Mexico, 1970), The Human En-
    counter: Readings in Education (New York: Harp-
    er and Row, 1969), Patterns of Power: Social
    Foundations of Education (New York: Pitman Pub-
    lishing, 1968), and School, Society, and the Pro-
    fessional Educator (New York: Holt, Rinehart &
    Winston, 1968).
11. See note 8.   Ronald G. Corwin teaches in the sociology
    department at the Ohio State University and James
    G. Anderson conducted his study while a student of
    educational administration at Johns Hopkins.
12. Ronald G. Corwin, Militant Professionalism: A Study
    of Organizational Conflict in High Schools (New
    York: Meredith, 1970).
13. Myron Lieberman, Education as a Profession (Engle-
    wood Cliffs: Prentice-Hall, 1956 and The Future
    of Public Education (Chicago: University of Chi-
    cago, 1960).
14. T. B. Bottomore, Critics of Society: Radical Thought
    in North America (New York: Pantheon Books,
    1968), 138.

PATRICIA MILLS

12. WHICH WAY IS UP?
SOME CAUTIONARY NOTES TO MODEL
BUILDERS IN TEACHER EDUCATION

Man invented the crystal ball and the soothsayer long
before the wheel and the horse collar. His need for the
magic of the future has not diminished as technology has advanced and change become more imminent. In teacher education as elsewhere, the desire to probe the future has
grown increasingly keener. It is therefore not surprising
to find teacher educators employing a variety of futuristic
methods, such as trend, technological, political, humanistic,
and visionary forecasting.

Each of these activities is perceived to have a contribution to make: first, in the improvement of teacher education programs; and eventually, in the increased efficacy of
schooling as a valid form of human enterprise. There are,
however, a number of hidden dangers lurking in the application of these probe mechanisms, and those of us concerned
with designing teacher education curricula must remain alert
to their limitations and illusions as well as to their promise.
Kenneth Boulding, for example, has warned us of the sur-
prises or turning points in the development of social systems (he refers to them as "systems breaks") that defy almost all possibility of prediction.[1] If only to protect our
reputations, we may want to qualify any forecasts we make
with the demurrer Van Til offered in his futurist scheme,
"All bets are off if such major system breaks ... occur."[2]

We might also want to expand our projections to a
series of alternate futures. If we make certain choices,
then certain outcomes are more probable, but even then,
logical inconsistencies may trap us. If we assume that the
universe is orderly and cause and effect are not just infer-

*The Journal of Teacher Education, Vol. XXI, No. 4,
(Winter 1970), pp. 494-97. Reprinted with permission.

ences derived from accidents of time and space, just as
soon as we crystallize the future upon the known present
and then proceed to dabble with the present we alter the basis for our prediction. When we posit alternate futures
based upon presently held assumptions, and then predict the
implications of certain choices, we produce a priori probabilities only.

Most importantly, however, we need to remember
that as we increase our success in exerting rigid control
over eventual outcomes, and thus reach congruency with predetermined aims, we negate the possibility of emergence,
the generation of new forms that are neither predictable nor
explainable by the functions or processes of known forms.
Thus the third and most dangerous pitfall we must avoid is
that of being caught up in the utopian promise of an educational future derived from a kind of technological rationality
in which we fall victim to Herbert Marcuse's syndrome of
one-dimensional man,[3] means become ends and the system
closes upon itself, eliminating the possibility of transcen-
dence beyond its now irrational whole. Our power to accomplish selected objectives--in fact, to invent the future--
is stronger than many of us realize; and we often overlook
the fact that each year we are living in a world more of our
own making. With each decade, we plan and implement a
greater proportion of our environment than ever before. We
must not become so enamored of our ability to develop more
and more intricate systems that we fail to realize any system may become anachronistic; we must not become so skill-
ful in planning and implementing what now appear to be perfect educational environments that we become locked into our
present, and possibly quite limited, perspectives.

Fortunately, because of their growing recognition of
the inadequacies of man to cope effectively with many of the
complexities his superior intellectual powers have created,
many educators, in thinking of the future, are paying increased attention to domains of human development, to questions that relate to the shaping and realization of the person
as well as of the society. Thus, a crucial and yet only
vaguely formed mode of inquiry, humanistic forecasting, is
gaining emphasis. This future probing is concerned with
such phenomena as needs, values, life styles, beliefs, attitudes, and motivations as a means for describing alternate
futures. This trajectory, which has as yet been less trav-
elled than the trend, technological, or political types of forecasting, has undeniable relevance to education. But there

are also dangers to avoid in traversing this route, not the least of which is the propensity of educators sensitized primarily to the problems of an interdependent humanity to allow emotionality and sensation to eclipse rationality or to project what ought to be from what is, and then to assume that what ought to be will be. Although an integration of people and things appears desirable, its actualization does not necessarily follow. This propensity for educators to translate wishful thinking into descriptive and prescriptive statements appears to be another occupational hazard. And yet, without intuitive leaps, discovery is stymied, and for this reason, wishful thinking (visionary forecasting) may be a useful component to planning in teacher education. Surely no one can deny the impact made by such openly fictitious renditions as Skinner's Walden Two or Orwell's 1984.

If any absolutes are to be entertained from probing the future, however, one may very well be that change will continue to be the prevailing constant. Although it may seem paradoxical to assert that the vital tenet for teacher education appears to be derived from the conclusion that the only certainty is uncertainty and that stability lies in the presence of change, this is the universal that consistently reappears in every category of future projection. Because human beings, especially those steeped in western culture, tend to abhor divergency and find it exceedingly difficult to entertain disjunctive concepts,[4] they have traditionally demonstrated an affinity for unity and order that, in turn, has been a great impetus propelling them toward the development of highly organized, complex, and technologically advanced societies.[5] But respect for the dignity and worth of man and the realization of a greater humanity now seem to depend upon accommodating diversity, plurality, and individuality as counterbalance to the forces of conformity, unity, and organization.

Despite its limitations, probing the future does offer possibilities by which teacher educators may escape the even greater restrictions of unforeseen change. Although man may neither be able, nor want, to control his future entirely, neither does he want to be the victim of circumstance. But the major concern in teacher education must be that of devising programs that are not merely adaptive to the future but that can remain open to permit the emergence of new conceptualizations which are beyond the boundaries of even the most carefully derived predictions.[6]

Educational planning, thus, would not be limited to concern for adaptation; it would recognize that without emergence survival is truly threatened. This vital concept of emergence must be translated into educational theory in the form of experimentation, completely open-ended endeavors, which, as Polanyi noted[7] are impossible if a lower level controls the boundary conditions of the higher level.

However, there is an even more promising way of enhancing both the adaptation and emergence factors in teacher education. Contrary to popular opinion, it is not by giving priority to the restructuring of institutions; when organizational changes rather than the reconstruction of people have been made the focal point of change, historical analysis repeatedly shows that these means typically have become ends in and of themselves. The thesis advanced here is that the primary goal in teacher education must be preparing teacher-persons who are able to interpret their environment through application of knowledge and understanding, who act intelligently and sensitively in the midst of dilemmas created by changing patterns and conflicts of a dynamic universe, and who aid their students to do likewise. The problem of teacher education is, in the words of one teacher educator, the "problem of preparing teachers who can learn with everybody else how to live in a breathtaking vortex of change in the cultural and material conditions of the human community."[8] The priorities in designing innovative or experimental teacher education programs for the future must be established with this end in mind; in fact, the entire structure of teacher education programs must be consistent with this outcome.

If the thesis advanced here has validity, and if teacher educators can meet the challenge of shaping their programs in the image of the teachers they aim to create, it will be relatively unnecessary to be able to predict accurately what the year 2000 will bring in terms of technology, trends, or politics. The teacher of the year 2000 will be equal to it.

Notes

1.   Boulding, Kenneth. "Expecting the Unexpected: The Uncertain Future of Knowledge and Technology." Prospective Changes in Society by 1980. (Edited by E. L. Morphet and C. O. Ryan.) Designing

Education for the Future, No. 1. New York: Citation Press, 1967. p. 203.

2. Van Til, William. The Year 2000: Teacher Education. Terre Haute: Indiana State Press, 1968. p. 10.

3. Marcuse, Herbert. One-Dimensional Man: Studies in the Ideology of Advanced Industrial Society. Boston, Mass.: Beacon Press, 1964.

4. See, for example, Bruner, Jerome S.: Goodnow, Jacqueline J.; and Austin, George A. A Study of Thinking. New York: Wiley, 1956. pp. 156-81.

5. See, for example, Dewey, John. The Quest for Certainty: A Study of the Relation of Knowledge and Action. New York: Minton, Balch & Co., 1929.

6. Adaptation in this context refers to the facility of a system to change positively along with or in advance of its environment; emergence refers to the facility to create higher forms that transcend the| environment and add new dimensions to the potentialities of existence.

7. Polanyi, Michael. The Tacit Dimension. New York: Doubleday, 1966. p. 45.

8. Cottrell, Donald P. "The Long View of Teacher Education." Theory into Practice 6: 230-35; December 1967.

CONTRIBUTORS

PART I

Frederick A. P. Barnard (1809-1889) was the president of Columbia University from 1864 to 1889. The books which he wrote include: A History of the United States Coast Survey (1859), Recent Progress of Science (1859), and The Metric System (1871).

William Harold Payne (1836-1907) was the chancellor of the University of Nashville and the president of the Peabody Normal College from 1887 to 1901; he then served as professor of education at the University of Michigan until his death. Among his publications are The Education of Teachers (1901) and Chapters on School Supervision (1875).

John Dewey (1859-1952) was a professor of philosophy at Columbia University from 1904 until his retirement in 1930. Among his numerous books are: Moral Principles in Education (1909), Democracy and Education (1916), and Experience and Education (1938).

James Bryant Conant is a president emeritus of Harvard University and was the director of the study of American Education, Carnegie Corporation, New York (1960-63, 1965-69). His recent writings include: The Comprehensive High School (1967), Scientific Principles and Moral Conduct (1967), and My Several Lives: Memoirs of a Social Inventor (1970).

Richard M. Millard is the director of Higher Education Service, Education Commission of the States. His major publications are: Types of Value and Value Terms (1949), "Whitehead's Aesthetic Perspective," Educational Theory (1961), and "Insuring the Future of the Liberal Arts," Educational Record (1966).

Peter A. Bertocci is a professor of philosophy at Boston University. His major books are Empirical Argument for God in Late British Thought (1938), Introduction to Philosophy of Religion (1951), and Personality and the Good (1953).

Mary Anne Raywid is a professor of foundations of education at Hofstra University. Her major writings are: The Ax-Grinders (1962), and "Subjectivism: The Self-destructing Philosophy of Education," Educational Forum (1970).

Edward Franklin Buchner (1868-1929) was a professor of education at Johns Hopkins University. He wrote A Study of Kant's Psychology (1897) and translated and edited The Educational Theory of Immanuel Kant (1904).

James L. Kuethe is Associate Professor, Education Department, State University of New York at Albany. Among his principal writings are "The Acquiescence Response Set and the Psychasthenia Scale and Social Schemas," Journal of Abnormal and Social Psychology, and "The Positive Response Set as Related to Task Performance," Journal of Personality.

David P. Ausubel is a professor of psychology at the City University of New York. His leading books include: Theory and Problems of Child Development (1958), Educational Psychology: A Cognitive View (1968), and School Learning: An Introduction to Educational Psychology (1969).

John Walton is a professor of education at Johns Hopkins University. Among his major books are: Administration and Policy Making in Education (1959), Toward Better Teaching in the Secondary Schools (1966), and Introduction to Education: A Substantive Discipline (1971).

John A. Laska is a professor of educational studies at the University of Texas and Director, Center for International Education. He is the author of Planning and Educational Development in India (1968) and Foundations of Teaching Method (1973).

PART II

Harry S. Broudy is Professor of Education at the University of Illinois and editor of The Educational Forum. His many publications in the Foundations include Building a Philosophy of Education (1954, 1961) and he is co-author of Psychology for General Education (1957) and Exemplars of Teaching Method (1964).

Andrew F. Skinner was for many years Professor of Education at the University of Toronto. Dr. Skinner has written mainly on the philosophy of education but his interests range broad and deep in history and comparative studies in education.

J. P. Powell. Formerly of the University of Manchester, Dr. Powell is now a member of the Education Department at the University of Papua and New Guinea, Boroko, T. P. N. G.

Maxine Greene is Professor of English and a member of the Department of Philosophy and the Social Sciences at Teachers College, Columbia University. Dr. Greene, who is a past-president of the American Educational Studies Association and the former editor of Teachers College Record, is author of The Public School and the Private Vision (1965), Existential Encounters for Teachers (1967) and Teaching and the Humanities (1970).

Margaret Gillett is Professor of Education at McGill University, Montreal where she teaches in the Department of Social Foundations of Education.

Theodore Brameld, a distinguished philosopher of education, has also made many contributions to the anthropology of education. Emeritus Professor of Boston University, Dr. Brameld is now a Senior Fellow at the East-West Center, University of Hawaii. Among his recent works are Cultural Foundations of Education (1957), Education as Power (1965), and The Climactic Decades (1970).

Leonard Marsh is Professor Emeritus, University of British Columbia. His publications include Canadians In and Out of Work (1940) and Communities in Canada (1970).

Philip H. Phenix, Professor at Teachers College, Columbia University, is well known for his works in the philosophy of education including his text Philosophy of Education (1958), Realms of Meaning (1964) and Man and His Becoming (1964).

Christopher J. Lucas is Associate Professor of Education at the University of Missouri and editor of What is Philosophy? (1969).

N. C. Bhattacharya holds degrees from universities in India, the U.S. and Australia. He is Professor of the Philosophy of Education at the University of Alberta.

Edmund J. King of King's College, University of London, is author of World Perspectives in Education (1962), Other Schools and Ours (1963), Education and Social Change (1966), Education and Development in the West (1969) and The Teacher and the Needs of Society in Evolution (1970).

Saul B. Robinsohn. Until his death in 1972, Dr. Robinsohn was Director of the Institute for Educational Research in the Max-Planck Institute and Free University of Berlin. He was also Vice-President of the Comparative Education Society of Europe.

Floyd G. Robinson is a professor in the Ontario Institute for Studies in Education and co-author (with David P. Ausubel) of School Learning: An Introduction to Educational Psychology.

PART III

Paul Nash, Professor of Education at Boston University, is a past-president of the American Educational Studies Association. His publications include Culture and the State: Matthew Arnold and Continental Education (1966), Authority and Freedom in Education (1966), Models of Man (1968) and History and Education (1970).

R. Freeman Butts, founding president of the American Educational Studies Association, is Associate Dean for International Studies at Teachers College, Columbia University. Professor Butts is author of A Cultural History of Western Education (1947, 1955) and, with Lawrence Cremin, A History of Education in American Culture (1953). His new study of civilization and education is to be published by McGraw-Hill in 1973.

James W. Wagener is assistant vice-chancellor for academic programs at the University of Texas, Austin.

Ralph A. Smith is Professor of Aesthetic Education in the Bureau of Educational Research at the University of Illinois, Urbana-Champaign. Founder and present editor of The Journal of Aesthetic Education, he has edited Aesthetic

Concepts and Education (1970), Aesthetics and Problems in Education (1971), and Meaning and Judgment in the Arts (forthcoming).

Edward Weisse is Professor in the College of Education, Wisconsin State University and author of Environmental Studies in Education (1970).

Moses Stambler is a professor of education at Southern Methodist State College.

Herbert K. Heger, when the paper reproduced here was written, was a teaching associate in the Curriculum and Foundations Faculty, Ohio State University.

Margaret Gillett is author of A History of Education: Thought and Practice (1966) and Educational Technology: An Essay in Demystification (1973). She is also founding editor of the McGill Journal of Education.

Robert J. Mulvaney and Roger J. Sullivan teach at the University of South Carolina.

Andreas M. Kazamias, a past-president of the Comparative and International Education Society, is editor of the Comparative Education Review. Dr. Kazamias is Professor of Education at the University of Wisconsin.

Wayne J. Urban is Associate Professor of Educational Foundations at Georgia State University, Atlanta.

Patricia Mills is a professor in the College of Education at Bowling Green State University, Ohio.

INDEX

Aesthetics of education, 276-277, 326-349
American Educational Studies Association (AESA), 11, 122, 135
Anthropology of education. <u>See</u> Social foundations of education
Ausubel, David P. , 9-10, 99-118, 416

Bailyn, Bernard, 269
Barnard, Frederick A. P. , 3-4, 6, 14-21, 415
Baumgarten, Alexander, 277
Bertocci, Peter A. , 8, 51-60, 415
Bhattacharya, N. C. , 145, 229-232, 418
Biological studies, 278
Brameld, Theodore, 146, 199-210, 417
Broudy, Harry S. , 143, 149-161, 416
Bruner, Jerome S. , 138
Buchner, Edward Franklin, 8, 82-87, 416
Butts, R. Freeman, 270-271, 300-319, 418

Comparative education
    purpose and content, 63, 173-174, 236-241, 271-272, 393-401
    utility of, 233-234, 236-244
Conant, James Bryant, 7-8, 39-50, 136-137, 415
Cremin, Lawrence, 270-271

Dewey, John, 4-5, 11-12, 23-38, 415

Eckstein, Max, 271
Ecology, 372-387
Education, art of, 22-24, 218
Educational psychology
    criticisms of, 245-247, 250-255, 261-266
    methods of teaching, 257-262, 267
    purpose and content, 44-49, 63, 99-118, 169, 249-261
    utility of, 249, 257, 288, 325
Educational studies, 11-12, 130
Environmental studies, 277, 355-356

Flexner, Abraham, 137-138
Foundation studies in education
  criticisms of, 135-137, 140-141, 159, 188, 191-193, 216,
    222, 230-231, 264, 288-289, 294-295, 303, 317, 320-
    322, 324-325
  definition and delimitation, 2-4, 6-7, 11, 39-41, 61-65,
    124-125, 149-150
  dependent field, 6-8, 12, 33, 39-81, 276, 303-304, 320-321
  independent field, 8-9, 12, 82-133, 322
  purpose and content of, 287-300, 307, 315-318, 320
  teaching of, 291-299
  utility of, 134, 137-140, 143-147, 179, 181-190, 197-198,
    205, 212, 218, 233-244
Fuller, Buckminster, 278
Future of education, 273, 278-280, 410-414

Gillett, Margaret, 134-148, 188-198, 264-282, 374-387, 417,
  419
Greene, Maxine, 144, 179-187, 417
Greer, Colin, 270

Heger, Herbert K., 272-273, 372-373, 419
History of education
  criticisms of, 269-270
  methods of teaching, 193-197
  purpose and content, 19-20, 43, 63, 169, 172, 179-181,
    192, 269-271, 304-317

Katz, Michael B., 3
Kazamias, Andreas M., 271-272, 393-401, 419
King, Edmund J., 233-234, 418
Koerner, James D., 136-137
Kuethe, James L., 8-9, 88-98, 416

Laska, John A., 2-13, 122-133, 416
Leacock, Stephen, 264
Levit, Martin, 272
Lucas, Christopher J., 145, 147, 221-228, 417

McClellan, James E., 147
McLuhan, Marshall, 275
Marsh, Leonard, 146, 417
Millard, Richard M., 8, 51-60, 415
Mills, Patricia, 410-414, 419
Mulvaney, Robert J., 388-392, 419
Mumford, Lewis, 273

Nash, Paul, 267-269, 283-299, 418
Noah, Harold, 271

Oakeshott, Michael, 142

Payne, William H., 4, 22-27, 415
Peters, R. S., 142
Phenix, Philip H., 145, 219-220, 417
Philosophy of education
 methods of teaching, 231
 purpose and content, 42-43, 51-60, 63, 169, 172, 220-
  229, 388-392
Powell, J. P., 144, 177-178, 417
Psychology of education. See Educational psychology

Raywid, Mary Anne, 8, 61-81, 416
Robinsohn, Saul B., 147, 235-244, 418
Robinson, Floyd B., 245-263, 418
Russell, William, 6

Skinner, Andrew F., 144, 162-176, 417
Smith, Ralph A., 277, 326-354, 418
Social foundations of education
 criticisms of, 357-358, 403-405
 methods of teaching, 205-209
 purpose and content, 43-44, 65-76, 169, 207, 213-215,
  217-218, 357-371, 402
Sociology of education. See Social foundations of education
Soltis, Jonas, 142
Specht, Robert, 278
Springer, Ursula K., 135
Stambler, Moses, 273, 357-371, 419
Stanley, W. O., 280
Sullivan, Roger J., 388-392, 419

Talbott, John, 269
Teaching, art of. See Education, art of
Toffler, Alvin, 279

Urban, Wayne J., 280, 402-409, 419

Wagener, James W., 272, 320-325, 418
Walton, John, 10, 119-121, 416